KANSAS CITY, KANSAS COMMUNITY COLLEGE

0 0005 0119385 8

Y0-CUO-751

PQ   Literate women and the
276   French Revolution of
.L57   1789
1994b

840.9 L776w

DISCARDED

SUMMA PUBLICATIONS, INC.

Thomas M. Hines
Publisher

William C. Carter
Editor-in-chief

Editorial Board

William Berg
University of Wisconsin

Germaine Brée
Wake Forest University

Michael Cartwright
McGill University

Hugh M. Davidson
University of Virginia

Elyane Dezon-Jones
Washington University

John D. Erickson
Louisiana State University

Wallace Fowlie (emeritus)
Duke University

James Hamilton
University of Cincinnati

Freeman G. Henry
University of South Carolina

Norris J. Lacy
Washington University

Jerry C. Nash
University of New Orleans

Allan Pasco
University of Kansas

Albert Sonnenfeld
University of Southern California

Orders:
Box 20725
Birmingham, AL 35216

Editorial Address:
3601 Westbury Road
Birmingham, AL 35223

Literate Women and the French Revolution of 1789

Literate Women and the French Revolution of 1789

Edited by

Catherine R. Montfort

840.9
L776w

SUMMA PUBLICATIONS, INC.
Birmingham, Alabama
1994

Copyright 1994
Summa Publications, Inc.
ISBN 1-883479-07-X

Library of Congress Catalog Number 94-69023

Printed in the United States of America

All rights reserved.

Contents

Illustrations	vii
Acknowledgements	ix
Introduction	1
1. Women's Voices and the French Revolution —Catherine R. Montfort —Jenene J. Allison	3
2. Women's Experience of the French Revolution: An Historical Overview —Suzanne Desan	19

I
Revolutionary Women Inscribed in History

3. Charlotte Corday: *femme-homme* —Nina Corazzo —Catherine R. Montfort	33
4. *La Déclaration des Droits de la Femme:* Olympe de Gouges's Re-Writing of *La Déclaration des Droits de l'Homme* —Janie Vanpée	55
5. The Circe of the Republic: Mme Roland, Rousseau, and Revolutionary Politics —Mary Trouille	81
6. From Private to Public Sphere: The Case of Mme de Sévigné and Mme de Staël —Catherine R. Montfort	111

Contents (cont'd)

II
Women of the Revolutionary Period Writing on History

7. Radical Compromise: The Political Philosophy of Isabelle de Charrière
   —Jenene J. Allison ... 129
8. Spectatrice as Spectacle: Helen Maria Williams at Home in the Revolution
   —Mary Favret ... 151
9. Charlotte Robespierre: A Sister's Perspective
   —Marilyn Yalom ... 173
10. From Reform to Revolution: The Social Theater of Olympe de Gouges
    —Gabrielle Verdier ... 189

III
To Interpret History: Mme de Staël and George Sand

11. Liberating Exchanges: Mme de Staël and the Uses of Comparison
    —Susan Tenenbaum ... 225
12. Speech Acts: Germaine de Staël's Historiography of the Revolution
    —Karyna Szmurlo ... 237
13. Unmasking *Indiana:* George Sand and the French Revolution(s)
    —Lauren Pinzka ... 253
14. Mad Sisters, Red Mothers, Wise Grandmothers: Women's Non-Realist Representations of 1789
    —Margaret Cohen ... 283

Contributors ... 297

Works Cited ... 299

List of Illustrations

1. Tassaert (after Hauer), "Marie-Ann-Charlotte Corday," 1793   37
    Engraving
    Bibliothèque Nationale, Cabinet des Estampes, Paris
2. Anonymous, "La Mort du Patriote Marat," 1793   38
    Engraving
    Bibliothèque Nationale, Cabinet des Estampes, Paris
3. Quéverdo, "Marie Ann Charlotte Corday," 1793   46
    Engraving
    Bibliothèque Nationale, Cabinet des Estampes, Paris

Editor's Note

The MLA Style Manual was adopted for preparing the manuscript. However, when there was more than one work per author, the author-date system was preferred, with several consequences throughout the volume: 1) parenthetical references include the author's last name and the year of publication (unless given in the text); 2) in the list of Works Cited, entries are listed chronologically, rather than alphabetically, with the year of publication immediately following the author's name; 3) when two or more works per author were published in the same year, their order is alphabetical, and the dates are assigned lower case letters a, b, c, etc.

Introduction

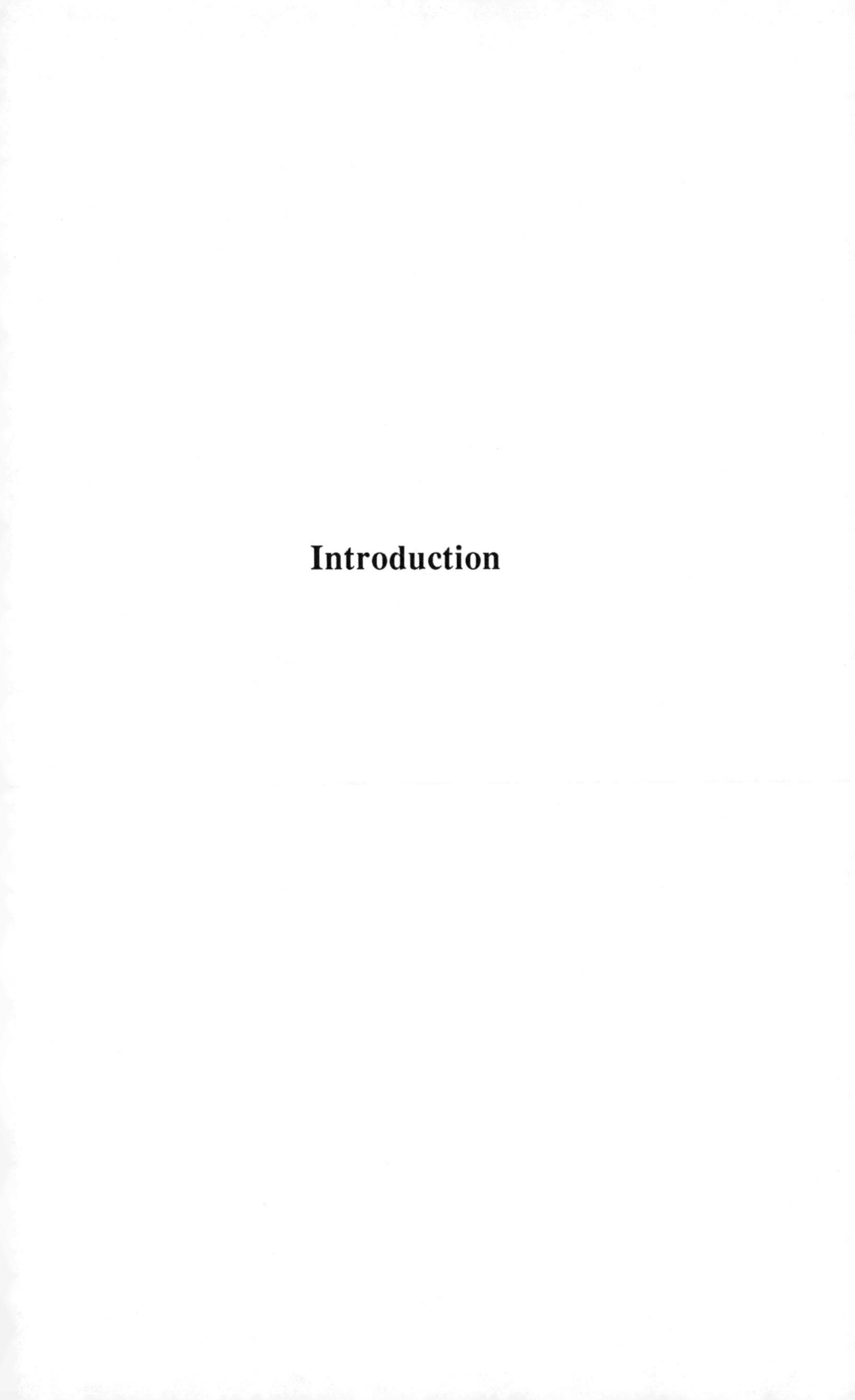

1

Women's Voices and the French Revolution

Catherine R. Montfort
J. J. Allison

> "Voulez-vous ressembler aux Muses
> Inspirez mais n'écrivez pas."
> —Lebrun, *Aux belles qui veulent devenir poètes*, 1796.

This volume was conceived during the bicentennial of the French Revolution. Conferences, colloquia, seminars, and special sessions mushroomed across the United States and France. The combined efforts of historians, literary critics, and historians of art and music resulted in considerable new knowledge about an important period of French history. In particular, scholarly studies on women—whether it be studies on women in general, on subgroups, or on individuals—have been invaluable in raising consciousness and restoring a fullness to the historical event.[1] One area, however, has not received the full attention it deserves: the contributions of "literate women" to the culture and politics of the French Revolution. When Sylvain Maréchal wrote in his *Projet d'une loi portant défense d'apprendre à lire aux femmes*, "Reason dictates that women who write books should not be permitted to have children" (qtd. in Harten 1989, 160-61), he expressed a deeply rooted obsession of many revolutionary men. In the ideal Republic, women were meant to be "mothers" not writers; in other words, women were expected to remain in the private sphere as moral guardians of the Republic rather than play a public role, be it political or literary. Men justified women's exclusion in part on the grounds that women, through the institution of sexual favoritism, had contributed to the corruption of monarchical power (Outram 1989, 125-26). The legitimacy of the new order could therefore only be predicated "not on an inclusion of the female, but on its exclusion" (126).[2] However, the Revolutionaries' ideology of gender roles did not die with the Revolution. In fact it has survived so well that, as pointed out by Yvonne Kniebielher, traditional history has remembered the women's march to Versailles in October of 1789 (women demanding "bread" for their families, a corollary of their motherly duty) as an important contribution, a "véritable fait historique," but has forgotten Olympe de Gouges's *Déclaration des droits de la femme* (1984, 52).[3] The same can be said of most women's writing of the period, a phenomenon that led to the neglect of works such as Helen Maria Williams's *Letters from France* (1791-96), a frontline account of Paris during the Terror, or Olympe de Gouges's large dramatic production. Criticized in the eighteenth century and neglected afterwards, "literate women" must be brought back to the historiography of the Revolution. This collection of essays is a step in that direction.[4]

In this volume we use "literate women" to mean women who share two characteristics, the first being education—even Olympe de Gouges who lacked formal schooling was far from being illiterate.[5] Some of the women studied here were educated in convents (Charlotte Corday, Charlotte Robespierre, George Sand), others at home by an influential family member, a governess or tutors (Mme Roland, Isabelle de Charrière, Helen Maria Williams, Germaine de Staël); still others were self-taught (Olympe de Gouges), or received their education from a combination of these sources. Education for women was not a given.[6] Although it is well known that schools multiplied in the seventeenth and eighteenth centuries, recent studies have shown that in general women were less literate than men, and that women of the upper classes were more literate than women of the lower classes.[7] One is struck by how little education schools provided. As Martine Sonnet remarks, "One avoids, like the plague, educating women who may become as sand in the well-oiled wheels of family and society" (233).

The second characteristic of our "literate women" is that all wrote texts meant for publication, whether it be an aristocrat writing anonymously such as Charrière, an outspoken author such as de Gouges, a late bloomer writer such as Roland, or a criminal's last message such as Corday.[8] In a letter to Benjamin Constant in 1794, Charrière acknowledged the importance of a public: "In speaking one must be, or believe oneself to be, heard" (1981, 4: 565). De Gouges stated in the preface to her first published play: "I am a woman and an author; I manifest all the activity of an author" (*Le Mariage inattendu de Chérubin* published in 1786). She even pleaded the cause of authors' rights for female writers.[9] As for Roland, when a friend predicted early in her life that she would one day write a book, she replied: "It will be under a pseudonym because I had rather eat my fingers than become an author" (1966, 321). But later in prison, subverting Rousseau's feminine ideals, she proudly declared: "If I had been allowed to live, I would have had only one temptation: to write the *Annales du siècle*, and thus become the Macaulay of my country" (1966, 338-39). Finally, and unexpectedly, even Corday expressed the wish to see her prose widely read in her last letter to Barbaroux written in prison: "Upon my arrest, I carried a speech addressed to the friends of peace; I cannot send it to you, I will ask for its publication" (qtd. in Walter 23-24).[10] Given that common base, the differences are striking. These authors include some who wrote on a full-time basis, such as Staël and Sand, as well as some who happened to write for a variety of reasons triggered by the Revolution. Even within this second category there are differences. The *Mémoires* that Mme Roland wrote in prison and the "Adresse aux Français" that Corday penned the eve of her assassination of Marat are substantially dissimilar forms of self-expression. The contrast between these two texts provides a concise example of the range of women's writing discussed here, a range that covers traditional genres for women, correspondence, novels, and memoirs, and what was new and daring—treatises and political tracts.

Utilizing these women's texts, we are able to address a number of interesting questions: Were literate women passive onlookers or active participants in the historical drama? What was their attitude towards domesticity and the ideology of separate spheres for men and women? What methods, ploys, and channels were used by these women to counteract the dominant role of men in society? How was the Revolution inscribed in post-revolutionary nineteenth-century women's texts? The goal of this volume is to analyze some of the forms in which literate women expressed their reactions to the 1789 Revolution; these forms may be structured primarily by their experiences, their writings, or their interpretation of events. We have chosen to tailor our study to the transitional period that links eighteenth- and nineteenth-century France; thus we are following Béatrice Didier's lead in *Ecrire la Révolution* and not arbitrarily dividing authors with a common focus who happen to fall on different sides of the year "1800."

Furthermore, the essays presented in this volume are also concerned with the question of a possible gendered response by women to the events of 1789 and their aftermath, an issue whose importance extends beyond the confines of feminist studies. A woman is always a woman biologically, but the ways in which she can be one are constructed by her culture. Gender, then, is a valuable gauge of cultural change.[11] The French Revolution is a particularly good context in which to assess change in this way, because it is not only an historical event crystallized around extraordinary occurrences on specific dates, it is also a social evolution embodied in the slow deterioration of the *Ancien Régime*. As Dorinda Outram remarks, "The meaning of the Revolution has to be found in the values it produced" (1989, 37-38). Thus, in considering the transition from Enlightenment society to post-revolutionary capitalism, a focus on the reactions of women to this transition gives us not *a* view but rather an overview of what was taking place at the most basic level of cultural identity; the optic of gender gives us a picture that is doubly fine-tuned.

All the essays revolve around the Revolution even when dealing with writers such as Charrière or Sand who, because of spatial or temporal constraints, might have ignored the event. Quite the contrary: Charrière, although she resided in Switzerland, is correctly termed by Isabelle Vissière "une aristocrate révolutionnaire" and Sand, writing in the century following the Revolution, is still engaged in the issues it raised, as Yves Chastagnaret has shown (Vissière 1988, Chastagnaret 431-48). By bringing together in this anthology a variety of literate women, the selection highlights the different ways in which women experienced the Revolution. The differences are important because the framework in which these women are featured resists the perpetuation of any essentialist notion of a common "woman's experience." What these individuals have in common is that they were literate, but that quality ranged from the barely literate to the super-literate and manifested itself in a broad range of reactions. Thus Charlotte Corday may be considered the keystone in this group of women, although her literacy led to action rather than the production of texts.

The focus of the first section, REVOLUTIONARY WOMEN INSCRIBED IN HISTORY, is the women themselves as text. The women in this section include an assassin, two activists, and two authors. Three of them are famous.[12] They are all victims. Corday, de Gouges, and Roland were executed. Staël was exiled. All are representatives of what the majority of revolutionary men hated most, the "public" woman. Interestingly enough, the deaths of Corday, Roland, and de Gouges in 1793 points out the insignificance of class differences: Corday was born an aristocrat, Roland and de Gouges came from the *petite bourgeoisie*.[13] One aspect of their "crimes" was their transgression of traditional gender barriers, subtle for Mme Roland, aggressive for Corday and de Gouges. Corday transgressed "human" boundaries as well. In the first essay, "Charlotte Corday: *femme-homme*," Nina Corazzo and Catherine Montfort, chronicle the life of Charlotte Corday, an individual whose experience serves as the starkest possible illustration of the problem confronting women of the revolutionary period in their search for political self-expression. Shortly after Marat's assassination, Corday was the subject of a play in which she is seen during her interrogation asking: "Am I therefore not a woman?" (qtd. in Corazzo and Montfort's essay). Corazzo and Montfort argue that the accusation implicit in the question attributed to her subtends a more global condemnation of Corday, that of being a *femme-homme*. This condemnation of Corday went far beyond the murder she committed to include all elements of her life and lifestyle. In late eighteenth-century France, a woman not being a "woman" was some sort of failure within the system; a woman being a man was viewed as a threat to the system, even if it was a system in the throes of revolutionary change. Corday, then, represents the most extreme case: a woman whose values and political actions were so alien to the concept of woman that she was categorized as a monster. Single, self-supporting, educated, and politically informed—all characteristics far afield from the ideal of domesticity—her counter image could be considered to illustrate the revolutionary era's definition of woman; everything that Corday was not.

Similarly, Olympe de Gouges both 'failed' to be a woman and 'threatened' to be a man. In her case, however, she not only lived this new gender identity, she theorized about a place for it in society. In "*La Déclaration des droits de la femme*: Olympe de Gouges's re-writing of *La Déclaration des droits de l'homme*," Janie Vanpée suggests that de Gouges's role in the Revolution was to designate the limits of change. Her insistence on being treated as a political subject brought about her incarceration and execution. The result, in terms of social change, of her experience was that woman's assumption of the status of political subject was identified as a threat to the evolving social order. Working on a text recently studied by Joan Wallach Scott (1989), Vanpée brings a different light to bear on her reading of de Gouges as a figure in the Revolution. Vanpée sees de Gouges's manifesto, the *Déclaration des droits de la femme*, as a brilliant rhetorical device that was doomed to failure because it was structured and undermined by the accepted patterns and rules of discourse and proper literary style of the period. Besides, it was addressed to a constituency of women who did not yet exist as a political entity.

Like Corday and de Gouges, Mme Roland also contested the gender-specific constraints that dictated her possibilities as far as political self-expression was concerned. This is especially illuminating when one considers early documents such as the personal letter written when she was twenty-nine, in which she asserts, "I can imagine no destiny more rewarding than that of assuring the happiness of one man alone" (qtd. in Mary Trouille's essay). While this could stand as a one-sentence summary of Rousseau's views on the role of woman, Mary Trouille shows in "The Circe of the Republic: Mme Roland, Rousseau, and Revolutionary Politics," that once the Rolands were swept up in the political struggle of the Terror, Mme Roland's superior intelligence and education, coupled with her political and literary activities, eventually caused her to be a "woman" who embodied ideals very different from the womanly perspective advocated in *La Nouvelle Héloïse* or *Emile*. She literally rewrote Rousseau's role for women. She transmuted herself from housewife to ghost writer, from homekeeper to (political) salonnière, and through this rewriting she created the chance to impose her republican ideology on public opinion. Contrary to Martin Sydenham in *Les Girondins* and Dorinda Outram (1989, 130-31) who adopts his assessment, Trouille argues that Mme Roland's political influence was very real and that she had an important impact on the course of events.

Corday, de Gouges, and Roland all shared the grim fate of being executed just as male political activists were. As for Mme de Staël, she was exiled most of her life. In "From Private to Public Sphere: The Case of Mme de Sévigné and Mme de Staël," Catherine Montfort examines how history has treated women such as those discussed above, and demonstrates how the images which history presents are largely drawn from an ideology that dates from 1789. Choosing one writer whose life began before the eighteenth century (Mme de Sévigné) and one whose life continued after its close (Mme de Staël), she describes how their contribution to French literature has been evaluated partly according to the degree to which they were, or failed to be, a "woman." More specifically, Montfort shows that Sévigné was praised in newspapers, plays, prefaces, etc. as a role model for women of the time—the perfect mother with no political ambition and no pretension to being a writer. The praise of Sévigné as "mother" constituted an important image transformation, considering that in the eighteenth century, the *public mondain* had been shocked by her overly passionate love.[14] Montfort argues that Staël, on the other hand, was severely criticized because she was an exceptional woman, a believer in the "philosophie des Lumières" and the antithesis of a model for women. She aspired to more than marriage and motherhood; not only did she choose to be a writer, but she also thought that a writer should be political. Critics perceived her as a threat and thus resorted to a gender stereotyping that, often in the same breath, conveniently belittled her while exalting Sévigné.

Taking a step back from the literate women who were, in some way, directly engaged in the social changes which culminated with and following the Revolution, the second section in this collection of essays, WOMEN OF THE REVOLUTIONARY PERIOD: WRITING (ON) HISTORY, focuses primarily on texts written by women. This section departs from the myth of events—supposedly pure and uninterpreted—and turns to women's reading of these events—from Charrière's immediate response to the events happening in Paris to Charlotte Robespierre's belated commentary written in her old age. In each case we find the authors writing in effect on two issues: The subject at hand and a discussion of what it meant to be a woman dealing with the subject at hand. Some of the women represented in this section have received very little critical attention, and except for de Gouges, all survived the Revolution. Interestingly, de Gouges was the only woman of the Revolution to be condemned and executed for her writings.[15]

Isabelle de Charrière was an aristocrat whose social and literary connections enabled her to maintain a diverse network of correspondents linked in varying degrees to the political scene in Paris. As a result, her political fiction chronicles, in almost documentary detail, the transformation that was taking place. In her recent anthology of Charrière's political writings,

Vissière has produced a collection of texts that read like a journal of Charrière's changing ideas about the Revolution. Vissière makes the important point that the well-known split between Charrière and the young Benjamin Constant was the result of a political, not an emotional argument, thereby rescuing Charrière's image from that of sentimental biographies that have hindered a full appreciation of her as an intellectual. In her essay on Charrière's political fiction, "Radical Compromise: The Political Philosophy of Isabelle de Charrière," Jenene Allison discusses Charrière's commitment to moderation in matters of political change. While Charrière was unafraid to advocate what would have been a radical compromise in the eighteenth century (lessening the distinction between the upper and lower classes) in order to make contemporary society more equal, she was unwilling to endorse egalitarianism. Allison argues that such moderation is due to Charrière's understanding of the role of gender in society. An astute observer of events in France, Charrière nonetheless writes first and foremost as an observer of the feminine condition. In this capacity, she never loses sight of the way in which woman's exclusion from the public sphere inevitably becomes a matter of public policy.

In contrast to Charrière who viewed the Revolution from afar, Helen Maria Williams, an English poet and novelist, may be said to have viewed the Revolution from the most dangerous vantage point possible—Paris during the Terror. She first arrived in Paris on 13 July 1790, and began what Sandra Adickes has labelled "a thirty years' mission in France" (67). The length of her stay, her full command of the French language, conspicuous in her various translations of French texts into English, and more importantly her transformation into an accomplished political essayist and historian explain why she was included in a volume devoted to literate women and the 1789 Revolution. In "Spectatrice as Spectacle: Helen Maria Williams at Home on the Revolution," Mary A. Favret describes Williams's life in Paris during the Terror and the active role she made for herself as salonnière, correspondent, and go-between. Her *Letters from France* (1791-96) not only record contemporary events, they reverse the logic of revolutionary ideology by placing both the woman and the domestic sphere at the center of the public spectacle. Rather than composing the feminine and domestic as a retreat from the turbulence of political activity, Williams elides the home with the public institutions: theater, prisons, parliament. In doing so, she finds herself and other women at home in the Revolution and she confronts the changes and possibilities of that position. Women in Williams's text, especially women writers, occupy the center of revolutionary politics not only as representatives of the nation but as agents of communication and socialization.

In Charlotte Robespierre we find a woman who was as close to the Revolution as was Williams, and yet was distanced from it in a way that Williams never could be. Charlotte Robespierre did not question the rights of men to determine the destiny of women and by almost any measure is the most "average" of the women studied here. Yet Marilyn Yalom's account of the sister of Maximilien and Augustin Robespierre, "Charlotte Robespierre: A Sister's Perspective," has little difficulty in convincing us that Robespierre's sister is more interesting than merely a footnote to her brothers' lives. In her 1828 *Memoirs*, she is first a hagiographic biographer of her brothers, but also a woman who periodically bares an anguished face and portrays herself as a hapless victim of a revolution gone mad. Yalom concludes that the memoir, a literary genre increasingly exploited as a means of self-expression, provided her entry into recorded history through the life of a famous male relative, and thus permitted her ironically, to have the last word.

While Williams and Charlotte Robespierre both reflect on contemporary political issues in letters and memoirs, the last woman presented in this section chose a more challenging form of political self-expression. Gabrielle Verdier's discussion of the theater of Olympe de Gouges, "From Reform to Revolution: The Social Theater of Olympe de Gouges," makes a case for reevaluating the unthinking dismissal of her plays. Unlike Vanpée (in this volume), Verdier concentrates strictly on the texts produced by de Gouges rather than on her activism. However, playwriting as de Gouges practiced it was in itself a political act since she did it so publicly: She proclaimed her authorship, battled with the Comédie française, and against all odds managed to have ten plays published and four performed. Verdier's essay is the first study to treat de Gouges's dramatic production seriously, within the context of the dramatic production of male and female playwrights of the period and recent theoretical reevaluations of bourgeois drama.[16] Her reading highlights the plays' thematic and formal originality. She describes how de Gouges used stock characters from contemporary theater and rewrote many lines which divided the masculine and the feminine. In her dramatic treatment of some of the most provocative issues of the time (in particular forced religious vocations, indissoluble marriage vows, and women's active participation in public political debate and in war), de Gouges set on stage characters who increasingly challenge assigned functions, particularly women's passivity and victimization, and thereby dislocate formal patterns as well. Her plays feature strong, mature, and united women who are shown enlightening the paternal figure and sharing authority with him, in defiance of the place which revolutionary ideology reserved for women in the bourgeois republic. Her innovations, by which she contested traditional gender identities, provoked the ridicule and abuse of her contemporaries, but anticipated both literary and social changes that would occur much later, and perhaps still remain to be achieved.

The focus of the last section, TO INTERPRET HISTORY: MME DE STAËL AND GEORGE SAND, is further removed from the women whose experience inscribed them in the history of 1789. Here our concern is with women whose writing serves to situate the history of 1789 in a larger context. Only two authors appear in this section, Mme de Staël and George Sand, both prolific writers. The selection of Staël is easy to explain. First, she was undoubtedly one of the foremost female interpreters of the Revolution. Second, in light of contemporary criticism, she is today a fundamental reference for scholars in the field of women's studies, political theory, and social history. In this section it is because of her methodology in her political writings and of her interpretation of history through language that she is pertinent. In the first essay, "Liberating Exchanges: Mme de Staël and the Uses of Comparison," Susan Tenenbaum analyzes Staël's use of the comparative method to defend the Revolution of 1789. Tenenbaum demonstrates that, while intellectually, Staël sustained the vigor of a tradition of comparative analysis reaching back to Montesquieu, she infused it with a female perspective and adapted it to the problems of a revolutionary age. Staël's arguments presaged the shift from early rights-based defenses of the Revolution to the empirically grounded strategies of legitimation employed by Restoration liberals. Through such arguments Staël enlarged the role of the salonnière as shaper of public discourse, transforming the use of comparison from literary technique to polemical weapon. In Karyna Szmurlo's essay, "Speech Acts: Germaine de Staël's Historiography of the Revolution," it is Staël's contributions to theories of language that are of interest, the focus being the study of revolutionary rhetoric. Inspired by studies exploring semiotics within a social praxis and especially recent interpretations by Sandy Petrey (1988 and 1989a), Szmurlo interprets Staël's *Considérations* (1818) as a peculiar speech act in the context of "performative" theory. She argues that it demonstrates the relationship between the process of language acquisition and the seizure of power. Szmurlo discusses Staël's association of the revolutionary crisis with an ongoing linguistic crisis, especially notable at the time of the Terror, when speech's new found freedom was suppressed—a process that particularly victimized women (including herself). She also shows how consecutive linguistic impasses ("infelicities" and "misfires" in the Austinian sense of the word) undermined revolutionary goals. Both of these essays indicate that Staël must be viewed as an expert at what contemporary feminists call "appropriation:" using what is considered as objective and therefore ungendered methodology to undermine patriarchal ideology in some form.[17]

The volume concludes with an evaluation of the aftermath of the Revolution in the writings of the nineteenth century's most noted female author. Although Sand did not live through the 1789 Revolution, she was unable to escape being drawn back to this fountainhead of the 1830 and 1848 revolutions. Central is her attempt to come to terms with women's failed struggle for civil equality in 1789—a task which obviously did not interest male writers of historical-realist novels such as Balzac (*Les Chouans*) and Hugo (*Quatre-vingt-treize*). Both Lauren Pinzka and Margaret Cohen are concerned with an aspect of Sand that is at odds with the image of an author of idyllic *romans champêtres*. In "Unmasking *Indiana*: George Sand and the French Revolution(s)," Pinzka's close reading of *Indiana* reveals two distinct levels: First the conscious means by which Sand creates political symbols for her time in her attempt to make sense of the Revolution of 1789 and the subsequent political upheavals; and second the significant "subtext" of her novel which includes revealing lacunae and unexpected associations in that portrayal. Pinzka argues that a look at Sand's sometimes surprising political beliefs as well as at the historical context of Romanticism in which her first novel was written throws a new light on a violent side to the author of bucolic *romans champêtres*. She concludes that as a woman, Sand was conditioned to repress an attraction to violence culturally perceived as "masculine," hence its subverted novelistic expression. Similarly, in an essay bearing the most provocative title in the anthology, "Mad Sisters, Red Mothers, Wise Grandmothers: Women's Non-Realist Representations of 1789," Cohen elucidates the subversive strategy underlying the text of *La Petite Fadette*. In the course of a comparison between Sand and Balzac, our last contributor shows how the seemingly neutral ground of a 'realist' narrative suppresses woman's divergent point of view concerning political change. She argues that in *La Petite Fadette* Sand subtly attempted to appropriate and subvert the discourses of sentimentalism and morality (the appropriate language of bourgeois femininity) to forge a powerful feminine language of political change. Instead of interpreting *La Petite Fadette* as Sand's flight from the failed revolution of 1848 into a fairy tale world, Cohen demonstrates that it is an historical novel of the 1789 Revolution in which the heroine eventually subverts the patriarchal order that had disgraced her.

With Cohen's compelling analysis of a tale for children, we have reached, once again, the beginning: What did it mean for literate women to live the Revolution? To write about it? To read the Revolution? To a certain degree, the contributors featured in this volume have done nothing more than to "begin at the beginning" as Lewis Carroll advocated. They have addressed the educated, literate, articulate, and propertied classes whose male spokesmen favored silence and domesticity for their female classmates. Obviously, even in this category, more 'literate women' need to be studied: Mme de Genlis, Mme Campan, Louise de Keralio, Vigée Lebrun, to name but a few of the better known women who took part in or commented later on the Revolution. There is also a full study to be written on women as petitioners, as producers of newspapers, as authors of hymns, poems, pamphlets, and letters to the press—all women who had a crucial role in creating revolutionary political culture. However, within the limits of this volume, in the disparity between the young woman who contested the political status quo by killing a man in his bath and the *belle dame de Nohant* who put into question the way in which political revolution is represented, the variety of narratives that may tell of the relationship between gender and revolution is provocative. Within this variety, nevertheless we find consensus—and foremost the existence of a gendered response to the Revolution and its aftermath. Given that the liberal discourse of the rights of man was subtended by a redefinition of woman that precluded most of all her political self-expression, all the contributors demonstrate that none of the "literate women" studied in this volume—with the exception of Charlotte Robespierre—accepted without a fight the work of asymmetrical gender. The collection moves from a real assassin (stabbing a man in the heart) to a fictional one (trying to take the heart out of a symbolic bourgeois family of the nineteenth century), from action to talk, from open revolt to hidden and subversive attacks—and contrary to pessimist interpretations of women's experience of the Revolution,[18] points to early nineteenth-century women ready for a long resistance. In restoring to the Revolution of 1789 the overlooked words of a group of literate women, we have brought into focus significant pages of history on which the full complexity of the Revolution is recorded. The next essay will paint a backdrop for the articles that follow.

Notes

1. See, among many others, the general studies (all published in 1989) by Badinter, Didier, Harten and Harten, E. Kennedy, Hunt, Marand-Fouquet, and Outram. On subgroups of women, see Godineau (1988), Yalom, and Vray. On the debate over *femmes-auteurs*, see Fraisse. On specific women, see the monographs by Roudinesco on Théroigne de Méricourt, Chaussinand-Nogaret on Mme Roland, Boissel on Sophie de Condorcet. Finally, see the bibliography for a more complete selection including not only earlier seminal studies by Duhet 1971, Levy et al 1979, and Hunt 1984, but also later major contributions in the field.

2. See also Joan Landes's analysis of the historical passage from French absolutism to bourgeois society and her selection of *The Oath of the Horatii* as symbolizing the opposition between family and state, private and public life, characteristic of the new Republic. For a critique of Landes, see Goodman 1992.

3. On the *Déclaration des droits de la femme*, see Scott 1989 and Janie Vanpée's essay in this volume.

4. The recent study *Rebel Daughters,* which appeared as this volume was close to completion, is an interdisciplinary collection of essays analyzing the paradoxical relationship between women and the French Revolution. Although it includes essays on de Gouges, Staël, and Helen Mary Williams, there is very little overlapping with the present volume which emphasizes "literate women" and literary analysis. Besides, two sections of *Rebel Daughters* deal with different issues: the exclusion of women in early nineteenth century texts by men, and the birth of feminism in the aftermath of the Revolution.

5. On the myth of de Gouges as "illiterate," see, in this volume, the essays by Janie Vanpée and Gabrielle Verdier. Both critics show that de Gouges's lack of formal education was offset by important factors, mainly a wide range of eclectic reading (Verdier), and a knowledge steeped in oral tradition, gleaned informally from listening to the ideas, words, and commonplaces that were being discussed on stage, at the national assemblies and in salon discussions (Vanpée).

6. On education, see Spencer, "Women and Education" 83-96; Julia; and Sonnet. On the salon, which was viewed by some women as a socially acceptable substitute for the formal education generally denied them, see Goodman 1989, esp. 333-34. In her essay, Goodman argues that the eighteenth-century salons were transformed from a noble leisure institution into an institution of Enlightenment.

7. See Knibielher et al.: "Il faut se souvenir que jusqu'au 18ème siècle, le taux d'analphabétisme féminin est pratiquement, à classe égale, toujours le double de l'analphabétisme masculin et que leur degré d'instruction élémentaire, même s'il croît proportionnellement plus vite que celui des hommes au 18ème siècle, ne rattrapera pas complètement celui-ci avant la seconde moitié du 19ème siècle" (1983, 34). See also Badinter's study *Emilie, Emilie* in which she quotes figures taken from R. Chartier et al., in *L'éducation en France du XVI^è siècle au XVIII^è siècle:* 95% men and 80% women of upper classes can write their names at the end of the Old Regime, while only 54% men and 19% women of the lower classes can (1983, 14).

8. On the question of anonymity, pseudonym, choice of first name or periphrasis, see Delon 1988, 277-94.

9. On this point and on the concept of "text as property" recognized with the law of 19 July, 1793, see Hesse 474-76.

10. On this point, see Montfort: "For the Defense: Charlotte Corday's letters from Prison," forthcoming in *Studies on Voltaire and the Eighteenth Century.*

11. The definition of gender at the origin of current feminist debate is still that which is outlined in Simone de Beauvoir's introduction to *Le Deuxième Sexe.* She asks, "Si sa fonction de femelle ne suffit pas à définir la femme, si nous refusons aussi de l'expliquer par 'l'éternel féminin' et si cependant nous admettons que, fût-ce à titre provisoire, il y a des femmes sur terre, nous avons donc à nous poser la question: qu'est-ce qu'une femme?" (1976, 13). Beauvoir propose que "En vérité pas plus que la réalité historique la nature n'est un donné immuable. Si la femme se découvre comme l'inessentiel qui jamais ne retourne à l'essentiel, c'est qu'elle n'opère pas elle-même ce retour" (18). A more recent definition is Myra Jehlen's entry for "Gender" in *Critical Terms for Literary Study.* See also Miller 1987, 63-73.

12. See the portraits of Corday, Roland, and Staël in Michelet's *Les Femmes de la Révolution* n.d.

13. On de Gouges at the time of her marriage, see Blanc: "Le jeune couple se range dans une catégorie sociale de petits bourgeois" (1981, 24).

14. On how Sévigné was judged in the eighteenth century and early nineteenth century, and on the important point of whether she wrote with publication in mind, see Montfort 1982 and 1992a.

15. They include plays (*La France Sauvée, Mirabeau aux Champs-Elysées* and *L'Entrée de Dumourier à Bruxelles*) as well as her political pamphlet, *Les Trois Urnes,* that showed sympathy for the federalist movement and the Girondins.

16. In contrast with someone like Chantal Thomas who condemns de Gouges for weaknesses which are common to most eighteenth-century theater (1988, 308-12).

17. On "appropriation," see Toril Moi 117-32.

18. See, for example, Marand-Fouquet and Yalom (1989).

2

Women's Experience of the French Revolution: An Historical Overview

Suzanne Desan

A band of market women marching to Versailles in the early October rain, calling for bread and hurling insults at the queen. A sketch by Jacques-Louis David of that same Queen Marie-Antoinette, stripped of her finery, en route to the guillotine four years later. Olympe de Gouges, feminist writer and revolutionary, composing an egalitarian marriage contract and demanding "Rights of Women" to match those of men. Charlotte Corday, dramatically thrusting her knife into the startled Marat in his bath. The club of *Citoyennes Républicaines Révolutionnaires,* radical proponents of popular sovereignty and price controls, suddenly stunned and silenced by the news that the National Convention had outlawed all women's clubs in October 1793. All of these are classic images of women's experience of the French Revolution.

Diverse images with mixed messages, for the impact of the Revolution on women was nothing if not varied and ambiguous. French women played an integral role in creating the revolutionary context and ideology. From the Parisian women rioting for bread and a republic, to the young women embodying goddesses of liberty and reason in provincial festivals, to political leaders, like Madame Roland, Claire Lacombe, or Madame de Staël, French women shaped the course of revolutionary events. Yet their relationship to the Revolution always held certain contradictions. For large groups of French women, the dechristianization campaign, the economic and personal strains of the war effort, and the fundamental restructuring of

French society took a deep toll.[1] Some of these women would turn against the Revolution. Moreover, liberal legal reforms and the creation of female citizenship had a paradoxical effect. The revolutionary movement improved women's status as legal individuals in certain ways, contributed to women's political education, and created a context in which they petitioned for various causes, organized, published, spoke in public, rioted both for and against the Revolution, and even appropriated revolutionary ideology to demand equal social and political rights for women. Yet, in both ideology and practice, women's newfound role as citizens stood in tension with the ideal patriotic role of women as republican mothers and moral guardians of the Revolution within the home. Wary of women's increasing activism outside the home, both Jacobin and Thermidorean leaders took steps to exclude women from the public sphere of politics; and the emerging cult of domesticity transformed women's private lives as well.[2]

In short, while the French Revolution constituted an unusual opening for female political activism, cultural expression, and feminist demand, it also brought severe physical hardship to many groups of women, curtailed religious freedom, and, despite its promises of citizenship, set patterns limiting the political and public rights of women and reinforcing their essentially domestic role.[3] To provide historical background for the essays in this volume, this section of the introduction will explore women's experience of the Revolution. I will highlight not only their crucial role in forging revolutionary political culture, but also the ambiguities and difficulties that stemmed from women's position on the border between the public and private spheres.

In the early years of the Revolution, the optimism surrounding the reform of society and politics in general seemed to encompass women's issues as well. Many women echoed the confident expectation of Marie Dorbe of the women's club of Bordeaux, when she declared in 1792, "Before the Revolution we were forgotten, reduced to housework and the education of our children; deprived of the benefits of the law, we lived in abject obscurity, painfully enduring our degradation . . . [Now] the blindfold which hid the truth from us has been lifted; in turn, we too have become free citizens." "Your chains are broken," declared the anonymous pamphlet *Adresse au beau sexe, rélativement à la révolution présente,* "You were, according to all accounts, slaves; now, behold, you are citizens!" (qtd. in Proctor 43). Indeed, the revolutionary refashioning of political structures, family law, and educational systems seemed to promise improvements in women's status as "citizens" of the new nation. In an attempt to protect individual rights, limit paternal authority, and reduce the power of the church, the national legislature transformed the laws governing marriage and inheritance. By making marriage a civil contract, lowering the age of marital consent for women to twenty-one, and legalizing a form of divorce relatively accessible to women and men, these laws increased women's legal potential to control their personal lives. The abolition of primogeniture mandated equal inheritance for both sons and daughters throughout France, and new laws governing paternity allowed single mothers to press charges for paternal support of illegitimate offspring. Liberal changes in law granted women the right to testify in court, while educational reforms seemed to promise more attention to primary school education for girls.[4] In short, although revolutionary legislation did not grant women full political rights as citizens, its challenge to the hierarchical and patriarchal structures of Old Regime society, monarchy, and church led to an expansion of certain elements of women's rights.

Furthermore, the new politics which validated popular activism and gave an unprecedented role to the power of public opinion opened up possibilities for women of various classes to influence revolutionary events and ideology. Women's collective action played a crucial role in directing and influencing the course of the Revolution at key political turning points. The "October Days" of 1789 offer the most well-known instance of female activism. Already angered by the shortage of bread in the fall of 1789, Parisian market women heard rumors on October 4 that the King's soldiers at Versailles had trampled on the national tricolor cockade. Early on the following morning, a group of women of the *menu peuple* rang the tocsin, marched to Versailles, poured into the National Assembly, and demanded more bread for Paris and the king's unconditional confirmation of the recent decrees of the National Assembly. The king received a small delegation of women, agreed to accept the Declaration of the Rights of Man and the August decrees without change, and promised that he had already ordered more grain to be brought to Paris. Yet the crowd of women, now joined by the National Guard, remained unconvinced. The following morning, an armed crowd of women and men, some disguised as women, broke into the palace, killed several royal bodyguards, and demanded an audience with Marie-Antoinette as well. Some fishwives threatened to "open [the queen's] belly ... and rip out her heart" or "to cut off her head and *fricasser* her liver," while others cried out "To Paris! to Paris!" (qtd. in Colwill 1990, 19; Schama 467). Finally, the king and his family made their way to Paris, accompanied by a crowd some 60,000 strong of national guardsmen and militant women waving bread on pikes and chanting gleefully about "the baker, the baker's wife, and the baker's son" (Levy et al. 1980, 36-54).

In the particular context of the fall of 1789, the activism of these Parisian market women cemented the constitutional role of the National Assembly and placed the royal family and the Assembly under the watchful scrutiny of Parisian crowds. The incident established patterns that would recur in later riots, particularly the women's potent fusion of economic and political demands and their critical role in mobilizing armed men to action. As the Revolution progressed, militant leaders of the *sans-culottes* women in Paris increasingly gave priority to political demands, such as the defense of popular sovereignty, the call for the Constitution of 1793, and, to a lesser extent, the right for women as well as men to arm themselves in defense of the Nation. Paradoxically, even as these women lobbied for popular sovereignty, they themselves could embody the "sovereign people" only at moments of insurrection; in ordinary times, their status as *citoyennes* had to remain purely passive.[5]

Women's political participation could take on a more official structure as well. Early in the Revolution, leading feminist activists, including Etta Palm d'Aelders, Théroigne de Méricourt, and Pauline Léon, used their memberships in political clubs, such as the *Cercle Social* or the *Société fraternelle des patriotes de l'un et l'autre sexe,* to lobby for women's education and the reform of marriage and inheritance laws (Kates 1990; Soprani 1988). In about sixty cities and towns across France women of middle class or artisanal backgrounds founded political clubs which combined charitable and ceremonial activities with political discussion and activism. These clubs usually dedicated themselves to Jacobin goals, such as support of the war effort, agitation for price controls, and the development of patriotic education programs for their families. In some instances, women's societies expanded their goals to include explicitly feminist demands: A handful of women's clubs demanded the right to vote, while quite a few more clamored for the right to bear arms or seconded Mary Wollstonecraft's call for female education. Yet, by their very structure as formal political organizations, these societies challenged existing conceptions of female roles. By petitioning the national government, pressuring municipal figures, organizing public demonstrations, and corresponding with the press, other clubs, and various government officials, the women's clubs entered the public sphere beyond the traditional female realms of ceremony, riot, or charity (Desan 1992; M. Kennedy 88-100; Villiers).

Female club members recognized that public structure gave them official voice. As the *citoyenne* Blandin-Desmoulins of Dijon wrote to the journalist Prudhomme in the winter of 1793, a republican government called on each individual to cooperate on behalf of the *bien public*. *Citoyennes* too "should make themselves useful to the public good. . . . To contribute in the surest and most advantageous fashion, we had to meet together; for what can individuals do if they remain isolated from each other? . . . We do not limit ourselves to singing hymns to liberty, as you advise us; we want also to partake in civic acts" (qtd. in *Révolutions de Paris*). The most well-known women's society, the Parisian *Citoyennes Républicaines Révolutionnaires*, played a crucial role in 1793 in garnering popular support for the Mountain, ousting the Girondins, and promoting the sans-culottes' platform of direct democracy and price controls (Godineau 1988, 129-77).

The written word offered literate women another means to participate in the emerging public sphere of politics. The declaration of freedom of the press in 1789, the gradual abolition of censorship, and the intensely politicized atmosphere of the early Revolution all encouraged a deluge of publications.[6] Both male and female writers largely set aside the traditional genres of the novel and poetry in favor of more explicitly political forms of expression. In looking at women's writing in the early 1790s, one is struck not so much by the publications of leading authors, as by the sheer numbers of unknown literate women who discovered the power of the pen to engage in revolutionary politics and call for action. "I was obsessed by the desire to write, and also to publish," wrote de Gouges (qtd. in Thomas 1988, 309). Her fervent desire to use the written word to influence public or legislative opinion was echoed by the hundreds of women who flooded the national legislature with petitions, wrote letters to the press, produced newspapers of their own, composed *mémoires justificatifs* in defense of themselves and their loved ones, and published pamphlets promoting everything from a separate all-woman legislature to the glories of a stable monarchy.[7] The outburst of popular press in 1789 to 1791 included several journals written by and for women. Fashion-oriented weeklies shared the market with more explicitly political and even feminist newspapers, such as the *Etrennes nationales des dames*. The *Courrier de l'hymen* offered an unusual combination of marriage advertisements, feminist appeals for improved civil and educational rights, and letters from female readers. In 1790-91 Madame Mouret's *Annales de l'Education du Sexe* articulated the demand for female education, prevalent among women writers in this era; Mouret backed up her words with action, opening a school for girls in 1791 (Bellanger I: 495-96, 536-37; Duhet 1971, 92-99; Sullerot).

While the years 1789 to 1793 were marked by highly politicized and engaged writing, the Terror, not surprisingly, witnessed a precipitous drop in publications by women. The Thermidorean and Directorial periods, in turn, saw the increasing emergence of memoirs looking back on the revolutionary turmoil, and above all, a marked resurgence of the novel by authors such as Madame de Genlis, Madame Cottin, and Madame de Staël. In this era when the lines between public and private were under so much debate, women's novels articulated conflicting visions of women's domestic role and public possibilities. While a few works, such as Madame Quinquet's *Illyrine* (1799), critiqued women's socially inferior position and called for a continued reform of marriage laws, many more works, such as Madame Booser's *Triomphe de la saine philosophie ou la vraie politique des femmes* (1795), seemed to glorify women's familial role as the underpinning of an orderly society. Madame de Staël's *Corinne, ou l'Italie* (1807) perhaps best captured the dilemmas and frustrations of a woman who aspired to public literary success and found herself limited by domestic expectations (Krief; Maza 1989 b).

Indeed, as many of the essays in this volume make clear, female writers throughout the revolutionary era found themselves in a difficult position. Despite the radical changes of the revolutionary era, neither the law nor public opinion offered much support for the role of the women writer. The law of 19 July 1793, which gave male authors property rights over their written texts, offered no such legal assurances to women. Husbands retained legal rights over the publications of their wives. Some women writers, such as Louise de Kéralio, turned to the use of pseudonyms in order to control their publications and establish their independence as authors (Hesse).

Moreover, women's ambivalent position on the hinge between the private world of the home and the public world of politics opened female authors up to suspicion and attack for transgressing gender norms and meddling in public affairs. Keenly aware of their uncertain position, some women, such as Madame Roland, expressed mixed emotions about making their writing public. Yet, many of these literate women, perhaps Madame Roland and Madame de Staël above all, nonetheless sought as salonnières to act as influential power brokers, taking maximum advantage of their stance with one foot in the public and one in the private realm. Many female authors explicitly defended their right to publish as a means of staking out their identity as well as their opinions.[8] In a pamphlet debate in 1797 over the role of *femmes-auteurs,* Constance Pipelet bemoaned the desire to consign women to the role of inspiring muses. She wrote, "A thousand voices blame us for audacity; they are astonished and agitated, they murmur and produce threats; . . . O women! take up the pen and the paintbrush; the arts, like happiness, belong to everyone."[9] Many of the authors in this volume shared Pipelet's certainty that women should have a literary voice. Yet, in this era when women's relationship to the public sphere was under constant scrutiny and redefinition, they also shared the difficulties of taking words written in private and making them public.

Women also participated actively in the elaborate new revolutionary festivals. Living women often represented revolutionary ideals, such as Liberty, Reason, Nature, or Victory, and the allegorical female figure of Marianne came to represent the Republic.[10] Revolutionary parades most often included groups of women: at the 1790 festival of the Federation in Strasbourg 400 adolescent girls dressed in white rode a flotilla of tricolor ships up to the "altar of the nation," while in Estampes in Burgundy a large group of mothers and daughters performed an elaborately orchestrated choral ceremony in honor of their sons and brothers at war in the summer of 1792. Revolutionary festivals often encouraged women above all to be republican mothers who would bear and raise young patriots to be good citizens and soldiers of the Republic. One mother who had borne 25 children had the honor of carrying the national flag to the cathedral of Rouen in a special ceremony in the spring of 1791; likewise, in one revolutionary festival a patriotic banner proclaimed, "Citizenesses! Give the Fatherland Children!"[11]

Women's portrayals in festivals highlight also the ambivalent aspects of women's position in the French Revolution. The revolutionary ceremonies, like much of republican ideology more generally, set up specific models for female behavior which conflicted with the public, political actions of women as club members, rioters, authors, and petitioners. Abstract, philosophical depictions of women as Liberty or Marianne distanced women from involvement in the pragmatic, everyday workings of politics and set up a model of femininity that was aloof, moral, and abstract.[12] Even more importantly, the recurring celebration of the cult of republican motherhood, which lay at the heart of patriotic visions of women's contribution, emphasized domestic virtues of sensibility, gentleness, self-sacrifice, intuition, and patience. These idealized forms of female behavior in the home did little to validate the political activism of women in clubs, streets, assemblies, or the Lycée des Arts.

In fact, particularly as the Revolution progressed, women from a wide range of political positions found their *public* actions come under close scrutiny or even attack. Invariably, when women were accused for political reasons, suspicions of counter-revolutionary sympathies mingled with the perhaps more deeply threatening notion that they had stepped beyond their gender roles in an unfeminine and too public fashion. Accusations which combined the political with the personal in this way were made against women from the whole gamut of political positions, including the queen herself, vilified as a sexual monster and bad mother, "a disgrace to her sex"; the vocal Olympe de Gouges, whose audacious texts apparently proved that she had forgotten "the virtues that suit her sex"; and finally, the radical *Citoyennes Républicaines Révolutionnaires,* whom the Jacobin Chaumette indicted in the Paris Commune as "denatured women [and] viragos."[13]

The radical Revolution called gender roles into question because the revolutionaries of various political stripes sought to redefine the relationship between public and private spheres and to refashion both public politics and the family. Joan Landes has argued that male republicans gradually excluded women from the public sphere in order to create space and legitimacy for male democratic politics.[14] In October 1793 the National Convention outlawed women's clubs altogether: The *Citoyennes Républicaines Révolutionnaires'* link to the Enragés was an irritating political challenge to the moderate Jacobin leadership, and women's formal participation in public politics seemed to threaten social stability (Godineau 1988, 163-77). "The social order results from differences between men and women," thundered Amar in his appeal to the Convention to close the clubs and relegate women to the domestic sphere (qtd. in Levy et al. 1980, 216). Despite the fall of the

Jacobin leadership in thermidor, the exclusion of women from formal politics only intensified in the year after the Terror. After the germinal and prairial uprisings in the spring of 1795, women were barred from the galleries of the National Convention or any other political assembly, and forbidden to assemble in public in groups of more than five.

This assault on women's public participation in revolutionary politics was fundamentally intertwined with a reformulation of women's domestic role and identity as well. Many men and women believed that republican women could act particularly well in the private realm as wives and mothers because of their *sensibilité*. This *sensibilité* gave women peculiar power over morals and the ability to touch and evoke the emotions of others—crucial characteristics in a cultural revolution which sought to "regenerate" human beings to their very essence. "The power of women," asserted Françoise Sanson of Caen in 1791, "is in their *sensibilité;* let us use this valuable arm" (qtd. in Villiers 127-28). This role as moral guardians gave women a certain power in the private realm; some speakers called on republican women not just to educate their children, but even to politicize the bedroom and "refuse their caresses" to men who were not true patriots. But private patriotic authority was a peculiarly ambiguous and limiting power. It opened women up to even closer moral and sexual scrutiny, for they had to be morally pure in order to exercise political persuasion and moral judgment within the family on behalf of the *patrie*.[15] Moreover, many revolutionaries began to develop the notion which would flourish in the nineteenth century: Women's moral authority would remain strong only if they left the somehow tainted and corrupting business of public politics to men.[16] Finally, the private power of women could become dangerously close to the seductive, mysterious influence of elite women in the Old Regime court; by definition, private power was somewhat secretive and suspect in contrast to the revolutionary ideal of transparency, publicity, and openness (Hunt 1984, 44-46; Hunt 1991; Maza 1991). Therefore, according to republican ideology, this form of moral suasion could be exercised only in the home by women whose sexual and social practices conformed to domestic and familial norms.

In the aftermath of the Terror and its social disorder, the desire of revolutionary leaders to define and limit the domestic role of women seemed to increase.[17] The radical revolution, with its intense politicization of every aspect of life, had obscured and altered the line between public and private:

Private decisions, from the naming of children to the choice of religion, were loaded with public political meaning and each individual's public legitimacy became dependent on his or her private morality. Such conflation or confusion of the private and public led in part to an intense anxiety about gender roles as the underpinning of social stability and nourished a corollary desire to strengthen the lines separating public politics from the private realm.

Thermidor and the Directory witnessed an escalating debate among the deputies and the public at large about the social legislation which had increased women's individual rights within the family. Post-Thermidorean governments dismantled some of the most radical revisions of family and property law: Family courts were eliminated on 3 brumaire an IV (26 October 1795); the retroactive clauses of the most egalitarian inheritance laws, attacking primogeniture and guaranteeing even illegitimate offspring an equal inheritance, were revoked by the laws of 9 fructidor an III (26 August 1795) and 15 thermidor an IV (1 August 1796). Above all, the national legislature repeatedly debated the validity of divorce based on incompatibility and eventually made it slightly more difficult to obtain in 1797.[18] This mood of growing social conservatism culminated after the Revolution in the drafting of the Napoleonic Code of 1804. This far-reaching civil code extensively reinforced the legal patriarchal control of husbands and fathers, made it particularly difficult for women to obtain divorces, and curtailed the control of married women over their wages, property, and inheritance.[19]

We are left, then, with an ambiguous picture of the impact of the French Revolution on women's private lives and public voices. It was an era of both possibilities and disillusionments, and most women found themselves scrambling to adapt to the rapid transformations in their legal status, proposed cultural role, and economic position. Yet, women did more than simply react to revolutionary change, they helped to create the revolutionary dynamic, including some of its paradoxes. And while the later years of the Revolution and the Napoleonic period did not witness the unprecedented opening for female activism and organization of the years of 1789 to 1793, the changes in legal and political structures could not erase women's political education and growing literary voice. The diverse women examined in this volume—including an aristocratic author like Isabelle de Charrière, a foreign observer like Helen Maria Williams, a politician and salonnière like Madame Roland, and a novelist and political analyst like Madame de Staël—

all bear witness to the rich complexity of women's experience of the French Revolution.

Notes

1. This essay will not explore women's extensive role in the counterrevolution and in religious resistance. On these topics, see Hufton 1971 and 1992, ch. 3; Vray 1989; Yalom 1989; Desan 1990, ch. 5.

2. On women's exclusion from the public sphere, see Landes. Landes's emphasis on the public sphere needs to be balanced by a closer look at women's changing position in the private sphere. See Darrow; Fulchiron; Hunt 1985 and 1992.

3. As Karen Offen points out, recent historiography mirrors this ambiguity, as different authors choose optimistic or pessimistic portrayals of the impact of the Revolution on women. See Offen 909-22.

4. On legal changes in women's private lives, see Darrow 3-13; Fulchiron; Garaud and Szramkiewicz; Kates 1990; Ronsin; Sledsiewski 99-126; *La Révolution et l'ordre juridique privé* esp. vol. I: pt. IV. On education, see Julia 310-31; Palmer 95-98, 122, 231. The various proposals for educational reform debated or adopted by the successive national legislatures advocated only primary education for girls; not even Condorcet's proposal called for secondary education.

5. For varying accounts of the paradoxical nature of women's citizenship, see Godineau 1988, 110-11, 163-69, 305-32; Godineau 1990; Levy and Applewhite 1990 and 1992; Levy et al. 1980, 15-17.

6. On steps to abolish censorship of press and theater, and on the limits of this abolition, see Popkin 25-29, 38-39, 169-79; E. Kennedy 1989, 182-85, 316-17; Reid 572-79. The king's minister Brienne had initially eased royal censorship of pamphlets in July 1788. The Declaration of the Rights of Man and Citizen declared a (limited) freedom of speech, writing, and publication in general; royal censorship of plays was abolished on January 13, 1791. Obviously, these guarantees of freedom of public expression were not always maintained in the heat of revolutionary politics.

7. The history of women as petitioners and as authors of "mémoires justificatifs" during the Revolution remains to be written. For an example of innovative use of these sources in the Old Regime, see Hanley. For the revolutionary period, see Andries; Jodin; Lézardière. For an overview of women writers' topics and changing choice of genres, see Slama. For excerpts from newspapers, pamphlets, and petitions written by women, see Duhet 1981; *Les femmes dans la Révolution française;* Levy et al. 1980; Yalom 1989.

8. On Madame Roland, see Thomas 1988, 309 and the essay by Mary Trouille in this volume. On Madame de Staël's salon, see Orr. On writing, identity, and salons, see Goodman 1989a and 1989b.

9. Salm, 1: 11, 13, & 20. See also her "Boutade sur les femmes-auteurs," 2: 245-48, and "Rapport sur un ouvrage intitulé: *De la condition des femmes dans une république*," 4: 131-56. On the debate over "femmes-auteurs," see Fraisse ch. 2; Planté.

10. On women and revolutionary allegory, see Agulhon; Hunt 1984, 61-66, 93-119. For examples of female participation as allegories in Old Regime ceremonies, see Bryant.

11. Schama, 503 & 522; Baillot; Darnton 1989, 4. On the cult of republican motherhood, see Harten and Harten.

12. Multiple authors have explored this problematic. See Harten and Harten 38-45; Huet 35-38; Hunt 1984, 31, 61-66; Landes, 162-67.

13. On Marie Antoinette, see Colwill 1989; Hunt 1991; Maza 1991; Thomas 1989 b. Chaumette quoted in Levy et al. 1980, 210.

14. Landes esp. ch. 4. For critiques of Landes, see Goodman 1992; Gordon 899-911; Maza 1992; Nathans 634-36.

15. On appeals to women to politicize their private lives, see Desan 1992. On the limitations of the republican concept of female "virtue," see Outram 1987, 124-26.

16. On protecting women's domestic moral strength from the corruption of the public sphere, see Poovey 75-80.

17. For an insightful analysis of this phenomenon in the realm of republican art and festival, see Lajer-Burcharth.

18. On women during the Directory, see Marand-Fouquet 287-314. As Lynn Hunt points out, these legal changes moved not just toward curtailing women's familial rights, but also toward reinstating the power of fathers over sons. See Hunt 1992, ch. 6; Garaud and Szramkiewicz 83-87, 127-30. On anxiety about gender roles, politics, and the private revealed in debates over divorce during this period, see Desan 1993.

19. According to the Civil Code, women could not participate in lawsuits, serve as witnesses to contracts or as witnesses in court. Specific legal rights given to women by early revolutionary legislation were lost: women could no longer sue in paternity cases for the support of illegitimate offspring; it became virtually impossible for women to divorce their husbands (unless they literally brought a mistress into the home); yet women were subject to fines and imprisonment for adultery. Married women had virtually no control over their property; even their dowries lay under the husband's management, and the wages of women workers or profits of women in business immediately belonged to their husbands. For a succinct summary of the impact of the Napoleonic Code, see B. Smith 120-22; also, Garaud and Szramkiewicz 165-81.

I

Revolutionary Women
Inscribed in History

3

Charlotte Corday: *femme-homme*

Nina Corazzo
Catherine R. Montfort

"Seule tu fus un homme."
—André-Marie Chénier

On July 13, 1793, Charlotte Corday stabbed to death one of the leading figures of the French Revolution, Jean-Paul Marat, and was cast by her detractors as an arch-criminal who had brazenly transgressed the basic moral orthodoxies of her time. This judgment must not, however, obfuscate the condemnation of her equally abhorrent error—contravention of the idealized forms of female behavior emerging in late eighteenth-century France. Indeed, immediately after the death of Marat, the Revolutionary government vilified her as a woman who had renounced "the temperament, the character, the duties, the tastes and the inclination" of her sex (*Gazette de France Nationale*, July 20 1793).[1] Moreover, two months later in a tribute to Marat, the Marquis de Sade graphically described Corday as a hideous hybrid of male/female: "The barbarous assassin of Marat, similar to one of those composite creatures to whom one can assign no sex, vomited up by Hades for the unhappiness of both sexes, belongs solely to neither" (September 29, 1793). This description illustrates the dilemma that Corday posed for most of her contemporaries: Although she possessed the physical attributes of a woman, she had not acted like one. Therefore, she was characterized as a loathsome amalgam of the two sexes, the *femme-homme,* the "unnatural" woman.

In his *Education of the Senses,* Peter Gay discusses the notion of *femme-homme.* He declares the *femme-homme* to be an international phenomenon which came into full bloom during the middle of the nineteenth century (190-97). Gay notes that while moderation was a key element of the Seneca Falls convention in 1848, the response of the opposition to feminism was instantaneous and furiously irrational. In Rochester in 1852, a Protestant pastor characterized women activists as a "hybrid species, half man and half woman, belonging to neither sex" (190). And in 1853, an editorial in the *New York Herald* insinuated that "unsexed women" had become activists because they were too repulsive to find a husband (190-91). Gay adds that the English and French also voiced concern about the *femme-homme.* In France, the *femme-homme* was seen as being bloodthirsty and cruel by nature and "became a specter for terrified men to conjure with: She was the supreme enemy of the family, ruinous to man's self-confidence, and destructive of women's real vocation" (193). Finally in England, Montagu Burrows, Chicele Professor of Modern History at Oxford contributed another dimension to the critique of the *femme-homme*: "The one thing men do not like is the man-woman," proffering "the University-woman" as a case in point. He went on explaining that one must: "Keep the male and female types essentially distinct. For those young ladies who cannot obtain 'a higher education' through their parents, brothers, friends, and books at home, or by means of Lectures in cities, let a refuge be provided with the training governesses; but for heaven's sake, do not let us establish the 'University-woman' as the modern type" (Gay 193).

These statements support a prevailing nineteenth century male position which castigated female activists and intellectuals as *femme-hommes,* unsexed and therefore "unnatural." In a nutshell, these women were considered neither physically attractive nor gentle, but rather coarse and violent in their emotions and their actions. They did not envisage themselves as goddesses of the hearth, but instead as co-frequenters of the male dominated political, intellectual, and cultural spheres so long kept closed to them. However, this caricature of woman as *femme-homme* predated the nineteenth century and, in fact, was firmly established at the turn of the eighteenth century. According to Harten: "By 1794, the myth that the learned and politically involved woman must necessarily become 'a being against nature,' 'a fury' was born (19). We argue in what follows that although Corday ultimately lost her life for being the murderer of Marat, her vilification and condemnation as a *femme-homme* during the anti-Corday campaign that followed her death—in newspaper articles, images, verses, songs, and plays—stem as much from her noncongruence with the expected role of women in Revolutionary society as from her crime. The denunciation of Corday as a *femme-homme* by the Marquis de Sade was elaborated on further by other commentators using derogatory comments about her physical appearance. In addition, Corday was castigated for being violent in both thought and deed, thus violating the ideal of the silenced and domesticated woman. Finally, as a single woman who was also an intellectual, she did not fit the stereotype of the emotionally and economically dependent woman, and instead represented a frightening model of the informed and politically engaged woman of the future. This essay will explore each of these points in succession, starting with the physical appearance of Corday, continuing with her unladylike violence and independence, and ending with her above average education.

One particularly bitter invective against Corday was published by the revolutionary government in the *Gazette Nationale* on July 20, 1793, a scant few days after her assassination of Marat. The article was written by Fabre d'Eglantine. It offers far-reaching insights into the nature of the accusations made against her:

> Charlotte Corday was 25 years old, which is, according to our customs, almost an old maid, the more so with her mannish carriage and tomboyish stature [. . .] She had no fortune and lived a paltry existence with an old aunt; her head was full of books of every sort; she declared, or rather she avowed with an affectation which approached the ridiculous, that she had read everything, from Tacitus to *Portier de Chartreux* [. . .] This woman absolutely threw herself outside her sex; when nature recalled her there, she experienced only disgust and boredom; sentimental love and its soft emotions no longer approach the heart of a woman who has the pretention to knowledge, to wit, to free-thought, to the politics of nations, who has a philosophic mania and who is eager to show it. Sensible and amiable men do not like women of this type [. . .] Charlotte Corday is a remarkable example of the seal of reprobation with which nature stamps those women who renounce the

temperament, the character, the duties, the tastes and the inclination of their sex.

Corday's Physical Appearance

The first aspersion cast upon Corday in this text is that she has passed the age at which women traditionally marry. Twenty-five years old was considered old by revolutionary men who generally speaking denounced celibacy.[2] The implication in the text is that something must be lacking either in Corday's character and/or her appearance which would account for her abnormal condition. The comment that she has a "mannish carriage and tomboyish stature" implies that she lacked feminine charm. In fact, in the same article, the attack on her beauty is plainly stated: "This woman that some say was pretty was not pretty at all." Yet, as evidenced in the portrait of Corday executed by Jean-Jacques Hauer and engraved by Tassaert, she had an undeniable physical allure (figure 1).[3] Done from sketches made at Corday's request while in prison, this image was widely circulated. As a matter of fact, the potentially deleterious effect such flattering images of Corday might have upon the populace, prompted the Marquis de Sade to issue the following injunction against future production of such works: "A funerary shroud must envelop her memory forever; everyone must stop presenting, as they now dare, her effigy under the enchanting symbol of *beauty*. Artists you are too credulous, break, destroy, disfigure the features of this *monster* or offer her image to our indignant eyes only if it is placed amidst the furies of Tartar" (our underscore). In any event, the main point is that, whether or not she was beautiful, using beauty as a category in reference to Corday was irrelevant to her crime.

In a song accompanying an image picturing the death of Marat, *La Mort du Patriote Marat,* Corday's beauty was not suppressed (figure 2).[4] However, the verses warn that her appearance is deceptive ("false," "disguises"), masking her true nature which is treacherous and evil ("wickedness," "monster," "fury"). Corday is portrayed as a lovely, lethal *femme fatale:*

Tassaert (after Hauer), "Marie-Ann-Charlotte Corday," 1793, engraving. Bibliothèque Nationale, Cabinet des Estampes, Paris.

Anonymous, "La Mort du Patriote Marat," 1793, engraving.
Bibliothèque Nationale, Cabinet des Estampes, Paris

> . . . Satan created this wretch
> One can see in every feature
> Of this temptress, his portrait . . . (repeat)
> So as not to alarm
> She has a false appearance of sweetness
> Her manner is charming
> Which disguises her wickedness.
> Source of eternal tears
> This monster filled with fury
> Has robbed us of a benefactor . . . (repeat)[5]

These lines introduce the notion that Corday was one of Satan's creations.[6] In fact, Satan is but one in a series of males with whom Corday's name was linked, sometimes to her advantage. In an impassioned text written immediately after Corday was guillotined, Adam Lux, a young German sent to Paris on a political mission, referred to her as "GREATER THAN BRUTUS" and enraged her detractors further by adding: "Charlotte Corday, celestial spirit, unrivaled woman! . . . be triumphant France, be triumphant Caen, because you have produced a heroine the like of whom is not found even in Rome or Sparta." (Lux was jailed immediately after writing his eulogy, and guillotined on November 4th.)

Corday, herself, had drawn attention to the fact that her action was patterned after those of two men, Alcide and Brutus. The day before she murdered Marat, she wrote an "Address to the French, Friends of the laws and peace" which was found on her after she was arrested: "O France! your peace depends on the execution of the law; I am not undermining it in killing Marat; condemned by the world, he is beyond the law. What court will judge me? If I am guilty, Alcide was too when he destroyed *monsters*" (qtd. in Walter 28-29. Our underscore). She further justified her act by quoting at length from Voltaire's *La Mort de César* (Act III, scene 2), citing the passage in which Brutus explains that what is important is not whether his killing of Caesar is glorified or reproached, but that by doing so he will act according to his duty: "My duty is everything, the rest is insignificant." Like Brutus, Corday concluded it was her duty to kill Marat: "You will not miss a ferocious beast made fat with your blood." In singing praise to the noble spirits of Alcide and Brutus who likewise destroyed "monsters," Corday drew upon the past to furnish historical precedents to legitimize her action.[7]

The linking of Corday with Brutus is not unexpected, as the French Revolution alternatively patterned itself and its outstanding members after the Roman Republic. What is of interest to this discussion is that her comparison to Brutus made her action more palatable. Besides, this comparison was quickly assimilated into the literary tradition. Barely twenty-six days after the assassination, a play was performed in which Corday muses to herself: "So the day of my vengeance has arrived! Today I will deliver my country from the monster which governs it. My life, without a doubt, will pay as the price for this. What does it matter? Like another Brutus, I will have saved my country."[8] And in *Charlotte Corday oder Die Rebellion von Calvados* (1794), a dialogue between Corday and a fictional fiancé contains this apostrophe: "Strange creature who bears the spirit of Brutus disguised in the angelic form of a woman. . . ."[9] By following in the footsteps of Brutus, Corday's admirers were able to elevate her into the pantheon of male heroes who had eschewed traditional moral values for the higher good of humanity. Corday, in this instance, benefited from being a *femme-homme*.[10]

Corday's Violence

In 1793, such budding admiration by counter-revolutionaries was not to the liking of Jacobin leaders as demonstrated by the following two documents.[11] First, the minutes of the meeting of the General Council of the Paris Commune which recommended on July 21, 1793 that the article of the *Gazette Nationale,* quoted at length above, be reprinted, posted, and sent to all local authorities. Members thought that this article assigned "to this atrocious woman the place which is due to her and to trace her character, her immorality and her audacity, with the brush of truth and the appropriate colors."[12] Second, the note of July 22, 1793 from the Committee of Public Safety to Fouquier-Tinville echoing official concern about Corday's image: "We have received the interrogation and the abstracts of the documents of Charlotte Corday's trial. The Committee thinks that it is unnecessary and potentially dangerous to give too much publicity to the letters of this unusual woman who has already inspired too much interest . . ." (Arch. nat., W 277, dossier 82, pièce 18). As noted previously, the article of the *Gazette Nationale* alleged that Corday had renounced the "temperament" and the "character" of her sex, scorning "sentimental love and its soft emotions." The same conclusion was reached by the Marquis de Sade: "Sweet and timid sex, how can it be that your delicate hands could seize the dagger which enticement whetted? Ah! Your eagerness to come and throw flowers on the grave of this true Friend of the people, makes us forget that the crime was able to find a perpetrator amongst you!" (September 29, 1793). Shock reverberated throughout Paris that a woman could not only conceive of such an act but also *physically* execute it. A play written by Jean-Baptiste Salle, three months after the assassination, contains the following interchange between Corday and her interrogator, Barrère, secretary to the Committee of Public Safety:

Barrere: What! Alone and with such an inexperienced hand you could, without a guide, carry out such a crime?
Charlotte: The God of my country guided my arm. Do you want to know where this success with which I'm honored derives from? I struck hard; my hate was even stronger.
Barrere: A woman, however, understands little of these excesses.
Charlotte: Am I therefore not of my sex?[13]

The issue posed by this dialogue is that Corday is shown questioning her sexuality because she struck Marat with violence born of hatred. Impervious to the call for emotional moderation and physical restraint, Corday violated the traditional stereotype of feminine behavior which cast women as emblems of docility and frailty: A stereotype which could not accommodate a woman who acted and had emotions like Corday.[14]

One must keep in mind that women accounted for only about twenty percent of all crimes considered by the Châtelet during the last years of the Ancien Régime and that eighty-seven percent of female offenses were not premeditated acts of violence. Typical female offenses consisted of petty larceny. Rarely were women accused of premeditated homicides, violent assault, or house breaking—the "typical male crimes in eighteenth-century Paris" (Johnson 112). However, Corday's assassination of Marat was a carefully planned and orchestrated homicide. Furthermore, there is no doubt that Corday's premeditated crime arose from her deep hatred of Marat's politics. As early as July 7, 1793, Corday had told a neighbor: "No. It will not be said that someone named Marat will have ruled France!"

(qtd. in Melchior-Bonnet). She then initiated a plan to leave Caen and go to Paris, where she purchased a knife and made repeated efforts on July 13, 1793 to obtain an interview with Marat. She finally succeeded and stabbed him in his bathtub. The emotions which fueled her resolve had long been brewing. In March 1792, following mounting tension in Caen where a number of policies instituted by the revolutionary government began to affect Corday's life directly, she wrote to a friend, Armande Loyer (later Mme de Maromme): "I am thus not at peace, and besides, what is the fate which awaits us? Appalling despotism; and if the lower classes can be retamed, it will be like falling from the pan into the fire, we will keep on suffering" (615). In another letter written on January 28, 1793 (after the execution of the king) to Rose-Fougeron du Fayot (whose brother, a refractory priest, had just been sent to the scaffold), Corday bitterly indicted the powers-that-be:

> ... behold thus our France surrendered to the *wretches* who have already done so much evil [. . .] I *shiver* with horror and indignation. Everything *horrible* that we could dream of lurks in the future which such events prepare for us. It is very obvious that nothing worse can happen to us [. . .] All those men who were supposed to give us freedom have assassinated it: they are nothing but *executioners* [. . .] All my friends are being persecuted, my aunt is the object of all sorts of annoyances since they found out that she sheltered Delphin when he left for Britain. I would do the same as he did if I could, but God keeps us here for other purposes [. . .] the Republic should be taken in *horror* if one did not know that the crimes of men do not reach the sky (qtd. in Defrance 73-74).[15]

In this impassioned cry against the current tyranny, she refers to the leaders of the revolutionary government as "wretches" and "executioners" responsible for the evils, past and present, which have befallen France. Corday's forceful rhetoric and the strength of her convictions clearly indicate the extent of her growing estrangement from societal norms.

The stand of Jacobin leaders who advocated a limited domestic role for women, as opposed to the active, public stance adopted by Corday, is clearly evident in the well-known remarks of Amar made about the two sexes and their respective spheres of influence at the National Convention on October 30, 1793: "Man is strong, robust, born with great energy, audacity, and courage [. . .]; and as he is almost exclusively destined for agriculture, commerce, navigation, voyages, war, and all that requires force, intelligence, capability, so in the same way, he alone seems fit for profound and serious thinking which calls for great intellectual effort and long studies which it is not granted for women to undertake" (qtd. in Duhet 1971, 155-56). The character assigned to women, on the other hand, hinged on her "morals" and even on "nature," hence her confinement to the domestic foyer, where these same qualities will be transmitted to her husband and children. It was further argued that women had no place in the public arenas where political issues were at stake, as they would be abandoning both "reserve, source of all the virtues of their sex, and the care of their family" (Duhet 1971, 156). Women it was claimed were predisposed to an "over-excitation" which could prove deadly in public affairs, and interests of the state would soon be sacrificed to "error" and "disorder" (157). This gendered interpretation of nature prompted the Convention to declare women's associations dangerous and to vote to outlaw all popular women's clubs and societies as of that day. On the 17th of November 1793 at a meeting of the General Council of the Paris Commune, the arrival of a deputation of female activists sparked the following outcry from Chaumette:

> Since when is it permitted to give up one's sex? Since when is it decent to see women abandoning the pious cares of their households [. . .] Is it to men that nature confided domestic cares? [. . .] She (nature) has said to woman: "Be a woman. The tender cares owing to infancy, the details of the household, the sweet anxieties of maternity, these are your labors (qtd. in Levy et al. 1979, 219-20).

Clearly Corday did not fit the mold described by Chaumette. Not only did she strike Marat with an unladylike force, but she also astonished everyone by the strength of character she exhibited after the stabbing, during the trial, while emprisoned, and on the way to the guillotine. She displayed no histrionics, doubt, self-pity, nor remorse.[16] While her consistent composure won her many admirers, it shocked her opponents who found her serenity in the face of such calamitous events highly suspect and irregular. Barrère, the interrogator in Salle's play mentioned earlier, after describing Corday's attitude while in prison, concludes that her composure must be a sham:

> She pretends to face death without shuddering;
> She wants to affix glory to her name;
> Her virtue is only a sham. Indeed is it believable
> That so brilliantly one can defy destiny
> And that in the heart of a woman there be such shams?
> (qtd. in Vatel 2: 39)

Interestingly enough, her composure did not win her the admiration of the Citoyennes Républicaines Révolutionnaires. Aware that Corday's crime would worsen the suspicion that surrounded them, they emphasized that Corday was not one of them and even counterattacked by stating that their sex had produced "one monster" but, for the last four years, the country had been besieged by numerous male "monsters" (Godineau 267). Also, it should be noted that Corday was fully aware of her own vulnerability as a woman. In her letter to Barbaroux, written while in jail, she remarked: "We are such good republicans in Paris that one cannot conceive how a useless woman, whose longest possible life would be wasted, can sacrifice herself in cold-blood in order to save her country" (Arch. nat., dossier 82, pièce 15).

In addition to written sources, visual sources also attest to what was deemed appropriate behavior for women at the time. In her analysis of David's *The Oath of the Horatii,* painted in 1785, Landes underscores the model which Republican women were to emulate by contrasting the attitudes of the three seated women and the two children with the clump of males on the left. "Their (the women) drooping, soft, sensual bodies evoke an atmosphere of deep sorrow." They are present, but passive, and yet "they feel the gravity of the moment, symbolized by the grave deed of creating a political future, one in which they will not participate" (152-53). While the women are superfluous to the main action, their presence fixes sexual boundaries, setting up unmodulated oppositions between masculine strength and feminine weakness, between rationality and passion, between male and female spheres of influence (155). Woman as spectator, mute, docile, and maternal was the order of the day.[17] By contrast, Quéverdo's engraving of Corday presents an alternative view of this self-proclaimed Republican female (figure 3).[18] An agent of violent change, a woman actively participating in the forging of a new political future, a woman moved from spectator to star performer, Quéverdo's Corday viciously plunges her stiletto into Marat, helplessly soaking in his tub.[19] Corday, like the Horatii, embraced violence and its attendant emotions as the means to an end. In so doing, she entered a space in which gender stereotyping no longer prevailed and thus fundamentally challenged the accepted dichotomy of sexual roles.

The extreme measures adopted to suppress women's associations reflect a more profound fear, that of the all-too-newly empowered non-socialized republican female. The abortive efforts of women to establish a political identity must be seen against a backdrop of unprecedented female turbulence (Johnson 123). Women in the marketplace, housewives, laundresses, domestic servants, and other working women were increasingly entering into conflict with the authority bequeathed to and controlled by males. Female violence was endemic and means were needed to immediately contain it. Simon Schama describes this period as the "stormiest phase of sexual politics in the Revolution" (800). He attributes the rabid anti-feminism preached at this time to the pervasive ideas then in circulation: women were "ravening beasts" (Marie-Antoinette) and "barrels of infection" (Mme de Barry) (796 and 800). The trials of these two arch offenders of the Jacobin ideal of the wife/mother, coincided with those of Mme Roland and Olympe de Gouges, upon whom the image of women as impure in body, thought, and deed was also levied (798).[20] It is interesting to note that Corday also underwent such attacks. After her death, there was wide spread speculation upon her virginity. This was fueled by a rumor published in *Les Affiches, Annexes et Avis divers* (a journal published in Caen) which claimed, in its issue of July 21st, that Corday had been four months pregnant at the time of her execution. Chabot was the bearer of these mysterious tidings and swore to their veracity (Defrance 374-75, 405). It was felt that if Corday was proved *not* a virgin she was lying when she said there was no man in her life (thus, no male to push her into killing Marat). However, two doctors from the Hospital of Charity determined that she had, in fact, died a virgin. Needless to say her adversaries would have been pleased to treat her as a "public" woman—rather than to have to face her growing legend as a heroine comparable to Joan of Arc or Judith.[21]

46   LITERATE WOMEN AND THE FRENCH REVOLUTION OF 1789

Quéverdo, "Marie Ann Charlotte Corday," 1793, engraving
Bibliothèque Nationale, Cabinet des Estampes, Paris

Corday's Independence and Education

Corday's assassination of Marat formed one more link in the chain of violent actions increasingly being undertaken by women. However, in the selection of Marat, *l'Ami du peuple* [the Friend of the People] as the target of her indignation, Corday hit a sensitive nerve. On the symbolic level, her act was construed as constituting the slaying of the Patriarch and by extension, as life-threatening to the patriarchal structure as a whole. To insure that the public at large was aware of the broader implications of her crime, she was dressed in red (the color reserved for those guilty of killing a representative of the people) when paraded through the streets of Paris on the way to the guillotine. A few days after Marat's death, a new Credo was recited in churches starting with the words: "I believe in Marat." And litanies followed: "Marat, solacer of the afflicted, Marat, father of the poor . . . Have mercy on us!" (qtd. in Melchior-Bonnet 221-22). Corday, slayer of the "divin Marat," had committed a crime against nature which was aggravated by the fact that she was also a fugitive from the sanctuary of her paternal home. She had moved to a distant cousin Mme de Bretteville-Gouville's residence in Caen after quarreling repeatedly with her father over politics.[22] Single and independent, Corday's lifestyle offered an unsettling blueprint for the independent woman of the future. Unattached and with no prospects of marital alliance in the near future, Corday showed no signs of becoming the Jacobin ideal of the wife/mother. On the contrary, according to the *Gazette Nationale* article mentioned earlier, Corday fancied herself a *philosophiste,* and boasted to have read everything, "from Tacitus to Portier de Chartreux." Vatel notes that the reference to Portier de Chartreux implied she had a taste for frivolous literature and that the same smear tactic was also employed against Louis XVI, Marie-Antoinette, and Camille Desmoulins to discredit their literary pursuits (1: CCCLIX). The *Gazette Nationale* article further alleges that Corday had the "pretention of knowledge, 'to wit,' to free-thought, to the politics of nations." In the eyes of the Revolutionary government, Corday was an intellectual, and as the article states quite categorically: "Sensible and amiable men do not like women of this type."

Corday's education was not standard for women of the times. When she was thirteen, she enrolled at the Abbaye-aux-Dames, the convent school of Sainte-Trinité in Caen.[23] The course of study administered by the nuns included a grounding in Latin and literature. During this period, Corday continued to express admiration for Corneille,[24] while adding the names of Plutarch, Rousseau, Raynal, and Voltaire to her list of favorite writers and philosophers. Upon leaving the convent, she studied languages and maintained her interest in Corneille, Rousseau, and the standard Roman histories.[25] In addition, she immersed herself in contemporary politics. She subscribed to *Perlet,* and read *Gorsas,* the *Courrier Français,* and the *Courrier Universel.*[26] Her friend Bougon-Langrais also sent her many political pamphlets (Defrance 87-88). During her trial, Corday stated that she had read over five hundred political tracts, representing both revolutionary and counter-revolutionary views. Furthermore, the house she shared with Mme de Bretteville-Gouville was close to the Intendance where the Girondins made their headquarters. It was here that she met one of their leaders, Charles-Jean-Marie Barbaroux, and other Girondins. She attended their meetings and developed a political consciousness nourished by her readings of the Classics. Essentially, she wished to see a republic established in France, but only if the people of France were worthy of a republic, for, according to her, a moral transformation of the populace would be required first (Defrance 64).

Corday was a perfect specimen of a rare breed, the politically informed, well-read Republican—a scourge to most revolutionary men who, at the time of her trial, could not believe that she had acted on her own and repeatedly asked her who instigated her crime. In one instance, true to her *femme-homme* persona, she proudly replied: "I would never have committed such a deed on the advice of others, I alone conceived the project and executed it" (qtd. in Walter 20).[27] Interestingly enough, Corday in her letters and her "Address to the French" expressed ideas similar to those of the republican leaders of France: rejection of patriarchal model of authority, condemnation of tyranny, desire for liberty and the public good, and fear of conspiracy. And yet, Revolutionary men so strongly disbelieved Corday's potential as an independent political thinker that they attributed her deed to a desire for revenge against Marat for the death of a man she was in love with: M. de Belsunce, nephew of the abbess of the Abbaye.[28] The idea was that political convictions alone could not have provoked such an act in a woman. Love or revenge, yes; convictions born out of patriotism, no. An informed woman was seen as a threat, in spite of the writings of Condorcet, Olympe de Gouges, and Mary Wollstonecraft, to name but a few feminist writers.[29]

Corday and other contemporary female intellectuals were viewed with deep suspicion and disdain. Armed with their erudition, they were considered formidable opponents of male supremacy, posing a threat as well to the traditional view that a woman's real vocation consisted in the establishment and maintenance of the domestic foyer. As clearly stated by Maréchal, a strict interpreter of Rousseau, there is an incompatibility between motherhood and intellectual pursuits: "Reason dictates that women who write books should not be permitted to have children" (qtd. in Harten 160-161).[30] As a result, the educated woman was likened to a freak of nature and reviled as a *femme-homme*.

In conclusion, it appears that *femme-homme* Charlotte Corday acted as a catalyst for those alarmed by the increasing inroads women had made into established patriarchal modes—women who actively claimed the fulfillment of the promise of inclusion in the universal community of equal human beings. She was the apotheosis of the threat posed by such newly empowered women: visible, vocal, and violent. Her death was the first in a string of executions of famous women aimed at destroying both the abhorred aristocratic woman and the newly empowered Republican woman.[31] Marie-Antoinette was guillotined on October 16, 1793, Olympe de Gouges on November 3, 1793, and Mme Roland on November 8, 1793. *Le Moniteur Universel* of November 19, 1793, asserts that the Queen was "a bad mother, a debauched wife," that Olympe de Gouges desired to be a "stateman," thus "forgetting the virtues that suit her sex," and that Mme Roland had "the desire to be learned," thus, also forgetting "the virtues of her sex" (qtd. in Duhet 205-06). It is ironic that these women who failed to gain political equality during their lifetimes were treated as equals to men only at the guillotine—their lives beset with the consequences of gender ended in a genderless death. As for Corday, her assassination of Marat had implications far beyond the death of an individual. Condemned as a monster and admired as a man, this audacious woman was a powerful precursor to the equally marginalized *femme-homme* of the nineteenth century.

Notes

1. Trans. Marrinan 160-61. All translations are the authors's except when otherwise stated. Corday's life is well documented. Documents on her life are preserved in the

Archives nationales, côte W no. 277, dossier 82. For one of the earliest biographies, see Couet de Gironville. In the nineteenth century, see the unfinished work of Vatel who spent a great part of his life searching for and collecting documents on Corday. In the twentieth century, see Defrance's thorough history, Melchior-Bonnet, and Dauxois. Also on Corday, and related to the ideas developed in this essay, see Thomas's article, "Heroism in the Feminine: The Examples of Charlotte Corday and Madame Roland" (1989a, 67-82).

2. On the average age for marriage at the time of the Revolution and its impact on demography, see Solé "Did the French Revolution undermine the traditional family?" (209-15). See also Harten for the content of Meriyon's address to the Convention in which he proposes a law which would force all girls unmarried at the age of twenty-one to choose a husband within three months (166).

3. The engraving is in the Cabinet des Estampes at the Bibliothèque Nationale. According to the *Journal de Perlet* of July 20, 1793, the portrait was of the most complete resemblance (Alméras 253-54). On Corday's beauty, see Mme Loyer de Maromme's description of Corday's complexion, eyes and voice, with as a conclusion to her portrait: "enfin c'était assurément une femme superbe" (604). See also Pierre Notelet's letter to his brother after seeing Corday on the way to the guillotine: "Elle était superbe dans sa longue chemise rouge que la pluie plaquait contre son corps. On eût dit une statue tant son beau visage était calme" (qtd. in Decours 480).

4. The engraving, which is anonymous, is in the Cabinet des Estampes at the Bibliothèque Nationale.

5. The complete title of the song is "La Mort du patriote Marat, l'Une des plus fermes Colomnes de la Constitution Assassinée par une femme du Calvados le 13 Juillet 1793, l'An 2e de la République Française, Dédiée aux Braves sans Culotte, Soutiens inébranlables de la Liberté." Air: Cœurs sensibles, cœurs fidèles de Figaro.

6. See also Chabot's commentary, at the July 14 meeting of the National Convention (Chabot was a representative of the Committee of Public Safety): "Elle (Corday) a l'audace du crime peinte sur sa figure; elle est capable des plus grands attentats. C'est un de ces monstres que la nature vomit de tems en tems pour le malheur de l'humanité. Avec de l'esprit, des grâces, une taille et un port superbes, elle paraît être d'un délire et d'un courage capables de tout entreprendre." *Gazette Nationale,* July 16, 1793.

7. See also her mention of Brutus in her letter to Barbaroux which she wrote while in jail: "Une imagination vive, un cœur sensible, promettent une vie orageuse; je prie ceux qui me regretterais de le considérer et ils se réjouiront de me voir jouir du repos dans les Champs-Elysées avec Brutus et quelques anciens." Arch. nat., côte W no. 277, dossier 82, pièce 15.

8. *L'Ami du Peuple ou la Mort de Marat, fait historique en un acte, suivi de sa Pompe funèbre, représenté pour la première fois sur le théâtre des Variétés amusantes, le 8 août 1793, par le citoyen Gassier Saint-Amand* (Vatel, 1: CLXV). Our underscore.

9. *Charlotte Corday ou la Rebellion du Calvados, tragédie républicaine en quatre actes, épisode du temps de la Révolution française, en iambes.* Stettin: Chez Jean-Sigismond Kaffke, 1794. Vatel attributes the play to Henri Zschokke (1: CXCI).

10. Further on this point, see Michelet: "Le vieux patron des meurtres héroïques Brutus, pâle souvenir d'une lointaine antiquité, se trouve transformé désormais dans une divinité nouvelle plus puissante et plus séduisante. Le jeune homme qui rêve un grand coup, qu'il s'appelle Alibaud ou Sand, de qui rêve-t-il maintenant? Qui voit-il dans ses songes? Est-ce le fantôme de Brutus? Non, la ravissante Charlotte, telle qu'elle fut dans la splendeur sinistre du drapeau rouge dans l'auréole sanglante du soleil de juillet et dans la pourpre du soir" (1854, 221).

11. This budding admiration soon developed into a full canonization of Corday in the late 1790s. See the early testimony in Camille de Malarmey de Roussillon's letter to Mme de Charrière (September 28, 1793): "Je voudrais qu'on peignît Charlotte Corday un poignard à la main et le plongeant dans le sein de l'anarchiste Marat. Le trait d'héroïsme de cette généreuse citoyenne mérite cet hommage de ses concitoyens. Les formes gracieuses du sexe féminin servaient d'enveloppe à une âme grande, courageuse et mâle, aussi ferais-je écrire au bas de ce tableau: 'Erreur de la nature' " (qtd. in Vissière 1988, 290). See later the anonymous play *Charlotte Corday ou la Judith Moderne, tragédie en trois actes et en vers.* Caen: l'Imprimerie des Nouveautés, 1797. In this play, Corday is described as a widow whose Royalist husband died for his country. The anonymous author has Corday say (qtd. in Vatel 1: CCXX):
> Nous ne combattons point pour ravir des trésors,
> Mais pour défendre Dieu, Louis et la Patrie.

12. See Couet de Gironville's biography for a facsimile of the article and the comments of the General Council of the Paris Commune.

13. *Charlotte Cordai, Tragoedie en cinq actes et en vers par Salle, l'un des proscrits* (Vatel 2: 27).

14. On this point, see also in Vatel 1: CLXXXVIII, the "Poëme à la gloire de Marat" by Dorat Cubières which was read at the meeting of the General Council on Sunday August 11, 1793, and printed by its order:
> ... Une femme pourtant, l'horreur de la nature,
> Une femme a plongé le poignard dans son sein.
> Une femme s'armer d'un poignard assassin!
> O sexe intéressant qui nous tient dans les chaînes,
> Toi que forma le Ciel pour adoucir nos peines,
> Pour charmer notre vie en la semant de fleurs,
> Pour calmer nos chagrins, pour essuyer nos pleurs!
> Faut-il qu'une mortelle, au quatrième lustre,
> Par un forfait horrible ait cru se rendre illustre!
> Que par la perfidie et la férocité
> Elle ait cru parvenir à l'immortalité?

> Jouissez de ce crime, ô tyrans que j'abhore!
> Marat n'existe plus, cent rois vivent encore!"

Finally, in a milder vein, see Louvet's *Mémoires* in which this moderate republican praised Corday for traditional feminine characteristics: beauty and modesty (1:114-15).

15. Our underscore. See Hunt's analysis of the rhetoric of revolution, in particular the passage about the language of the heart: "In the oratory of the Convention . . . the verb 'frémir' (tremble, quiver, shake) appeared again and again; orators spoke directly to the hearts of the auditors . . . and they expected to produce in them immediate emotion" (1984, 45).

16. See Chauveau-Lagarde's commentary on Corday during her trial: "Il ne faut pas essayer de donner une idée de l'effet qu'elle parut produire sur les jurés, les juges et la foule immense du peuple qui remplissait l'enceinte du Palais; ils avaient l'air de la prendre elle-même pour un juge qui les aurait tous appelés à un tribunal suprême" (qtd. in Vatel, 1: LVI). See also Helen Maria Williams's description of Corday in her *Letters from France* (1975, 2:128-35).

17. On David as propagandist in revolutionary France, see Crow. See also Marrinan who points out that David took a consistently 'hard line' towards the murderess in his painting of *Marat Dying*. He simultaneously excluded her from the picture visually, but included her by writing her name on the note held by Marat. Although Corday's pleading note was never presented to Marat, David used it to portray Marat as the victim of a deceitful women (161-62).

18. Quéverdo's engraving, "Marie Ann Charlotte Corday," 1793, is in the Cabinet des Estampes at the Bibliothèque Nationale.

19. Quéverdo's publicizing Corday's action can be interpreted in two ways. Either he agreed with David's condemnation, but, unlike the famous painter, chose to depict the enormity of her crime, or he genuinely admired Corday and decided to portray her as an exemplary criminal.

20. Schama's book has been severely criticized by historians, not only for its one-sided negative view of the Revolution, but also for its generally slipshod treatment of women exemplified in the book's horrific ending. See the review of Alan Spitzer in *Journal of Modern History*, 65 (1993), No. 1, pp. 176-92.

21. See Outram and her analysis of the differences of meaning of "public" when referring to a man or a woman. A public man was a man who sacrificed himself for a life of service to the patrie. A public woman, who assumed a public role in public arenas, was a courtisane or prostitute (1989, 127).

22. Corday was not a Royalist as shown by the following anecdote. When her elderly relative organized a dinner party in an attempt to heal the rift which had developed between Corday and her father, Corday refused to raise her glass to toast the King, explaining: "Je le crois vertueux, mais un roi faible ne peut être bon, il ne peut empêcher les malheurs des peuples" (qtd. in Maromme 610).

23. This institution did not ordinarily educate young women from the community, but upon recommendation from the King, select girls from impoverished nobility in Normandy (a maximum of five at a time) could be admitted on an honorary basis (Defrance 30-33). According to Sonnet, "les demoiselles confiées aux prestigieuses abbayes féminines se comptent sur les doigts des deux mains" (13).

24. A distant forebear whom she had learned to appreciate earlier under her uncle's tutelage. According to Villiers, she learned how to read from Corneille's works (20).

25. Corday's level of education far surpassed that of the typical middle and upper-class woman of the eighteenth century. For a more detailed discussion, see Spencer 83-96, Rousselot, and Snyders. See also the recent monograph by Sonnet. According to Sonnet, schools provided first and foremost religious education, followed by basic intellectual skills (such as reading and writing), and basic manual skills (such as needlecraft). Only a few privileged students received additional instruction in drawing, music, grammar, geography, and history. Altogether, Sonnet notes how little education was provided: "Partout l'on se garde, comme de la peste, de former des femmes qui en sachent trop (233).

26. It is difficult to know for sure whether she read *Gorsas*. Defrance says she subscribed to it (89). However, if one carefully examines Corday's statements at her first interrogation (on the 16th of July) and at her trial (on the 17th of July), a discrepancy appears: at first she admits reading it occasionally and later denies reading it at all.

27. In a play *La Mort de Marat, tragédie en trois actes et en vers, suivie de son Apothéose, en un acte et en vers, par Jean-François Barrau, représentée pour la première fois à Toulouse le 15 pluviôse de l'an II de la République française (3 février 1794),* Toulouse: l'imprimerie Jean-Florent Baour, Corday is portrayed as a devoted disciple of the Gironde deputies who acts on their behalf (Vatel 1: CLXXVI-CLXXXVI). But, although the Girondins admired Corday, they did not approve of her action. They generally thought that Marat's death was useful to the ambition of men such as Robespierre and Danton. Mme Roland's commentary about Corday is a case in point: "Une femme étonnante, ne consultant que son courage, est venue donner la mort à l'apôtre du meurtre et du brigandage; elle mérite l'admiration de l'univers: mais faute de bien connaître l'état des choses, elle a mal choisi son temps et sa victime" (qtd. in Vatel 1: LX).

28. See the letter of Fouquier-Tinville to the Comité de Sûreté Générale: "Citoyens, Je vous observe que je viens d'être informé que cet assassin femelle (Corday) était l'amie de Belsunce, colonel, tué à Caen dans une insurrection, et que depuis cette époque elle a conçu une haine implacable contre Marat, et que cette haine paraît s'être ranimée chez elle au moment où Marat a dénoncé Biron, qui était parent de Belsunce, et que Barbaroux paraît avoir profité des dispositions criminelles où était cette fille contre Marat pour l'amener à exécuter cet horrible assassinat" (qtd. in Vatel 1: CCXCI).

29. On Condorcet, see Badinter 1988. On Gouges, see Blanc 1981, and Scott 1989. As far as Mary Wollstonecraft is concerned, she proposed in her *A Vindication of the Rights of Women* (1792) that the goal of education should be to make women autonomous,

whether functioning within or outside of the family unit. Wollstonecraft was well aware that drastic upheavals in the existing political, social, economic, and legal orders would be necessary before women could become independent, yet, she maintained that it was primarily through the vehicle of education that the status of women would improve.

30. On Rousseau's views on women, see, in this volume, Mary Trouille "The Circe of the Republic: Mme Roland, Rousseau, and Revolutionary Politics."

31. According to Giroud, 374 women were executed in Paris during the months of the Terror (41). On Marie-Antoinette, see Thomas 1989b; Maza, "The Diamond Necklace Affair Revisited: The Case of the Missing Queen," and Hunt, "The Many Bodies of Marie-Antoinette: Political Pornography and the Problem of the Feminine in the French Revolution," the last two essays in Hunt 1991, respectively 63-89 and 109-30.

4

La Déclaration des Droits de la Femme et de la citoyenne: Olympe De Gouges's Re-Writing of *La Déclaration des Droits de l'homme*

Janie Vanpée

> "... la femme a le droit de monter sur l'échafaud; elle doit également avoir celui de monter à la Tribune."
> —Article X, *Declaration of the Rights of Woman*

Death Rites

October and November 1793 were fateful months for women of the Revolution.[1] The Queen, one of the last important symbols of the hated old order, was guillotined on October 16; Olympe de Gouges, arguably the period's most politically outspoken woman, lost her head on November 3; and Mme Roland, perhaps the most powerful woman behind the scenes of the Revolution, was executed on November 8. As was true in many of the trials of the Revolution, none of these accused women received what today would be considered a "fair" judgment. Evidence was shaped and twisted to confirm the predetermined decision to condemn them.[2]

In the case of Olympe de Gouges, her accusers culled immediate evidence from "Les Trois Urnes, ou le salut de la patrie," a political pamphlet she had attempted to distribute. It called for a plebiscite to choose from among three forms of government—a republic, a constitutional monarchy, or a federation—to put an end to the ongoing and debilitating factionalism (EP II, 243-48). Supportive evidence came from one of the last plays she had written, *La France sauvée ou le tyran détroné,* which presents a critical yet intimate perspective on the Queen's desperate attempts to save the monarchy during the last hours before its overthrow on August 10, 1792.[3] As transcripts and records from her trial show, she and her accusers disagreed fundamentally on the meaning and intentions of these texts.[4] Where the accusers, interpreting as literally as possible, saw proof of seditious intentions and royalist tendencies, de Gouges insisted that the very same texts were, on the contrary, proof of her republicanism, her desire to put an end to the factionalism threatening the nation, her patriotism, and her "solemn hommage to the national sovereignty" (Tuetery, entry no. 828 and 829).

The real issue, however, was not one of holding opinions from the wrong side of the political spectrum, but rather of articulating political opinions at all. Had she played innocent, denied the authorship of the incriminating pamphlet, *Les Trois Urnes,* not led the police to the study where she kept all her writings, which would serve as further evidence against her, in short, moderated her political zeal, the authorities might have ignored her case. Certain facts indicate that they were willing to forget her in prison. First, her two pretrial cross-examinations reveal that the Tribunal gave her several chances to recant or to plead ignorance of the laws violated by her pamphlet's call for a plebescite. Second, during the three months of her incarceration she was transferred twice to increasingly minimum-security prisons. As she commented in her last letter to her son, "I was as free as at home. I could have escaped; my enemies and persecutors were not unaware of it."[5] However, instead of capitalizing on the opportunities that would help the authorities forget her, she did everything she could to the contrary. In a series of invective letters and pamphlets, she boldly claimed responsibility for her political actions and called attention to her situation. She continued her activism from prison; she managed to smuggle out, have printed, and distributed at least two pamphlets decrying prison conditions, attacking Robespierre, and defending her patriotic fervor.[6] She herself requested to be judged as quickly as possible, believing that the trial would correct the authorities' misinterpretation of her writings, prove without a doubt the patriotic and republican intentions of her texts, and vindicate her.[7] Far from being paralyzed by the danger of her arrest and impending trial, de Gouges saw her case as a means of testing certain principles of the

Revolution. In pretrial interrogations she invoked as her right the freedom of opinion and speech granted by the *Déclaration des droits de l'homme*.[8] In short, she was determined to use her imprisonment and trial to implement once again her right to participate in the political arena. She was not about to let herself be ignored or forgotten, nor to efface the political identity she had fought so hard to forge through her writings.

De Gouges was certainly not the only defendant in the trials of the Revolution to have felt that her political writings, misinterpreted, led to a misunderstanding of her true patriotic identity. But given her repeated efforts to have her identity as a politically active citizen recognized and acknowledged, the Tribunal's attempt to reshape that identity according to its own interpretation and political needs takes on an ironic, as well as tragic, dimension. In the final account, the Tribunal did recognize her as a political individual, but not for the reasons that she had wanted. It is precisely because she insisted on maintaining her political identity that de Gouges had to be executed. Thus, she was silenced, not for her particular opinions, but simply because she had a political stance.

In the great drama of the Revolution, Olympe de Gouges's trial is but a minor scene. Yet, the Tribunal's willful misinterpretation could itself be interpreted as part of a larger pattern that would prove to be particularly significant for the status of women. During the same fateful month of October, the Committee of General Security was debating the question of women's political rights, their role in government, and more specifically, their right to found and participate in political associations such as clubs. Upon receiving the Committee's conclusions that women's nature called them to more important concerns of family and home, and that, according to the universal laws of nature, they could not claim political rights, the Convention voted to ban women's clubs.[9] A year and a half later, in May 1795, it reinforced this decision by voting to exclude women from its assemblies, and then by outlawing all public congregation of five or more women (Duhet 1971, 163-64). The politically expedient death sentences were thus sustained and grounded in theoretical reasoning that legally excluded women from further political activity. Both theory and practice colluded to cut women off from the body politic.

Now, while Marie-Antoinette, Madame Roland, and Olympe de Gouges each held very different views and could in no way be grouped together politically, the conjuncture of their death sentences and the government's debates on the political status of women cannot fail to have been read on a symbolic level by a public deeply engaged in inventing a new symbolic order for society. The combination of the government's deliberations and condemnations sent the message that whatever political positions women may have represented, they were lumped together and condemned, not for their specific opinions, but for their active engagement in politics. That is indeed how the press interpreted the events.

Here, for example, is how the *Moniteur universel* conflates the very different political significations of the trials of these three women to extract one symbolic meaning and warning:

> In a short span of time, the Revolutionary tribunal has just given to women a great example that will not be lost on them: for justice, always impartial, metes out its lessons severely.
>
> Marie-Antoinette, raised in a perfidious and ambitious court, brought the vices of her family to France. She sacrificed her husband, her children and the country that had adopted her to the ambitious views of the House of Austria.... She was a bad mother, a debauched wife ... and posterity will forever look down in horror upon her name.
>
> Olympe de Gouges, born with an exalted imagination, took her delirium for an inspiration of nature. She wanted to be a statesman and it seems that the law has punished this conspirator for forgetting the virtues that suit her sex.
>
> [And as for Madame Roland] ... the desire to be learned led her to forget the virtues of her sex, and this forgetfulness, always dangerous, led her to her death.[10]

October and November 1793 thus marked a turning point in the participation of women in revolutionary politics. If, for four years, they had been included in the political upheavals, if their voices had been heard and at times heeded, from then on their voices would be silenced.[11] In this historical context, de Gouges's trial and judgment take on an ironic significance; she did succeed in being taken seriously enough to be executed for her politics, but she failed to have her political texts understood as she intended them to be, let alone have any effect.

Speaking Rights

Olympe de Gouges had seized the occasion and tried to play a political role in the events that were unfolding, and, most importantly, she had argued vociferously for the recognition of women in the creation of the new republic. Other women were politically active, especially during the first three years of the Revolution. Besides the famous roster—the Queen, Mme Roland, Théroigne de Méricourt, and Etta Palm—countless women participated in many of the important events.[12] What makes the case of Olympe de Gouges exceptional and important is that, of all women activists, she alone, through her writings, left a very complete public record of her involvement. Unlike Mme Roland who made astute political observations in her personal journal and private correspondence, and unlike both Théroigne de Méricourt and Etta Palm who did not commit much of their political ideas to paper, Olympe de Gouges was a prolific and public writer.

Before the Revolution, she had begun to write for the theater and to fight the theatrical establishment to have her plays accepted and produced.[13] Although her theater was neither original nor sophisticated from a dramatic perspective, her subjects were always topical and often in the vanguard. She was, for example, one of the first to confront the problem of slavery in a dramatic production, representing blacks on stage. She repeatedly turned her attention to the underprivileged, the old, the poor, the disenfranchised, and the forgotten. With the advent of the Revolution, de Gouges seems to have found her true calling. The immediate and concrete political and cultural changes activated by the Revolution initially allowed women such as de Gouges much more freedom and opportunities to express themselves. Although this freedom would eventually be rescinded, as we have seen, at the beginning of the Revolution it had very real consequences for women. For example, once the National Assembly abolished royal censorship and the exclusive privileges of the Comédie Française in January 1791, de Gouges managed to have more of her plays produced.[14] After 1788, as the social turmoil intensified, she turned towards more overtly political writings. She became a prolific pamphleteer, plastering the walls of Paris with posters expressing her views on current political issues including the debate on the vote in the Etats-Généraux ("Le Cri du sage, par une Femme" and "Pour sauver la Patrie" [EP 1993a, 73-76 and 83-85]), the debate between the Jacobins and the Girondins on excluding Robespierre from the

Convention ("Grande éclipse du soleil Jacobiniste" [EP II, 110-20]), the upheavals caused by the dismissal of ministers ("Départ de Monsieur Necker et de Madame de Gouges" [EP 1993a, 145-62]), and the fate of the King whom she courageously offered to defend at his trial ("Olympe de Gouges défenseur officieux de Louis Capet" [EP II, 191-94]).[15] She also volunteered practical solutions to some of the period's pressing social and cultural problems, such as how to raise revenue for the depleted national treasury ("Lettre au peuple ou projet d'une caisse patriotique par une citoyenne"), how to care for the homeless and the unemployed ("Remarques patriotiques"), how to reform the sclerotic theatrical establishment, and how to encourage women to participate more actively in the literary and theatrical domains by establishing a theater reserved for them only ("Projet d'un second théâtre et d'une maternité" [Groult 1986, 69-82]). In this broad range of interests, de Gouges returned repeatedly to one concern above all—the status of women, their lack of power, of voice and of recognition in both the old and new order. Acutely aware that the Revolution offered an unprecedented opportunity for women to redefine their role and status in the newly emerging society, she undertook to articulate the needs of women, to secure their right to speak in both cultural and political arenas, and to forge their independent political identity.

She paid dearly for her outspoken political activism, for not only was she silenced, but so were her works. Already at the time of their publication, and with increasing frequency after her death, her writings were criticized for their illogical arguments, their digressive personal anecdotes, and their excessive tropes of passion and pathos. Despite some of her valid suggestions and commentaries on events, she was often spurned or ridiculed. Later, nineteenth-century historians and critics would dismiss both her and her texts as irrelevant to what they considered the essential history of the Revolution and the literature it produced.[16] Such reactions to her and her texts raise questions. Why, we need to ask, was de Gouges taken seriously enough as a political entity to be executed, and yet not seriously enough to have any of her texts remembered? How is it that she came to occupy such an ambiguous place in the history of the Revolution?

In a recent seminal article, "French Feminists and the Rights of 'Man': Olympe de Gouges's Declarations," Joan W. Scott advances a convincing hypothesis (1989, 1-21). Using de Gouges as her primary example, she analyzes why, during the Revolution and after, feminist writers who tried to establish political rights and equality for women were doomed to emit paradoxes, at best, and nonsense at worst. She argues that the period's prevailing philosophical discourses defined the terms and determined the logic of any feminist dissent and attempt at articulating a counterposition. The problem was particularly evident with the concept of natural rights, which served equally to establish the principle of universal equality and to prove the existence of sexual difference, and therefore, inequality. As Scott demonstrates, de Gouges was not at liberty to fashion an argument without referring to and tacitly adopting the established terms of philosophical discourse, with all their unresolved ambiguities, for her own discourse. In a close reading of de Gouges's *Déclaration des droits de la femme et la citoyenne,* Scott discloses the manifesto's paradoxes and sometimes apparently nonsensical statements to be the logical result of this discursive quandary.

In this essay, I would like to follow up on Scott's line of inquiry. If, as Scott argues, the ambiguous philosophical principles of the Revolution's political discourses subtended and ineluctably subverted feminist discourses such as de Gouges's, their form was similarly structured and undermined by the accepted patterns and rules of discourse and proper literary style of the period. Thus, the success or failure of de Gouges's texts depended not only on her manipulation of accepted, if self-contradictory, philosophical commonplaces, but also on her ability to implement, imitate, play off of, or parody specific textual strategies established by current literary tradition. To write outside or against those rules was to court failure. In the following pages I will consider some of the general textual strategies de Gouges relied on as well as the more specific ones she used in her most memorable, and hence successful text, *La Déclaration des droits de la femme.* As we will see, de Gouges walked a fine line between adherence to and deviation from established literary practices.

Born and raised in Montauban until she left when she was widowed at age eighteen, her background and the independent, unconventional life she led thereafter in Paris did not predispose her to become the *femme de lettres* she proudly claimed to be at her trial. Being from the south, she was geographically removed from the center of cultural activity in Paris and her native language was not French. Unlike the majority of eighteenth-century women of letters, she was uneducated and had absolutely no literary formation. As she proclaimed in the preface to her play, *Le Philosophe corrigé,*

"I do not have the advantage of an education; and, as I've already said, I know nothing" (1788, I, 1). The illegitimate child of an aristocrat who refused to recognize her, she was further hindered by a lack of the social connections key to deciphering the codes and conventions of public and literary discourses (Blanc 1981 and Groult 1986, 11-64). Yet, against these odds, de Gouges managed to absorb enough information and knowledge about the most popular cultural and literary commonplaces of the period to scatter references to them throughout her writings. Reflecting uncritically contemporary literary, philosophical, and political ideas, debates, and clichés, her texts have the unexpected, but most interesting effect of functioning like a mirror of the tastes and interests of the period's uneducated, yet engaged, common people.

Whatever genre de Gouges turned to, she invoked, imitated, indeed competed against, its leading practitioner. A few examples can illustrate this point. When she started writing for the theater in 1784, she pitted herself against Beaumarchais, then at the height of his popularity. Following the example of countless other authors who themselves were reflecting just how completely Beaumarchais's play had captured the French imagination, she wrote a sequel to *Le Mariage de Figaro, Le Mariage inattendu de Chérubin* (OCT 1993c, 43-66). Other plays she wrote reveal that despite the amateurishness of their dramatic composition, she was aware of some of the rules and clichés of the most popular dramatic genre, sentimental drama, and tried hard to achieve effects of tearful sentimentality. Both *L'Esclavage des nègres* and *Le Philosophe corrigé* (OCT 1993c, 23-42, 105-42) showcase the most blatant conventions of the genre—lost children and lovers, improbable coincidences, shipwreck (in *L'Esclavage*), and tearful reunions. In the case of the novel, de Gouges's choice to format her two attempts at the genre in the epistolary and oriental subgenres reflects the popular taste of the moment. *Mémoires de Mme Valmont* (1788, II), alludes constantly, albeit awkwardly, to Laclos's bestseller, from the straightforward stealing of the names of characters, to the imitation of the epistolary form, certain characters, and segments of the plot. As for her political texts, she had numerous models to repeat, imitate, or continue in the discourses and debates that she heard at the sessions of the various national assemblies that she attended faithfully. Not only do her political tracts invoke the great orators, Mirabeau among them, but they repeat the most current vocabulary and clichés of revolutionary discourse. Finally, in the domain of philosophy, her emulation of

Rousseau underscores the extent to which he had become a popular cult figure. Her philosophical essay, *Le Bonheur primitif de l'homme, ou les Rêveries patriotiques* (1788, I) refers to many of the striking ideas he had advanced in his two discourses, but rearticulated as the common platitudes to which popular interpretations had reduced them.[17]

Had de Gouges actually read, let alone studied, Rousseau and the other writers she referred to and whose styles and thoughts she emulated? It is impossible to determine exactly what or if she did read. What is clear from her references to other writers and their texts is that her knowledge was superficial, limited to the popular commonplaces the works had spawned and that were repeated everywhere. Thus, if de Gouges appears to have been cultivated enough to recognize and repeat the conventions of some of the period's most popular genres, thereby giving her texts a semblance of adhering to accepted literary rules, her education was not formal enough for her to have mastered those rules in any critical fashion. Her knowledge was steeped in oral tradition, gleaned informally from hearing whatever ideas, words, commonplaces were being bandied about on stage, at the national assemblies, in street and salon discussions. In this sense, de Gouges was very much a product of her times, reflecting in both the content of her knowledge and the manner by which she gained that knowledge, the explosion of speech, discourse, and oral communication of all types that occurred at the advent of and during the Revolution (Hunt 1984, 19-51).

The oral basis of her knowledge is evident throughout her writings, not only in the ideas she articulates, but also in the rhetorical strategies she deploys. Indeed, one of the most striking features of her texts is the overriding presence of the author's voice, which strains to be heard and understood. Given that oratorical discourse was the preferred genre of the revolutionary period and that her texts often mimic the tone and the topic of the day, it makes perfect sense that they communicate an oral urgency. The deputies and legislators that de Gouges heard speak at the bar of the National Assembly and later of the Convention strove for spontaneity and immediacy in their speeches. But such effects were the results of carefully honed rhetorical devices, culled from the rules of classical rhetoric and prepared in written texts before their actual oral delivery. Unlike her, the representatives were all educated, many of them lawyers, trained specifically in the art of rhetoric and argument.[18] De Gouges was aware that her lack of education impeded her ability to write as effectively as the orators she admired and made it more difficult for her to be considered seriously by the literary and political establishment. But she was also clever enough to capitalize on her ignorance. Turning her weakness into a strength, she claimed that ignorance lent her voice the authority of "nature" and the authenticity of unadulterated truth. In the preface to her play, *Le Philosophe corrigé,* she writes: "I am a student of nature; I've said, and I repeat, that I owe nothing to the learnings of men: I am my own creation, and when I write, there is nothing on the table but ink, paper, and pens" (1788, I, 2). And in a later political pamphlet, "Départ de Monsieur Necker et de Mme de Gouges," she repeats: "I am, in my writings, a student of nature; I might be, like her, irregular, even bizarre; but yet always true, always simple" (EP 1993a, 145-62). Was she conscious or not here of invoking one of Rousseau's famous paradoxes? Was she cleverly basing her claim to authenticity on an ignorance that masked a knowledge of a well-known philosophical tradition? In other words, was she feigning ignorance or was she ignorant of the philosophical feint behind her claim? What is certain is that de Gouges was walking a fine line between two contradictory rhetorical strategies. On the one hand, she invoked knowledge of literary and philosophical traditions as a way to have her works taken seriously; yet on the other hand, she invoked ignorance for the same reason.

To what extent, then, is thematizing her ignorance of the rules of literary discourse an effective strategy?[19] One of its most evident consequences is that it allows her to deemphasize the importance of writing and emphasize and value her "voice" in its place: "I do not possess the art of writing, I can only speak a natural language," she proclaims in a "Lettre de Madame de Gouges à la Comédie Française" (1986a, 140-41). De Gouges can thus circumvent the laws and customs that made it difficult if not impossible for women to speak in public forums and from the stage, and write as if she were speaking directly to her public. Indeed, she addresses all of her texts to someone. Nearly all of her pamphlets follow the format of an address or a letter, and the texts and plays that do not are dedicated to particular individuals. The Assembly, the Convention, different ministers and delegates to the Assembly, the Queen, Robespierre, French patriots, and, with increasing urgency, French women were all, at different moments, the interlocutors of her texts. Within the texts, she frequently apostrophizes her interlocutors, making their presence, and hers, all the more palpable. Apostrophe is a traditional rhetorical device of oratorical discourse. I would argue, however, that de Gouges implements it literally rather than rhetorically. What I mean by this is that while her texts evoke a relationship between speaker and interlocutor that she would like to actualize in reality, her actual practice of dictating her ideas to a secretary realizes her desire. Thus, the spoken immediacy of her pamphlets is not simply rhetorical artifice, but the actual reproduction of her working method.[20] De Gouges's practice subverts the rhetorical device of "writing as if one speaks," breaking it down into two separate operations of speaking and writing by two different people. In this way, de Gouges manages to mask the personal disadvantage of being incapable of writing behind a devaluation of writing in general and a revaluation of speaking.

Such an oral method of composing emphasizes the communion of the author with her audience more than the communication of ideas. This shift of emphasis, however, is the source of several problems. First, the more de Gouges strives to maintain contact with her interlocutor, the more the reader/interlocutor is lost and frustrated. "Speaking" as she does to her interlocutor, de Gouges uses rhythm and long periods to carry forth her "voice." Her "style" appears uncontrolled, devoid of the rules of argumentation and dominated by the organizing principle of one figure above all—metonymy—with its illogical turns, unexpected jumps, and frequent free association of ideas. The audience/reader feels directly interpellated, yet may not understand the logic of the ideas being articulated by her insistent "voice." The text's *énonciation* is very much present, indeed, threatening, but its *énoncé* remains unclear, and therefore unconvincing by more traditional standards of logic and argumentation. But for de Gouges, it is less important that her text communicate a coherent meaning than it preserve the physical link between author and interlocutor created by the "signifier." Hence, critics who deride the nonsense of her arguments miss the point. Her texts serve more as a conduit to a relationship than as a means to communicate a meaning.

The second problem arises from the difficulties of the interlocutor's recognition of himself, and in this case, often herself, as such. In other words, communion cannot take place unless both parties are conscious participants. The problem is particularly acute in the case of women, to whom and for whom de Gouges speaks. For the female author at this moment in history who claimed the right to active citizenship for women and all the responsibilities obtaining, including participation in the national debate, had no leaders of her sex to follow, no models to imitate, no established constituents to listen to her. As de Gouges's texts addressed to women repeatedly bemoan, French women, far from identifying as a group, have no consciousness of the commonality of their needs, demands, and identity; on the contrary, their jealousies and their incessant petty criticisms of one another fracture their solidarity. In "Préface pour les dames, ou le portrait des femmes," a text that precedes *Mémoires de Mme Valmont,* she chides women for their lack of group consciousness: "We need, my very dear sisters, to be more generous with each other for our shortcomings, hide them from one another together, and try to become more consistently supportive of our sex" (1788, II). But without a constituency that recognizes her as one of them and as their spokesperson, Olympe de Gouges's claims to represent French women are ineffective, if not moot. The "voice" in her texts, no matter how insistent or strident, becomes eccentric and unconnected to the group for whom she speaks, in total contrast to her aim of establishing communion and solidarity. Far from creating the constituency necessary from which her texts can derive their authority and meaning, her "natural" voice simply isolates her. As we will see, this basic failure of communion will be the undoing of her most celebrated text.

Righting the "Rights"

If de Gouges is remembered at all today, it is for her radical manifesto, *The Declaration of the Rights of Woman,* written in 1791 as a cutting response to the 1789 *Declaration of the Rights of Man* and the text that best exemplifies her attempts to speak both to and for women. Before analyzing how de Gouges deploys her various rhetorical strategies in this text, it may be helpful to situate it in its historical context.

During the two years since the original act of declaration, it had become increasingly evident that the rights described within would not pertain with equal force to all citizens. The founding document of the Revolution, the *Rights of Man* established the inalienable rights of the individual and the philosophical principles according to which the Constitution and the new legislative order would be built. The *Declaration of the Rights of Man* and the Constitution emancipated both men and women from the group identifications that governed society under the *ancien régime* and conferred equally upon both the new legal status of separate and free individual. Some of the new laws that the *Assemblée constituante* and then the *Assemblée legislative* enacted clearly presupposed the civil autonomy and equality of both sexes. For example, the law establishing civil marriage based on the contract is founded on the equal capacity of women as well as men to enter into a contract. In the same vein, the March 1791 law granting women the right to inherit reinforced the status of women as individuals by giving priority to the individual, of whatever sex, over the family group. As the September 1792 law on divorce by mutual consent proved further, the Revolution did transform the legal status of women.[21] But although the overthrow of the laws and social fabric of the *ancien régime* was equally liberating for men and women, the Constitution and the laws upon which the new society would be built did not grant equal political rights to both. Indeed, while the Constitution and the new laws were being drafted in the two years following the *Declaration of the Rights of Man,* it became clear that the "man" to which the Declaration referred was not mankind, but rather certain particular individuals who could take on the responsibilities of the active citizen, to wit, propertied and moneyed men. The rights instituted by the very "declaration" of those rights proved to be valid for only those who had actually participated in the performative act of declaring them. Others were decreed to be passive citizens, and denied the right of participating actively in the political process. A few voices (Condorcet, Etta Palm, Mlle Jodin) rose to argue for a broader conception of "man" and "citizen" and to point out the logical inconsistencies between the claims of the *Declaration* and the restrictions and exclusions actualized in the new Constitution, but to no avail.[22]

Such were the circumstances when Olympe de Gouges published her own *Declaration of the Rights of Woman* in a last attempt at influencing the way the Constitution conceived of the legal and political status of women just before its proclamation in September 1791.[23] Although several of her previous plays and pamphlets had already advocated women's participation and empowerment in both the public domain and private life,[24] sensitivity to the needs of women was often an aside or part of an argument, but rarely the main point of the text. In contrast, The *Declaration of the Rights of Woman* was her most explicit text yet, and, significantly, throughout its addenda, notes, preamble and postscripts, consistently aggressive in its demands for the equal rights of women.

In an open but playful act of piracy, de Gouges usurped the pre-existing *Declaration of the Rights of Man* and used it as a template for her own text, inflecting it with a woman's voice and point of view. As we have shown, reference to or imitation of a well-known text or author was one of de Gouges's favorite tactics to persuade her public that she was cognizant of current ideas and tastes. In this case, she used the tactic for more complex and rhetorical purposes. She deliberately played with imitation to obtain certain effects. Having purloined the original document, she copied almost word for word the preamble, imitated closely its seventeen articles, except at crucial points where she substituted "woman" for man, added "woman" to man, or changed the statement to redefine the right under discussion to fit the particular needs of women. At its core, then, the manifesto is like the original. It follows the same format; it uses the same performative language that enacts as it declares; it echoes the same vocabulary invoking the same principles of equality, justice, freedom, rights, and laws. The manifesto's frame, however, is significantly different than the original document. De Gouges appended two prefatory remarks, a letter dedicating the manifesto to the Queen followed by an introductory statement on the rights of woman, and a long double postscript, beginning with an apostrophe to women pleading that they become aware of their oppression and ending with an appeal for the emancipation of "men of color." In the detailed argument on society's unfair treatment of women, de Gouges also inserted a prototype of a contract for a civil marriage. The changes, of both form and meaning, operate a radical transformation on the original *Rights of Man* as they create a totally different and new document. And yet, the original document never disappears beneath the changes; it controls the structure and referents of the new text. As in a many layered palimpsest where different texts are superimposed one upon another, *The Declaration of the Rights of Woman* is at once, and often simultaneously, a literal and figurative interpretation of the *Rights of Man,* a critique, and a rewriting. De Gouges's intertextual experiment thus calls for a careful re-reading of both texts side by side.

On a first reading, the *Declaration of the Rights of Woman* appears to be as literal an interpretation of the original *Rights of Man* as possible. As its authors were well aware, one of the most radical implications of the first article's declaration of equal rights was to legitimize the overthrow of a society of privilege, structured on the hierarchical differences between social orders, to establish in its stead a society based on equality. Debate over the wording of the text between partisans of an entirely new order and those who merely wanted reforms had underscored the document's potential and to some, dangerous, ambiguity.[25] De Gouges's manifesto interprets the declaration of equality as some of the more conservative deputies to the National Assembly had most feared; it takes the *Declaration*'s first article conferring equal rights to mean literally that equality applies to all—men, women, and, de Gouges suggests in the postscript, men of color. Furthermore, it acts on the presumption that such a founding document must be consistent with the consequences of the principles it articulates. It cannot establish a society founded on equality and, at the same time, retain hierarchical differences within that society. In order to erase the inconsistencies that the original *Rights of Man* harbors, de Gouges's manifesto alters the original document, adding "woman" or "la citoyenne" to the neutral, or as her additions reveal, the gendered terms "man" and "citizen." In de Gouges's literal interpretation, equal rights must be spelled out each time as the equation "woman is equal to man." The first article of the original text, "Men are born and remain free and equal in rights" thus becomes "Woman is born free and remains equal to man in rights."[26] To be consistent with this first declaration, de Gouges must then rectify any latent contradictions in all the subsequent articles. As will shortly become evident, such alterations, even if for the purpose of eliminating contradictions, generate other contradictions.

Not only does de Gouges read the original document's philosophical principles literally, she also takes its rhetorical strategies at face value, repeating them uncritically in her own manifesto. One of the problems that most vexed the members of the National Assembly was how to legitimize its actions and documents. By what authority did the Assembly declare the *Rights of Man?* And who could guarantee that the act of declaring them would institute them legitimately? Article 11, which grants "one of the most precious rights of man . . . (the right) to speak, to write, to publish freely," is the legitimizing principle by which the *Rights of Man* posits itself as the founding document of a new society. This article basically authorizes and empowers the Assembly's right, as the representative of French citizens, to enact the declaration that it articulates. De Gouges faced a similar problem of legitimacy with her manifesto. By what authority would her declarations be enacted? Understanding that the original *Rights of Man* legitimized itself through its very declaration in the Assembly, de Gouges opts to repeat the same means to legitimize her own *Declaration*. As its imitation of the original document's title and the format of the preamble emphasize, her manifesto follows the same tactic of empowerment through the performative act of declaring. Just as the preamble of the *Rights of Man* begins by constituting a community for and from which to speak, the preamble of de Gouges's text first addresses the problem of creating a constituency, in her case, of women, to represent and to authorize the declaration made for and by them: "The mothers, daughters, sisters, the nation's female representatives (*représentantes*) ask to be constituted into a national assembly." De Gouges ends the preamble, exactly as does the original, with a double performative act of recognizing and declaring: ". . . the sex superior in beauty as in courage, in maternal sufferings, recognizes and declares, in the presence and under the auspices of the supreme Being, the following Rights of woman and female citizens (*citoyennes*)." To guarantee even further that her manifesto would be legitimized and thereby enacted, de Gouges adds these instructions beneath the title: "To be decreed by the National Assembly at its last gathering or in that of the future legislature." However, as the need for these instructions already hint, and as soon would become evident, to declare and decree without a constituency from which and for which to speak would void the enactment of the declaration.

One consequence of de Gouges's modeling her text so literally on the original *Rights of Man* is that it produces a double text. Just as the *Rights of Man* refers to the previous "text" of laws and practices under the *ancien régime,* simultaneously deconstructing the principles and practices of the old order as it constitutes the foundations of a new society, so does the *Declaration of the Rights of Woman* implicitly relate in various ways to the document it interprets; it censures the omissions and contradictions of the *Rights of Man* as it corrects them; it parodies its rhetorical strategies as it imitates them; and it uncovers new, and most likely unintended, meanings as it amends the original text.

Some of de Gouges's alterations, primarily aimed at extending the right under discussion equally to women, also function powerfully as a critique of the original document, systematically uncovering its lacunae and revealing the limits and failures of its claims of universality. Consider Article IV from the original Declaration:

> Freedom consists of being able to do everything as long as it does not harm others. Thus, the exercise of man's natural rights has no limits but those that assure that other members of society enjoy those same rights; these limits can only be determined by the law.

De Gouges modifies the text:

> Freedom *and justice* consist of *giving back to others what belongs to them;* thus the exercise of the natural rights of *woman* has no limits but *man's perpetual tyranny*. These limits *must be reformed* by the laws *of nature and reason*. (The additions are underlined.)

Proving herself to be a careful reader of the *Declaration of the Rights of Man,* de Gouges calls upon the universal principles of nature and reason, the same principles to which the *Declaration* appealed, to rectify that text's narrow and self-serving concept of freedom. Her rewriting exposes the inherent contradiction of defining the freedom of the individual according to the rights of others to that same freedom, without universally extending participation in society. Indeed, de Gouges states that a freedom limited to only certain individuals actually deprives others of what justly belongs to them also. By adding "justice" to the text, she underscores the fundamental "injustice" or, as she puts it, the "perpetual tyranny" of a definition of freedom that appeals to universal principle without universal application.

As the above example demonstrates, the additions to or deviations from the original text do not simply replace one meaning with another. Rather, they signify in at least two ways. The addition of "justice" in article IV, first signals the absence of justice and then the injustice of that absence. In a similar vein, the addition of the word "woman" in many of the articles comes to mean both that something is missing and what it is that is missing; woman signifies both a void and that which can fill the void. Appending *citoyenne* to *citoyen* has a similar effect of drawing attention both to the exclusivity of the citizenship granted by the *Rights of Man* and to the way to open up citizenship to be more inclusive. De Gouges's "alterations" of the primary document thus produce at one and the same time both a negative and a positive reading, in other words, a double text that is simultaneously a critique and its emendation.

The manifesto's insistence on establishing and maintaining a strict equality between the sexes creates some odd alterations in the original text that lead, in turn, to more ambiguous and even contradictory double meanings. For example, Article IX of the original reads as follows:

> Tout homme étant présumé innocent jusqu'à ce qu'il ait été déclaré coupable, s'il est jugé indispensable de l'arrêter, toute rigueur qui ne serait pas nécessaire pour s'assurer de sa personne doit être sévèrement réprimée par la loi.
> (Every man being presumed innocent until he has been declared guilty, if it be judged indispensable to arrest him, the law must severely restrain any harshness not necessary to secure his person.)

"Tout homme" here is clearly meant to signify every man or all men in general. It establishes the right of innocence of all men until judged guilty. In de Gouges's version it becomes: "Toute femme étant déclarée coupable, toute rigueur est exercée par la loi." Her substitution of "guilty" for "innocence" in the original text produces multiple, conflicting readings. On the one hand, it can be read as a general indictment of women by society: society declares all women guilty. In this case, de Gouges's rewriting parodies the original. On the other hand, the alteration of the word "innocence" affects the word that does not change from one version to the other. The "tout," which in the original text means all or every in the general sense, becomes any or every in the singular sense in de Gouges's text: "Any woman declared guilty must feel the full extent of the law." In this reading, de Gouges's concern is not only that laws be ignored, abused, or ineffective in protecting some citizens, but rather that women be treated as equals according to the law; that they be accused, punished, and declared guilty strictly according to the law. This claim for equal treatment leads paradoxically to the right to be guilty and punished. Yet another, less paradoxical reading is also suggested by de Gouges's rewriting. "Toute rigueur est exercée par la loi," can be a demand that the law be rigorously followed and that no excesses or unlawful acts be allowed. However contradictory the readings are, they concur in their demand that both the law and women be held accountable in relation to one another, that women be taken seriously and be held responsible for their acts and that the law follow the strict letter of the law for both men and women.

De Gouges's insistence on absolute equality and the unique perspective she brings as a woman lead her to claim rights that the original *Rights of Man* had not even conceived. The addenda as well as the core of the manifesto make evident that equal rights mean not only the political and civil rights decreed in the *Rights of Man,* but also economic and sexual rights. The need to establish sexual rights makes it necessary to deviate substantially from the original document, which never even alludes to such a potentially revolutionary right. Article XI is a case in point. In the original document the article establishes freedom of speech:

> The free communication of thoughts and opinions is one of the most precious rights of man; every citizen can therefore speak, write, and publish freely . . .

De Gouges is faithful to the beginning and the end of the article, but deviates completely in the middle:

> The free communication of thoughts and opinions is one of the most precious rights of *woman, since this freedom guarantees the legitimacy of fathers and their children.* Every *citoyenne* can therefore *say* freely, *I am the mother of a child that belongs to you, without a barbarous prejudice forcing her to hide the truth* . . . (The changes are underlined.)

As de Gouges rewrites the article, true freedom of speech must include the right to name, and to legitimize the names, of one's progeny. Although the right to name openly the father of one's child appears to stem from a very limited understanding of the right to free speech and its importance, in fact such an interpretation invokes a most fundamental law. Given that law in general originates in the need to protect and legitimize property, of which the most basic is one's progeny, the right to name, to ascribe paternity and property rights, is fundamental. De Gouges is not demanding that women name their children after themselves nor that a matriarchy supplant the traditional patriarchy, but simply that women be free to name the rightful fathers of their children born out of wedlock. This decree is in fact most conservative, for it demands that the law abide by its own law. If the law institutes and protects the right to name, then it should be consistent with itself and protect that right in all circumstances.

The claim to this right presupposes equal sexual rights, that is, the right to dispose of one's body and sexuality according to one's will. In the prototype of a marriage contract that she inserts in the postscript of her manifesto, de Gouges substantiates the claim to sexual rights by redefining marriage as a limited and renewable social contract between two free and willing parties. Moreover, as she writes it, such a contract would allow both partners the right to engage in other sexual relations and guarantee the offspring of any such union their rightful paternity and inheritance. De Gouges thus insists that inheritance laws be adhered to literally, and that a father's and mother's property be transferred to their child, be it legitimate or not. By thus holding the law (and fathers) to the letter of the law, she eradicates the concept of illegitimacy and extends rights to both disenfranchised children and women. The explicit inclusion of sexual rights makes de Gouges's conception of a contractual marriage much more radical than the civil marriage instituted by the revolutionary government. Indeed, the sexual freedom and equality it grants equally to both men and women threatens to redefine completely the conception of the family and society. As a matter of fact, the 1791 Constitution's new law instituting civil marriage and the 1792 law of divorce by mutual consent, both of which embodied part of de Gouges's conception of a contractual marriage, would be severely restricted in subsequent legislatures (1795 and then again with the enactment of the Napoleonic Code) precisely because they were considered to be too threatening to social stability (Sledziewski 115-23).

However successful de Gouges's insistence on absolute equality and her attempts to amend the latent inconsistencies of the *Rights of Man* are, when it comes to the practical results of enacting her declaration, the right that matters the most is freedom of speech. As her comments in the manifesto's supplements attest, she was acutely aware of the importance of this right. Her opening remarks to the Queen announce that "(her) goal is to speak frankly . . .", and her introductory preface on the rights of woman challenges man to revoke her right to speak and to question: "Man, are you capable of being just? It's a woman who asks you this; at least you will not deprive her of this right." De Gouges thus states and enacts her right to speak, to question and to critique in a public forum. And yet, despite the fact that the publication of the *Declaration of the Rights of Woman* actualized a woman's right to speak and to publish freely, the text failed to achieve its goals. Neither the Queen nor the General Assembly and its deputies, whom de Gouges apostrophized directly, responded seriously to her text. Nor, for that matter, did the women whom she sought to represent and to whom she had appealed throughout the text for solidarity.

By the time she wrote her *Declaration* in September 1791, it had become evident that the Revolution was proceeding by a series of speech acts just as much, if not more, than by violent actions. The Tennis Court Oath of June 1789, the revocation of feudal privileges on August 4, and the declaration of the *Rights of Man* at the end of August 1789 had all demonstrated how effective language could be in actually achieving immediate change. But, as the debates among the deputies in the Third Estate and then in the National Assembly had made clear, the effectiveness of their language acts—oath, revocation, and declaration—had not been guaranteed. On the contrary, it had been a calculated gamble that their speech acts would be granted the legitimacy and authority they needed to be actualized as acts. As it turned out, the Nation, for whom the deputies spoke, recognized the deputies as its representatives and thus legitimized their declarations and pronouncements.

In the case of Olympe de Gouges's *Declaration,* the absence of a constituency would prove to be the failing of her text. Without the authority that the recognition of a constituency would bring, de Gouges's speech act remained a simple statement, a critical interpretation of the original *Rights of Man* but more an academic exercise than an effective action. No matter how cogent some of her rhetorical strategies were, her manifesto would not be included in the series of successful speech acts upon which the French Revolution was founded.

Notes

1. I would like to thank Smith College and the Jean Picker Fellowship for their generous funding of the research for this paper.

2. Marie-Antoinette's trial aptly demonstrates how the predetermined political imperative to delegitimize her as queen obliged her accusers to resort to the scurrilous accusation of incest and to the more than doubtful testimony of the nine-year-old Dauphin. For a transcript of the Queen's trial, see Walter 96. For an analysis of how an underlying misogynist and xenophobic current led the popular imagination to transform the myth of the fashionable queen into one of a nymphomaniac and a monster, see Thomas 1989b. In "The Many Bodies of Marie-Antoinette," Lynn Hunt analyses the Queen's trial to show

how the sexualized body of the Queen functioned as the most efficient of political metaphors (1991, 108-30).

3. The one and a half acts, dated 1792, is an unfinished manuscript of what was projected to be a five-act play and was found among de Gouges's possessions when she was arrested in July 1793 (OCT 1993c, 329-46).

Since this article was completed in 1991, new editions of some of de Gouges's works have appeared, one as recently as the fall of 1993. My citations refer to the following editions: *Œuvres complètes: Tome I Théâtre* (1993), ed. Castan, abbreviated OCT, for all the published theater and the plays in manuscript. For the pre-1789 prefaces to the plays and other paratexts (not included in OCT but forthcoming in Vol. IV) I refer to the original *Œuvres* (1788). My citations of the pre-1791 political texts refer to *Ecrits politiques 1788-1791* (1993), ed. Blanc, abbreviated EP. For the post-1791 political pamphlets, I refer to *Ecrits politiques II 1792-1793* (1993), ed. Blanc [EP II]. When no other current edition is available and for the reader's convenience, I refer to the Groult edition (1986) if useful, although the scholarship is unreliable and the texts are cut and edited without warning.

4. The records—letters from Olympe de Gouges and transcripts of the various official procedures are in the French National Archives: W 293, no. 210. For a summary of the documents and proceedings, see Tuetery Vol. 10, entry nos. 812-846. See also Blanc 1981, 160-84.

5. Letter to Pierre Aubry, November 2, 1793, French National Archives, W 131, qtd. in Blanc 1981, 173.

6. See "Olympe de Gouges au Tribunal Révolutionnaire" (EP II, 254-60). For public reactions to this pamphlet and another one she had plastered all over Paris in September, see Blanc 1981, 171-72.

7."Mais convaincue que toute la malveillance réunie pour me perdre ne pourrait parvenir à me reprocher une seule démarche contre la Révolution, j'ai demandé moi-même mon jugement. . . " Letter to Pierre Aubry, qtd. in Blanc 1981, 173.

8. The transcript of her interrogation quotes her indirectly: ". . . elle ajoute qu'après avoir lu l'article sept de la *Déclaration des droits,* 'Le Droit de manifester sa pensée et ses opinions, soit par la voie de la presse', cela a laissé à ses bonnes vues une carrière libre . . . " Document de la Commune de Paris, 20 July 1793, National Archives, W 293, no. 210. See also de Gouges's pamphlet (EP II, 254-60).

9. See Deputy Amar's report to the Convention on 9 brumaire an II of the discussion that occurred in the Committee of General Security, *Le Moniteur universel,* t. XVIII (1 November 1793), qtd. in Badinter 1989, 170-79. For eighteenth-century views on women's relation to nature, see M. Bloch and J. H. Bloch 25-41, and L. J. Jordonova 42-69.

10. Originally published in *La Feuille du salut public* and reprinted in *Le Moniteur universel,* t. XVIII, 29 brumaire an II (19 November 1793), qtd. in Badinter 1989, 184-86. All translations are mine unless otherwise noted.

11. One of the best sources for a documentation of women's participation in the Revolution remains Duhet 1971. For a recent analysis of the interaction of society and the public activism of women during the eighteenth century that led up to their involvement in the Revolution, see Landes.

12. In "Women, Democracy and Revolution in Paris, 1789-1794," Harriet B. Applewhite and Darline Gay Levy argue that the political activity of nonelite women at the center of revolutionary politics developed naturally out of their traditional involvement in public life and their sharing of the public space (1984, 64-79).

13. Although de Gouges claims to have authored thirty plays, of the nineteen that have been inventoried only twelve are extant (OCT 1993c). Before the end of 1789, she had already written the following plays: *Zamore et Mirza ou l'heureux naufrage* (1784), reworked and retitled *L'Esclavage des nègres* (1789); *L'Homme généreux* (1786); *Le Mariage inattendu de Chérubin* (1786); *Le Philosophe corrigé ou le cocu supposé* (1788); and *Molière chez Ninon* (1788). All five plays, with the exception of the revised *Esclavage* were published in *Œuvres* (1788); the rewritten *L'Esclavage des nègres, ou l'heureux naufrage* was published separately in 1792. After waiting three years, she had succeeded, albeit with great difficulty, to have the former troupe of the Comédie Française produce her play *L'Esclavage des nègres* at the newly baptised Théâtre de la Nation. Responses to the first performance on December 28, 1789 were extreme, with one half of the audience in support of the play and the other half strongly opposed to it. Both sides loudly expressed their opinions, making for a riotous performance. The play lasted only three showings. For the controversy concerning this play, see the Archives of the Comédie Française.

14. Records show that at least three other of de Gouges's plays were produced during the Revolution: in 1790 the Théâtre Comique et Lyrique put on her play, *Le Couvent, ou les vœux forcés;* in 1790 the Comédie Italienne produced her one-act play, *Mirabeau aux Champs Elysées,* which was subsequently staged in the provinces; and in January 1793, the Théâtre de la République staged her play, *L'Entrée de Dumouriez à Bruxelles, ou les Vivandiers.* For details concerning these productions, see Blanc 1981. For a discussion on the difficulties women of letters encountered having their plays produced in a theatrical world dominated professionally and socially by men, see English Showalter 1988, 95-111. See also Carla Hesse 1989, 469-87, for an overview of the evolving legal status of women writers.

15. For a detailed bibliography of the more that seventy political pamphlets that de Gouges wrote from 1788 to her death in 1793, see Blanc 1981, 223-30.

16. Two weeks after her death, Chaumette, in an address to the Paris Commune against a group of women present, characterized Olympe de Gouges, among other politically active women, in the following manner. "Rappelez-vous, hier cette virago, cette femme-homme, l'impudente Olympe de Gouges, qui, la première, institua des assemblées de femmes (sic), voulut politiquer et commit des crimes." *Révolutions de Paris,* no. 216, 27 brumaire an II (17 November 1793), t. XVII, qtd. in Badinter 1989, 181-182. For a contemporary

judgment of her theater, see *Mémoires de Fleury*. A nineteenth-century assessment can be found in Monselet. Léopold Lacour dismisses her literary efforts: "Malheureusement, elle n'arriva jamais à écrire, n'eût pas même le désir d'y arriver. Et le style, par quoi seul durent les pages les plus hardies même d'inspiration, l'a fatalement punie de l'avoir méprisé. Elle périt avec son œuvre, qui ne pouvait lui survivre" (1900). Dr. Alfred Guillois enlists medical science to judge her literary productions: "Ce côté politique de l'œuvre d'Olympe de Gouges est surtout caracterisé par un curieux mélange d'idées tantôt saines et prophétiques, tantôt réellement démentes: A tout propos, ce sont des digressions sans fin. . . " He is most critical of her writings on women: "Ses idées sur le féminisme sont déjà moins raisonables; empreinte d'une bizarrerie excessive, elles servent de trait d'union entre la raison et la folie" (1904).

17. For an incisive analysis of Rousseau's influence on de Gouges's *Le Bonheur primitif*, see Erica Harth's study of women writers and philosophers before the Revolution (213-34).

18. See Béatrice Didier's "Une Langue de juristes," an analysis of the interpenetration of two distinct modes of discourse—oratorical and written law—in revolutionary texts (1989, 43-56). Also pertinent is Hunt 1984, 33-34.

19. In her preface to the play *L'Homme généreux* she confesses: "Je crois, sans m'abuser sur mon compte, que le plus grand reproche que l'on peut me faire, est de ne savoir pas l'art d'écrire avec élégance qu'on exige aujourd'hui. Elevée dans un pays où l'on parle fort mal sa langue, et ne l'ayant jamais apprise par principes, il est étonnant que ma diction ne soit pas encore plus défectueuse. Si je croyais cependant qu'en adoptant la manière des autres, je pusse gâter le naturel que m'inspire des sujets neufs, je renoncerais à ce qui pourrait m'être le plus indispensable. Peut-être me pardonnera-t-on en faveur de la nouveauté, ces fautes de style, ces phrases plus sensibles qu'élégantes, et enfin tout ce qui respire la vérité" (OCT 1993c).

20. It is clear from examining the few documents, mostly letters and short notes (French National Archives, W 293, no. 210) that have come down to us in de Gouges's own handwriting that for her the physical act of writing was not an easy or a practiced one. Her handwriting in these letters is awkward, unsteady, not uniform, and greatly slanted on the paper, the sheets of paper spotted with ink stains, some words crossed out. Written while she was imprisoned, the almost illegible letters could simply reflect the duress of prison conditions. Yet, as I have argued, such difficulties did not prevent her from pursuing her political activism by writing and publishing at least two more pamphlets from her prison cell. The other manuscripts that I have been able to examine of her works, the unfinished play *La France sauvée* in the French National Archives and a copy of *L'Esclavage des nègres* in the Archives of the Comédie Française, are both written in different, but extremely clear, legible, "professional" handwriting. These manuscripts are undoubtedly the work of professional scribes and seem to support de Gouges's contention that she preferred to "write" by dictating to a secretary.

21. For a summary of the legal status of women under the *ancien régime,* see Adrienne Rogers (1984, 33-48). See Elisabeth G. Sledziewski's excellent analysis of how the Revolution's concept of civil marriage and divorce as a contract agreed upon by the mutual consent of both contracting parties granted women a juridical status equal to that of men (99-126).

22. Condorcet's essay, "Sur l'admission des femmes au droit de cité," originally published in *Journal de la Société de 1789,* no. 5, July 3, 1790, has recently been reprinted in Badinter 1989, 53-62. Mlle Jodin's address to the National Assembly requests the establishment of a separate legislative code for women and a tribunal to be run by women and exclusively for women. In effect, she thus claims judicial rights for women—the right to testify and judge, the right to be judged and sentenced by one's peers. In her address of July 1791 to the National Assembly, Etta Palm presents the program of social welfare for women that her *Société des amies de la vérité* had drafted, thereby proposing both social rights and the right of women to participate in governmental responsibilities and undertakings. Both texts are reprinted in Duhet 1981, 183-204.

23. A note expressing her joy at the King's acceptance of the Constitution, and which de Gouges appended to her brochure while it was still in press, allows us to date the composition of her text before the September 13 royal acceptance. The text is reprinted in full in Duhet 1981, 205-223.

24. See, for example, her three plays, *Le Philosophe corrigé, ou le cocu supposé, Molière chez Ninon, Le Couvent ou les Vœux forcés* (OCT 1993c); and the pamphlets "Action héroïque d'une Française, ou la France sauvée par une femme"; "Dialogue allégorique entre la France et la Vérité, dédié aux Etats-Généraux"; and "Sera-t-il Roi, ne le sera-t-il pas?" with its appended "Projet d'une garde nationale de femmes" (EP 1993a, 120-21, 62-72, 187-97).

25. For a summary of the debates, see Marcel Gauchet, "Droits de l'homme" 685-95.

26. Throughout the essay references are to the complete version of the document, reprinted in Duhet 1981, 205-23. All translations are mine.

5

The Circe of the Republic: Mme Roland, Rousseau, and Revolutionary Politics

Mary Trouille

The enthusiastic response of eighteenth-century women to Rousseau's sexual politics presents an intriguing paradox. How can one explain the puzzling fact that his views on women's nature, role, and education—views that seem reactionary, paternalistic, even blatantly misogynistic today—had such tremendous appeal and influence among women of the revolutionary era? More intriguing still is the passionate admiration for Rousseau and his writings expressed by talented and independent-minded women such as Mme de Staël, Mme Roland, Mary Wollstonecraft, and Olympe de Gouges. Their turbulent lives and political and literary activities seem incompatible with the feminine ideals of domesticity and self-effacement set forth in *Julie* and *Emile*. To probe Rousseau's paradoxical appeal to women readers, I will examine how one woman of the revolutionary period—Marie-Jeanne Phlipon, who later became Mme Roland—responded to his views on women and, specifically, how she interpreted his cult of domesticity as an empowering discourse.[1] Her case is a particularly striking illustration of Rousseau's influence, since, of the women mentioned earlier, Mme Roland was the one who made the greatest effort to conform her outward behavior to the limited role he prescribed. Yet, while seeming to conform to these feminine ideals and norms, she in fact undermined them by blurring the gender dichotomies and the distinction between public and private spheres that lay at the very core of Rousseau's discourse on women. Her subtle transgression of traditional gender barriers did not go unperceived, and was capitalized on by the Rolands' political enemies in the campaign of slander and persecution that eventually led her to the guillotine.

A Passionate Disciple of Rousseau

Born in 1754, Marie-Jeanne (or Manon as she was affectionately called) was the only child of a Parisian engraver. M. Phlipon's small but thriving trade permitted him to provide his gifted daughter with an education far above that customary for her sex and social rank, as well as excellent marriage prospects. However, M. Phlipon's reckless business speculations after the death of his wife considerably dimmed Manon's hopes for the future. It was at this critical juncture in her life, at the age of twenty-one, that she first read *Julie*. By then, Manon had perused the works of an impressive number of authors, in virtually every period, field, and genre, including all the major *philosophes*—except for Rousseau, conspicuous by his absence. Mme Phlipon, who in general had given her daughter complete freedom in the choice of her readings, seems to have taken special care to prevent her contact with Rousseau, apparently fearing the negative influence he might have on Manon's passionate, sensitive nature.[2] The novel made a profound impact on her and was to have a determining influence on the course of her life. In her *Mémoires,* she recalls: "It seemed to me that I then found my true substance, that Rousseau became the interpreter of feelings and ideas I had had before him, but that he alone could explain to my satisfaction. . . . Rousseau showed me the domestic happiness to which I had a right to aspire and the ineffable delights I was capable of enjoying." (Roland 1966, 302). At a time of stress and crisis in her own life, when Manon had practically given up hope of finding a suitable husband because of her modest personal circumstances and idealistic expectations, Rousseau renewed her faith in the future through his appealing picture of the domestic felicity and motherhood to which a virtuous woman could aspire. Far from being considered a trap, this ideal of motherhood and of enlightened domesticity seemed to offer a new power and dignity to women, regardless of their socio-economic status.

After reading *La Nouvelle Héloïse,* Manon devoured Rousseau's works one after the other. Her correspondence of the period expresses the enthusiasm he inspired in her. In a letter to a friend, she wrote:

> I find it strange that you are surprised by my enthusiasm for Rousseau. . . . Who else portrays virtue in a more noble and touching manner? Who makes it more appealing? His works inspire love for truth, simplicity, and goodness. I truly believe that I owe him the best part of myself. His genius has inspired me; I feel myself elevated and ennobled by him. . . . His *Héloïse* is a masterpiece of sentiment. (To Sophie Cannet, 21 March 1776, *Lettres* 1:393)

In the course of this same letter, each of Rousseau's works is praised in turn, including *Emile*. Nowhere in her writings does Mme Roland explicitly criticize the ultra-conservative, repressive view of women set forth in the fifth book of *Emile*. However, when raising her daughter Eudora, Mme Roland would conscientiously apply the principles outlined for the education of Emile, while ignoring the far more limited education prescribed for Sophie. Like Rousseau, Mme Roland felt that a woman's place was in the domestic sphere; however, contrary to Rousseau's view in *Emile,* she did not feel that a woman's activities should be limited to purely domestic tasks. In this respect, she was not unlike other Rousseau fans of the period, who did not hesitate to adapt and even distort his views according to their own needs and values.

Mme Roland's response to *La Nouvelle Héloïse* has generally been described by her biographers as a revelation or even as a conversion experience.[3] However, as Mme Roland herself observes in her *Mémoires,* she was predisposed both by her character and her upbringing to embrace Rousseau's ideal of domesticity, as well as his pre-Romantic, prerevolutionary spirit. Rousseau simply confirmed—and gave eloquent expression to—her deepest convictions and aspirations: "When I read Rousseau or Diderot, but especially the first, I felt transported by a tremendous enthusiasm; they seemed to have captured my deepest convictions, expressing them in ways I myself would no doubt have been incapable of matching, but that I could fully appreciate because they were feelings I shared" (Perroud, 2: 422).[4] That Manon Phlipon was a firm believer in the ideal of domesticity long before she read Rousseau is borne out by the following passage of her memoirs where she recalls Sunday walks with her parents as an adolescent and her growing aversion for the crowded public promenades of the capital:

After these walks, I felt a terrible emptiness, anxiety, and disgust. . . . Is it merely to attract attention and to receive vain compliments that the members of my sex acquire talents and are schooled in virtue?. . . Do I exist only to waste my time with frivolous concerns and tumultuous feelings?—Oh, surely I have a higher destiny! . . . The sacred duties of wife and mother will one day be mine: my youth should be spent preparing me for these roles; I must study their importance and learn to control my inclinations, so that I can direct those of my children. Above all, I must become worthy of the man who will one day win my heart and be able to assure his happiness (Roland 1966, 264).[5]

Although Manon's domestic ideals may seem self-limiting to modern readers, her refusal to be reduced to a *femme-objet* and to engage in the frivolous games of vanity and ostentation, so prevalent at that time, constituted a conscious act of revolt on her part against what she considered an oppressive gender system. Above all, this passage reflects an independent mind and a strong desire for dignity and for a useful, meaningful life.

In her quest for happiness through companionate marriage and motherhood, Manon seemed to take Julie as her model by accepting as her husband an erudite and austere man twenty years her senior. During their six-year stay at Le Clos, Roland's modest country estate, Manon took great pleasure in emulating the sober domestic virtues embodied in Julie's life at Clarens. Like the Wolmars, Mme Roland viewed the domestic sphere and rural life as the privileged locus of happiness and virtue. During her peaceful retreat at Le Clos, which she affectionately referred to as "mon Ermitage," Mme Roland conscientiously fulfilled her role as wife and mother—educating her daughter (whom she had dutifully nursed in infancy), running her household, serving as doctor and benefactress to the local peasants, and overseeing the farm work when her husband was away on his frequent tours as regional inspector of manufactures.

Roland's Early Writings: The Specter of *Emile* and the Proper Lady

In addition to these domestic and maternal tasks, Mme Roland actively collaborated with her husband on numerous technical and scholarly works, including his three-volume *Dictionnaire des Manufactures, Arts et Métiers* for the revised edition of Diderot's *Encyclopédie*. Manon had a direct hand in the research, writing, and proofreading of every article. Yet, far from satisfying any personal ambition on her part, this work was in her eyes merely an extension of her devotion to her husband:

> It was almost as natural for me to write with him as it was to eat with him. Existing only for his happiness, I devoted myself to what brought him the greatest pleasure. If he wrote about industrial arts, I wrote about them too, although they bored me. Since he liked scholarship, I helped him in his research. If it amused him to send a literary piece to an academic society, we worked on it together. (Roland 1966, 154)

Although well aware of her intellectual and literary talents, Mme Roland consistently refused to publish anything (even works entirely her own) under her name, preferring to remain anonymous or to hide behind her husband's signature. She seems to have subscribed wholeheartedly to Rousseau's ideals of female modesty and self-effacement and to his views of the "natural" superiority and domination of the male sex. Her interiorization of female inferiority and of traditional prejudices against women writers and scholars is particularly apparent in a letter written to a male family friend in the early years of her marriage:

> I believe in the superiority of your sex in every respect. . . . You have strength, and everything that goes with it: courage, perseverance, wide horizons, and superior talents. It is up to you to make the laws in politics and discoveries in the sciences. Govern the world, change the face of the globe, be proud, terrible, clever, and learned. You are all that without our help, and because of it you are destined to be our masters. But without us, you would not be virtuous, loving, loved, nor happy. So keep your glory and authority. For our part, we have and wish no other power than over your morals, no other throne than in your hearts. I will never claim anything beyond that. It often irks me to see women claiming privileges which suit them so poorly. Even the name of author . . . strikes me as ridiculous when applied to them. However gifted they may be, women should never show their learning or talents in public.

And she concluded her Rousseauistic credo by declaring: "I can imagine no destiny more rewarding than that of assuring the happiness of one man alone" (to Bosc, 29 July 1783, *Lettres,* 3:257).

Mme Roland firmly believed that women who pursued ambitions and desires outside the domestic sphere jeopardized not only their happiness, but their reputation as well. She was, moreover, acutely aware of the double standard and prejudices affecting women writers:

> I never had the slightest temptation to become an author; it became clear to me very early that a woman who earned this title for herself lost much more than she gained. She is disliked by men, and criticized by her own sex. If her writing is bad, people make fun of her, and rightly so; if her works are good, people deny that she wrote them . . . [or] they attack her character, morals, behavior, and talents to such an extent that they destroy her reputation as an author through the notoriety they give her. (Roland 1966, 304)

When a friend predicted that she would one day write a book, she retorted: "Then it will be under someone else's name; for I would eat my fingers before I ever became an author" (Roland 1966, 321).

Despite her passion for learning and the intense pleasure Mme Roland experienced as a writer, she carefully avoided calling attention to her scholarly and literary activities, fearing the ridicule and censure generally encountered by *les femmes de lettres:* "I am not interested in becoming a scholar, nor is it my goal to earn a reputation for wit or talent or the pleasure of being published; I study because I need to just as much as I do to eat. . . . My work brings me happiness and much pleasure, or at least some consolation for my troubles" (to Sophie, 27 March 1776, *Lettres,* I:396). When Manon wrote to Rousseau to try to arrange a meeting with him, she carefully kept her plans secret: "I had no desire to make a spectacle of myself by calling further attention to my interest in philosophy: enthusiasm for celebrated writers always appears ridiculous to those who do not share it," she explained in the same letter to Sophie (*Lettres,* I:383). Convinced that a woman's place was out of the public eye, Manon voluntarily relegated herself to the domestic sphere both before and after her marriage: "I like the shadows, and twilight is enough for my happiness. As Montaigne says, one is only at ease in the backshop" (to Sophie, 2 October 1776, *Lettres,* I:492).

The six years spent at Le Clos unquestionably represent the most serene period in Mme Roland's life. With peaceful resignation, she looked forward to finishing out her days in tranquil domesticity, enlivened by readings from her favorite authors: "Yes, I feel that I will spend my whole life in the country, in peace and contentment," she wrote her husband, "all I need are the works of Jean-Jacques; reading them will make us shed delicious tears and rekindle feelings that will bring us happiness whatever our fate may be" (to Roland, 22 and 18 November 1787, *Lettres,* 3:709 & 695). Her formerly keen interest in political events waned under the influence of domestic preoccupations. To a Parisian friend who kept her informed of the latest news, she quipped: "I no longer dabble in politics" (to Bosc, 10 June 1783, *Lettres,* 3:254). However, Mme Roland's political apathy was not destined to last, for the events of 1789 jolted her out of this comfortable and secure routine and, in their wake, brought to the surface unfulfilled aspirations and talents that had lain dormant during her nine-year retreat into domesticity.

The Revolution's Impact: Breaking Out of the Domestic Mold

Fervent disciples of Rousseau's political and social thought, the Rolands greeting the Revolution with immediate and unbounded enthusiasm: "The Revolution took hold of all our ideas and subjugated all our plans; we devoted ourselves entirely to our passionate desire to serve the public welfare" (Roland 1966, 337). All personal feelings and private activities were relegated to the background in favor of the national events that were making history. The *aurea mediocritas*—the notion that happiness can be found only in obscurity—by which she had lived for so many years, now seemed totally forgotten in the flurry of excitement and exhilaration. In her memoirs, Roland recalls: "I was seduced by the Revolution, . . . penetrated by the desire to see my country prosper, and seized by a feverish and continual preoccupation with public affairs" (Roland 1966, 154). Mme Roland's repeated use here and elsewhere of amorous terms and images to describe her revolutionary zeal underlines the extent to which her libidinal urges were sublimated in her political fervor. More than once in the course of her memoirs, the Revolution is personified as a seductive, but ultimately faithless lover.

Under the pressure of events, Mme Roland's life and writings underwent a radical politicization. Her character and tone grew more energetic and direct, even brusque at times, as a result of her revolutionary zeal. In her letters from Le Clos to friends in Paris, her charming vignettes à la Sévigné gave way to urgent exhortations and warnings expressed in a trenchant, sometimes violent style "It is true that I no longer write of our personal affairs: where is the traitor who today has other affairs than those of the nation?" (to Bosc, 26 July 1789, *Lettres,* 4:53).[6] When some of her letters disappeared in the mail, censured perhaps because of their radical antimonarchism, she angrily warned the culprits: "If this letter does not reach you, let the cowards who read it blush with shame upon learning that these words were written by a woman, and let them tremble to think that she can inspire a hundred men who will in turn inspire a million others" (53).

Increasingly conscious of the power of words and of her own ability to use them to further the revolutionary cause, Mme Roland became a regular, albeit anonymous contributor to republican journals. In 1790, Roland was sent to represent Lyon in the Constitutional Convention in Paris, where he became an active member of the Jacobin Society. When he was appointed secretary of the club's correspondence committee, Mme Roland eagerly shared his work. Convinced that shaping public opinion could play a vital role in the success of the Revolution, she put all her literary skill into answering the many letters from provincial correspondents. After Roland's unexpected appointment as Minister of the Interior, her collaboration became even more crucial to the success of his career. She was not only the moving force behind the propaganda bureau set up by her husband, the famous "Bureau d'Esprit Public," but also served as Roland's secret political advisor and ghost writer.[7] She composed many of the key documents of his ministry, including his protest to the Pope concerning French prisoners in Rome, as well as his famous letter of protest to Louis XVI. Published by the Assembly (at Mme Roland's urging), Roland's letter to the King led to the dissolution of the first Cabinet and played a significant role in turning the tide of public opinion against the monarchy.

As in her earlier journalistic endeavors, Mme Roland remained resolutely anonymous: "It was with intense pleasure that I wrote these pieces, because I felt they could be useful. I found greater satisfaction in doing it anonymously. . . . I have no need of glory" (Roland 1966, 155). As before, she claimed that her work was simply an extension of her devotion to her husband. In response to charges that she had secretly run her husband's ministry, she loyally defended Roland's probity and capabilities. She insisted that she merely served as his secretary and had always refrained from influencing his decisions: "I never meddled in administrative affairs. . . . Why should it detract from a man's professional reputation or merit if his wife serves as his secretary?" (Roland 1966, 305). However, from Mme Roland's own testimony elsewhere in her *Mémoires,* it is abundantly clear that she was much more than a mere scribe and that charges that she was the hidden power behind her husband's ministry were not unfounded.

It is also clear from her *Mémoires* that Mme Roland derived a secret pleasure and amusement from the important role she played behind the scenes: "A letter to the Pope, written in the name of the Executive Council of France, secretly composed by a woman in the austere office that Marat liked to call a boudoir—the situation struck me as so amusing that I laughed about it quite a while afterward. It was the secrecy of my participation that made these contrasts so amusing." (Roland 1966, 304) At one point in her memoirs, she could not resist discretely poking fun at Roland's tendency to take her talents and efforts for granted and to appropriate them as his own: "If one of his pieces was singled out and praised for its graceful style, . . . I took pleasure in his satisfaction without remarking that I had written it, and he often ended up convinced that he had truly been inspired when he had written a passage that I myself had composed" (304). Although on the surface, this passage suggests that Mme Roland was being exploited by an ungrateful and egotistic husband, her ironic tone conveys quite a different impression—that if Roland became the powerful political figure that he was, it was due less to his exploitation of her than to her clever manipulation of him. He became in a sense her mouthpiece, just as she was his hidden voice. Moreover, this subtle subversion of her husband's authority can be seen as an indirect challenge to Rousseau's male-centered view of power relations between the sexes.

In the early years of their marriage, Mme Roland had felt intimidated by her husband's greater age, knowledge, and experience. Eventually however, she gained enough confidence in her abilities and judgment to voice her own opinions. She began to resent Roland's autocratic, self-centered manner, and the fact that she had always sacrificed her happiness for his;

but she carefully repressed any resentment behind a mask of submission and devotion to him and his work:

> After considering only my partner's happiness for so long, I finally realized that there was something missing in my own. . . . I often felt that our relationship was unequal, due to Roland's dominating character and the twenty-year age gap between us. If we lived alone together, I sometimes had a difficult time with him; if we went out into society, I was admired by people, some of whom I sensed might attract me. I plunged myself into my husband's work—another excess which had its disadvantage, for he became too dependent upon my help, . . . and I wore myself out. (Roland 1966, 332-33)

This passage suggests that Mme Roland plunged herself into her husband's work not simply to prove her devotion and worth to him, but also to fill emotional and intellectual needs that her marriage had not satisfied, as well as to protect herself from the attractions of younger men. Her collaboration on her husband's work may also have helped compensate for the disappointments of motherhood. For despite all Mme Roland's efforts, Eudora remained a rebellious and indolent child of mediocre intelligence, utterly lacking in intellectual curiosity and artistic gifts.

The Revolution gave Mme Roland a unique opportunity for self-fulfillment outside the domestic sphere—the chance she had secretly longed for to play an active role in shaping the ideal republic she had dreamed of ever since she first read Plutarch at the age of eight. As a young woman, she had lamented the powerlessness and obscurity to which she seemed condemned by both her sex and her inferior social status:

> I am truly vexed to be a woman: I should have been born with a different soul or a different sex or in another century. I should have been born a woman in Rome or Sparta, or else a man in France. At least then I could have chosen the republic of letters as my country, or another of those republics where as a man, one only needs to obey the law. . . . I feel imprisoned in a class and an existence that is not at all mine. . . . Everywhere I turn, my mind and heart run up against the constraints of opinion and prejudice, and all my strength is consumed in vainly struggling against my chains. . . . My enthusiasm for the

welfare of society seems utterly wasted, since I am unable to contribute anything to it! (To Sophie Cannet, 5 Feb. 1776, *Lettres*, 1:374-75)

Conscious of her rich inner gifts, Manon felt stifled and out of place in the petit bourgeois world of her father. For lack of proper training and a stimulating environment, she felt that her intelligence and imagination were being wasted.[8] Ardently she aspired to a higher level of existence, to a place in the "republic of letters" where her intellectual and literary endeavors would be appreciated and encouraged. She bitterly resented the socio-economic and gender barriers that prevented her from traveling abroad and from participating actively in the cultural life of her period. In several letters to Sophie Cannet, she fantasized about dressing like a man in order to gain greater freedom to study, to travel, and to develop her talents.[9]

Parallel to Manon's frustrated intellectual and artistic ambitions as a young woman of the *petite bourgeoisie* were her frustrated political aspirations—her desire to participate in the political life of her country, to contribute actively to the public good in accordance with her republican convictions. At the age of twenty, she had written to Sophie: "It seems to me that man's vocation is to be useful to his fellow creatures, that the first and most admirable virtue lies in working for the public good. . . . You can imagine how frustrated I feel to be confined to the narrow circle of my private life, living only for myself and totally useless to others" (to Sophie Cannet, 9 May 1774, Lettres, 1:195).

Mme Roland's Revolutionary Salon: Fusion of Public and Private Spheres

Mme Roland's important contribution to her husband's work during his two terms as Minister of the Interior enabled her to participate covertly in the public sphere and to help shape the future of the new French republic without having to sacrifice her outward conformity to Rousseau's ideals of female modesty and domesticity. When her husband first became active in the Jacobin Club in early 1792, Mme Roland's home served as an informal gathering place for Brissot, Robespierre, and other deputies who at the time constituted the radical Left. After Roland became minister, she had dinner gatherings twice a week for his political associates.

As a hostess, Mme Roland maintained a simple, almost Spartan style of entertaining. There were generally no more than fifteen guests at a time. Moreover, women were strictly excluded from the gatherings in her home—in accordance with Rousseau's dictum concerning the segregation of the sexes and his notion of separate spheres.[10] Mme Roland justified her exclusion of women from her home on the grounds that it helped create an atmosphere suitable for serious political discussion, free from frivolity and intrigue (both amorous and political). She also viewed it as a means of preserving her independence and privacy, in keeping with her ideal of domesticity. For the same reason, she refrained from participating in the social life of the capital. In maintaining this austere lifestyle, she claims to have merely followed the positive example set by Mme Pétion, wife of the mayor of Paris. However, her exclusion of women from her home and refusal of their invitations suggests that Mme Roland had interiorized her male contemporaries' distrust and scorn for women.

During the discussions that followed dinner, Manon officiated with simplicity and tact and—what was even more appreciated—in silence. In her *Mémoires,* she insists that she never allowed herself to utter a word until the meetings were over, although occasionally she had to bite her lip to keep from disagreeing with what was being said. Deliberately seating herself outside the circle of men, she quietly did needlework or wrote letters while the debates went on. Yet, despite her voluntary self-effacement, Mme Roland does not deny that she listened attentively to all that was said, nor did she hesitate to offer her opinion when it was asked for. Moreover, since Roland's associates tended to call on him at home rather than at his office, political matters were frequently discussed in his wife's presence. Under the pretext of leaving messages for the absent Roland, they got in the habit of calling on Manon and presenting their case to her, for they were well aware that she would be consulted anyway. In her *Mémoires,* Mme Roland tries to repudiate accusations that she was running her husband's ministry by insisting that since she was nearly always at home and enjoyed her husband's fullest confidence, she found herself quite naturally "in the midst of things without intrigue or vain curiosity" (Roland 1966, 72). But, she hardly needed to resort to intrigue or subterfuge to impose her views, for in the intimacy of the Girondin circle her opinions carried increasing weight.

The Virtuous Martyr: Reliving Julie's Passion

Mme Roland's "secret" collaboration in the political affairs of the Girondists seemed to offer the ideal opportunity to satisfy her unfulfilled political ambitions. However, by putting her in contact with dynamic young men, her role as Egeria of the Girondist party exacerbated the equally painful dilemma of her unfulfilled desire for romantic love and sensual pleasure—desires which Mme Roland recognizes quite openly in her *Mémoires*.[11]

In the fall of 1792, when the Girondists were under constant attack from the Montagnards, Manon fell passionately in love with the Girondist deputy François Buzot. Young, handsome, eloquent, and dynamic, he was everything Roland was not: a worthy Saint-Preux-like foil to the aging and "sexless" Roland. Despite her disenchantment with marriage and motherhood, as well as her growing disillusionment with the Revolution, Mme Roland stoically resisted yielding to her passion, which was shared by Buzot with equal ardor. Like Julie's death, Mme Roland's imprisonment and execution resolved her moral impasse. By allowing herself to be imprisoned in place of her husband, Mme Roland was able to free herself from conjugal duties and to give full expression to her love for Buzot, without restraint or remorse. In a letter to Buzot from prison, she expressed her secret joy:

> I was not greatly distressed to be arrested. They will be less angry and vindictive toward Roland. . . . If they put him on trial, I will be able to defend him in a manner that will enhance his reputation. And in this way I can pay the debt I owe him for his sorrows. Don't you see that by being alone, it is with you that I remain? Through imprisonment I can sacrifice myself for my husband and keep myself for my friend, and it is to my persecutors that I owe this reconciliation of love and duty. Don't pity me! Others may admire my courage, but they don't know my joys. (22 June 1793, *Lettres*, 4:484)

Mme Roland firmly rejected all plans for her escape, for she was convinced that freedom would not bring her happiness, "but only replace [her] chains with others that no one can see" (to Buzot, 6 July 1793, *Lettres*, 4:498). In a final message to Buzot (embedded in her "Dernières

Pensées") she wrote: "And you whom I dare not name! ... who respected the barriers of virtue in spite of the most overwhelming passion, will you grieve to see me go before you to a place where we will be free to love each other without crime, where nothing will prevent us from being united? ... There I will await you. ... Adieu. No, in leaving the earth, I am not leaving you, but bringing us closer together."[12] The parallels with the dénouement of *La Nouvelle Héloïse* are of course striking, for on her deathbed, Julie had expressed herself in almost identical terms in a letter to Saint-Preux.[13]

Dorinda Outram convincingly argues that through her intense identification with Julie, Mme Roland "was able to turn a potentially threatening physical outcome, such as in her relationship with Buzot, into a verbal performance" and that "by substituting the verbal for the physical, she could overcome the contradiction between the unchastity of her desires and the self-portrait she cherished, as chaste wife, and could keep to herself the heroine's role in her domestic drama" (Outram 1989, 138-39).[14]

Roland's Subversion of Rousseau's Feminine Ideals

In her final farewell to the man she loved, as throughout her adult life, Mme Roland had followed the inspiring example of Rousseau's heroine. Like Julie, Mme Roland had conscientiously devoted herself to an idealized view of marriage and motherhood, and like her—rather than accept moral defeat or disenchantment—had heroically sacrificed her life in order to preserve the precarious balance between duty and passion, virtue and sensibility. However, while seeming to conform to the feminine ideals and norms advocated by Rousseau in his novels, Mme Roland in fact subverted those models by undermining the gender dichotomies (public/private, self-assertion/self-effacement, reason/sensibility) that lay at the very core of his discourse on women. While appearing to relegate herself to a role of silence and self-effacement in the domestic sphere, she in fact transformed her home into a public forum, her tiny office into the unofficial center of Roland's ministry, and her devotion to her husband into a dynamic political partnership—thereby giving herself the power to influence public affairs in a very direct and dramatic manner. Furthermore, through her ability to combine qualities traditionally reserved for men (reason, authority, energy, superior intelligence, and strength of character) with traits traditionally ascribed to women (sensitivity, charm, intuition, and persuasiveness), Mme Roland was able to command the respect of her husband and colleagues and to make herself valuable, indeed indispensable, to their political cause. As Mme Roland herself remarks in her *Mémoires:*

> Roland would have been no less a fine administrator without me; his capabilities, diligence, and probity are entirely his own. With my help, he caused more of a sensation because I infused his writings with that special mixture of strength and gentle persuasiveness, that blend of reason and authority with the charms of sentiment, which perhaps only a sensitive woman with a sound mind is capable of achieving. (Roland 1966, 155)

Mme Roland's elevated opinion of her husband's capabilities is disputed somewhat by biographers and historians. They generally agree that Roland was a dedicated, hard-working administrator, but that without his wife's conviction, boldness, literary talents, and shrewd judgment of character "he could be rated barely higher than a superior clerk" (May 1970, 206).

That Mme Roland was a woman of exceptional talents—with a distinctly androgynous character and style—is confirmed by numerous contemporary accounts, including a review of her *Mémoires* in the *Analytical Review* of 1795: "She possessed a mind uncommonly vigorous and masculine, and her situation as wife of the minister Roland in a moment of great peril called forth all her energy [to display] talents which will not fail to rank her among the distinguished ornaments of her sex."[15] As for the "virile" quality of her writing, even Rousseau had been fooled by it. After an unsuccessful effort to meet her idol during his last stay in Paris, Manon's disappointment had been somewhat allayed by the fact that Rousseau had mistaken her letter of introduction for that of a man. "Surely it was not you who wrote a letter like that," reported Thérèse, as she blocked the door. "Even the handwriting looks like that of a man."[16]

Contrary to traditional eighteenth-century views of women as victims of their imagination, emotions, and sexual desires (views clearly reflected in Rousseau's portrayal of Sophie), Mme Roland underlines her belief in the primacy of reason and consistently portrays herself as in control: "I kept my imagination in check and followed lines of reasoning. . . . I channeled my imagination through studying" (Roland 1966, 303 & 346). Her "masculine" firmness, self-possession, and strength of character inspired even her strongest critics with a grudging sort of admiration, mixed with deep ambivalence and distrust.

Gita May maintains that Mme Roland's transgression of traditional gender restrictions was involuntary and largely due to the unusual circumstances in which she found herself. If Mme Roland contradicted her own convictions regarding the proper role of women, argues May, it was not through any personal ambition or will to power on her part, but through a disinterested, self-sacrificing devotion to the revolutionary cause.[17] She goes on to defend Mme Roland against the criticism of pro-Jacobin historians who, in May's view, unjustly question her intentions and motives. While there is little doubt that these historians were unduly harsh and often misogynic in their judgment of the Girondists' Egeria,[18] May seems to give too much credence to the mask of modesty and self-effacement that Mme Roland assumed in an effort to defend herself against similar attacks by her contemporaries. She tends to take Mme Roland's self-justification at face value and to ignore or minimize the importance of passages in her memoirs and correspondence where she momentarily lets her mask fall, revealing a woman of intense personal and political ambitions. The passages expressing her desire to develop her talents to the fullest, her secret pleasure at manipulating power relations behind the scenes, and above all her deep satisfaction at fulfilling her adolescent dream to escape the confines of her sex and class in order to help shape the future of the new French Republic—all these passages reveal the woman behind the mask who consciously subverted the limited gender role imposed upon her by society.[19]

On Trial: Misogynic Attacks by the Press and Revolutionary Leaders

Mme Roland's subtle transgression of traditional gender barriers did not go unperceived and was capitalized on by the Rolands' political enemies in the campaign of slander and persecution that eventually led her to the guillotine. As the Girondins' popularity declined, Jacobin politicians and journalists multiplied their attacks against the Rolands. Joan Landes underlines the extent to which the schism between Jacobins and Girondins was fought out in gendered terms, with Mme Roland as a key figure (Landes 118). As a woman, she was particularly vulnerable to denunciations and satire. No insult or innuendo, no matter how far-fetched or obscene, was spared to destroy her influence and to belittle her party by picturing the Girondists as wholly dominated by a scheming female—a form of ridicule particularly withering to the Gallic ego. For example, in an issue of his highly popular *Ami du peuple,* Marat inserted "Un mot à la femme Roland" which read: "Roland is only a ninny whose wife leads him by the nose; it's she who is Minister of the Interior" (Marat 230).

Ten days later (in late September 1792) Roland went before the Assembly to resign as Minister in order to become a simple deputy; however, upon the urging of a majority of the deputies, he agreed to retain his post. Hearing this, Danton rose from his seat and launched his famous sarcasm: "No one does justice to Roland more than I, but if you invite him to be Minister, you should also extend the invitation to Mme Roland; for everyone knows that he was not alone in his department! As for me, I was alone in mine." He then added: "We need ministers who see through other eyes than those of their wives." (Cited by Chaussinand-Nogaret 1985, b, 263.) The following spring, Danton would again make Mme Roland the butt of his sarcasm in an effort to save the Girondists from an assassination plot hatched by Varlet: "Those glib talkers [*beaux parleurs*] are not worth such a fuss," quipped Danton, "they are as enthusiastic and flighty as the woman who inspires them. Why don't they choose a *man* as their leader? That women will lead them to their destruction. She's the Circe of the Republic!" (263).

Following Danton's lead, the Jacobin press tirelessly harped on the theme that it was not M. Roland but Mme Roland who actually ran the Ministry of the Interior. Day after day, the popular press echoed with outrageous reports of the "orgies" over which Mme Roland had presided, and of the sexual and political favors she had distributed in order to maintain her influence. In his popular *Père Duchesne,* Hébert artfully exploited both the anti-feminist and anti-aristocratic sentiments of Mme Roland's enemies by comparing her to Marie-Antoinette and to various royal mistresses—minus their beauty, for he later describes her as a toothless, balding old hag:

> The tender wife of virtuous Roland is ruling France just like the Pompadours and the du Barrys. Brissot is the grand squire of this new queen,

> Louvet is her chamberlain, Buzot her chancellor. . . . [Barbaroux, Vergniaud, Guadet, Lanthenas, are then each assigned a role.] This is the new court that is running things today. Like our former queen, madame Coco, stretched out on a sofa, surrounded by all those *beaux esprits,* talks on endlessly about war, politics, supplies. It is from this den of corruption that daily proclamations issue forth to the public. (202 [20 Dec. 1792])

In the midst of Hébert's grotesque slander, one recognizes a man who is perceptive and well-informed and who does not strike at random. All the politicians who were among Mme Roland's circle of close friends are named. Moreover, Hébert rightly guesses that several of them (and Buzot in particular) might be enamored of her and that she might not be insensitive to their admiration. In the following issue of *Père Duchesne,* Brissot is "overheard" saying to Buzot:

> Admit that you are fortunate to serve as the right-hand man of someone like me. I got you in with the *beaux esprits* that are governing France. If it weren't for me, you wouldn't be the favorite among the admirers of the virtuous wife of the virtuous Roland. What a pleasure it must be to rehearse at her feet the role you will play at the Convention the following day, to hear her applaud you when you recite a fiery tirade against Robespierre, to see her swoon in your arms when you have passed some fine decree banishing loyal revolutionaries or encouraging civil war (204 [25 Dec. 1792]).

In general, Mme Roland chose to maintain a dignified silence in response to such slander. Referring to Marat's repeated attacks, she told her husband: "He is foolish enough to imagine that I would be sensitive to such nonsense, that I would answer him in writing, and that he would have the pleasure of dragging a woman into the public forum in order to ridicule her husband." And defiantly, she declared: "Let them slander me as much as they like; I won't complain or even concern myself with them" (Roland 1966, 90). In prison, however, she felt physically threatened by the danger of mob violence that might result from the increasingly inflammatory articles published by Hébert. When an angry group began to shout insults and threats outside the window of her cell, she dashed off a fierce letter of protest to Garat, who was then Minister of Justice.

The viciousness and frequency of the attacks against Mme Roland reflect the degree of power and influence that were attributed to her.[20] Like her subsequent imprisonment, trial, and execution, they constitute a paradoxical tribute to her importance as a political figure. The misogynic nature of the charges made against Mme Roland by both the periodical press and the revolutionary government—the fact that she was condemned more for alleged moral transgressions and for overstepping traditional gender barriers than for any specific political act—illustrates how women's political and intellectual activities were associated with moral and social deviance. It is interesting, moreover, to note how in their allusions to Roland's writing her enemies make use of double entendres to equate literary self-revelation with sexual promiscuity. For example, in one of his articles in *Père Duchesne*, Hébert recounts how Mme Roland "unbuttoned herself/spoke frankly to" Père Duchesne, and "lui a découvert le pot aux roses"—that is, revealed her secret plots/private parts (243 [20 June 1793]). Similarly, in the formal act of accusation against the Girondists, Amar refers to the "prodigieuse facilité" with which Mme Roland provided the "Bureau d'Esprit Public" with propaganda pamphlets in order to corrupt the public. Once again, ease of writing in a woman is associated with easy virtue, and both are directly linked to corruption of the public mind and morals. The connection between women's writing and female sexuality (and promiscuity) is illustrated most graphically—and grotesquely—in another issue of *Père Duchesne* in which Hébert reports an alleged visit to the Rolands on New Years Eve:

> It was around midnight and, in the arms of her lackey Lanthenas, the virtuous Mme Roland was diverting herself from the moral pleasures provided by her feeble old husband. Pregnant with a discourse that the billboarders would deliver in the morning, she was right in the midst of her labor when little Louvet rushed in and interrupted their lovemaking. (205 [1 Jan. 1793])

In this passage, Hébert evokes the hackneyed comparison of writing to childbirth in order to mock Mme Roland's literary and political activities more effectively. By appealing to misogynic prejudices and stereotypes (women writers and politicians as witches, whores, and monsters), he and his colleagues added highly effective ammunition to their campaign of verbal terrorism against the Girondins and their ill-fated Egeria.

Well aware of the misogynic tenor of the charges against her, Mme Roland strove to counterbalance them by underlining her strict conformity to traditional gender roles. In the speech prepared for her trial she maintained:

> I took a keen interest in the public welfare and in the progress of the Revolution, but I never went beyond the limits prescribed for my sex. It was no doubt my talents, knowledge, and courage that turned people against me. . . . Only odious tyrants would sacrifice a woman whose sole crime was to possess a few merits about which she never boasted. ("Projet de défense," Roland 1966, 371-73)

Much to her chagrin, Mme Roland was never permitted to deliver her speech or indeed to utter more than a few words at her trial. However, during the two interrogations that preceded it, she cleverly turned the antifeminism of her examiners against them. When questioned about her husband's political activities, she replied that as a woman it was not her role to meddle in public affairs and that her only knowledge of events had been through the newspapers. This, of course, was hardly the case; but when her examiners insisted that she must have had more information than the average citizen, she coolly observed that a woman was not expected to make special inquiries into matters that did not concern her sex ("Interrogatoire de Mme Roland," Roland 1966, 95). When asked about various pamphlets distributed by Roland's propaganda bureau, she maintained that they were available for anyone to read and that it was up to the public and not to her, a mere woman, to pass judgment on them. She also firmly denied accusations that she had directed the propaganda bureau or any other of her husband's political operations ("Notes sur mon procès," Roland 1966, 367). Finally, when her interrogators demanded to know Roland's whereabouts, she responded that no human law could force her to betray her loyalty to her husband—another dictum of the Rousseauistic code. She then attempted to defend her husband's probity as an administrator and his loyalty to the Revolution, but was rudely interrupted, accused of being a chatterbox, and ordered to respond to all further questions with a simple yes or no. Resisting the prosecutor's efforts to intimidate and silence her, and rejecting the self-incriminating script he tried to impose on her, Mme Roland appealed to higher principles of justice and reason to affirm her innocence.[21] She even tried to seize control of the proceedings by ordering the court clerk to write under her dictation. But this open defiance of the prosecutor's authority only served to infuriate him so much that he abruptly ended the interrogation, thereby silencing her definitively.

That Mme Roland was imprisoned and condemned to death more for overstepping traditional gender barriers than for any specific political act is clearly underlined by newspaper accounts of her execution. For example, *Le Moniteur Universel* wrote: "In a short period of time, the Revolutionary Tribunal has given women several valuable examples that will not be lost for them." After unflattering epitaphs to Marie-Antoinette and to the feminist Olympe de Gouges (both executed the same month as Mme Roland, along with Mme du Barry), the memory of Mme Roland was then evoked in blatantly misogynic terms.

> That woman Roland, who fancied herself a great mind with great plans, a philosopher, was in every way a monster. Her disdainful attitude, her proudly opinionated replies, her ironic gaiety, and the firmness she displayed on the way to her execution prove that she was devoid of any grief. She was a mother, but she sacrificed nature. . . . The desire to be learned led her to forget the virtues of her sex. Such negligence is always dangerous and caused her to perish on the scaffold. (*Le Moniteur universel* [19 Nov. 1793]), quoted in Dauban 537-38)

In other accounts of her execution, Mme Roland's courage was invariably construed as proof of her insensitivity and baseness: a truly virtuous woman, a truly loving wife and mother, would have shown regrets, weakness, tears.[22]

It is clear from all these commentaries that Mme Roland's execution, like that of Olympe de Gouges and other "public" women, was being used as a warning to women activists: If they did not give up their political activities and conform to the passive domestic role prescribed for them by the revolutionary government, they, too, would risk imprisonment and death. After pointing to Mme Roland's example, the article in *Le Moniteur Universel* ended with the following exhortation:

> Women, do you wish to be true republicans? Then love, follow, and teach the laws that guide your husbands and sons in the exercise of their rights. . . . Be diligent in your housework; never attend political meetings with the intention of speaking there; but let your presence serve as an example for your children. The fatherland will then bless you, for you will truly have given what it expects from you. (19 Nov. 1793; quoted in Dauban 538)

Similarly, in the ruling banning women's participation in political clubs and meetings, Chaumette, head counsel of the Paris Commune, pointed to the cases of Mme Roland and Olympe de Gouges as irrefutable justification for the ban: "Remember *la Roland,* that haughty wife of a stupid, perfidious husband, who thought herself fit to govern the republic and who rushed to her downfall. Remember the impudent Olympe de Gouges, who . . . abandoned the duties of her household to meddle in politics, and whose head fell beneath the avenging knife of the law " (quoted in Levy et al. 1979, 220).

It is indeed ironic that Mme Roland—who had so painstakingly conformed her outward behavior to Rousseau's ideal of domesticity—should be frequently cited along with the militant feminist de Gouges as a pernicious example for others of their sex by revolutionary leaders and journalists.[23] The charges against the two women were surprisingly similar, despite the striking differences in their lives and characters. Both were accused of neglecting their duties as wives and mothers in order to meddle in politics, of attempting to usurp male powers and prerogatives and, graver still, of forgetting their proper place as women. Both were victims of the revolutionary government's increasingly repressive policies toward women—policies strongly influenced by Rousseau's writings.[24] Given the concerted effort to represent these women as dangerous deviants from the prescribed norms of domestic life, it is quite striking, as Simon Schama has noted, that both Roland and de Gouges—like numerous other female victims of the Terror—presented themselves as tender and conscientious mothers following the Rousseauistic model in their parting letters to their children (802).

Rousseau's Paradoxical Influence on Roland's Life and Writings

Above all, Mme Roland was a victim of long-standing tensions within herself between the Rousseauistic ideals of domestic happiness and female self-effacement and an irrepressible urge to develop her talents to the fullest—an urge that impelled her, almost in spite of herself, to take an active part in the intellectual and political life of her period. As the attacks against her in the press became increasingly frequent and violent, Mme Roland bitterly lamented the loss of her anonymity: "Those who have lifted the veil under which I wished to remain have done me an ill turn indeed! . . . If they had judged the facts as they really were, they would have spared me the kind of celebrity for which I had no desire. Instead of having to defend myself against their slander by writing my confession, I could brighten the solitude of my imprisonment by reading the essays of Montaigne" (Roland 1966, 304-05).

Yet despite all her protestations of modesty, Mme Roland was secretly grateful to her persecutors for giving her the ideal pretext to write her autobiography. For it was an opportunity not only to justify herself in the eyes of posterity, but also to fulfill her talents and ambitions as a writer. Recounting her life's story and the political personages and events she had witnessed proved to be a richly rewarding experience. Despite the gloom of prison and the specter of impending death, Mme Roland ended her *Mémoires* with a proud affirmation of her powers as a writer, mixed with the regret of being unable to develop her talents more fully: "If I had been allowed to live," she declares, "I would have had only one ambition: to record the annals of my century and to be the Macaulay of my country; I was going to say the Tacitus of France, but that would be immodest, and . . . some might say that I am not quite up to his level" (Roland 1966, 338-39). Overtly mocking the conventions of modesty and inferiority imposed upon women—conventions to which she had always previously deferred—she then expressed her confidence that with time and practice, and on a subject of equal richness, she might well have rivaled the writings of Tacitus. By composing her memoirs and correspondence, Mme Roland was in fact able to fulfill her ambitions at least partially, for together they provide a vivid chronicle of her period and a rich sampling of what she might have accomplished as a writer had she lived longer and pursued a literary career.[25]

Despite her special fondness for Tacitus and Plutarch, it is Rousseau who is most often evoked by Mme Roland as her literary and spiritual father. From her prison cell, she wrote to a friend: "These memoirs will be my *Confessions,* for I will not conceal anything. . . . I've thought about it carefully and made up my mind. I will tell all, absolutely everything. That is the only way to be useful" (to Jany, October 1793, *Lettres,* 4:527-28). Following Rousseau's example in his *Confessions,* Mme Roland gave free rein to her thoughts and feelings in her memoirs and, like Rousseau, attempted to justify herself in the eyes of posterity by presenting an authentic self-portrait and self-analysis to counter what she perceived as misrepresentations of her character and motives by her contemporaries. In the course of her autobiographical venture, Mme Roland emerged from anonymity as her husband's secret political advisor and ghost writer to become a writer and public figure in her own right, as well as a woman with passions and ambitions outside the domestic sphere to which she had voluntarily—on the surface at least—confined herself until them. However, without the Revolution and the Terror, without the creative impulse provided by the constant threat of death and the desire to justify herself in the eyes of future generations, would Mme Roland have felt impelled to write her memoirs? Given her earlier reluctance to pursue a literary career and to publish under her own name, this appears rather doubtful.

Rousseau's influence on Mme Roland's life and writing is therefore crucial, yet paradoxical. For although on the surface she appeared to conform to his ideals of domesticity and sensibility, her superior intelligence and education, coupled with her political and literary activities, made her a very different woman indeed from the feminine model advocated in *Julie* and *Emile*. In fact, because of her involvement in politics, she was the very kind of woman Rousseau would have been inclined to criticize. Perhaps the most paradoxical aspect of Rousseau's influence on Mme Roland is that, following his bold example in the *Confessions,* she dared to transgress social and literary conventions of female modesty and silence to reveal her most intimate thoughts, feelings, and experiences in ways that both shocked and thrilled her readers.

Notes

1. An earlier version of this essay appeared in *Eighteenth-Century Life* 13, 2 (May 1989): 65-86 under the title "Revolution in the Boudoir: Mme Roland's Subversion of Rousseau's Feminine Ideals."

2. "My mother, who no doubt understood that my mind needed a challenge, made no objection to my study of philosophy, even at the risk of exposing me to a bit of atheism," Mme Roland later surmised. "But she no doubt felt that it would be unwise to expose my overly sensitive and passionate nature to Rousseau's writing. Alas, what useless precautions to save me from my destiny!" (Roland, *Mémoires*, 1966, 277). [All translations are mine.]

3. See in particular May 1970 and May 1964. Also see May 1984, 309-17. Gita May's work on Roland has been a source of great inspiration to me, but my approach differs from hers in several important respects. May views Roland's response to Rousseau as a conversion experience that inspired a lifelong effort to live up to his idealistic views on women. In contrast, I see Roland's initial enthusiasm for Rousseau as a confirmation of the deepest convictions and longings of her youth. This enthusiasm gradually gave way to a questioning and subversion of his narrow ideals under the pressure of external events and in response to her own evolving aspirations—political, literary, and romantic—as a mature woman. It is this gradual evolution in Roland's response to Rousseau, from young militant to married conformist to subverter of his ideals, that I have sought to trace in my essay.

4. In this passage, Mme Roland negates gender differences at the experiential level, but not at the creative level. She recognizes women's (and specifically her own) ability to experience the same thoughts and aspirations as men, but underlines the superior ability of male writers (and specifically Rousseau's) to express them.

5. Similarly, recalling the Sunday dances at Soucy (the estate of a farmer general where her great aunt and uncle Besnard had worked as housekeeper and intendant), Roland writes: "I never stayed long. After an hour, escaping from the curiosity of the guests, I withdrew with my parents to continue our walk, the sweet joys of which I would never have sacrificed for the boisterous, but empty pleasures of such appearances in public" (Roland 1966, 276).

6. The shift in her character and tone brought about by the Revolution is particularly well reflected in the following passage of her *Mémoires:* "So long as I remained in a peaceful condition in the domestic sphere, my natural sensibility dominated or masked my other qualities. My chief desire was to please and to help others. . . . Since then, however, political storms and other circumstances have shaped my character. Frankness has become my dominant trait. . . . I am not afraid to tell people the blunt truth about themselves, and I do it without showing emotion or anger, whatever the effect may be on my listeners" (Roland 1966, 202).

7. See de Roux, p. 93, n. 1: "Arrested August 4, 1793, Champagneux had to defend himself against the accusation that he had directed this propaganda bureau, whose actual director was probably Mme Roland."

8. "I am distressed that my imagination remains useless, for lack of talent and opportunities to exercise it. . . . To be truly happy, I would need to immerse myself in serious study and have access to all kinds of resources that are denied me. I'll never amount to anything. I'll always feel miserably incomplete, displeasing to those of my kind for failing to resemble them, but lacking the culture necessary to raise myself to the level of others. I am as out of place as one can possibly be" (to Sophie Cannet, 10 Dec. 1776, *Lettres*, 1:527-28).

9. "Sometimes I'm tempted to put on pants and a cap so that I might have the freedom to seek out the talents of others and to cultivate my own," she confided to her friend. A few months later, in another letter to Sophie, Manon expressed her enthusiasm for d'Holbach's *Système de la nature* and then added: "I can't tell you how much I wish to study physics, astronomy, and other subjects to which I'll probably never have access. What a bore to be a woman! If I were a bit bolder and crazier, I would disguise myself as a man in order to throw off my fetters and I would immerse myself in the pleasure of scholarly pursuits." However, the conclusion of her letter clearly suggests that Manon did not really feel the need to be a man in order to engage in serious study: "The die is cast, for now that I've begun to reason and to search for answers, I'll never stop. I've set up my own rules and standards to guide my actions, and I'm convinced that happiness depends less on the opinions of others than on one's own character and determination" (to Sophie Cannet, 25 Aug. and 13 Nov. 1776, *Lettres*, 1:465 & 519).

10. "When my husband served as Minister of the Interior, I carefully followed the rule of never paying visits to women or inviting them to my home," Mme Roland later recalled. "This entailed no great sacrifice for me, since I had never had any taste for high society. For I loathe boring people, gaming, and game-playing almost as much as I cherish serious study and solitude. Accustomed to spending my days at home in the domestic sphere, I shared Roland's work and cultivated my own scholarly interests. By establishing this strict code in our residence, I was able both to preserve my usual way of life and to avoid all the problems caused by the crowd of hangers-on that usually surround people in high office" (Roland 1966, 72). Throughout this passage, one senses a thinly veiled misogyny.

11. In her self-portrait, Roland underlines her natural sensuousness: "As for my chin, it has all the characteristics that physionomists generally associate with sensuality. . . . I doubt that anyone was ever better suited for sensual pleasure, yet enjoyed it less" (Roland 1966, 253).

12. "Mes Dernières Pensées," (Last Will and Testament written by Mme Roland 8 Oct. 1793), reprinted in de Roux's edition of her *Mémoires*, 1966, 342 & 346.

13. "No, I am not leaving you; I shall wait for you. The same virtue that separated us on earth will unite us in heaven. . . . I am only too happy to sacrifice my life for the right to

love you forever without crime, and to be able to say it to you freely once again" (Rousseau, *Julie*, 2:743).

14. Outram presents her chapter on Roland as a case study to illustrate her central thesis that, during the French Revolution, shifting attitudes toward the body—and specifically the female body—had a determining influence on the unfolding of events. She maintains that, despite the efforts of modern feminists to recapture the female body from male appropriation, "recent women's history of the Revolution has considered its female actors as without embodiment"—as unconscious of their physical specificity and its consequences. She further maintains that modern historiography has failed to show how the effort to exclude women from the public sphere was "inextricably linked to the way that the pre-Revolutionary culture of the eighteenth century had given drama and visibility to women's physicality" (1989, 129).

15. "Madame Roland's Appeal to Impartial Posterity," review of *An Appeal to Impartial Posterity* [English translation of Mme Roland's memoirs], in *The Analytical Review* 22 (July-Dec. 1795): 145. The reviewer's compliments were however double-edged, since s/he then added: "while her husband continued in office, she assisted him in his political labours, and by her uncommon exertions, rendered herself the centre of a numerous group of enthusiastic admirers." The lengthy four-part review was signed "E. D."—initials sometimes used by Mary Wollstonecraft, who was a frequent contributor to the *Analytical Review* at the time Mme Roland's *Mémoires* were published, as well as a passionate observer of the French Revolution. If indeed Wollstonecraft wrote the review, her ambivalence toward Roland's political role—reflected in the repetition of the term *uncommon* and in the sexist phrase *distinguished ornament of her sex*—would strikingly illustrate the power of traditional gender stereotypes over even the most progressive minds of the period.

16. Anecdote recounted in a letter to Sophie Cannet, 29 Feb. 1776, *Lettres*, 1:384.

17. "It was through genuine devotion to the revolutionary cause rather than to satisfy any personal ambition on her part that Mme Roland came to contradict her restrictive principles concerning women and their proper role in society and politics," writes May. "Extraordinary events in a sense forced her hand. After witnessing the eternal hesitations and waffling of the Girondists and the ineffectiveness of their political program, she could not help but play an increasingly important role in their private deliberations and provide them with support and counsel" (May 1964, 187).

18. See, for example, Walter's note on Mme Roland in his critical edition of Michelet's *Histoire de la Révolution Française* 1952, 2:1521; Mathiez, 2:46-47 & 3:85; and Madelin.

19. These passages are all cited and discussed in the course of this article. See, in particular, Roland's *Lettres*, 1:195 & 374-75 and her *Mémoires* 1966, 155; 305; 338-39.

20. In *The Girondins*, Martin Sydenham argues that Mme Roland had very little real political influence. He maintains that the "myth" of her negative effect on the Girondist

cause was used by her contemporaries (as well as by later historians) to absolve the Girondins of responsibility for their own downfall. According to Sydenham, this myth also had the merit, for the hard-pressed historian, of easily defining just who *were* the Girondins; by definition, they became the group of politicians known to Mme Roland. Adopting Sydenham's assessment, Outram claims that Mme Roland's political influence was "virtually nil," but that (as in the trials of Marie-Antoinette and Charlotte Corday), her example was used by the Jacobins as a warning to women who sought to play an active role in the public sphere. (See Outram 1989, 127, 130-31, & 151.)

Contrary to both Sydenham and Outram, I would argue that Mme Roland's political influence was very real and that she had an important impact on the turn of events, as I have sought to illustrate in my article. I agree, however, with Sydenham that her influence was at times exaggerated by her political enemies and then used by various historians to absolve the Girondins of responsibility for their downfall.

21. "My interrogator loaded all his questions with insulting epithets and tried to prevent me from providing any evidence in my defense. Both he and the judge . . . used all possible means to reduce me to silence or to force me to say what they wanted to hear. I was indignant and insisted that, once my case was brought to trial, I would protest this outrageous mode of questioning. I added that I would not let myself be silenced by authority and that I acknowledged only the higher authority of reason and nature" ("Notes sur mon procès," Roland 1966, 367).

22. Commenting on Mme Roland's execution in *Journal universel,* Audouin remarks: "True courage does not jest" (9 Nov. 1793). Similarly, in *Le Calendrier républicain* the same day, Sylvain Maréchal insists: "A truly virtuous woman, a woman who had sacrificed her life to the Republic, would not have behaved in this manner. Not surprisingly, the most insulting commentary on Mme Roland's execution is found in Hébert's *Père Duchesne:* "It's better to kill the devil than to let the devil kill us first. . . . The sans-culottes were smart to call your bluff, Dame Coco, because if your old cuckold of a husband had not been thrown out of office, you would have become the second Marie-Antoinette" (9 Nov. 1793).

23. The negative portrayals of Mme Roland by hostile journalists and politicians form a curious contrast with the glowing description of her shortly before her death by Count Beugnot, a fellow prisoner at the Conciergerie. Despite his political differences with her and his natural aversion for intellectual, aggressive women, he was rapidly won over by her dignity and charm. He was especially moved when she spoke of her family: "No one defined better than she the duties of a wife and mother and proved more eloquently that a woman knows happiness only in the accomplishment of these sacred duties. The picture of domestic life took on ravishing colors when she painted it; tears fell from her eyes whenever she spoke of her daughter and husband" (Beugnot 139).

24. Rousseau's home-and-hearth ethic was enthusiastically advocated by the revolutionary government as a vehicle for its program of social reform. The public discourse of the period is filled with references to the bourgeois ideals of simplicity, efficiency, and fru-

gality extolled in *Julie* and *Emile*. The Rousseauian cults of motherhood and domesticity and the principle of separate spheres underlying them were frequently invoked by revolutionary leaders (notably Mirabeau, Robespierre, and Chaumette) to justify the continued subordination of women, as well as the persecution of feminist militants and the suppression of women's revolutionary clubs.

For further discussion of the influence that Rousseau's views on women had upon the leaders of the revolutionary government, see Cerati and Blum, especially Blum's chapter titled "The Sex Made to Obey," 204-15.

25. "Mme Roland's memoirs of the Revolution constitute without a doubt one of the most energetic and evocative texts of the period," remarks Gita May. "More valuable still are her *Mémoires particuliers*. A chronicle of the private life of the Parisian artisan class between 1760 and 1780, her personal memoirs present us with a splendid inside view of the lifestyle, ideas, sensibility, and tastes of the *moyenne bourgeoisie parisienne* at the end of the ancien régime. In these memoirs, we discover a writer who is alert and often enchanting" (May 1964, 30). Mme Roland's writing was of course greatly admired by important writers and critics of the Romantic period including Sainte-Beuve, Lamartine, Brunetière, Stendhal, and the Goncourts.

6

From Public to Private Sphere: The Case of Mme de Sévigné and Mme de Staël

Catherine R. Montfort

> Malheur à une femme qui veut devenir un grand homme.
> —*Journal des Débats,* mars 1800.[1]

Throughout the ages, few French women writers have been accepted into the literary "canon." This proposition is clouded by several individuals with outstanding reputations, such as Christine de Pisan and Mme de la Fayette.[2] But even Christine de Pisan, who earned a well-established reputation as a writer in the Middle Ages, was subjected to repeated attacks and innuendo when she not only defended women against medieval misogyny, but also affirmed the intellectual capacity of the "feminin sexe" (Albistur and Armogathe 1: 72-85).[3] A century later, Louise Labé seemingly partook of the Renaissance in that she received a liberal education, but her relative independence after marriage gave rise to widespread denunciation and eventually subjected her to calumny. She was accused, among other things, of publishing Maurice Scève's works under her name and of being a courtisane or "plebeia meretrix," by Calvin, among others (Albistur 1: 158).[4] And although Montaigne thought highly of Mlle de Gournay and called her his "fille d'alliance," she was heavily criticized throughout her life. Her writing was not taken seriously, and her *Egalité des hommes et des femmes* written in 1622 had no impact on the "Grand Siècle" (Albistur 1: 179-88).

In contrast, in the seventeenth century proper, Mme de Sévigné and Mme de la Fayette were ladies of the salons and were well thought of in their lifetime, but, interestingly enough, Mme de Sévigné wrote only personal letters published after her death,[5] while Mme de la Fayette's famous novel, *La Princesse de Clèves,* was published anonymously. As far as the "Précieuses" were concerned, their trial to promote a new image of woman was offset by plays like Molière's *Les Femmes Savantes* or the very conservative views of Fénelon in *De l'éducation des filles.*[6] Finally, even in the eighteenth century, a century well known for its remarkable women— Mme de Lambert, Mme de Tencin, Mme du Châtelet, Mme Du Deffand, Mlle de Lespinasse, Mme d'Epinay, Mme Necker—learned women were viewed as amateurs in intellectual circles. As pointed out by Evelyn Bodek, the *salonnière* "wrote, but rarely for a wide audience (a woman could respectably write for a circle of admirers or friends who might suggest publication, but she could rarely seek publication herself); she spoke, but carefully modulated her voice; she questioned, but hardly ever pursued the unquestionable" (191-92). As for the main women writers of the century, such as Mme Dacier, Mme de Genlis, or Mme de Staël: "Their books were sold and were read; but history, more sexist than the time, has hardly remembered their names" (Rosa 46). Nina Rattner Gelbart argues that even the panegyrics on women written by men were socially innocuous, because the authors were defending a weak, subservient group that could not defend itself: "They gallantly exercised their licenses to speak for women who were condemned to be mute, both by the social system and by women's acceptance of their own inferiority" (9). Elisabeth Badinter has concluded in *Emilie, Emilie: L'ambition féminine au XVIIIème siècle* that, even today, Mme du Châtelet is still mainly known as Voltaire's mistress, and Mme d'Epinay as the lady who protected Rousseau (475). These examples are far from exhaustive, but underscore a long standing state of affairs: In the centuries-old patriarchal system that governed sexual roles and rights, there was very little room for women writers.

At the time of the Revolution, there was great hope for a change in the status of women in general and women writers in particular.[7] Clearly, the willingness of Enlightenment intellectuals to question previously sacrosanct beliefs, values, and institutions had potentially revolutionary implications for the status of women.[8] In addition, the revolutionary movement, which politicized every aspect of life, led some women to assume the right to participate alongside men in civil life: These women rioted, petitioned for various causes, spoke in public, published, and demanded equal social and political rights. However, in spite of important feminist publicists such as Condorcet, Théroigne de Méricourt, Olympe de Gouges, and Etta Palm d'Aëlders, neither the law nor public opinion offered much support for the role of the woman writer. The law of July 19, 1793 gave male authors property rights over their written texts—but not female authors (Hesse 469-87). Moreover, October and November 1793 marked a turning point in the participation of women in revolutionary politics. The Jacobin dictatorship closed down women's political clubs and sent to the guillotine female political activists such as Mme Roland, Olympe de Gouges, and Théroigne de Méricourt. The goal of the present paper is to investigate the criterion used in the literary evaluation of French women writers immediately after the Revolution. I proceed by analyzing the literary fortunes of two well-known authors, Mme de Sévigné and Mme de Staël. These two women, currently well within the "canon," underwent diametrically opposed literary evaluations at the turn of the century. At first sight, the selection of Sévigné and Staël might seem arbitrary since one was dead while the other was still alive, but in doing so I follow the lead of Staël's contemporaries who, faced with an increasing number of women writers, particularly novelists, liked to refer to the past to evaluate modern writers. My modus operandi is to analyze the extent to which female literary figures were evaluated, at least partly, on the basis of their congruence with traditional feminine roles. I argue that divergence from the "norm" was very costly in terms of a woman's lasting literary success.

Mme de Sévigné and Mme de Staël had much in common.[9] Although each was raised in a bourgeois family, each belonged to the aristocracy through either birth (Mme de Sévigné) or marriage (Mme de Staël). Both were well educated and at ease in salons, where, due to vivacious conversational skills, they were much appreciated. Paris was the city of choice for each. Both married according to the mores of the time: love was not a consideration, rather the family name or wealth of the spouse. Both had children—Mme de Sévigné two, Mme de Staël five. Mme de Sévigné developed a strong and lasting attachment to her daughter.

Although Mme de Staël loved her children, her strongest attachment throughout her life was to her father. Both were religious and both wrote.

The similarities stop there. Mme de Sévigné married and was quickly a widow. She never remarried and refused lovers. In contrast, immediately after her marriage, Mme de Staël began a lifetime of taking lovers: Louis de Narbonne, Benjamin Constant, Prosper de Barante, and John Rocca, to name but a few. Mme de Sévigné was Catholic, leaning towards Jansenism. Mme de Staël was a strong Protestant who believed that Protestantism was the only religion compatible with a republic in that it promoted morality and reduced dogma to a minimum. Mme de Sévigné travelled within France, primarily to her estate in Brittany, and to visit her daughter in Provence. Mme de Staël was essentially exiled from Paris from 1792 to 1814. Besides England, where she had gone early in life, she travelled extensively—to Germany, Italy, Austria, and eventually to Russia and Sweden. Her exile and consequent travelling ultimately gave her a cosmopolitan outlook in spite of her strong Franco-centrism. Finally, and most importantly, Mme de Sévigné's primary audience was her daughter. Publication never crossed her mind.[10] Mme de Staël wrote to be published—from her *Lettres sur J. J. Rousseau* in 1788 to the posthumously published *Considérations sur la Révolution française*.

The contrast in how these women were judged as literary figures at the turn of the century is illuminating. Of course, one must be aware of the aristocracy's radically different standing in society after the Revolution. Recent events had been shocking: the king beheaded, upper classes exiled, and the poor rioting in the street. The aristocracy was held to be responsible for much of the moral decay which led ultimately to the Revolution and the associated societal chaos. For this, the upper classes were castigated as having been living a sinful life with too much freedom outside the family, not enough religious practice, too much sexual freedom, and too much leisure (Pope 301-02).[11] Moreover, a new cultural paradigm was consolidated by the Revolution, a paradigm based on stronger lines between the public sphere of politics and the private sphere of the family: Women were seen as "mothers," with the education of the young as their primary role—all under the guidance of men.[12] This role demanded staying at home: Mothers could not and should not have a public role. The key words were gentleness, passivity, submissiveness, abnegation, and faithfulness to the husband. Three points are noteworthy here: First, this view of women was identical among men whether one was a Republican and inspired by Rousseau, or whether one was a Royalist who had come to accept the judgment of Rousseau. A generally accepted ideal of womanhood triumphed in spite of severe class differences.[13] Second, most women internalized Rousseau's views on woman's nature, role, and education. Even Mme de Staël, as is evident in her novel *Corinne,* was haunted by self-doubt and self-censorship—yet she had come of age before 1789, and was raised with much liberty and intellectual freedom.[14] Third, Napoleon held and supported these same ideas concerning the role of women.[15] In March 1800 the *Journal des Débats* summarized the prevalent opinion on women—including women writers—at the turn of the century, when it stated: "Is it proper for a woman whose most sacred duty is to be a faithful wife and a tender mother, whose first virtue must be modesty, is it proper for her to leave this pleasant darkness imposed upon her by her sex to hand her whole life over to a public, who after having judged her writings, has the right to judge her actions?"

The fact that Napoleon supported the new ideal is especially important because of the large number of edicts and laws he enacted from 1800 to 1815.[16] In addition, Napoleon wanted to control opinion and, in particular, the press. Under his rule, writers were sponsored only if they did not criticize the new order. Newspapers came under strict scrutiny.[17] Some writers tried to please him. Others were censured or exiled. The newspapers which managed to survive were either official newspapers of the state such as the *Moniteur* or those favoring literature over political and religious topics. The *Mercure de France* was one of these primary literary newspapers. Newly reestablished in 1800, one of the hopes expressed in its "Prospectus" of Messidor an VIII was to "contribute to the destruction of those barbarous texts that the influence of the 18th of Brumaire steadily purges from revolutionary law." And in 1801, Fructidor an IX, the same journal chose the seventeenth century as a model to be emulated: "Imagination and good taste like to reflect and dwell on the good old days of Louis XIV's century."

In this climate of domesticity, censorship and longing for "the good old days," Mme de Sévigné's letters appeared particularly attractive. They were published in their entirety in 1801 by Vauxcelles, again in 1806 by Grouvelle,[18] and also in *Sevigniana* and in numerous *Lettres Choisies.* The *Lettres Choisies* were published mainly to be read by the young as part of their education. Levizac, in the 1803 edition of his *Lettres Choisies de Mme de Sévigné et de Mme de Maintenon* boasted to be the first editor to offer such a selection. The reasons for Sévigné's popularity were numerous: She was a representative of the seventeenth century—a century which, in contrast to the recent past, appeared to be a model of tranquillity and order with one king (Louis XIV), one religion (Catholicism), and a structured society. She had never rebelled against the state government nor aspired to a political role. She was religious. She wrote delightful and unpretentious letters, with no public in mind but her daughter, relatives, and friends.[19] Above all, she loved her daughter. The latter points are important as can be seen by Geoffroy's remark, in 1806, that one of the charms of Mme de Sévigné is that "she is always a woman, never an author, never pedantic, never a woman of letters" (*Spectateur français* III, 319), or Dussault's comment that "her destiny, due to a superiority of mind, elevated her above those of her sex, and above the ambitions of males thanks to her lack of ambition. One has contested nothing to this woman who has never contested anything herself" (*Journal des Débats,* 1806).

The upshot of Mme de Sévigné's seemingly perfect alignment with the current social mores was that she was repeatedly praised by critics for her role as *mother,* an important turnabout considering that, in the eighteenth century, the "public mondain" was shocked by that very love.[20] It is interesting to contrast the following typical criticism expressed by La Rivière in the early part of the eighteenth century: "I realized that the mother's expressions of love for her daughter are repetitive and resemble passion, so much so that one believes that it is a lover writing to his mistress" (letter to his correspondent the abbé Papillon, August 18, 1735),[21] with Ballanche's commentary in 1801, in his *Du Sentiment considéré dans ses rapports avec la littérature et les arts:* "I will not forget Madame de Sévigné who has had no model to emulate and who has been one for all [...] It is a beautiful embroidery where one can find Fontenelle's subtlety, Marivaux's wit, Montaigne's negligence and above all the heart of a *mother*" (213, my emphasis). And again in 1806, Grouvelle, wrote in *Notice sur la vie et la personne de Mme de Sévigné:* "She had not been a happy wife; she was a rich widow, and moreover a passionate *mother*" (307, my emphasis).[22]

On top of the various comments found in newspapers, books, and the editions of her letters, plays were written in which Mme de Sévigné was the major figure. It is important to note here that plays where Mme de

Sévigné had a role were written before the 1800s, for example, Olympe de Gouges's *Mirabeau aux Champs-Elysées* (1791).[23] But in these plays Mme de Sévigné did not have the leading role, nor was she chosen as the symbol of maternal love. In contrast, after the 1800s, both Bouilly and Dupaty wrote plays where the famous "épistolière" had the main role and is depicted as the perfect mother. As Bouilly said in the Preface of *Madame de Sévigné* (1805): "Who is the tender hearted *mother* who does not notice that patience and gentleness are the surest ways to elicit love from one's children, to win their trust and to save them from the fire of passion?" (245, my emphasis). Bouilly's play emphasized Sévigné's devotion to her children. For example, the character Mme de Villars mentions that Mme de Sévigné did not let youth, beauty, or wit distract her from devoting her entire life to the "education of her children" (257). When M. Darmenpierre, the tax collector in the play, asks Mme de Sévigné about her daughter, she replies that "the heart of a *mother* is an altar meant for many sacrifices" (332, my emphasis). Finally, she is addressed as "la meilleure des mères" [the best of *mothers*] by her son Charles. In Dupaty's play written in 1808, *Ninon chez Madame de Sévigné,* the author has Ninon, the famous courtesan, giving up the love of Mme de Sévigné's son for the sake of Mme de Sévigné and of the son's chosen bride:

> Instead of a fickle love which lasts only a few days,
> Learn to deserve the two immortal loves:
> That of a spouse, and that of a *mother.*
> Far from blinding you the latter enlightens you! (57, my emphasis)

Napoleon was surely pleased.[24] The point is that, although praised, Sévigné's life as mother and writer was distorted to fit the mores of the time. Being a good mother should have been irrelevant for her lasting claim to fame. Besides, and more importantly, her exceptional maternal love was interpreted to be the norm, while her letters clearly indicate that her "passion" for her daughter was extraordinary and even "abusive."[25] In addition, the wide spread circulation of *Lettres Choisies,* carefully selected and edited for the education of the young, gave the reader little indication of the richness and variety of her genius. The *Lettres Choisies* played a major force in the development of an antiseptic persona for Mme de Sévigné, a heavy price to pay for her letters to be easily integrated into the canon.

In contrast to Mme de Sévigné, Mme de Staël did not fit the new ideal.[26] For one thing, she held that education for women was essential: "If women rising above their fate dared to aspire to the education of men, if they knew what to tell men to do, if they had the conviction of their actions, what noble destiny would be theirs!" (qtd. in Balayé 1979, 31). Further, she aspired to far more than marriage and motherhood. Not only did she choose to be a writer in spite of her father's disapproval and that of society at large, but worse she believed that a writer should be political. She was never able to remove herself as writer from social events, nor could she remove literature and philosophy from the domain of political action (Balayé 1979, 13). Consequently she wrote on many topics, from literary criticism, to political issues, to philosophy, and in doing so became a threat to male writers and the new literary marketplace. For this reason, her writing, and her public and private behavior came under intense scrutiny. In 1794, when she published her *Réflexions sur la Paix adressées à M. Pitt et aux Français,* followed in 1795 by her *Réflexions sur la Paix Intérieure,* the Comité du Salut Public was outraged and exiled her to Switzerland.

A few years later Napoleon also thought that Staël was a threat to the new order he was in the process of establishing. This conflict between Napoleon and Mme de Staël spanned most of his reign and is epitomized in the well-known confrontation in which Mme de Staël asked the new ruler: "What would be for you the best woman?" Napoleon answered: "The one who would bear the most children" (qtd. in Diesbach 202). Virtually everything about Mme de Staël bothered Napoleon: her far above average education, her belief in the "philosophie des lumières," her sexual freedom, her desire to play an active role in politics, and finally her expression of these ideas in writing. Her first novel, *Delphine* (1802), with its defense of divorce and protestantism; her second novel, *Corinne* (1807), with its support for the independence of nations and its praise of England; and finally, *De l'Allemagne* (1810), with its praise of German writers and philosophy—all disturbed him immensely. "Never will Necker's daughter come back to Paris," he exclaimed after the triumph of the first novel. When Mme de Staël came to the vicinity of Paris in 1806 to correct the galleys of *Corinne* and to see friends, Napoleon took the time to write from Prussia to his chief of police Fouché: "Do not let this rogue of a woman, Mme de Staël, come close to Paris" (qtd. in Gautier 185). Finally in 1810, he ordered *De l'Allemagne* to be seized and destroyed.

Although Staël's problems with Napoleon were mentioned first, it is worth stressing here that the leader of France was far from being her only detractor. For example, on 24 July 1797, Fiévée refers to her in the *Gazette française* as "A foreigner as ugly as mortal sin," a comment he elaborates upon on August 19 of the same year:

> Some wish that one would respect political women, others wish to have them ridiculed [. . .] Let us not involve in our political quarrels women whose charms belong to all parties, but political viragos, orleanist schemers, why would we respect them when they do not even respect themselves? [. . .] Let us talk of Mme de Staël as Marat; if she is grieved by the attack, she will reform, if she does not reform, she will share this in common with her patron. A woman who has written puns on the influence of passions must have calculated the passions that a foreigner excites against herself when she shakes the torch of discord in an already split family.[27]

However, emboldened by Napoleon's condemnation of Staël, her detractors proliferated as the years went by. Whether one reads newspaper articles, plays, or novels—criticism abounds. For example, and to name but a few, Mme de Staël's novel *Delphine* triggered criticism from Villeterque in the *Journal de Paris,* Féletz in the *Journal des Débats,* and Fiévée in the *Mercure de France.*[28] Fiévée in an article of Nivôse an XI in the *Mercure de France* was the harshest of them all. Not only did he criticize the novel because the heroine is a "philosopher," "deist," "talkative," "passionate," adding that "a passionate woman is not against nature; but she is against the nature of well brought up women"—but he also attacked the author as a woman, a foreigner, and the ultimate horror, an anglophile: "Born in a country which no longer exists, wife of a Swedish man, French by circum--stance, with no homeland but that of her delusion, it is possible that she cannot imagine any other." Fiévée's antifeminist attacks in 1802 should not come as a surprise since he already attacked Mme de Staël as early as 1797 as mentioned above. What comes more as a surprise is Guinguené's article in *La Décade philosophique.* Written out of indignation at the treatment of the novel by the press, Guinguené nevertheless ends up criticizing the heroine and eventually the author—not out of subservience to Napoleon, but out of belief.[29] He is shocked by Delphine's behavior and her desire to be a brilliant and eloquent conversationalist: "Besides, a woman who plays that role in society really abandons the role that nature and society both prescribe to her sex." Delphine appears to Guinguené as dangerous as "a comet which whirls around and disturbs the whole system." It could not be clearer: the "system" did not favor ambitious women.[30]

Besides the numerous newspaper articles, *Delphine* triggered a number of novels and plays in reprisal. Two examples are J. B. Dubois's novel *Delphinette ou le mépris de l'opinion* and Radet's play *Colombine Philosophe Soi-Disant*. In Radet's play, Staël's *Delphine* is criticized both indirectly and directly; indirectly through the behavior of his heroine, Colombine, and directly in the comments of other characters. Before Colombine's arrival on stage, she is depicted as "crazy," a state brought about by reading the novel and accepting the beliefs of its main female character. In addition, one of the characters notes that Delphine is a woman "for whom wit is used only to talk wildly and to act irrationally" and that "all the characters of this novel are more or less in a frenzy" (5). As the plot develops, Colombine is abandoned by her lover Leandre, because Leandre prefers an "old-fashioned," "sweet," and "modest" wife (24). Following Delphine's footsteps, Colombine attempts to kill herself as a ploy to be in the spotlight. When the attempt fails, she suddenly becomes "reasonable" and is immediately rewarded with a husband. Her last tirade is a "mea culpa" for her past behavior:

> Finally I give up Delphine's
> principles and manners,
> I abandon this heroine
> and come back to reason. (47)

"Reasonable" behavior for Colombine is clearly spelled out and entails submission to her father, elimination of "mauvais livres," abandoning any idea of writing, and subservience in marriage.

Although Staël spent most of her adult life in exile, she tried innumerable times to return to Paris, her intellectual home.[31] One can understand the frustrations of this exceptional woman, torn between women's traditional role and that of activist author, by reading her largely autobiographical novel *Corinne*—the portrayal of a woman of genius. On the one hand, the mother figure is either absent or very harsh, and men are depicted as weak and powerless. On the other, the novel reeks with self-doubt and self-censorship. In any event, though this second novel did not trigger as much criticism as *Delphine,* it nevertheless was not spared an antifeminist barrage. Féletz, in an article of May 7, 1807 in the *Journal de l'Empire,* is a case in point. He begins by noting that Corinne is extraordinary and worthy of admiration, but then adds a caveat of condemnation: "This extraordinary woman is Corinne: probably an admirable woman, if the greatest charm and even the greatest glory of women was not in the practice of all the gentle, sweet, and modest virtues, if her most beautiful or rather her entire destiny was not to be foremost a timid and respectful daughter, then a sweet and virtuous wife, a tender and sensitive *mother"* (my emphasis). Another critic, Auger, is even more biting when he comments in the *Revue philosophique, littéraire et politique* that Corinne is not "une femme intérieure, c'est une femme toute *publique"* [not a domestic woman, she is a public woman], with as a striking conclusion, "this is so far from the true role of women, that custom has given this name to those who put their sex to shame" (472, my emphasis).

Auger's comment summarizes what bothered most critics of the time: Staël was not a domestic woman, but a public woman, in spite of her five children.[32] The reverse was true of Sévigné. As a matter of fact, I mentioned earlier that in selecting Sévigné and Staël I was following the lead of Staël's contemporaries. Palissot, for example, in an article on Mme de Genlis, mentioned that among the illustrious writers of the past, Mme de Sévigné was the best, adding interestingly: "Her glory is to have written immortal letters without even having thought that she was writing a book" (357). He then contrasted the unpretentious women of the past (Sévigné among others) with those of the present (Graffigny, Boccage, Ricconboni, Necker, Staël, Genlis): "Nowadays everything is different. Modesty has been replaced with proud pretensions of all sorts" (359). Another critic, Dussault, defended Mme de Sévigné as "la meilleure des mères," and ironically pointed out how different she was from modern "philosophers in petticoats." Not only would the latter despise Sévigné for "sots préjugés" [stupid prejudices], that is, for believing in an afterlife and being religious (reading Pascal and sermons, etc), but also for being unaware of the *Système de la perfectibilité* and a stranger to *De l'influence des passions* (1807, 49-51). The attack on Mme de Staël is obvious.[33] Still another reason I have chosen to contrast the fortunes of Sévigné and Staël is that they reside at opposite ends of the spectrum of feminine behavior, and illustrate perhaps better than any other pair of women writers that, after the Revolution, gender stereotyping was regularly used as a tool against women writers—in this case, it conveniently exalted Sévigné and belittled Staël.[34] Mme de Genlis, the only rival of Staël at the time, would be another possible candidate to contrast with Sévigné. (Interestingly enough, she praised the former and criticized the latter.)[35] However her case is not as clear cut as the Sévigné/Staël comparison. For example, Genlis believed in the education of women and argued that women should be allowed to become authors, but, clever enough to understand the constraints and mouth the pieties expected, she stated in her "Réflexions préliminaires sur les femmes" in *De l'influence des femmes:* "One must admit that in general women are not made to rule nor to meddle in serious political issues" (20). Consequently, although as a writer she had her share of detractors, she was never as bitterly criticized as Staël.[36]

In conclusion, for women writers of the time conformity with the existing zeitgeist distorted "les fortunes littéraires" as much as nonconformity. Mme de Sévigné's life and work was distorted in the sense that her "abusive" maternal love was interpreted to be the norm, at a time when motherhood was being exalted within the framework of a patriarchal society. She thus became the symbol of "motherly" love. On the literary side, her genius as a writer was praised, but never analyzed in depth. Most commentators merely repeated what had already been said in the eighteenth century by men such as Voltaire, Perrin, Suard, and La Harpe.[37] Eventually, since the epistolary genre was no threat to male writers, she was selected to inaugurate the "Grands Ecrivains de la France" series published by Hachette in the middle of the nineteenth century. On the other hand, Mme de Staël's life and work experienced the opposite type of distortion. Because she was a threat to male writers and because she believed in the "philosophie des Lumières," critics magnified her flaws, belittled her qualities, and in general, attacked her as not conforming to the existing feminine mold. Stendhal best summarizes the opinion of the time in a letter to his sister: "Mme de Staël has lost charm by showing her superiority; she wanted to be loved as a woman after having shone as a man" (letter of March 22, 1806, 315-16). Although Staël played a major role in French Romanticism, she was ignored after her death by nineteenth-century literary cognoscenti, and until recently was relegated to secondary status in anthologies of French literature. Being the victim of gender stereotyping appears to have been the fate of women writers until very recently—a fact fully understood by Mme de Staël herself when she wrote: "When a woman publishes a book, she becomes dependent on opinion, and those who control this opinion make their power severely felt" (1967, 1: 302).

Notes

1."Cursed be a woman who wants to become a great man." All translations are mine. An earlier analysis of some of the ideas of this essay will appear as "French Women Writers and the Revolution: Preliminary Thoughts," in *The French Revolution of 1789 and Its Impact* (Greenwood Press).

2. For an investigation of canon making which focuses on the exclusionary politics regulating the transmission of French literature—in particular the question of exclusion by gender, see DeJean and Miller 1-258.

3. On Christine de Pisan, see also Bell's essay on the problem of a studious woman (173-84).

4. On the Renaissance, see Kelly-Gabol's still interesting article, "Did Women have a Renaissance?" Kelly-Gabol was one of the first critics to challenge traditional periodization and to demonstrate that the modern relation of the sexes with its subordination of women made its appearance at that time (137-64).

5. With the exception of the thirteen letters that her cousin Bussy included in his *Mémoires* sent to Louis XIV. For a detailed account on when and how the letters were published, see R. Duchêne 1792, 1: 756-830.

6. On the "Précieuses," see Richmond and Venesoen, Pelous, and Stanton 107-34.

7. On the Revolution and women, see the basic studies by Levy et al. 1979, Duhet 1981, Landes, and Godineau 1988. See also, among the numerous books and articles published in 1989, the studies by Outram, Hunt, Didier, and Marand-Fouquet.

8. On feminine writing in the press in the eighteenth century, see Gelbart's study on *Le Journal des Dames,* in which she shows that the editors of the paper tried to combine the legitimacy of the protected papers with the challenging attitudes of those produced outside the system of censorship (11). Unfortunately, the *Journal des Dames* was suppressed in 1778, and "no truly feminist papers were printed on French soil" (299). On the contribution of the Grub Street milieu of intellectuals to the Revolution, see Darnton 1982.

9. For biographies of Sévigné and Staël, see R. Duchêne 1982 and Diesbach, respectively.

10. "Elle n'a jamais écrit pour le public, sachant combien elle était loin d'écrire comme devait écrire un auteur. Et, de fait, on ne l'imprima qu'après l'avoir minutieusement corrigée afin de la rendre conforme au goût du temps et aux règles du genre de la lettre" (R. Duchêne 1982, 462). On this important point which has been debated among Sevignists for several decades, see the concurrent studies by R. Duchêne 1970 and Montfort (-Howard) 1982, 14-31. See also Bray, Cordelier, and more recently Farrell, who argue to the contrary. But none of this really matters here: What is important to this essay is that her readers at the turn of the century believed (unanimously) that she did not write for publication and, as shown below, praised her for that very reason.

11. See Mme de la Tour du Pin's later testimony. She was a former court lady of Marie-Antoinette and wrote in her *Mémoires* (begun in the 1820s): "The older I grow, the more sure I become that the 1789 Revolution was but the inevitable consequence and, I might almost say, the just punishment of the vices of the upper classes" (46).

12. On the public and private sphere, see Landes, Hunt 1985, and Goodman 1992.

13. See, for example, on the Royalist side, Louis de Bonald's statement on women: "Les femmes entendent mieux que les hommes la conduite des affaires domestiques, ce qui prouve mieux que de longs raisonnements que la nature ne les appelle pas à diriger les affaires publiques" (qtd. in Albistur 2: 365).

14. For a critical comment on women's attitude as a whole at the turn of the century, see, in 1808, *l'Athénée des Dames* bemoaning their submissive behavior (Albistur 2: 374-75). Before 1793, Mme Roland is an interesting case in point. On the one hand, she tried to conform to Rousseau's ideal and stated in her *Mémoires particuliers:* "Le bel esprit, la réputation, le plaisir d'être imprimé n'étaient pas mon but. [. . .] je ne voulais pas être auteur; j'avais vu de très bonne heure qu'une femme qui gagnait ce titre perdait beaucoup plus qu'elle n'avait acquis. Les hommes ne l'aiment point et son sexe la critique" (qtd. in Cornevin 62). On the other, as pointed out by Mary Trouille in this volume, she transgressed traditional gender barriers which eventually led her to the guillotine.

15. Napoleon's ideas on women are well documented and can be partly explained by his personal history. He was raised in a patriarchal society. His mother, married when she was fourteen years old had thirteen children, and was widowed at thirty-five. At the imperial court, she became a model for him: her austerity, her lack of ambition, and her discretion—the perfect role model in contrast with the coquettish Joséphine de Beauharnais.

16. Directly affecting women was the founding of "lycées" in 1802 and the organization of the University in 1806, both done under his guidance and both forbidding admission to women. His plan for the "Ecole de la légion d'honneur" at Ecouans prepared women to enjoy the legal status he gave them in the Code Civil, that of minors. See the *Revue de l'enseignement des femmes* where the following conversation between Napoléon and Mme Campan is cited. Napoléon: "Les anciens systèmes ne valent rien. Que manque-t-il aux jeunes personnes pour être bien élevées en France?" Mme Campan replied: "Des mères." Napoléon: "Le mot est juste. Eh bien! madame, que les Français vous aient

l'obligation d'avoir élevé des mères pour leurs enfants" (10). Even in 1806 when he founded the first chair of gynecology, seemingly a step forward for women and science, his ulterior motive was to produce more soldiers for the "Grande Armée" (Kniebielher and Fouquet 163-68).

17. Almost immediately after the "coup d'état" he suppressed sixty newspapers and permitted only thirteen to continue publication (*Histoire générale de la presse française* 1: 550).

18. In his ten-volume edition, Vauxcelles was not motivated by the discovery of new letters. In fact, he followed the 1790 edition published in Rouen, adding only his *Réflexions* in the last volume. In his edition, Grouvelle ordered the letters chronologically instead of grouping them according to correspondent, as traditionally done. Both Vauxcelles's *Réflexions* and Grouvelle's *Notice sur la vie et la personne de Mme de Sévigné* are invaluable to any effort to chart Sévigné's image transformation at the turn of the century.

19. On this point, see n. 10.

20. On this point, see Montfort 1982, in particular chapter 3, and its conclusion: "Peu de lecteurs se doutaient en 1734-1737 que cet amour serait un jour porté aux nues et considéré comme l'un des titres de gloire de Mme de Sévigné" (54).

21. See also Anfossi's complaint: "La tendresse pour sa fille forme un caractère bien singulier, on souhaiterait quelquefois qu'elle eut suivi là-dessus la morale de Mr. Arnaud, cela lui aurait épargné des répétitions qui fatiguent les lecteurs" (Montfort 1982, 53).

22. See also Mme de Genlis's praise of Mme de Sévigné as mother in her *De l'influence des femmes:* "C'est en se livrant au plus pur de tous les sentimens [amour maternel] et à la plus tendre affection de son cœur, que madame de Sévigné s'est immortalisée" (136-39).

23. I would like to thank Gabrielle Verdier for bringing this play to my attention.

24. His own judgment on Mme de Sévigné turns out to be rather stern. In his *Mémorial de Sainte-Hélène,* he wrote that he prefers the letters of Mme de Maintenon: "Mme de Sévigné certainement restera le vrai type; elle a tant de charmes et de grâces, mais quand on a beaucoup lu, il ne reste rien. Ce sont des œufs à la neige dont on peut se rassasier sans charger son estomac" (6 September 1816). On Napoleon's thoughts on Sévigné, see 2: 171-72, and 6: 107.

25. On this point, see J. Duchêne and Montfort 1992b.

26. On Staël, see the basic studies by Gutwirth 1978 and Balayé 1979. See also Diesbach's biography.

27. For further examples, see in 1791 the anonymous play written by a Royalist, *Intrigues de Madame de Staël à l'occasion du départ de Mesdames de France,* in which the following diatribe is delivered by Mirabeau: "Et cette femme étrangère, cette fille d'un Ministre justement exécré, cette femme laide et ridicule, intrigante, et qui va promettant à chacun ses faveurs, que nous importent ses lascives amours!"

28. See Balayé's article on *Delphine*, although some of the references are incomplete and several dates appear to be incorrect (1986).

29. According to Kitchin: "C'est le rédacteur qui reste le plus fidèle aux principes républicains et qui exprime le plus librement sous l'Empire des opinions susceptibles de déplaire à l'autorité" (8). He was eliminated from *La Décade philosophique* this very year.

30. See also, in 1800, Fontanes's criticism of *De la littérature*. As pointed out by Winegarten, Fontanes condemned Staël because she was aiming to function outside her proper feminine sphere (Winegarden 86).

31. When as a condition for her return, she was asked to write something favorable about the Emperor, she flatly refused.

32. See Outram's analysis of the differences of meaning of "public" when referring to a woman and a man. A public man was a man who sacrificed himself for a life of service to the patrie. A public woman, who assumed a public role in public arenas, was a courtesane or a prostitute (1989, 127).

33. See also Joubert's *Pensées* in which I noted his early admiration for both women (in 1795): "De toutes les femmes qui ont imprimé, je n'aime qu'elle [Mme de Staël] et madame de Sévigné," his constant admiration for Sévigné (in 1800 and 1807), and his criticism of Staël (particularly in 1807 and 1817) (2: 221, 250, 276, 434-35).

34. It should be noted that gender stereotyping did not prevent women from being prolific writers, mainly in the area of sentimental novels. But, writing sentimental novels, if practiced quietly and in private, was a perfectly acceptable business (Maza 1989b).

35. See Genlis's praise of Sévigné in the already mentioned *De l'influence des femmes* and her criticism of Staël in *La Femme philosophe*, 1804.

36. On Genlis, see "Portraits et jugements" (Broglie 475-82). See also two reviews of a play, "Delphine," where she is represented on stage with Mme de Staël, one by L. C. (La Chabeaussière) in the *Décade philosophique*, one in the *Journal des Débats*, 22 mai 1803: "Quant à la femme de lettres, auteur de plusieurs traités d'éducation et de romans moraux, j'ignore absolument les qualités de son cœur; je ne connois d'elle que ses écrits qui ne sont pas toujours le portrait fidèle du caractère; mais je sais que sa doctrine est utile aux mœurs, nécessaire à la société, précieuse pour la jeunesse [. . .] en un mot, je sais qu'elle est aussi sensée, aussi raisonnable que Delphine est folle et inconséquente."

37. For a more detailed study on how Sévigné was judged between 1800 and 1815, see Montfort 1992a, 447-53.

II

Women of the Revolutionary Period Writing on History

7

Radical Compromise: The Political Philosophy of Isabelle de Charrière

Jenene J. Allison

In a telling description of how one woman's political activism in September of 1789 was perceived, Isabelle de Charrière reports to her friend, Jean-Pierre de Chambrier d'Oleyres:

> Speaking of remarkable . . . Mme de Staël has made herself so assiduous at the Assemblée nationale, approving, advising, etc., that her father has told her to choose between that hall and his house, no longer wanting her to return to the one if she wishes to come back to the other. (3: 149)[1]

It is true that before and during the Revolution, Frenchwomen were participants and sometimes agents of political change, at least until the Convention began to engage in law-making that excluded them from such activity (Landes 143). For example, most history books record the famous march on Versailles in October of 1789 by women demanding food for their families. A more complex form of women's political expression has been pinpointed by Madeleine Rebérioux, who sees 1792 as the apogee of their activism, a moment when women "defined their citizenship" simply "through the evidence of their presence in the city" (XI). However, recent research on the effects of the French Revolution of 1789 on women (their social status, their rights, even their perception of their own bodies) has tended to emphasize those forces that served to erase women from political activity in the course of the Revolution. Thus, Dorinda Outram sums up the consequences of the Revolution as "validat[ing] the political participation of men and culpabiliz[ing] that of women" (1989, 156), a situation that is evident in the paternalistic ultimatum intended to quell Mme de Staël.[2]

In the context of this most recent assessment of the Revolution, an apt representation of woman's participation in the political debates of the Revolution, is Mme Roland's description in her *Mémoires* (written in prison) of herself actually writing political commentary.[3] She recounts how the room next to hers was often the scene of "lengthy orgies that lasted four or five hours" when certain police officials arrived to visit (1967, 279). Horrified by "the brutish joy, the obscenity of the remarks . . . the disgusting kisses of those mouths full of wine, planted noisily on the face of the new arrivals . . . the dirty jokes of men without manners and without shame. . . ." Mme Roland spends these moments writing "notices historiques:" "I had written several vigorous tirades under the very eyes, so to speak, of the wretches who would have massacred me if they had heard a single sentence thereof." While the experience of incarceration was certainly not limited to women during the Revolution, the scene as she describes it accurately portrays the fate of the women who aspired to political expression. Woman was in effect set off in a room by herself, while men controlled both her life and the events around her, severely curtailing her political expression.[4]

Given the repressive circumstances surrounding women in France, the political writings of the Dutch-born Isabelle de Charrière (1740-1805) are of considerable interest. Although she is perhaps best described as a European, she considered herself a type of non-resident Frenchwoman:

> [W]hile preferring in some ways my nation [the Netherlands] to any other, yes, to *any other* . . . I don't like my country at all. A humid ground, a servile *republic* displease me no end; [also] I am biased in favor of France. . . . It is their language that I speak the best, it is their books that I know the best, it is with them that I am most comfortable. It is their heroism, when they have it, that seduces me the most. (emphasis in the original; 3:92)

As a child she received a privileged education, being tutored by a governess with whom she corresponded after they parted company. A Protestant,

Charrière came to view her religion in very loose terms.[5] Her *Œuvres complètes,* only published in 1981, run to ten volumes and include letters, plays, musical scores, novels, and political treatises. During her lifetime, Charrière achieved notoriety as the author of several works of fiction in which her peers (whether aristocrats or simply her Swiss neighbors) were ridiculed.[6] After her death, she came to be admired as a cosmopolitan figure who represented the social ideals of the Enlightenment, and whose complex relationships with men such as James Boswell and Benjamin Constant added to her fame.[7] Today, studies of her work have expanded into areas other than biographical research.[8] More and more it is read in the light of feminist studies.[9] Current interest in a new way of reading women writing, one that goes beyond a focus on women-centered novels or women authors, accounts for her growing importance.

Charrière is relevant to a consideration of women's involvement in the Revolution of 1789 for several reasons. Reading her extensive correspondence (five volumes) one is struck by her active concern with events in France.[10] This concern stems, in part, from a sense of déjà vu. As Isabelle Vissière points out in her anthology of Charrière's political writings, she is an astute observer of the Revolution in France because she has the advantage of having observed an earlier one in the Netherlands (1988: 36 and 170).[11] A resident of what is today a part of Switzerland (Neuchâtel), Charrière also had the advantage of both living at a safe distance from the violence so that she was never in any personal danger, and of having the independence of means to publish. Considering the bloodbath that was taking place in Paris, and then in Europe as a whole, her situation was in fact remarkable:

> A single small state miraculously escapes from the general upheaval: . . . Neuchâtel, which is provisionally sheltered . . . by its status as Prussian principality. From this guarded balcony, Isabelle, a lucid and saddened spectator, watches the conflagration of Europe going up in flames. (5: 8)

Thus, at a time when women in France were being censored, exiled, and executed for their political expression, there was a woman intellectual across the border actively writing on revolutionary events and ideas (and having her husband copy her manuscripts). Furthermore, Charrière lived until

1805, a life span that encompassed both the Revolution and the Terror. This meant that she was able to witness the long-term results of the political changes in France.

Clearly Charrière's circumstances enabled her to have a unique perspective. (In December 1791 she wrote to a correspondent, "no one thinks about anything except politics; sometimes I think about politics too but in a manner that pleases nobody" (3:328).) In addition to her unique perspective on the actual political events of the Revolution, one might expect, in approaching Charrière's political commentary, that one would find some consideration of women's rights. Unlike someone such as Olympe de Gouges, for example, Charrière had the freedom to write without fear of being arrested. We know from her novels that she is adept at describing the finest nuances of the feminine condition. One critic, Alice Parker, goes so far as to claim that Charrière's fiction "deconstruct[s] the grammar of gender relations and denominations" (75). It seems paradoxical, then, to find that in her political writings only once, in an unfinished satire, "Lettre d'un Anglois à un député de l'Assemblée nationale de France (Letter from an Englishman to a Deputy of the National Assembly of France [?1790]), does she address the issue of women's rights. While the social reforms that Charrière proposed all seem fair and just, the lack of any treatment of the problem of sexual inequality is puzzling. She had a clear understanding of the rules that governed the status of men, and of those that governed the status of women, so it is hard to believe that she could have thought that the reforms she advocated would, if implemented, benefit both groups equally.[12] Why, then, do her political works seem to neglect women's issues? Even in her letters one is surprised to not find any comment on the execution of the author of *The Declaration of the Rights of Women* even afther Constant mentions it: "Poor Olympe de Gouges caused me a moment of sadness. I say a moment because one does not have the time to feel sorry for victims who succeed one another so quickly" (4:266). Could it be that Charrière felt that the political change under way left so little hope for justice, for either the people or the aristocracy, that to even mention the special case of the status of women, in a discussion of this change, was pointless?

In the following consideration of her political philosophy, I would like to suggest that far from disregarding the status of women in this area of her thought, Charrière sees sexual inequality as the limiting factor that precludes any type of idealism. I will first describe her concrete suggestions on how to make contemporary French society less unjust as outlined in "Lettre d'un évêque français à la nation" ("Letter from a French Bishop to the Nation" [1789]). Her understanding of revolutionary politics was exceptional for the acuity with which she saw both the need for reform and the limits to what could be accomplished by her contemporaries. Moving on to three texts which are more theoretical, "Bien-né" ("The Well Born One") (1787-88), "De l'esprit et des rois. Trois Dialogues" (Of Spirit and Kings. Three Dialogues" [1798]), and "Les deux Familles" ("The Two Families" [?1789]), I will examine this more general aspect of her political philosophy. While Charrière believed in the possibility of progress, she also believed in the inevitability of inequality. This pessimistic component of her philosophy leads to her rejection of utopian ideas, including egalitarianism. I argue that her understanding of sexual difference as an insurmountable basis for inequity in society is what accounts for the pessimism that limits her belief in the possibility of progress. Finally, I look at the one text that she wrote to create, rather than to just discuss, political change: "Lettres trouvées dans la neige" ("Letters Found in the Snow" [1793]). This epistolary novella/political treatise illustrates the practical application of her political theory as elaborated in the three above-mentioned texts. The manner in which woman is presented in what was intended to be an instrument for political change represents Charrière's perception of the negative role of gender in social relations. Seen in this light, the work of this Dutch/Swiss/French intellectual may be considered to confirm what Judith Gardiner noted in her contribution to *Writing and Sexual Difference:* "Many women writers feel that women remember what men choose to forget" (188). As the equality of men was being proclaimed on all sides, Charrière refused to forget that that of women was not, and would not be, included.

Lessening Social Justice

Charrière's plan for social reform in France is spelled out in the greatest detail in "Lettre d'un évêque français à la nation." Composed at the time of the convocation of the Etats Généraux, and published at the author's expense (10:127), this text is similar to the genre of Jean-Jacques Rousseau's *Letter to d'Alembert*.[13] An important difference is that in "Lettre d'un évêque français à la nation," the author assumes a voice that is not her own, but a man's voice. Charrière did not wish to antagonize the majority of readers for whom politics was a masculine subject matter (Vissière 1988, 43). The narrator introduces the need for a pluralistic, rather than an egocentric, point of view in the very first sentence, asserting that "although I am a bishop and a gentleman, I am nonetheless human and patriotic. . . ." (132).[14] In the six letters that follow, the clergyman details the reforms that are needed to integrate the church into a more just society.

The bishop bases his ideas on the principle of moderation: in reference to the plan, of which he approved, to abolish the tax on salt and on tobacco, he specifies "a *gradual abolition*" because violent change is against his principles (emphasis in the original; 150n). His is the cautious political philosophy of Charrière; as Jeroom Vercruyesse describes it "her true religion" was to "write to propose, rather than to impose, things in a world of greed, violence, fanaticism, and lies, even while being ignorant of the true fortunes of mankind" (77). The bishop's insistence on moderation in reforms reveals a perspicacity that does credit to Charrière's understanding of the economics of the situation in 1789: "one cannot *suddenly* take away from the bishops a great part of their revenue and their luxury, without making suffer the very same third estate . . . in whose favor one would do well to deprive us *to a certain degree and little by little*" (emphasis in the original, 132).

For a narrator whose dominant theme is moderation, the bishop can be aggressive and even extreme at times.[15] For example, he underlines the urgency of the social reform that Charrière wanted to advocate when he specifies instituting this reform "starting today" (136). The most extreme suggestion he formulates concerns a kind of alchemy he himself has conducted and one which he would see imitated across the country: "What could I convert into money ["argent"]? Silver ["argent"] itself; a sterile money into a fertile money. . . . Oh would that I could melt down or sell some of the ornaments of our temples!" (134-35).

The depth of Charrière's understanding is nowhere more evident than in the analysis of the psychological factors that would accompany the reforms for which the bishop wished. She was perfectly impartial with regard to the emotional weakness of both the upper and the lower class. Thus the bishop, for all his admirable eagerness to begin ameliorating the daily life of the poor in a concrete fashion, is frank about his own unwillingness to be reduced to squalor: "[B]ut the rest of my . . . daily luxuries, I have kept . . . and [this] despite a feeling perhaps more disagreeable than that which would have been experienced by the poorest and greediest man of my diocese upon seeing the luxury of his bishop" (133).[16] The precise detail with which the fictional bishop's emotions are described, while making "Lettre d'un évêque français à la nation" an unusual political tract, lends a greater psychological complexity to Charrière's understanding of the situation in France. Those whose poverty the bishop would relieve are by no means exempt from emotions that will interfere with political reform. Speaking with one of his poor parishioners, an old man whose son works in the church kitchen, the bishop balks at employing yet another one of the man's sons, Jeannot. He advocates instead the value of agricultural labor over domestic service for the good of the nation. The old peasant selfishly rejects the proposal, telling the bishop to not send Jeannot back to the family farm until the government has made working the earth a less onerous chore (134).[17] Clearly the self-indulgence of both the bishop and the old man will prevent progress from "starting today."

The importance that Charrière accorded to this psychological factor was a fundamental feature of her political thought. In fact, in one instance she goes so far as to list this single factor as one of three causes for the failure of the Old Regime. In a note to her 1790 "Eloge de Rousseau" ("In Praise of Rousseau"), arguing that neither Rousseau nor Voltaire should be held accountable for the Revolution she asserts that "in order to bring us to where we are, all that was needed were the vices of the high and mighty, the misery of the people, and the all too common ambition of people who are neither the people nor the high and mighty" (10:582n30).

Her belief, as expressed in "Lettre d'un évêque français à la nation," that gradual change was the only possible solution, was confirmed by the Terror. Charrière had realized that any approach other than gradual change would simply substitute one agent of social injustice for another, while leaving intact the structure enabling this injustice. In her epigram about "this good people of France" (1789), she correctly anticipated that this turnabout is, in fact, what the Revolution will bring: "I am, they say, the human race above all / sensitive, generous, polite, full of sweetness. / Everything, however, in their hands becomes the wheel or a gallows / Everywhere I hear cries, everywhere I see tears" (10:372). It is the urgency of preventing such an error that leads Charrière to emphasize the role of education in her later political works.[18] As was noted in the discussion of "Lettre d'un évêque français à la nation," both the bishop and the peasant, whose son he employs, are dominated at some point by feelings that are inimical to the necessary reform. Only by changing the way people think, could there be a structural change in society. In a later work, "Lettres trouvées dans la neige," Charrière asserts "it's not our government, it's us that must be changed" (10:249).

Education is to be the means by which society will change in order to become more, albeit not absolutely, just. Charrière's discussion of education as such a political instrument appears in several contexts. In "Les Deux familles" (9:617-20), an allegory about the upper and lower classes, she writes about the role of educating the citizenry; also, in "Bien-né" (10:82-84, 87-89) and "De l'esprit et des rois" (9:233-53), she details how to teach a king to be just. As we shall see, she did not dismiss the possibility of a monarchy for the new society she imagined. In fact, in 1791 she wrote to a friend, "I would like for there to be a patriarch in France and for us to put an end thus to quarrels that are as fatal as they are ridiculous" (3:344).[19] On the other hand, she had a specific context in mind for this head of state: A society that had been structured so the king was one part of its machinery rather than the force driving it. Such a change would have changed not just the government, but the status of women in particular. As Annette Rosa has pointed out, under the Old Régime submission to the king and to the head of the family were both ultimately based on the idea of submission to God (16). To appreciate the role of education in Charrière's political philosophy, and the limits to what it can accomplish, we need to look at the above-mentioned texts.

To Increase Equality

As we shall see, there is a fundamental difference between the three texts in which Charrière describes her political philosophy. In "Bien-né" and "De l'esprit et des rois" the possibility of making society more equal is presented as theoretically feasible, just as the reforms proposed by her 'French Bishop' were presented as a way to lessen real social injustice. In contrast, "Les Deux familles" presents the possibility of making society more equal as doomed from the start. The lack of pessimism in "Bien-né" and in "De l'esprit et des rois" results from the focus on reducing the status of one person, the monarch, rather than elevating that of the disenfranchised (as in "Les Deux familles").

"Bien-né" is a short fairy tale in two parts about an unfortunate king "whose bad education had left his good qualities uncultivated and useless" (10:82). He will be visited by a fairy, Wisdom, who will make seven suggestions to him to re-educate him.[20] "De l'esprit et des rois" consists of three brief dialogues between two interlocutors, Basilagogue and Amphidoxon.

In both texts we find an emphasis on counteracting the way in which the king traditionally is isolated. Thus Wisdom, at the crucial turning point in the king's re-education, invokes the character of Henri IV, in order to win her pupil over completely to her way of thinking. She reminds him that Henri IV, the ancestor he most admires, "owed his most desirable and precious qualities only to the equality in which adversity had forced him to live with other men, and at the level, so to speak, of their passion" (10:88). The definition that Basilagogue in "De l'esprit et des rois" gives of kings resembles this description, but is given in negative terms. He pities kings because although they are "a class of men like other men" they are "less able to become a part of other classes" (9:239). The method by which the monarch is to be educated, so as to prevent his being isolated, differs in these two texts only in that one concerns a king who is already on the throne and the other concerns a young prince.

In "Bien-né," Wisdom begins by making what appear to be trivial and arbitrary demands of the unhappy king: First he must give up swearing (10:83), then drinking (84), and finally hunting (87). Significantly, the long-term effect on her pupil is to change his relationship to others: On the fourteenth day of practising his new lifestyle, he notices the "physiognomies" of those who are around him. He makes the decision to surround himself with those men whose faces are "open" and to disregard the other courtiers (88). While it may seem that he is reducing the number of people around him, and thereby increasing his degree of isolation, in fact, the king is more integrated into the social structure of his court as a consequence of this decision. No longer the decorative centerpiece of the entire court, he becomes a participant in a group of well-socialized individuals. This is the development that leads to the turning point in his treatment, for Wisdom then comes to him with a demand of an entirely different nature, one that is suitable for a head of state: "Now you must establish more liberty between you and the citizens who are most worthy of your confidence: One must be able at all hours, and on all occasions, to speak to you about what it is important that you know . . . the citizen must converse with the king. . . ." (88).[21] Initially the king resists, but in the end, he obeys and the nation prospers.

Within the context of raising a prince, who has not yet been the victim of a pernicious education, Charrière outlines a similar formula for preventing him from being an isolated leader. In "De l'esprit et des rois" Basilagogue explains that isolation makes the monarch vulnerable. He then describes how a future king may be raised so that he avoids the tragic fate of a gladiator, who is thrown alone into a combat to the death (9:237).

Essential to the success of a prince's education is a careful selection of men who will live with him.[22] The right type of man is characterized as someone who is "occupied with interesting projects that cannot augment his fortune" or who, when he tries to get something for himself, goes about it in a clumsy way (247). (Amphidoxon objects that in accordance with Basilagogue's precepts, the future king will be surrounded by men who are "peculiar, ridiculous, and almost crazy" (248). In fact, Basilagogue is describing the type of men that Charrière imagined in the meritocracy described in her novel, *Lettres écrites de Lausanne* (*Letters written from Lausanne* (1788)). The candidates for this class would form the middle class or second order of the meritocracy, and they include types like "such and such a man who would have distinguished himself by some good action, a foreign gentleman, a rich merchant, the creator of some useful invention" (8:142).[23] The task for which these companions are selected is to provide a cacophonous chorus of opinions: "These people will speak to each other, they will quarrel among themselves, and apart from the possibility that truth could spring from the shock of their opinions, this very shock will awaken the spirit of the prince. . . ." (248). In this way, the man who eventually occupies the throne will be more able to "become a part of other classes" having thus acquired such a degree of human understanding.

Should the princes who are the object of such an education lack any aptitude for it, Basilagogue would have them resign: "let them . . . make us pass with the least amount of shocks and upheavals from a government against which on all sides the people are cautioned to a government towards which on all sides their inclinations and wishes are directed" (253). The conclusion of "Bien-né," then, presents what Charrière envisaged as a viable form of government in the shape of an absolute 'either/or': either a monarchy with a king who is qualified by his greater degree of human understanding or else a republic.

We have seen that in "Bien-né" and "De l'esprit et des rois," education has a political function. Its purpose is to integrate the monarch into the social microcosm of the court, and of society in general. This greater degree of integration would gradually lessen the rigidity of social hierarchization, and would work from the top down, as far as rank is concerned. Similarly, we shall see that in "Les Deux familles" the purpose of education is to make society more equal, although in this case, the process is intended to work in the opposite direction.

This parable chronicles the development of two families on a desert island who found themselves in a hierarchy paralleling that of the Old Régime: One group toils, the other recreates. The way in which she depicts the inevitable conflict between these two groups is notable for its complexity in an otherwise terse narrative. It is not simply the one group versus the other:

> After a certain time, this whole state of affairs greatly displeased some members of the [lower class]. They [i.e. these few individuals] said to their so-called friends (for a bit of good luck had put them in a situation quite different from that of the majority) . . . : the island should belong to you, and it seems that you are tolerated here only out of kindness. (9:617)

The actual revolt by the lower class family is not described. Charrière halts the proceedings with a discourse spoken by disembodied voices: "It was not clear what would come from this mixture of rights and wrongs . . . when some voices that had not yet been heard were raised" (618). These voices will attempt to arbitrate, interrogating both sides and pointing out that extreme demands cannot be met. They advocate instead a gradual revolution on the island, one that involves a radical compromise: blurring the division between the two families. Recognizing that the agitators can no longer be refused admission to the ranks of the leisure class, the voices suggest that there should be less distinction between the two classes. How will this be implemented? The brightest children of the agitators are to be educated alongside the children of the upper class family (618-19).[24] This would both placate the agitators, and begin creating a more egalitarian society. The education per se would not necessarily be designed to benefit the children. Learning is not the issue here. What is required is that it make them equal to exercise the "great prerogative" of the upper class: The right to be employed in a capacity for which they have no aptitude whatsoever ("thus one often sees [the members of the upper class] doing what they do not know how to do" [9:619]).

The idea of transplanting children from one class to another also appears in the meritocracy described in *Lettres écrites de Lausanne* but, with a significant difference. For this meritocracy, Charrière proposes a government council that would be representative of three social classes, including one that would be supplemented as appropriate by the type of creative, self-made men previously described. Significantly, the children of *all* council members "would enter by right into the noble class" (8:142). The major difference between the change proposed in *Lettres écrites de Lausanne* and that in "Les Deux familles," apart from the fact that the former is more detailed, is that one is a more negative description than the other. Whereas in the parable the transplanted children would acquire the right to be incompetent, in the novel these children are described as acquiring a positive attribute: "ennoblement" (8:143).

There is no happy ending for the two families in the parable. After the disembodied voices make their suggestions for reform to the upper class, the members of this class refuse to agree, preferring revolution and death to compromise. Once again, Charrière makes psychological weakness an impediment to social justice. After this negative development, she abruptly concludes, "We ceased hearing them [the members of the upper class], and we do not know what will become of the two divided families" (9:620).

While "Bien-né" ends well and "De l'esprit et des rois" ends with the possibility of a better society (whether monarchy or republic), "Les Deux familles" ends on a pessimistic note. Charrière terms this text "a tale," yet it does not have an ending such as we found in "Bien-né," also "a tale." Similarly, the notion of integrating children from the lower to the upper class, presented in a positive light in *Lettres écrites de Lausanne,* is here presented in a negative light. While she could have ended "Les Deux familles" before the upper class refused the suggested reform, so that the ending could at least offer some hope as it does in the alternative suggested at the end of "De l'esprit et des rois," she chose to not do so. The intransigence with which the upper class turns down the compromise proposed by the voices is unmitigated: "surrender gracefully what you *cannot and should not keep any longer*" (9:620, my emphasis). It is evident that in her assessment of the results to be expected from her plan for education in the service of increasing equality, Charrière reveals a greater pessimism when it is a question of changing society from the bottom up. In other words, she presents as more plausible the idea that a prince or king could be taught how to function having been lowered from the pinnacle of social hierarchy rather than that citizens could be taught how to rise above the idea of a less rigid social schism. What is the limiting factor that precludes the creation of a more egalitarian society, in theory, by working from the bottom up?

The way in which Charrière formulates the prejudice of the upper class family against the lower class one places the emphasis on the absurdity of using differences that are imperceptible to justify social inequity.

> [The upper class family] spoke . . . of their ancestors, and one saw clearly that, despite the sameness of features, hair, legs, arms, needs, diseases, despite the extreme equality in ways of being born and of dying, one saw, I say, that they well and truly believed in a distinction made in heaven between the two families. (9:618)

This formulation closely parallels her claim for the equality of women in "Lettre d'un Anglois à un député de l'Assemblée nationale de France," although in this case it is perceptible differences that serve to perpetuate social inequity. In this text the narrator suggests that "*all men . . . are born equal*" means the same as "*all human creatures are born equal*" (emphasis in the original). He proposes that:

> [I]f it is a question of the capabilities of man when he is born and such as he comes from the belly of his mother, one cannot deny that they are very similar in both sexes and that *the differences that one perceives do not entail the inequality that one does not perceive.* (10:317 my emphasis)

A digression is in order here to consider the rhetorical status of this claim, which might be considered ambiguous since "Lettre d'un Anglois à un député de l'Assemblée nationale de France," a satire in the vein of Jonathan Swift's "A Modest Proposal," is a complex work. However, one can justify taking at least the above-quoted statement at face value because Charrière situates it in between two extremes presented at the beginning and the conclusion of her text. The beginning of "Lettre d'un Anglois à un député de l'Assemblée nationale de France" is the fictional Englishman's complaint that the revolution among the "horses" over in France has created similar disquiet among the English horses, a disquiet that has had serious consequences. "This shaking off of the shackles among the equine population has got our ladies thinking; they do not see why no declaration of rights has yet proclaimed their equality to us. . . . " (10:317). He worries that this spirit of contestation will cause trouble: "Our women will want to vote at the very least if they don't take it upon themselves to be voted for." While at first it might seem that Charrière was advocating women's suffrage, the inclusion of the extremist "if they don't take it upon themselves to be voted for" would tend to undermine this interpretation. (An educated woman, she may have feared the consequences of allowing uneducated women to vote.) Like her 'French Bishop,' Charrière was committed to moderation in social reform—women voting, perhaps; women being elected, probably not. In turn, the conclusion of "Letter from an Englishman" consists of the actions of a ridiculous character who manifestly represents the opposite of what Charrière believed. This man, a philosopher who is smitten with the new ideas that have emerged from France, takes the concept that we are all born equal to an impractical extreme. To implement the revolutionary ideals he espouses, he becomes a vegetarian and moves to the country, all the while worrying that he will murder "a crowd of his peers" should he walk on the grass (318). The philosopher is presented as absurd and even contemptible. Thus, the justification of his squashing the insects in the grass is as follows: "Since it will not be his fault he flatters himself that his conscience will not be burdened by it." Clearly with this vegetarian philosopher Charrière is describing what not to believe, for he claims that "an incontestable principle cannot be destroyed by any of its most extreme consequences" and what mattered to her was precisely insuring that the consequences of any principle be limited to what was as fair as humanly possible. From this consideration of what Charrière is mocking in "Lettre d'un Anglois à un député de l'Assemblée nationale de France," I suggest that she is indeed asserting the undeniable validity of the fact that we are all born equal regardless of the extremes to which this idea may be taken, whether it be women's aspiration to political office or a philosopher's objection to assassinating ants.

To return to the question of the pessimistic outlook presented by "Les Deux familles," then, we find that in two texts that were probably composed within one year of each other, there is a similar claim for equality based on the idea that we are all, upper and lower class citizens, men and women, born equal.[25] Taken together, "Les Deux familles" and "Lettre d'un Anglois à un député de l'Assemblée nationale de France" condemn using difference, real or imagined, to legitimate the social division that translates into inequity. The presence of a common element of such importance in these texts makes it possible to hypothesize about what precluded there being a happy ending to "Les Deux familles." In this parable, Charrière found it necessary to dismiss the idea that social inequity could be overcome working from the bottom up because, in the last analysis, humans in society consistently use difference to institute and perpetuate this inequity. Thus, real equality is not possible. According to this theory, the model of the disenfranchised in a divided society would be women because they constitute the one class whose difference, regardless of social status, is unavoidably perceptible. A consideration of "Lettres trouvées dans la neige" will illustrate what Charrière perceived as a plausible scenario for the application of her political theory. We shall see that the image given of woman in this context does not differ significantly from the treatment that was, in fact, accorded to her during the aftermath of the Revolution of 1789.

Utopia and the Failure of Egalitarianism

Charrière wrote "Lettres trouvées" in response to a request from the chancellor of Neuchâtel who feared the consequences of imported Jacobin fervor.[26] Therefore, it represents an effort on her part to exercise political power directly: to *change* the situation then and there.

"Lettres trouvées" consists of all letters between a Frenchwoman wishing to flee post-Revolutionary France and a Swiss friend of his, who vetoes Switzerland as a refuge. It starts with a description of the intolerable political situation in France. Then, when the two correspondents conceive the idea of emigrating in order to start a more ideal society, Charrière is drawn into a commentary on utopia. The end of the novella is a letter from the Swiss to the king of Prussia, in which he humbly requests that the government in Neuchâtel be made more open. The structure of the text presents, in effect, two options for a person who is unhappy with society: Flee to a utopia or try to change society. Charrière will undermine the very idea of a utopia, thereby placing the emphasis on the idea of practical reform. The refutation of the notion of a utopia makes of "Lettres trouvées" a pessimistic text similar to "Les Deux familles."[27]

In fact, the utopia in question was doomed from the start. The Swiss suggests that they should go live in some land populated "if not by wise men, at least by more peaceable lunatics than our own. . . ." (10:231). In his acceptance of the proposal, the Frenchman defines the limits inherent in such a dream. He recommends that they take women along in order to found "a colony that could subsist for a few centuries before ending up in the state of affairs in which my homeland and yours are today" (233). Then the inevitable end to the utopia is anticipated:

> *Equality* will not reign there for long, because the strength and the talents of our children will be unequal. Nor will *freedom* such as they brag about it here every day while violating it incessantly exist there. I will govern my children until, having become weak in my mind and my body, it will be they who govern me. But I hope that all this will take place smoothly. (emphasis in the original; 233)

The failure of their utopia is predicated on real physical differences that *are* significant in the context of a developing society.

It is noteworthy that Charrière sets up two male correspondents using the epistolary form, since this form is traditionally associated with the voice of woman. In so doing, she writes what is slightly unconventional for an epistolary novel, but as a record of political discourse it is, on the contrary, exemplary, because it is a dialogue that excludes women. Significantly, before the two letter writers cease the discussion of running away to make a new society, another character is introduced. The Swiss tells the Frenchman that his niece, Rosine, will be the perfect wife for him to take on their journey. The way in which Rosine came to be available for marriage is pertinent to the issue of equality in a utopia.

Rosine, once engaged to a man she loved, is a political victim. During the course of an argument between her Republican father and her

Royalist fiancé, she was so disturbed by their animosity that she withdrew to the side and wrote a poem to the latter in which she suggested that if their neighbors across the border wished to be free, he should respect their aspirations (236). Upon reading this, he broke the engagement. Rosine recovered and eventually decided, "democrat or aristocrat, a lover so brutal was not worth regretting" (237). The structure of this sentence reproduces exactly one of Charrière's main political tenets: Replacing one oppressor with another is not progress.[28]

It is relevant that Rosine is a woman and that she steps back, writing in an effort to protect her hopes. In fact, sitting alongside two men who are arguing about politics and thereby deciding her fate, Rosine represents well eighteenth-century woman. The decisions made during the Terror disenfranchised her more and more, even as feminist demands were being made more publicly.[29]

The consideration of "Lettres trouvées" was introduced to illustrate Charrière's political philosophy 'in action.' We have seen that the obstacle to reform in "Les Deux familles" was the intransigence of the upper class. Despite the evident "sameness of features," they believed in the inferiority of the lower class, a prejudice which resembled the description of woman's irrelevant physical difference in "Lettre d'un Anglois à un député de l'Assemblée nationale de France." In "Lettres trouvées," as in "Les Deux familles," the outlook is pessimistic. Not only is the projected utopia characterized as destined for inequality, but the structure of the novella undermines the hope that is implicit in the very idea of imagining a utopia, since this idea is framed by references to actual, imperfect political situations. In "Lettres trouvées," the one political text in which Charrière explicitly assigns a role to woman rather than just speaking in general about citizens, woman is seen as the one who withdraws and writes, but who is victimized by a masculine political discourse.[30] Coming from an author whose female protagonists embody such a perspicacious understanding of the feminine condition, Rosine's significance cannot be overlooked. Her role, in what was meant to be an instrument of political change, serves to confirm Charrière's rejection of egalitarianism. A society structured on this principle will never be possible so long as sexual difference can be used to justify social inequality.

While Charrière believed in the possibility of reform, as her "Lettre d'un évêque français à la nation" makes evident, and even in the possibility of fundamental political change, as described in "Bien-né" and "De l'esprit et des rois," she set a definite limit on the extent of progress that her contemporaries could achieve. In "Les Deux familles" she emphasized the inevitable inequity that divides society, an inequity founded on the perception of difference. The model victim of the abuse of perceived difference is woman.

The presence of these two different lines in her political philosophy is best summed up in her succinct statement, "Il faut être en parlant ou se croire écouté" ("In speaking one must be, or believe oneself to be, heard" [4:565]). Written in anger to an increasingly inattentive Benjamin Constant at a time when his politics were becoming different from her own, it illustrates the particular disadvantage that women faced when participating in political discourse.[31] During the course of the eighteenth century, their discourse had been empowered, both in the institution of the salons and in the valorization of a certain 'feminine' style of writing.[32] Ultimately, however, their discourse was disempowered as men proclaimed the rights of men. Thus, 'to be heard' would be paradigmatic of man's experience, and the bifurcation embodied by 'to be or to believe oneself to be' paradigmatic of woman's.

Notes

1. This translation and those that follow are my own. All following references to Charrière's works are to her *Œuvres complètes*.

2. See also Hunt 1992 and Landes.

3. Outram devotes an entire chapter to Mme Roland emphasizing the importance of her stay in prison (1989, 147-49).

4. "Si les femmes ont réussi à se faire entendre pendant la phase ascendante de la Révolution, à partir de la Terreur—laquelle ne les a pas épargnées—, toute prise de parole leur est refusé" (Soprani 5).

5. When she was twenty-four years old she wrote, "I have doubts, I keep quiet, I would believe myself guilty of a crime for upsetting the faith of someone else to put in its place nothing but a worrisome doubt" (1:196).

6. For example, "Le Noble" (1763) (8:21-34) and *Lettres neuchâteloises* (1784) (8:47-89).

7. The first book-length treatment of Charrière was a biography (Godet), not a critical study, and in *The Second Sex*, it is in this biographical context that Charrière is discussed (Beauvoir 1949, 318-21). Lacy asserts that Charrière's "greatest claim to fame was . . . in

her contacts (i.e. conversations and letters) with James Boswell, Benjamin Constant, and David Constant d'Hermenches . . ." (1982, 154) and as recently as 1991 Vissière published the Charrière-d'Hermenches correspondence under the title *Une Liaison dangereuse*. Important archival research was undertaken by Courtney and by Wood.

8. A discussion of her novel *Caliste* appeared in *PMLA* (Rossard); there was a panel on her at the 1990 meeting of the Modern Language Association, and a special issue of *Eighteenth-Century Life* (Fink) was devoted to her. Jean Starobinski, wrote a lengthy preface to a 1970 edition pairing *Lettres écrites de Lausanne* with Jean-Jacques Rousseau's *Julie ou la Nouvelle Héloïse*.

9. Minier-Birk, for example, asserts that Charrière was not a feminist (1983, 27) although she later attenuates this view in her monograph (1987). Other critics (Jackson, MacArthur, and Stewart) see feminist strategies in Charrière's fiction.

10. For a discussion of the political content of her correspondence with Benjamin Constant, see Vissière (1989).

11. Vissière's approach to Charrière's political philosophy differs from mine in that her objective is to link the life of the author to her political writings (1988, 458).

12. For example, the definition of virtue that the narrator gives her daughter in *Lettres écrites de Lausanne* (8:160).

13. Vissière has chronicled how most of Charrière's works were published at her own expense, due in part to their anti-aristocracy tendency (1988, 65, 326, 331, 367, 458).

14. Deguise points out that Charrière is like her Bishop because they are both unable to be elected, and are thus reduced to the role of political observer (36).

15. This tone is characteristic of Charrière herself. Thus, she reacts to August 1792 with both a lack of partisanship and a disconcerting bloodthirstiness: "comme l'atrocité des Jacobins ne change en rien mon idée sur les aristocrates, sur les princes, sur les émigrés je souhaite qu'il y ait une guerre civile qui nettoye la terre de beaucoup de ces gens de l'un & de l'autre parti" (3:405).

16. Charrière defended her own wealth thus: "Un peu plus d'argent chez moi un peu moins chez d'autres fait des relations entre eux & moi qui leur conviennent autant qu'a moi" (3:363).

17. In light of Charrière's real concern about the victimization of the lower classes, it is disconcerting to find her writing to Constant about a serving girl as follows: "Elle ne m'a point du tout entendue mais elle m'obeit parfaitement. Et puis parlez au peuple de ses droits, de sa liberté!" It is clear, however, that this attitude merely represents her refusal of a sentimentalized concept of the people for she continues, "Pour peu [que le peuple] vous entendit il renverseroit vos propres plans, car de vous bien entendre & de concourir à quelque chose de sage avec connoissance de cause c'est impossible. Il faut non seulement avoir de l'esprit mais l'avoir exercé dès le berceau être capable de raisonnement" (3:283).

18. As with so many eighteenth-century authors, education in and of itself was an important theme for Charrière. Furthermore, she was also an avid reader of Rousseau (see Trousson).

19. Although her preference was for some type of monarchy, she did not feel that it would be good to have the Revolution reversed (3:256).

20. In "Aiglonette et Insinuante, ou La Souplesse" (1791), a work that she sent to Marie Antoinette, Charrière outlines a plan for the re-education of the queen. "Aiglonette" is not analyzed in my discussion because it is primarily an argument for flexibility in the face of adversity. This is an attitude that Charrière advocated to all those who had to live through the Revolution, regardless of who was destined to win. (In a letter in 1790, she wrote, "heureux ceux qui pouront vite se plier à tant de choses nouvelles...." (3:181).)

21. The publisher who printed "Bien-né" was imprisoned (Deguise 34 and Vissière 1988, 41).

22. Basilagogue does appear to exclude women.

23. See also "Lettres trouvées" (10:253).

24. In *Sir Walter Finch et son fils William* (1799/1806), Charrière describes a father who takes in a peasant boy as a companion for his son so that he will receive an ideal education.

25. Charrière offers the idea that we are all born equal in a letter giving advice to the mistress of the King of Prussia. Henriette L'Hardy, a young friend of Charrière's, was attached to the king's mistress and accompanied her when she left the Court in 1792, pregnant and in trouble with the king. Writing to L'Hardy, Charrière proposed that the countess needed "un cœur de Reine pour la noble fermeté & de Democrate pour l'amour de l'egalité et l'intime persuasion que veritablement nous naissons tous egaux & qu'une fortune inconstante met seule des differences entre un Roi & un Laboureur, Entre une femme de qualité & une paysanne" (3:367).

26. In the fall of 1792, Neuchâtel was suffering from a dangerous political crisis that might have provoked an act of aggression on the part of the King of Prussia (10:224).

27. It could be argued that Charrière wrote against the hopeless fantasy of a utopia because she had been asked to dissipate the revolutionary fervor. On the other hand, it is implausible that she would have contradicted her own political theory.

28. Hence the Frenchman's summary of the French Revolution: ".... tout ce qui a gouverné est devenu successivement semblable au roi soliveau, & ... les grenouilles montés sur le trône regnent non-seulement sur d'autres grenouilles, mais sur des lions" (10:232).

29. A woman sitting off to the side writing is an image that contrasts sharply with the images of women that entered into the iconography of the French Revolution. For example, in her analysis of the traditional festival crowning the rosière of Salency, Maza shows how a feminine folklore figure was transformed into a symbol of the modern state.

In the course of this process, what was originally a positive feminine quality became a neuter quality (1989a, 412).

30. In an important reading of a novel that is all too often interpreted as autobiographical, Bérenguier shows that Charrière's *Lettres de Mistriss Henley* in fact concerns the way in which women were victimized by another masculine discourse, namely that of conjugal bliss.

31. Regarding the rupture between the two of them, Vissière states unequivocally: "Contrairement à ce que l'on écrit généralement, la rupture entre [Charrière] et Benjamin n'est nullement sentimentale, mais idéologique, voire politique" (1988, 584).

32. Gutwirth (1989a), Parker, and Showalter (1977).

8

Spectatrice as Spectacle: Helen Maria Williams at Home in the Revolution

Mary Favret

> It was a rendezvous for the most famous orators, the best-known men of letters, the most celebrated painters, the most popular actors and actresses, the most fashionable dancers, the most illustrious foreigners, the lords of the Court, and the ambassadors of Europe; the old France had come there to end, the new had come there to begin.
> —Chateaubriand, *Mémoires,* Book 5

The Paris home of the English writer Helen Maria Williams was just the sort of rendezvous Chateaubriand recalled from the early days of the French Revolution. At Williams's dinners and teas, generals and diplomats, poets and philosophers, actresses, journalists, and educators mingled. There intellectuals, artists, and politicians of several generations and various countries united in a heady, head-turning society. There the young Peruvian Miranda, newly arrived in Paris, was introduced to Manon Roland and consequently, in whirlwind fashion, made a general in the French army (Williams 1828, 97).[1] Mary Wollstonecraft, new in the capital in 1792, immediately made the requisite visit to chez Williams. To her regret, Wollstonecraft never met the renowned Mme Roland, but through Helen Williams she encountered her old acquaintance Thomas Paine, Thomas Jefferson's friend Joel Barlow, as well as Jacques-Pierre Brissot, and other prominent Girondins. She also discovered Gilbert Imlay, the American adventurer who would become her lover.[2] While Imlay wooed Wollstonecraft, Lord Edward Fitzgerald, leader of the rebel United Irishmen, courted his future wife Pamela, protegée of Mme de Genlis and (rumor had it) daughter of the Duc d'Orléans (Woodward 82-86). But more than intriguing socializing was at work within Williams's four walls. "Often," she recounts, "conversation reached that certain pitch which only a feeling of personal danger could create" (Williams 1828, 50). After the Montagnard insurrection of 31 May 1793, she tells us, a desperate Rabaut Saint-Etienne sought asylum in her home; and Bertrand Barère, before betraying his Girondin associates to Robespierre, fell into her armchair and "wept bitterly over the fate of the country" (1975, II:1:171-73; 1828, 52-56). Later that year, when Williams herself was forced from home to prison, the inspector of police conveniently napped on her sofa while, in the next room, she burned "enormous piles" of incriminating documents left in her care.[3] Locating Helen Maria Williams's place within this intricate network of international hospitality, politics, romance, violence, dangerous manuscripts, and comfortable furniture should, therefore, be done with a good deal of circumspection. For Williams's salon was as unusual as the salon described above by Chateaubriand. His was no proper drawing-room by eighteenth-century standards: He was describing the Place de la Bastille, seen in the aftermath of its destruction.[4]

Comparing the social space created by Helen Maria Williams in the heart of Paris with the renowned Place de la Bastille interferes with our sense of public and private structures, of outdoor and indoor rendezvous. Her salon was a popular stopping place for foreigners visiting Paris in the years of the Revolution and the Directorate. It provided the setting for sentimental narratives and the site for dangerous alliances.[5] It was also the meeting ground of the old and the new—of an eighteenth-century salon society which imagined no barriers between public and private, between home and history; and a nineteenth-century romanticism which sought refuge from the public eye in domestic, feminine interiors (Landes 50-63). Her Parisian salon had not yet entered a world which, as Nancy Armstrong puts it, "represented the existing field of social information as contrasting masculine and feminine spheres" (9). Williams could, in a way that seems almost paradoxical to us, watch the world turn in her front parlor even as she represented the home as an asylum from the turmoil in the streets. In her published writings on the Revolution in France, she painted herself as the outsider/"spectatrice" of revolutionary events and politics, while simultaneously making a public and political spectacle of herself, her sentimental attachments, and the domestic virtues she espoused: "My love for the French Revolution is the natural result of . . . sympathy and therefore, my political creed is entirely an affair of the heart" (1975, I:1:66). Moreover, at the same time that her house shielded Girondins on the run and protected their valuable papers, her own writing broadcast their plight and reproduced their conversation. As a result, her works were dangerously double-edged, their notoriety transforming her house into a prison for herself, her sisters, and her mother during the Terror.[6] Like the Place de la Bastille with its demolished walls, like her high profile salon, the structures of Williams's *Letters From France* defy any careful separation of interior and exterior, public and private, political and sentimental.[7] There is no ideal refuge and no absolute prison in her representation of Revolutionary France. If, in the novels of the Marquis de Sade, the "privé . . .is almost always figured as a prison" and "privacy is only the theatrical form of solitude," in the contemporaneous works of Helen Maria Williams, the prison is almost always figured as a social place and domesticity is a private theatrical about society.[8]

Helen Maria Williams remains remarkably unknown two centuries after that conflicted period when her health was drunk at meetings of the Friends of Liberty, when she was denounced as "a scribbling trollope" and Jacobin "prophetess" with bloody talons (Walpole 15:25), and when her *Letters From France* made her "perhaps the best-known contemporary author to magazine readers of her generation" and "the overwhelming favorite among writers of popular history and biography" (Mayo 259). By virtue of her early poems, especially those denouncing tyranny and oppression (Peru, published in 1784 and *The Slave Trade* 1788), Williams had settled at the heart of liberal literary circles in London while still a young woman. But, in 1790 she determined to "renounce" the soothing enjoyments of "literary conversation, a fine library, charming music and sweet walks" found in assorted English country homes. She uprooted herself and her family in order to explore the "sublimer delights of the French Revolution" (letter to Col. Barry, 25 June 1790, qtd. in Woodward 32).[9]

Williams returned to England briefly in 1791, but never thereafter. For the next thirty years she lived and worked primarily in Paris, writing thirteen volumes of contemporary history as one of Europe's first foreign correspondents. Among other projects, she translated into English her friend Bernardin de Saint-Pierre's romance, *Paul et Virginie* (1795), and A. de Humboldt's *Personal Narrative of Travels* (1814) and *Researches* (1814), all three of which became extremely influential works in England and America. Two popular French poets, Boufflers and Esmenard, translated excerpts from Williams's early poetry for an eager French audience, since "renown had placed her . . . on the first tier of poets in England" (Advertising Notice; Woodward 202). And her *Poems on Various Subjects,* including the 1802 ode on the Peace of Amiens that had enraged Napoleon, was published in London in 1823. Of all her publications, however, none was more successful or significant than the eight volumes of *Letters From France* published between 1791 and 1796, which brought the French Revolution into the libraries, parlors, and sitting rooms of a generation of English readers.[10] Resting in their own armchairs and sofas, the English public viewed a France represented through the eyes of this female correspondent. They also watched an exile playing hostess to a world in revolution, a woman at home in the theater of politics.

Private Theatricals

> While you observe from a distance the great drama which is acting in France, I am a spectator of the representation.—I am placed near enough the scene to discern every look and gesture of the actors, and every passion excited in the minds of the audience. (Williams 1975, I:3:2)

The language of spectacle and stage fashioned popular response to the French Revolution from its earliest days. Even Edmund Burke initially saw events in France as a performance, and he expressed "astonishment at the wonderful Spectacle": "What Spectators! and what actors! England gazing with astonishment at a French struggle and not knowing whether to blame or applaud!" (6, 10). As the play developed, reaction in England became less ambivalent. Hester Thrale Piozzi, after reading Williams's *Letters,* bemoaned "this theater of massacres and follies" that had entrapped her friend (Woodward 87). The French themselves presented their revolution as theater. In the words of Jean Starobinski, the French saw "the history of the year 1789. . . . [as] a series of spectacular events linked together like the scenes of a tragedy and luridly lit" (8-9; also Hunt 1984, 34-38). It seems appropriate then that the new Republic would commemorate its first dramatic year with a staged pageant, the Fête de la Fédération, and that this Fête would become, in its turn, a revolutionary event. Indeed, the introduction of modern public ceremonial, together with the use of dramatic imagery for widespread propaganda, arises with the political culture of the French Revolution.[11] Yet private manifestations performed "in the minds of the audience" accompany and give weight to the public display. When Helen Maria Williams begins her *Letters From France* with an enthusiastic description of the processions and set pieces of the 1790 Fête, she represents for her audience the collaboration of public and private at play in political culture. The first letter opens with a dramatic flourish:

> I arrived at Paris by a very rapid journey, the day before the Federation; . . . had the packet which conveyed me from Brighton to Dieppe sailed a few hours later; had the wind been contrary; in short, had I not reached Paris at the moment I did reach it, I should have missed the most sublime spectacle which, perhaps, was ever represented on the theatre of this earth. (1975, I:1:1-2)

The "most sublime spectacle" is, of course, the Fête de la Fédération, the celebration of the first anniversary of the storming of the Bastille. But the spectator also celebrates her own dramatic entrance: It is her extraordinary experience and elation (paradoxically, as audience) that gain our attention. Indeed, our assistance is required for her successful performance:

> I am well aware how very imperfectly I shall be able to describe the images which press upon my mind. It is much easier to feel what is sublime than to paint it; and I shall be able to give you a faint sketch, to which your own imagination must add colouring and spirit. (I:1:2)

Playing to the theaters of our imagination, she models for us an emotional response to the scenes she displays: "I have beheld with awful enthusiasm the sun of Liberty spreading its broad blaze," and "My mind is overwhelmed with its own sensation—the paper is blotted by my tears—and I can hold my pen no longer . . ." Williams exploits the familiarity of the letter form to enlist the reader's feelings in her narration and to create a sense of commonly shared emotion: "You will rejoice with me. . . ." or "You, my dear friend, . . . who understand . . . can judge the feelings . . ." (I:1:109, 195). Indeed, the dramatization of personal feeling dissolves the barriers between reader, writer, and spectacle so that partisan politics are translated into universal, "human" sympathies.

Both the revolutionary spectacle of the Fête de la Fédération and the structure of Williams's *Letters* insist that the viewer/reader participate in this transformation:

> You will not suspect that I was an indifferent witness of such a scene. Oh, no! this was not a time in which the distinctions of country were remembered. It was the triumph of humankind; . . . and it required but the common feelings of humanity, to become in that moment a citizen of the world. . . . my heart caught with enthusiasm the general sympathy; my eyes were filled with tears; and I shall never forget the sensations of that day, "while memory holds her seat in my bosom." (I:1:13-4)

This passage sets several rhetorical gestures in motion, all of which complicate our sense of the author's place of the world of revolution. First, we recognize that the literary form she uses, the "letter to a friend," permits her to speak of political questions in the language of intimacy and familiarity. She dresses her own propaganda in the terms of friendship and feeling: "What, indeed, but friendship, could have led my attention from the annals of imagination to the records of politics," she protests elsewhere in her *Letters*. "That system of politics must be best," she asserts, "by which those I love are made happy" (I:1:196-7). We also note here the purely representative role performed by her feelings, evident in the fact that she concludes the passage above (characteristically) with a quotation, effectively de-personalizing and generalizing her response. She regards one nation (France) on behalf of another nation (England), her "common feelings" uniting them both.[12] Behind the apologetic voice of this "citizen of the world" rumble the broad tones of democracy and universalism. The sentimental experience allows the woman writer to imagine a general, undifferentiated political structure that includes her. Moreover, we hear in Williams's description of the Fête de la Fédération hints that "this was not a time" when "distinctions" between inner and outer self were "remembered" or easily negotiated. To be a citizen of the world was to capture the political "moment" in one's heart. At the same time that tears publicized one's emotional investment, memory began to hoard that investment within the bosom. These conflicted gestures underwrite Williams's *Letters,* appearing individually or mingling with the others in an extended dramatization of revolutionary France.

What marks Williams's representation of the early years of revolution is her theatrical display of spectators and their "inner state" as itself a display of the state of France. She delivers the Revolution to England as a "répétition" produced primarily for emotional effect:

> Future generations will celebrate, with grateful commemoration, the fourteenth of July: and strangers, when they visit France, will hasten with impatience to the Champ de Mars [site of the first Fête de la Fédération], filled with that enthusiasm which is awakened by the view of a place where any great scene has been acted. I think I hear them say, "Here the Federation was held! here an assembled nation devoted themselves to freedom! . . . I see them eagerly searching for the place where they have heard it recorded, that the National Assembly were seated! I think of these things, and then repeat to myself with transport, "I was a spectator of the Federation!" (I:1:107-08)

Williams places the national celebration at two removes: Future spectators will relive not the experience of revolution, but the experience of spectators at a commemorative event. Here again we see the blurring of individual with collective response, as well as the enlistment of the audience in the event described. Future generations—perhaps Williams's very readers—repeat her ecstatic response to the scenes she has witnessed and imaginatively recreated. In fact, their response becomes the spectacle to be watched. In other words, the experience of revolution is only realized as the experience of spectators, foreigners, and strangers (see also I:1:46, 67-68). While on the one hand, this seems a distancing strategy, on the other hand it allows Williams to bring the spectacle closer to herself, within the stage of her own imagination. In her *Letters,* outsiders are written into the revolutionary show by means of this imaginary and emotional "mise en scène."

The force of the *Letters* depends, like the revolutionary spectacles themselves, on the ability to reproduce a shared emotional state (or State). By means of this three-way theater of sentiment (between the revolutionary spectacle, the author, and the reader), Williams implicates herself in the rhetoric and strategies of the revolutionary government. "The sublimity of [the Fête de la Fédération] . . . depended much less on its external magnificence," explains Williams, "than on the effect it produced on the minds of the spectators. 'The people, sure, the people were the sight!' " (I:1:5). The sight was not necessarily a visible, but rather an internal, *felt* production: "How am I to give you an adequate idea of the behaviour of the spectators? How am I to paint the impetuous feelings of that immense, that exulting multitude?" wonders the writer (I:1:5). The affective state of the individual correspondent, her inner life, must serve "naturally" as the medium for understanding the people, and thus, the State itself: "My love for the French Revolution is the natural result of . . . sympathy and therefore, my political creed is entirely an affair of the heart" (I:1:66).[13]

In the early 1790s, Lynn Hunt explains, "a good public life depended upon transparent private hearts" (1990, 4:16). But this "transparency" has to be carefully and deliberately fashioned, and Williams is a skillful artist. She capitalizes on talents she shares with the leaders of the French Revolution, who, she tells us, "have studied to interest in their cause the most powerful passions of human nature," and whose ceremonies are "perfectly calculated to awaken that general sympathy which is caught from heart to heart with irresistible energy" (1975, I:1:62). Anna Seward, rereading Williams's *Letters From France* after reading Edmund Burke's terrifying *Reflections on the Revolution in France,* attests to the artificial, yet effective intimacy of her friend's letters: "These Letters . . . do not seek to reason, they only paint. . . . My own enthusiasm, which fear had frozen, was relit under the warmth of her sentiments and her imagination" (Seward 3:75). A laudatory note from la Société des Amis de la Constitution à Rouen (1791) repeats the paradox of Williams's obvious fabrication of a "pure" inner self:

> The French Revolution offers a sublime tableau, . . . but it demands a painter who can present its image to all the peoples of the world. It was left to you, Mademoiselle, to your pure and sensitive heart, to your soul . . . to express with dignity the noble transports of a great people

> at the very moment they became free. . . . If reading your first letters caused us to weep tears of admiration, your last letters have made us cry all the more copiously. What sorrowful tableaux . . . ! (Woodward 43)

Williams responds to this letter in typical fashion, redirecting the experience of a revolutionary people into a display of her own emotion: "May Virtue no longer be oppressed by those evils the telling of which has cost me so many tears!" (Woodward 46).

At the same time, Williams's response maintains that the figure of the sensitive woman best represents and ensures the good of the public: "For to understand the general good, one need not possess the wisdom of a philosopher, one need only the sensitivity ["sensibilité"] of a woman" (Woodward 45-46). In the *Letters* themselves, she assures her readers that "when a proposition is addressed to my heart, . . . I can decide, in one moment, points upon which philosophers and legislators have differed in all ages" (1975, I:1:196). Oddly enough, her heart and soul understand the French people precisely because she is a woman and a foreigner. This affective advocacy is especially pronounced in volume 2, where Williams discovers a curious kinship with the mountebanks and magicians, the comedians and motley characters she views in the town square of Orleans (I:2:10-40). But the significance of her outsider status is even more explicit in other episodes. When she and her sister first visit the National Assembly, for instance, they are admitted "without tickets" to the best seats in the hall: "We had no claim . . . except that of being foreigners and women; but these are, of course, the most powerful claims . . . to French manners" (I:1:42). Of course, the structures of Williams's prose present these claims as forcefully as, and more consistently than, any set of French manners.

In the early volumes, the distinction of being female and foreign forms a strange bond between the author and the French crowd. The central episode of Volume 2 involves an ingenious and self-conscious staging by a woman well aware of her symbolic value. From the window of an apartment in the Palais de Bourbon, Williams and her sisters look down upon a festival procession of "between three and four hundred thousand" Parisians. The people in the street perform an impromptu show for their elevated audience: [they] danced, they sung hymns to liberty, they filled the air with cries of 'Vive la nation!' " But the spectator does not remain at a safe distance from the volatile mob. The crowd immediately turns upon those who stand above them in the Palais de Bourbon, the edifice of monarchy:

> The people do not always reason logically. . . . they could associate no ideas of patriotism with the Palais de Bourbon, and accused us of aristocracy as they approached. (I:2:145)

The danger subsides when sympathy intervenes and the women are offered as an alternative spectacle:

> They [the people] soon perceived that we were entirely disposed to sympathize in their festivity, and also that part of our company were Englishwomen: While the gentlemen from our windows repeatedly called out in as loud voices as they could, "Vive la nation!" the people answered by crying, "Vivent les Anglaises!" (I:2:145-46)

The spotlight travels from the noisy crowd in the street to the silent women in the balcony, finally fusing the two as representatives of popular revolution. The response of the individual woman is eclipsed by the demands of national identity. Here we see the story of Williams's letters reduced to a set piece.

Williams not only fills a representative role, she plays director as well, managing both actors and audience from her unique position both outside (politically) and inside (emotionally) the scenes she depicts. She borrows from the contemporary practice of using young, unmarried women as "living allegories" of the nation, but then recasts those figures in a script she controls.[14] In doing so, she emphasizes once again the reciprocity between inside and outside, domestic and national theater. In the concluding pages of Volume 1, the author participates in a salon production of a play, "La Fédération, ou la Famille Patriotique"[The Federation, or the Patriotic Family]. Set within a family celebration, this play recalls and yet replaces the sublime Fête de la Fédération which opened the volume. It also demonstrates how, in the context of home, family, and friends, the outsider/woman occupies the central position. Williams, the Englishwoman, agrees to take a non-speaking part, "le beau rôle de la statue" [the coveted role of the statue]. Silenced (as in the balcony scene), she speaks for all: She plays Liberty, who stands "guarding the consecrated banners of the nation," while other actors heap decorations, scarves, hats, and words upon her and circle her in a dance (I:1:203-04). "Thus do the French," she slyly remarks, "appoint [female Liberty] not merely to regulate the great movements of government, but to mold the figure of the dance" (I:1:206). And thus, Williams herself places the spectacle of domestic pleasure and feminine "sensibilité" at the center of revolutionary France.

Visites Domiciliaires

> Sometimes, [Vergniaud] presented to us, in a language pure and sparkling, a sort of prelude to the admirable speeches he gave to the gallery, at the [hall of the] Jacobins. It seemed to me that he spoke in an irresistible tone; . . . It is one of my regrets not to be able to recall the expressions of this eloquent orator, who spoke at that time with the abandon of a private conversation while discussing the most profound political questions. (1828, 50-51)

Not only did Helen Maria Williams use the salon as the stage for national performance, the most brilliant orator of the National Assembly used her *soirées* to rehearse his speeches. There, the distinction between the language of private conversation and that of public performance was ignored. Visiting Williams's home, one participated at and in the spectacle of revolutionary politics. Reading Williams's prose, one recognizes the domestic dimensions of the national stage. The most profound political questions of the revolution, were, in fact, questions about the private life: home, family, affective discourse. It is no coincidence that Jacques-Louis David, pageant master of countless outdoor fêtes, set his most significant paintings within the confines of the home: his "Oath of the Horatii," "Lictors Returning to Brutus the Bodies of his Sons," and "Death of Marat." All of them explain public acts of Republican virtue as a violation of (feminine) domestic interiors and, in the two former, of familial sentiment. David's work graphically depicts the intrusion of state concerns into the realm of home, family and feeling—the artistic equivalent of the Terror's dreaded "visites domiciliaires".[15] Whereas David, Robespierre, and Saint-Just imagined a one-way avenue from the State into the home, Williams's work effects a dual movement. Even as statesmen begin to supervise interiors, she imagines interiors opening onto or replacing the public forum. While inviting politicians into the home, the woman writer nevertheless transports the language of domesticity, family, and psychological interiority to national issues, often challenging the assumptions that would impede such translation.

To understand the place occupied by Helen Maria Williams and created by her *Letters,* it helps to see the public sphere in terms of what she would call "domestic affections." "For," she explains, "we are so framed that . . . the tears of tenderness, the throbbings of sympathy, are reserved for that moment when, . . . amidst the loud acclamations of an innumerable multitude, we can distinguish the soothing sounds of domestic felicity" (I:2:1-2). At the same time that we harken to domestic sounds in the midst of multitudes, we understand ourselves as subjects "framed" by domestic settings, in a world that is fundamentally social. We are men and women of various nations, ages and professions gathered in an intimate space and interacting—under the aegis of a woman. In this way the home, but more specifically the welcoming salon, offers the model for an egalitarian, universal society. Yet, where Rousseau and later bourgeois ideology would imagine the home as refuge from "le monde" and from history, and would endorse "the solitude of personal existence" found at home, Williams refuses to shut the door on world, history and society (Starobinski 235). For her, isolated "personal existence" is evacuated to make room for shared social experience. The language of the salon blends with the language of the street.

This fusion is accelerated under the heat of insurrection and violence, where the principles of *politesse* fade and "something more than gallantry" overtakes conversation (Williams 1828, 19). In her memoirs, Williams recounts an evening when she watched social discourse being reconfigured at dinner with Pétion, then mayor of Paris,

> the conversation was lively and animated . . . . we hardly engaged in the ordinary chit-chat of society. The women seemed to forget the task of pleasing, and the men thought less about admiring them. . . . A mutual esteem, a common interest in the great issues of the day, were what manifested themselves most. We spoke of liberty in accents profound and sincere, which approached eloquence. The joy of this patriotic meal was augmented, rather than distracted, by the immense crowd that

surrounded the Place de la Ville, and a thousand voices carried up to us the repeated cry, "Pétion or death!" (1828, 19, 24-5)

This slippage between indoor society and the world out of doors, and the concurrent realignment of gender as well as class, winds its way through the narrative structure of the *Letters From France*.

At times, the challenge to interior and exterior structures expresses itself simply in the contrast between individual letters, as when Williams juxtaposes her accounts of a visit to the cathedral with a visit to a friend's home; of a tour of the dungeons of the Bastille with views of outdoor processions; of a walk within the halls of the Palais Royal with a walk past the coffeehouses outside. The contrasts can be quite sharp. Williams prefaces her description of the passages and apartments of Versailles by insisting we see "in the background of that magnificent abode. . . the gloomy dungeons of the Bastille" (1975, I:1:83). Both these "résidences privées" and the stories they contain are now opened to the speculations of a curious public.

At times the movement between private and public spheres is subtle, gliding back and forth with smooth elisions. In the fifth letter of the first volume, Williams describes her visit to the maison of Mme de Sillery (Félicité de Genlis), a woman "unrivalled in the arts of pleasing" (I:1:33). She then shifts, in letters six and seven, to the halls of the National Assembly, "whose fame has already extended through every civilized region of the world" (I:1:45). At tea with the pleasant Mme de Sillery, Williams discusses the question of the "distinction of ranks," the nature of nobility, and the fall of the Bastille—all "in the spirit of philosophy" (I:1:36). At the National Assembly, by comparison, she attends to the personal "virtue" and wit of the orators. She concludes her study of the Assembly by relaying a sentimental anecdote "warm from my heart," about an emotional speech given by a young man on behalf of his brothers and dying father. If, in the company of women, one discusses political philosophy and current events, amidst male politicians one lets familial sentiment and romance claim the floor. The ability to please runs round in a circle, uniting politics and feeling, men and women, author and reader: "If . . . you have fallen in love with this young Frenchman [the speaker]," Williams ventures at the close of this series of letters, "do not imagine your passion is singular, for I am violently in love with him myself" (I:1:60).

Williams is not disavowing politics here. Rather, she is claiming the heart, together with the entire realm of affective feelings and relations, as the "natural" terrain of politics. The socializing and unifying force granted to public demonstrations of personal affect allows Williams to intertwine the language of domestic sentiment with the discourse of revolution and liberty. This was the logic of much revolutionary propaganda and political reform: The "interior" life of the citizen provided the terms for understanding the state. "The soul of the republic," insisted Robespierre, "is virtue" (Blum 27). In parallel fashion, a 1793 Lyons Commission for Vigilance decreed that "to be truly Republican, each citizen must bring about in himself a revolution equal to the one that has changed France" (qtd. in Hunt 1990, 15). The revolutionaries, invoking Rousseau, asked for a "participatory subjection," "a new subjection," according to Jean Starobinski, in which individuals "were ruled over by the power of feeling and reason" rather than "bound by" an impersonal social structure defined by birth, title, and status (95).

To be "ruled over by the power of feeling and reason" meant that feeling and reason fell under the jurisdiction of political discourse. The spectacle of feeling which accompanied and represented the Revolution required a feeling subject which, in turn, could reinforce the idea of a humanizing, "natural" political system. Robespierre, of course, exploited this mechanism in speeches which emphasized the private virtue and morality of good citizens. Because the line between self and state was not fully articulated, "because politics did not take place in a defined sphere, it tended to invade everyday life," especially the domestic realm (Hunt 1984, 56). The revolutionary government felt free to legislate domestic arrangements, intrude upon matters of personal virtue, and dictate attitudes toward clothing, eating and sexual practice. Consequently, as Lynn Hunt and others have noted, the "ever-expanding publicity" of the private life in the early years of the Republic also promoted society's "romantic withdrawal" into a "more clearly defined feminine space"—the affective realm of family and the home.[16]

Through Prison Walls

The home, a woman's space, can then serve as political theater, where relationships and feelings perform the lead roles. Given that structure, the *Letters From France* nevertheless do not represent the home as a convincingly withdrawn or secure place. Nor do they imply that domestic pleasures are divorced from public passions and violence. For instance, Bernardin de Saint-Pierre drops by Williams's parlor for a cup of tea and entertains her with his fantasy of domesticity:

> I was listening to a description he gave me of a small house which he had lately built in the centre of a beautiful island of the river that flows by Essonne which he was employed in decorating, and where he meant to realize some of the lovely scenes which his fine imagination has pictured in the Mauritius [in his novel, *Paul et Virginie*]. (Williams 1975, II:5:6)

But Saint-Pierre's dream of seclusion receives little support in Williams's house:

> While ... listening ... , I was suddenly called away from this fairy land by the appearance of a friend, who rushed into the room, and with great agitation told us that a decree had just passed in the national convention, ordering all the English in France to be put into arrestation, ... and their property to be confiscated. (II:5:6)

The dream of privacy yields to the nightmare of incarceration.

Like the lively conversation at Pétion's [Pétion or death!"], the rooms and passages where Marie-Antoinette hid from vengeful Poissards, and the emotional speech by the young orator, Williams's account of her own imprisonment (II:5 and 6) points to the implicit violence that accompanies the interchange of interior and exterior, familiar and political. Williams refuses to let private space remain secure from public discourse. In the *Letters,* the prison, an enclosed society wrenched apart from revolutionary France, becomes, like the foreign woman, the symbolic center of political and social discourse. As an emblem of the nation, the home is another

Bastille—at once a reminder of the *ancien régime* and of its demolition—and the prison is another home.

This system of reversals becomes most apparent in the later volumes, where Williams's oscillations between private and public cast darker shadows and the specter of violence grows more tangible.[17] Robespierre himself spelled out the cost of linking the private life to the politics of the nation when he declared "virtue and its emanation, terror" as the fundamental principles of the new Republic (qtd. in Blum 26). Williams's later letters explore this realm of emanations—the danger zone of threat, violence, and duplicity known as the Terror. In the earlier letters, public spectacle and private theatre organized her reporting, but in volumes 5-8 these two structures repeatedly fold into that of the prison.

Williams focuses on the prison as an alternative salon. It provides the image of a home created by violence, an interior space provided by a totalitarian regime. A biting joke, which hinges on the word *foyer,* articulates Williams's sophisticated sense of this space. A liberal-minded countess, an acquaintance of the author, sends her fine marble hearth to be mended in the capital. An accompanying note declares "that the *foyer* must be repaired at Paris." The revolutionary committee, intercepting the countess' mail, reads in these words "the dark designs of aristocracy," "a daring plot," "a *foyer* of counter-revolution, and to be repaired at Paris!" Immediately, the countess, count, and their steward are "conducted to the maison d'arrêt," despite assertions "that no conspiracy lurked beneath the marble" (II:5:25-26).

The grim humor suggests that with its *maisons d'arrêt,* the Terror implicitly acknowledged the "hearth" as "the central point of a [political] system."[18] Williams develops and exploits this point by establishing the society of the prison—those excluded from citizenship, from representation, and potentially, from life—as a model for French society. In fact, her treatment of the prisons offers the possibility of a state institution constituted in terms of affective relationships. The contrast between her salon and her prison rooms in the Luxembourg Palace is "unutterable" (II:5:9) precisely because the two sites fuse into a single social vision which threatens Robespierre's: "Our prison was filled with a multitude of persons of different conditions, characters, opinions and countries, and seemed an epitome of the whole world" (II:5:18-19).[19] In some ways, the prison collapses the distinctions between workplace and home: "The mornings were devoted to business and passed in little occupations, of which the prisoners sometimes complained. . . . Everyone had an appointed task. . . ." (II:5:19). The prison also provided a self-regulating political system: "Every chamber formed a society subject to certain regulations: a new president was chosen every day, or every week, who enforced its laws and maintained good order" (II:5:19-20). In the prisons of Paris, Williams claims, "the system of equality, whatever opposition it met with in the world, was in its full extent practised": class distinctions were eased, goods were shared, responsibilities evenly distributed (II:5:20-1). Nor did prison life neglect social and cultural enrichment. In the public room of the building one found inmates "flirting together, . . . making appointments for card parties or music in their own apartments in the evening, and . . . relating . . . in pathetic language all they had suffered" (II:5:23). Storytelling, poem-writing, and singing punctuated the daily routine. Williams even spent time studying the magnificent tapestries that adorned her chambers (II:5:36-39) and translating French novels into English. Dispossessed and circumscribed by the threat of execution, the prisoners—like Pétion's dinner guests—seemed to glow with the promise of a utopian society unimagined on St. Pierre's island and unimaginable in Robespierre's Paris (II:5:54; also II:6:95-97).

Not surprisingly, these interior spaces permit Williams to give preeminence to women, since these communities emphasize "the fidelity of our [women's] attachments" (II:5:41). When the author is later transferred to the prison at the Couvent des Anglaises, she explains that women together make the best prisoners/citizens:

> [A] true spirit of fraternity . . . prevailed in our community, consisting of about forty female prisoners, besides the nuns [all Englishwomen]. Into how happy a region would the world be transformed, if that mutual forebearance and amity were to be found in it which had the power to cheer even the gloom of a prison! (II:5:185)

The women's ties of mutual suffering and shared nationality are redefined in terms of friendship—"We are born each other's friends"—and exhibited in acts of care and compassion (II:5:186-93).

As Williams's reports sweep in and out of the prisons of Paris, she takes particular note of those women who refuse to honor the barriers set up between *foyers privés* and *maisons d'arrêt*. "Those prisons from which men shrunk back with terror, . . . women . . . demanded and sometimes obtained permission to visit, in defiance of all the dangers that surrounded their gloomy walls" (II:5:41). Women transgress in simple ways: They smuggle letters between cells and salons; they carry food from dining rooms to prison rooms (II:7:181, 187-90; II:8:111-17); or, in the case of the English nuns, they maintain the prison as their residence, and walk to the outer gate arrayed in the outlawed signs of their order—the veils and cross. These simple transgressions can be symbolically potent. In one of the more moving episodes in the *Letters,* Williams recounts the fall of Robespierre from the vantage point of the men and women he had imprisoned. On the night of 9 Thermidor, cut off from the normal channels of communication, the prisoners hear nothing but the foreboding tones of the tocsin bell. The next morning, at last, the prisoners receive the first sign of hope from

> women who displayed upon the roofs of houses, which overlooked at a distance the prison walls, the names of Robespierre and his associates, written in such broad characters that the prisoners with the aid of glasses could read them plainly; and after presenting the name, the generous informer shewed by expressive gestures, that the head of him who bore that name had fallen. (II:7:179-80)

Woman can write the news of the nation upon their houses, communicating to those locked away from the world, the possibility of freedom.

For women especially, the distance between home and prison could be slight: "Home was but a milder prison," observes the author, "where we lived in voluntary seclusion, trembling at every knock at the gate, . . . afraid to venture out" (II:5:206). But the heroines of Williams's *Letters* do venture out, risking their lives in the process. She tells the stories of various unnamed women who coordinate the worlds of prison and home, and consequently reverse the threat of *visites domiciliaires*. But she gives the spotlight to those women who had "fixed on [themselves] the attention of the world": Jeanne d'Arc (I:1 and 2), Charlotte Corday (II:5:128-35), Marie-Antoinette (II:5:153-57), Madame du Barry (II:6:42-45), and Manon Roland (II:5:278-91; 6:232-66). In Williams's *Letters,* several of these women display both inner virtues and public effectiveness: Jeanne d'Arc, Corday, and Roland are not only representative figures, they also act with courage and communicate with eloquence.

But the risk of such display outweighs its celebration. We see a culmination of Williams's concerns—spectacle, prison, and women's space—when she recreates the final moments before these women's public executions.[20] Williams's adulation of her heroines is defined and reinforced by the prison walls which hold them: in the *Letters,* the moment of execution serves as both the motive and the result of their brief histories. Indeed, these women seem most vivid at the point of death. "Those philosophers who have met death with fortitude" fade before tyranny's female victims, who "have been peculiarly distinguished for their admirable firmness in death" (see II:5:212-20). But death also makes a silent spectacle of them, an allegorical figure like Williams's own rendition of Liberty. With good cause, Manon Roland would face the guillotine invoking this feminine allegory—"Oh Liberty! what deeds are committed in your name!" Watching several young women en route to the guillotine, Fouquier Tainville, the public accuser, nearly smacks his lips in perverse anticipation: " 'How bold these women look!' cried Fouquier, enraged at their calmness. 'I must go and see if they show the same effrontery on the scaffold . . . !' " (II:6:72). Ironically, these women hold our attention as soon as they stop moving. The prison and the scaffold serve as frames which, in Williams's prose, both elevate and contain heroic women. The movement between interiors and exteriors seems inevitably to lead to a show, making a spectacle of these remarkable women.

Of course, Helen Maria Williams is as much a heroine and a victim as the women she writes about. She too crosses the lines between intimacy and publicity, between private associations and public concerns. She smuggles messages into and out of prisons, reprinting the prison memoirs of Manon Roland, General Sernan, and Brissot (see Appendices to volumes 6 and 7). And she sends correspondence past enemy lines, insisting on communication between two countries at war. She places herself and her "sympathies" on stage, marking them as both public and political. And she pays the price. Having made a spectacle of herself in the 1790s, she is silenced by history. "What is she now?" writes a critic, William Beloe, in 1817. "If she lives, (and whether she does or not, few know, and nobody cares), she is a wanderer—an exile, unnoticed and unknown" (qtd. in Luria 18). Until a society that erases the walls between a woman's place and the public forum is realized, rather than imagined, the work of women like Helen Maria Williams may remain spectacular—and virtually unknown.

Notes

1. Williams's *Souvenirs* were written in French and published posthumously by her nephews. All translations from the French of the *Souvenirs* and of Woodward are my own. Portions of this essay appeared in *Studies in Romanticism* 32.2 (Summer 1993): 273-95.

2. See Mary Wollstonecraft's *Letters* and Godwin's *Memoirs* regarding her visits to Williams and her desire to study French. See also Woodward 77-78.

3. She understood the inspector's ploy and rushed into a neighboring room in order to destroy "enormous piles of papers, the discovery of which would have been disastrous for us: Mme de Roland's notes, Lasource's letters, and the correspondence of other conspirators" (Williams 1828, 81). Amongst the papers were also the notebooks of Mme de Genlis, who later complained that Williams was harboring them in order to publish them herself (Woodward 85-86).

4. For background on the eighteenth-century French salon and the powerful role it assigned to women, see Lougee and Landes 17-65.

5. A full list of the distinguished and curious visitors to Williams's salon in the 1790s and in the first decades of the nineteenth century would overwhelm a single footnote. I offer only a sampling: l'Abbé Grégoire, M. and Mme Roland, Benjamin Constant, Joseph Priestley, Charles Fox, William Godwin, Fuseli, Mrs. Siddons, Frances Burney d'Arblay, William Wordsworth, Percy and Mary Shelley. Williams was romantically linked with a number of eminent men, notably Bancal des Issarts, General Miranda, Barère, the Dutch preacher Marron and the Polish General Kosciusko, but she seems to have remained attached to John Hurford Stone throughout these years, though they never married. For details, see Woodward, especially chapters 2, 3, 6 and 8.

6. Williams, her sister and her mother, with whom she lived, were imprisoned repeatedly in the years between 1793 and 1802. At first they were sent to the prison du Luxembourg in the general arrest of all English citizens in Paris in 1793. From the Luxembourg they were transferred to the Couvent des Anglaises. They spent about three months in prison at this time. Later, due to the decree of 27 germinal, Williams was forced to move outside of Paris and report daily to the local magistrates. In June of 1794, she fled to Switzerland to avoid a "special proscription" against her, caused by her sympathetic accounts of Robespierre's enemies. At several points during Napoleon's reign, Williams's writings offended the emperor, and he placed her under house arrests for days at a time. For detailed accounts, see Woodward chapters 4, 6, 8, 9.

7. In *Women and the Public Sphere,* Joan Landes argues that the public sphere, which was produced by a growing print culture, and which organized social and political transformations during the Revolution, contended with *le monde* of salon society as "a mode of cultural production" and "organ of public opinion" (22-23; 39-40). According to this model, print culture was hostile to the idea of the stylish, spectacular, and politically

effective woman of the salon (31-8). Print culture fostered the idea of a "bourgeois interior" which substituted the familial foyer for the sociable salon (61-62). Williams's distinction, I argue, rests on her disregard of this conflict: She is a *salonniere* who belongs to the world of print. Her published *Letters* open the salon onto the larger, less select stage of the reading public, while at the same time exploiting the ideological force of domesticity, transparency, and femininity.

8. Roland Barthes's remark from *Sade, Fourier, Loyola* is quoted in Hunt 1990, 4:41.

9. Williams's "family" at this time included her mother and her two sisters, Persis and Cécile. Cécile subsequently married Athanase Coquerel, and when she died in 1796, Helen adopted her sons, Athanase and Charles.

10. The eight volumes were published serially between 1790 and 1796. The first two volumes, entitled *Letters Written in France in the Summer of 1790, to a Friend in England*, were published together after Williams's initial visit to France. The second two, *Letters From France, containing many new anecdotes relative to the French Revolution and the present state of french manners*, appeared in 1792. Four more volumes were published together in 1795-56 as *Letters Containing a Sketch of the Politics of France*. Together, the collected *Letters From France* cover Williams's experience of the Revolution from the Fête de la Fédération on 14 July 1790 to the fall of Robespierre on 28 July 1794. For a history of their publication and reception, see Woodward 207-11 and Todd 4-7.

11. For an elaboration of this point, see Starobinski 101-12; Hunt 1984a, chapter 2; Paulson 4-28; and Ozouf. I take the term "political culture" directly from Hunt.

12. At one point in her travels, Williams spots a sign over a shop, and reports, self-ironically, to her English audience: " 'Robelin, écrivain—Mémoires & Lettres écrites à juste prix, à la nation.' ['Robclin, writer—Memoirs & letters written for a just price, for [to?] the nation.' I am told that Robelin is in very flourishing business; and perhaps I might have had recourse to him for assistance in my correspondence with you" (1975, I:1:94-5).

13. For similar statements, see also I:1:60 and 222.

14. Young women were frequently used in place of statues in the secular ceremonies and spectacles of the new Republic. Moreover, these live, allegorical figures, especially female Liberty, replaced the figures of Catholic saints and French monarchs, which had hitherto functioned as symbols of community and nation. See Hunt 1980, 11-17 and 1984a, 64-65; and Agulhon 11-37.

15. In my characterization of these paintings I depart from the Landes argument that sees the masculine ethos depicted unambiguously within the domestic interior (Landes 154-65). Rosenblum and Paulson are more sensitive to the ambiguity of the domestic setting, acknowledging that the rhetoric of public activity may be violently inconsistent with, and nevertheless endorsed by the rhetoric of home and family (68-74 and 29-30, respectively).

16. Hunt 1984, 13; see also Blum chapter 2 and Armstrong 3-27.

17. See the opening pages of Volume 5: "Those scenes [of the Terror], connected in my mind with all the detail of domestic sorrow, with the feelings of private sympathy, with the tears of mourning friendship, are impressed upon my memory in characters that are indelible" (1975, II:5:23).

18. See Williams's own footnote to this tale, where she defines *foyer* in just these terms.

19. Compare this characterization of the salon/prison with Montesquieu's treatment of the seraglio/salon in *The Persian Letters*. Rica, a Persian noble, complains that the Parisian salon "is like a state within the state, and a man who watches the actions of ministers, officials or prelates at court, in Paris or in the country, without knowing the women who rule them, is like a man who can see a machine in action but does not know what makes it work" (Letter 107). The correlation between salon and seraglio is made clear in the course of Montesquieu's letters (qtd. in Landes 31-35).

20. Volumes 6 and 7 are devoted almost entirely to accounts of executions, but more especially, accounts of the condemned's behavior before death and the public's response to the various executions. Typically, Williams correlates the victim's demeanor in the prison with the reaction of the crowd assembled around the theater of the guillotine. And typically, she attends more often to female victims than male. See for example Corday's execution (1975, II:5:133-35).

9

Charlotte Robespierre: A Sister's Perspective[1]

Marilyn Yalom

Women's memoirs of the French Revolution constitute a rich, largely untapped resource for historians and literary critics. They range in scope from the ten-volume memoirs of the prolific writer Mme de Genlis to the sixteen-page testimonial of the Widow Bault, wife of the concierge in the prison where Marie-Antoinette spent her last days. Of the roughly eighty female-authored autobiographical works that evoke the Revolution, few are known to a general public. Only the memoirs of Mme Roland, Mme Campan, the Duchesse de Tourzel, the Marquise de la Tour du Pin, and the Marquise de la Rochejaquelein are regularly cited by historians, and only those of Mme Roland have received the serious attention of literary scholars.

One reason for the neglect of these works by literary scholars is that we have not known where to place them. Are they memoirs in the conventional French sense, that is, a narrative written from personal knowledge that focuses on public history? Are they autobiographies emphasizing the author's psychological development? Are they primarily biographies of the men to whom the women were attached? I have argued elsewhere that French women's post-revolutionary, first-person narratives are textual hybrids created from a mixture of the traditional memoir form, with its emphasis on public persons and events, and the newer Rousseauist autobiographical form, with its emphasis on the author's inner life.[2] Moreover, some of these female life stories were carefully screened behind the histories of their famous male relatives—husbands, fathers, brothers, generals, and statesmen—adding a biographical-cum-autobiographical strain to the general hybridization of memoirs and autobiography.[3] The case of Charlotte Robespierre is a troublesome one.

Thirty-three years after the execution of her brothers Maximilien and Augustin Robespierre, their surviving sister Charlotte was asked to write a memoir about her two famous siblings. Almost seventy, living in obscure poverty, she was warmed by the friendship of Albert Laponneraye, a young man determined to restore Maximilien's greatly tarnished image. Charlotte's 1828 encounter with Laponneraye eventuated in the production of a curious autobiographical document, published in 1835, a year after her death.[4] Historians, political scientists, biographers, novelists, and specialists in the French Revolution have subsequently made use of its 100 pages for numerous factual tidbits concerning the public and private lives of the two male Robespierres. And, some few have even professed interest in the sister as well.

Two decades after Charlotte's death, when historical romance was much in vogue, the Comtesse Dash wrote a fanciful novel around the name of Charlotte Robespierre. At the end of the century, she appeared again as the central figure in "La sœur de Robespierre, épisode de la Terreur," recounted by the scholarly G. d'Orcey. In our own time, she has become the classic spinster sister, as in Max Gallo's psychobiography of Maximilien. A more nuanced treatment appeared during the winter of 1989-90 in a two-person play based on Charlotte's relationship with Laponneraye, which had a successful run at La Vieille Grille Theater in Paris. But the only serious scholarly attempt to present her life is found in the 1910 edition of her memoirs, meticulously annotated and introduced by the eminent French historian Hector Fleischmann. Still, despite the exhaustive accumulation of documentary evidence, Fleischmann makes little effort to understand Charlotte Robespierre, much less to portray her sympathetically. He judges her as he judges all women: "She is a woman, and as such, no exception to the average nature characteristic of her sex" (11).

Today, with our interest in "average" women at an all-time high, Charlotte Robespierre's story takes on special meaning. What can be learned about the life of an obscure woman who has come down in history as a footnote to her brothers' lives? From her memoirs, which focus largely on her two brothers and their involvement in revolutionary politics, we are able to glean the historical facts of her existence and a sense of her temperament. Supplementing her memoirs with a few of her letters and several other texts written by her contemporaries, it is possible to piece together this life, so profoundly allied to the Revolution, and so deeply harrowed by its course.

Charlotte Robespierre was born in Arras in 1760, twenty months after her brother Maximilien. Within the next three years, her mother gave birth to another daughter, Henriette, and another son, Augustin. Charlotte lost her mother when she was only four. Shortly thereafter, her father, while travelling to forget his grief, also died. The children were then parcelled out to relatives, the girls taken in by paternal aunts, the boys by their maternal grandparents.

In 1768 Charlotte was sent to a convent school in Tournay, where she and twenty other boarders received the education considered suitable for young ladies from the provinces. In light of subsequent history, it is often forgotten that the Robespierres could claim noble status. The young ladies learned writing, religion, lace-making, and home economics. Charlotte was to remain in this cloistered setting for nine years, with her sister joining her there in 1773.

In the meantime, Maximilien had been sent, not to a second-rate provincial school, but to the prestigious Collège Louis Le Grand in Paris. While Charlotte's references to her own studies are skimpy at best, she lavishes upon Maximilien's school years copious adulation. He is presented as a brilliant student—a fact borne out by other accounts—with "a sweet and fair disposition that made him loved by all" (46). Here and elsewhere Charlotte's hagiographic attempts to promote her brother to sainthood fail through their excess. Her obvious idolatry, coupled with a desire to rehabilitate Maximilien in the eyes of history, colors all aspects of her account of their early life, retrospectively casting Maximilien, the child, into the role of family hero and savior. For example:

> Each year he came back to us for the holidays. We always saw him with transports of joy. How quickly the days we spent together passed, after the absence of a whole year! When the moment for him to return to school arrived, it seemed as if we had possessed him for only a few minutes. It was while Maximilien was studying in Paris that we had the misfortune of losing our little sister. It was thus decreed that our childhood would be bathed in tears and that each of our early years

> would be marked by the death of a cherished object. This fatal destiny had a greater influence than one can imagine on Maximilien's character; it made him sad and melancholy. (51)

And what of the influence of these events on Charlotte's character? Has she possibly projected upon Maximilien part of her own "sad and melancholy" nature? The death of her younger sister, when Charlotte was twenty, must have seemed like another form of orphanage. The most consistent companion of her youth, the one who had lived with her in her aunts' home and followed her to the convent school, was now gone. With both her brothers away in Paris, Charlotte must have felt more isolated than ever.

But a year later, in 1781, her life was to take a more fortuitous turn. Having finished his legal studies, Maximilien returned to Arras to practice law and took up residence with his sister. She became, for the first time, the mistress of a household, responsible for every detail in her brother's domestic life.

Imagine a young woman, orphaned in her fifth year, placed in a convent school from age eight to seventeen, and mourning the loss of her only sister. Then suddenly, at twenty-one, mistress of the lodgings she shared with an adored older brother, one of the most eligible bachelors of Arras. How she enjoyed her cozy family life and her new place in provincial society! Those were to be the happiest years of her life.

She describes, in her memoirs, a life structured around his needs:

> He worked a great deal, and spent long hours in his study when he wasn't at the hall of justice. He got up at six or seven, worked till eight. Then his wigmaker came to dress his hair. He had a light breakfast... and went back to work till ten, when he got dressed and went to the court. After the session, he came home for lunch; he ate little and drank only watered-down wine. . . . After lunch he went out for an hour's walk or a visit. Then he came back, closed himself once more in his study until seven or eight, and spent the rest of the evening either with friends or at home. (56-57)

Her portrait of Maximilien could be that of any hard-working, honest, sober member of the bourgeoisie. In his relationship with his sister and aunts, Charlotte portrays him as frequently preoccupied, uninterested in their light talk and card-playing, yet "naturally gay" and capable of "laughing till the tears flowed" (57). As for the fair sex, Maximilien definitely had his conquests, including a certain Mademoiselle Deshorties, whom he courted for two or three years. Charlotte assumes that he probably would have married her "if the voice of his co-citizens had not snatched him from the sweetness of private life and launched him upon a political career" (58-59). Politics were to be his deepest passion.

What were Charlotte's reactions when her revered brother was called to Paris by his election to the Estates General in 1789? She is clearly very proud of his political ascendancy, proud too that they remained in close contact through the mail, giving one example from his correspondence: "You are what I love the most after 'la patrie' (the fatherland)" (73). This fervent declaration is included so as to suggest both her value as his favorite person, and his worth as a patriot. We know from a document left by Pierre Villiers, Maximilien's secretary in 1790, that he sent a fourth of his salary every month to a "sister living in Arras of whom he was very fond" (Jacob 86).

While the older brother was making history in Paris, the younger one, Augustin, succeeded Maximilien as a fledgling lawyer in Arras and as his sister's joint tenant. Both followed their brother's dramatic rise to power in the National Assembly. They adopted his revolutionary ideas and tried to promote them among their fellow citizens in Arras.

We get a glimpse of Charlotte's interests and activities from a letter to Maximilien dated 9 April 1790. She reports that the good citizens of Arras are "pleased with the patriotic contribution," referring to a decree issued by the revolutionary government requesting all citizens to contribute a fourth of their income to the nation. She also notes that the municipal authorities have begun a campaign to raise money for the poor, but that "many people do not want to pay anything additional. They give as their reason that we shouldn't feed the poor to do nothing, that we should make them work" (Fleischmann 28). The concept of the dole was obviously as unpopular with many eighteenth-century individuals as it has been with like-minded citizens in our own time.

This letter also contains more personal information on Charlotte in her dealings with a certain Mme Marchand:

> We've had a falling-out. I allowed myself to tell her what all good patriots ought to think about her newspaper, what you thought about it. I reproached her for always putting in odious remarks about the people. She got angry. She maintains there are no aristocrats in Arras, that she knows them all to be patriots, that it's only hotheads who find her gazette aristocratic; she told me a heap of nonsense and since then she hasn't been sending us her paper any longer. (Fleischmann 28-29)

Whatever her ideological justifications, Charlotte does not appear in a very favorable light. She comes across as officious, self-righteous, even arrogant. It is the first of several fallings-out to take place in the next few years. As for the letter's style, it is considerably more colloquial than her memoirs, and filled with spelling errors. This, and a few other letters written in her hand, preserved in the National Archives, suggest that her memoirs were substantially corrected by Laponneraye.

This same Mme Marchand, editor of the *Affiches d'Artois,* published two ironic articles on the "patriots" of her city, including Charlotte and Augustin, on the occasion of Maximilien's visit to Arras in October 1791. In the first, she describes a missed meeting in a neighboring town:

> M. et Mlle de Robespierre went to meet him . . . at the head of a delegation composed of a number of their friends . . . A wreath was carried in a basket by two of the ladies. What a pity for the group! Robespierre did not arrive . . . Well, the group decided to dance. They were right to dance; one shouldn't go so far for no reason. . . . they came back to the city: the wreath was still at the head of the parade. (Jacob 91-95)

In the second article, published a week later, she reports Maximilien's belated arrival and the visit she received from several members of his entourage, who tried to persuade her to write about Robespierre with greater respect. This curious woman, publisher and editor of her own newspaper, presents herself as refusing to be cowed by masculine intimidation. Her articles suggest the mettle of a bold woman, whose outspoken political views contrast markedly with the more dependent nature of her contemporary, Charlotte Robespierre.

In September 1792, both Maximilien and Augustin were elected to the Legislative Assembly. Charlotte and Augustin left Arras for Paris, where they found Maximilien lodged with the Duplays, a family of ardent Republicans. For a time, Charlotte lodged at the Duplays as well. In recounting the story of Maximilien's involvement with the Duplay family and her own difficult relations with them, Charlotte finally assumes a leading role in her memoirs. The reader is presented with the situation of a woman in her early thirties, who had kept house for her older brother for almost a decade, and for her younger brother for three more years. She comes to Paris in the hope of establishing a household in which the three siblings can finally be together, and what does she find?

> When I arrived from Arras in 1792, I stayed with the Duplays, and I noticed right away the strong influence they had on him. . . . [T]his influence had as its source my brother's good nature, on the one hand, . . . and Madame Duplay's incessant and often tiresome endearments, on the other.
> I resolved to extricate my brother from her hands, and in order to do so, I tried to make him understand that in his position, occupying such as elevated political rank, he should have his own place. . . .
> Madame Duplay was very angry with me. I think she bore me ill will for the rest of her life. We thus lived together alone, my brother and I, for a short period of time, whereupon he fell ill. His sickness was not dangerous. He needed much attention, and I certainly saw to it that he wanted for nothing. I didn't leave him for a moment. I looked after him constantly. When he was better, Madame Duplay came to see him. . . . She started saying very disagreeable things to me. She told me that my brother did not have all the care he needed, that he would be better off in her family . . . and she pressed Maximilien to return to her home. . . . Robespierre, in spite of my protests, finally decided to follow her. "They love me so much," he said, ". . . they have shown me such great kindness, it would be ungrateful for me to reject them." (86-87)

For once, Charlotte is critical of Maximilien; she reproaches him for not putting her interests above those of another:

> [B]ut after all, should he not have thought that his preference for Madame Duplay would distress me at least as much as his refusal could have distressed that lady? Between Madame Duplay and me, should he have hesitated? Should he have sacrificed me for her? (88)

This is perhaps the truest personal moment in Charlotte's memoirs, the moment of release from sisterly obedience when the voice crying for love, recognition, and justice refuses to be stifled. For one passionate moment, Charlotte drops the veil of the hagiographic biographer and bares her own anguished face. Her cries sound like those of a wife abandoned for another woman. She calls upon the reader to empathize with her past injury: She, who had been briefly restored to what she considered as her rightful place as mistress of her brother's home, was abruptly replaced. It is understandable that she felt bitter, even against her revered brother, and especially against the woman whose maneuvers had caused his desertion. The rivalry between Charlotte and Mme Duplay was complicated by the fact that the latter had four daughters, one of whom—Eléanore—was reputed to have been either Maximilien's mistress or his fiancée. Charlotte insists that both opinions were equally untrue. Whatever his involvement with Eléanore Duplay, a gulf between Charlotte and Maximilien gradually developed, one so large that Charlotte, like many who came to call upon the great patriot at the Duplay residence, often found him sequestered behind closed doors.

Charlotte did have an ally in one of the Duplay daughters, Elisabeth. "She was not," Charlotte wrote, "like her eldest sister, set against me. Several times she came to wipe away my tears when Mme Duplay's indignities made me cry" (91-92). This friendship is supported by Elisabeth Duplay Le Bas's own autobiographical account. In her short memoirs, the Duplay younger daughter described her life in Paris during the early years of the Revolution and her close relationship with Maximilien and Charlotte Robespierre, who introduced her to her future husband, the deputy Philippe Le Bas.

During the winter of 1792-93, Charlotte's first in Paris, she did her best to maintain the family bonds. With Elisabeth Duplay she frequented the Legislative Assembly, and occasionally dined out with her brothers. A letter dated February 17, 1793, from Rosalie Jullien, the wife of a substitute deputy from the Dauphiny, offers a picture of the three Robespierres invited to dinner by another Jacobin family:

> I was delighted with the Robespierres. The sister is naive and natural... she came two hours before her brothers, and we had a chance to talk together as women. I got her to talk about their domestic habits; they're just as we are—unsophisticated and sincere. Her brother... is abstract, like a thinker, dry like a minister... He doesn't have our tender sensibility, but I believe he wants the best for the human race, more through a sense of justice than through love.... The younger Robespierre is more animated, more open, an excellent patriot, but common in his thoughts and petulant in disposition. (Jullien 345-46)

This rare close-up portrait of the three Robespierres zeroes in on their most pronounced features: Charlotte's simplicity, Maximilien's abstraction, Augustin's temper. These personal characteristics are to play their part in the final falling-out between Charlotte and her brothers. Charlotte records the circumstances of that unhappy break in a chapter describing a trip to the South of France in the company of Augustin and M. and Mme Ricord. Jean-François Ricord and Augustin Robespierre, both Convention deputies, were sent on an investigatory mission to Nice. In Charlotte's account, Augustin welcomed her proposal to accompany him "with joy" (100).

Their descent by carriage into the provinces during the summer of 1793, when the South of France from Lyon to Marseille was studded with counter-revolutionary uprisings, brought them close to peril on several occasions. Finding Lyon in full insurrection, the deputies feared imprisonment and made haste to move on. In order to make their presence less conspicuous, they took back roads, stopping in small towns such as Manosque, but even here their stay was "not without danger," given the menacing attitude of the population (102). In their next stop at Forcalquier, the patriots of that city offered their services, staying with them through the dinner hour, which was interrupted at eleven o'clock by an express message from the mayor of Manosque warning them that counter-revolutionary soldiers from Marseilles were on their trail. The foursome quickly made their way on horseback into the mountains, leaving their carriage behind. Accompanied by "a dozen patriots" serving as their guides, they travelled all night "on terrible paths, descending very rough hills" on horses that had difficulty finding their footing (105). After numerous adventures worthy of a picareseque novel, they arrived in Nice, which had a division of French troops capable of protecting them from harm.

At first, Charlotte enjoyed the company of Mme Ricord. While the men were engaged in official business, the two women occupied themselves with making shirts for the soldiers. In the evening, they explored the outskirts of Nice, either on foot or on horseback, but when their equestrian outings were criticized as "aristocratic" and word of this criticism reached Maximilien in Paris, Charlotte bowed to her brothers' demand that she give up "the pleasure of riding" (109).

From Charlotte's perspective, it was the machinations of Mme Ricord, intent upon seducing Augustin, that caused the rupture between the two siblings. She characterized Mme Ricord as a wicked coquette, who wanted to destroy the relationship between Charlotte and Augustin so as to rid herself of "a severe and rigorous witness" (110). And, she succeeded.

It is not difficult to imagine what the situation felt like for Charlotte, dismissed as Maximilien's housekeeper and now alienated from Augustin as well. She had cared for her younger brother in Arras, promoted his career in every possible way, come with him to Paris with the highest of hopes, accompanied him on his mission to the South, only to find herself an importunate intruder in his liaison with Mme Ricord. According to Charlotte, Mme Ricord engineered her dismissal through a letter from Augustin commanding her to return to Paris: "Imagine my astonishment! My brother, without seeing me, without saying good-bye, sends me away like an outcast" (115). The brother and sister were never to see one another again.

Was Charlotte simply perceived as a spoil-sport by her younger brother? Was she indeed the victim of another woman's coquettery and wiles? Did her own "chaste" habits as a respectable single woman come into conflict with those of Augustin and his mistress and the French tradition that allowed a married woman more sexual freedom outside the conjugal situation than an unmarried woman? Much of Charlotte's history and characteristics did not lend themselves to the looser private morality of a revolutionary milieu: her convent school upbringing, without the benefit of a mother; her lack of marital experience; her adherence to the prescriptive behavior for unmarried women, especially in the provinces; and her uncompromising ideals. She could not condone the boldness of some of her female contemporaries, particularly when it impinged upon her brothers' lives. She felt profoundly threatened by them, and deeply betrayed by her brothers' preference for one such woman.

A letter from Augustin to Maximilien preserved in the National Archives throws some light on the increasingly strained relations between Charlotte and her brothers:

> My sister has not a single drop of blood which resembles ours. I have learned and seen so many things about her that I consider her our greatest enemy. . . .
> We must take a stand against her. We must make her leave for Arras and thus distance ourselves from a woman who contributes to our mutual despair. (Fleischmann 54-55)

This damning letter, written in early 1794, was to condemn Charlotte to temporary exile. She was sent packing back to Arras, accompanied on her voyage by an old curate named Le Bon. Her memoirs are silent on this disgrace, which was terminated in less than a month; other sources reveal that Charlotte was brought back to Paris by the Convention member Florent Guyot. Here (and elsewhere) it is impossible to ignore the patriarchal aspects of her situation: Dependent on her brothers for financial and social support, she was moved about like a child, always under the surveillance of male authority figures. Her memoirs indicate that, unlike a few more daring women (for example, Mme Marchand or the pre-feminist Olympe de Gouges), she never questioned the right of men to tell women what to do.

The last chapter of her memoirs focuses on the last months of her brothers' lives, and mainly on Maximilien's. The author is anxious to place him firmly at the summit of the pantheon, above such figures as Danton and Saint-Just, all good revolutionaries but lacking—she averred—some of the virtues that made her brother superior to his contemporaries. It is possible that Laponneraye, himself the author of several treatises on the revolutionary years, expanded her notes for this chapter into a more substantial historical document. We are in the presence of unabashed political hagiography, designed to counter the ignominy visited upon Robespierre after his death.

The very last pages revert to the story of Charlotte as she herself experienced the terrible Thermidor days. Portraying herself as a hapless victim of a revolution gone mad, Charlotte's account is oddly similar to those written by female aristocrats with opposite political loyalties:

> The next day, the 10th of Thermidor, I rush into the streets, my head full of anxiety, my heart full of despair. I look for my brothers. I learn that they have been taken to the Conciergerie. I run there, ask to see them, plead with folded hands, get down on my knees in front of the soldiers. They push me away, laugh at my tears, insult me, strike me. Several people, moved by pity, drag me away. My reason became clouded. I no longer knew what was happening, what would become of me. Or rather, I found out several days later; when I came to myself, I was in prison. (144-45)

This passage reminds us not only of other contemporary memoirs, but also of numerous pre-romantic and romantic works of fiction in which the heroine is buffeted about by a relentless fate. She is all trepidation and sensibility, prey to the cruelties of masculine power. The conventional "black-out," often occasioned in novels by an attempted rape, ends when she wakes to the reality of imprisonment.

This account of how she came to be a prisoner is followed by an account of how she extricated herself from that situation. Her tale of a letter written from her cell at the urging of an unnamed coprisoner has a fictional ring: "Profiting from my horrible situation, my dejection, my despair, and my distraught spirits, she made me sign a statement containing things that were unworthy of me" (146-47). Charlotte fears that this letter, the exact contents of which she has forgotten, was used by Maximilien's detractors to further blacken his name.

Whether such a letter ever existed (it has never been found) or whether, as Fleischmann surmises, Charlotte confused it with another document, this last entry in her memoirs reveals an uneasy conscience. But while she expresses concern for the consequences of her letter, she refuses to take responsibility for it. Her destiny is always presented as determined by the diabolical machinations of someone else. This sense that fate was against her from the start is more than a romantic pose. Orphaned in childhood, Charlotte Robespierre began early in life to see herself as a victim of outside forces. Whatever the circumstances, she projected the blame on others, frequently women: Mme Marchand, Mme Duplay, Mme Ricord, or the mysterious woman in prison. The memoirs do not offer a single instance in which Charlotte tries to understand the ways in which she herself may have contributed to her personal tragedies (except for one incident in childhood centered around her laxity in caring for Maximilien's pet pigeons, the neglect of which led to their death). We are in the presence of a self-righteous elderly woman intent upon justifying herself to posterity.

Her self-justification is, of course, minor in comparison to the apology she has written for Maximilien. He is *always* portrayed as being in the right, except in the matter of Mme Duplay. It is always the other—the other members of the Committee of Public Safety, for example—who were responsible for the Terror. It was Danton, with his dissolute habits and lapsed hostility toward the nobility who brought about his own execution, not Robespierre who led the National Convention against the Dantonists. And it was Robespierre's jealous enemies who engineered the coup against her brothers, "against all the good Montagnards [the deputies on the extreme left] or rather against the people, of whom they were the purest representatives" (143). Her memoirs stand as a monolithic apology for a formidable public figure who continues to inspire controversy 200 years after the Revolution.

The memoirs end with Maximilien's death, although Charlotte was to live on for forty more years. She considered her own life worthy of documentation only to the extent that it was coterminous with her brothers' lives. The later period of her life was marked by a strange quirk of history: Charlotte Robespierre was to receive a pension from the French government that lasted, under various regimes, for at least fifteen years and probably longer. Issued by Napoleon, whom she had known through Augustin, and renewed by the restored Bourbon monarch Louis XVIII, a pension was granted to the sister of the regicide Maximilien Robespierre, whose speeches at the trial of Louis XVI had hastened the King's death and the destruction of the Old Regime! And Charlotte Robespierre, fervent Republican, was willing to accept support from the kings of France!

Elisabeth Duplay Le Bas, for one, condemned Charlotte for accepting this pension. In a note ringing with indignation, Mme Le Bas wrote that she preferred being a washerwoman to asking for help from her husband's enemies, whereas Mlle Robespierre—it pained her to report—had not refused their assistance. Laponneraye, on the other hand, defended Charlotte on the grounds of her advanced age, ill health, and material destitution. As he stated in the Introduction to her memoirs: "To have rejected the pension . . . would have condemned her to die of hunger and extreme poverty, since her brothers had not left her anything" (33).

She lived very modestly on this pension, her last years spent in a tiny apartment in the rue de la Pitié, with the companionship of a young woman named Victoire Mathon, who was named Charlotte's inheritor in her testament of 1828. In that same year, her meeting with Laponneraye was to transform her few remaining years. Laponneraye was to become not only a collaborator, but also a financial and moral helpmate, the son she had never had.

In accepting a small sum of money from him, she wrote a gracious thank you note that expressed her maternal sentiments:

> I accept then (this gift) from one who has for me the sentiments of a son, whom I consider as such, and for whom I have so much affection. . . . I accept with pleasure! That word says it all. I think you will be pleased with me. (172)

There is something quite touching about the kindness bestowed upon a seventy-year-old woman by a twenty-one-year-old man and her almost childlike desire to please him; in her last years, quite unexpectedly, a young man came into her life to bring her comfort and sustenance. One might say that she found in Laponneraye not only the son or grandson she never had, but the affection ultimately denied her by her brothers.

She was, of course, undoubtedly of interest to Laponneraye primarily as the Robespierre sister. Yet, while her memoirs are mainly a testimonial to Maximilien, they also allowed her to write her own life story, at least obliquely. The memoir form provided a means for Charlotte Robespierre—like many other women in the past—to enter into recorded history through the life of a famous male relative, and thus, ironically, to have the last word.

Notes

1. A slightly different version of this chapter appears as "The Other Robespierre" in *Blood Sisters: The French Revolution in Women's Memory* (Harper Collins Publishers, 1993).

2. See *Blood Sisters,* chapter 1.

3. I take up the subject of women memoirists screening themselves behind male relatives in "Biography as Autobiography: Adèle Hugo, Witness of Her Husband's Life." See Yalom 1990, 53-63.

4. All my translations are from the 1835 edition of Charlotte Robespierre's memoirs.

10

From Reform to Revolution: The Social Theater of Olympe de Gouges

Gabrielle Verdier

Je suis femme et auteur; j'en ai toute l'activité" ("I am a woman and an author; I manifest all the activity of an author"). By this opening statement in the preface to her first published work, *Le Mariage inattendu de Chérubin* (1786), Olympe de Gouges proclaimed in print her status as playwright.[1] Indeed she was an active author, "the only known woman author of the Revolution" (Thomas 1988, 309). Yet even after the research generated by the bicentennial, she is known primarily for a single political manifesto, *Déclaration des droits de la femme et de la citoyenne,* although she published more than sixty political texts, addressing them to political figures or plastering them all over Paris. After two centuries of derision, her large dramatic production is only beginning to emerge from oblivion. This is due in part to the fact that revolutionary theater and eighteenth-century bourgeois drama have been dismissed as inferior on esthetic grounds and that significant reappraisals are yet to appear.[2] De Gouges's plays, however, have been singled out for scorn because she dared to practice a genre that was a male preserve. In the absence of unbiased histories of this theater, reevaluations of individual authors remain tentative but some conclusions can be reached by comparing plays that treat similar themes. The aim of this article[3] is to provide an overview of de Gouges's plays, and suggest their thematic and formal interest. I begin with general remarks on her production, and a review of critical reaction.

Twelve of the plays she wrote between 1783 and 1793 have survived. The following lists titles, probable date of composition, and generic subtitle:

1783-84	*Zamor et Mirza, ou l'heureux naufrage* (retitled 1798 *L'Esclavage des nègres;* 1792 *L'Esclavage des noirs*)	3-act drama
1784	*Le Mariage inattendu de Chérubin*	3-act comedy
1785-86	*L'Homme généreux*	5-act drama
1786-87	*Le Philosophe corrigé ou le cocu supposé*	5-act comedy
1788	*La Bienfaisance récompensée ou la vertu couronnée*	1-act comedy
1788	*Molière chez Ninon, ou le siècle des grands hommes*	5-act "episodic play"
1790	*Les Démocrates et les Aristocrates*	1-act comedy
1790	*Le Couvent ou les vœux forcés*	3-act drama
1790	*La Nécessité du divorce*	3-act comedy
1791	*Mirabeau aux Champs-Elysées*	1-act comedy
1792	*La France sauvée, ou le Tyran détrôné* (unfinished)	5-act drama
1792	*L'Entrée de Dumourier* [sic] *à Bruxelles ou les Vivandiers*	5-act "play"

De Gouges managed to have ten published and four performed:[4] *L'Esclavage,* by the Comédie Française (renamed "Théâtre de la Nation") on 28 & 31 December 1789, and 2 January 1790; *Le Couvent,* by the Théâtre Française, Comique & Lyrique starting in October 1790 for over eighty performances; *Mirabeau,* by la Comédie Italienne on 15 April 1791 and in June by a company in Bordeaux; *Dumourier,* by the Théâtre de la République on 23 & 25 January 1793. In addition to the ten published plays, there are manuscripts of two others: *La France sauvée ou le Tyran détrôné* (1792), which was used by the Revolutionary Tribunal to accuse her of counter-revolutionary sentiments, and *La Nécessité du divorce* (1790), recently identified.[5] The inventory of her papers, which were seized and partly destroyed when she was arrested in 1793, suggests an even more prolific activity.[6] It lists some forty plays, among these several with provocative titles, which were apparently read by the Comédie Française after 1798, but refused: *Le Marché des noirs, Le Nouveau Tartuffe ou l'école des jeunes gens, Les Rêveries de Jean-Jacques ou la Mort de Jean-Jacques à Erménonville.*

This listing suffices to dispel the cynical view that this "galant woman" threw herself into literature when her charms began to fade at age thirty (she was born in 1748), and then threw herself into politics in 1789 when that became a better way to attract attention. Several observations can be made. It was indignation at injustice, not primarily vanity, that inspired Olympe de Gouges to write plays. Her first drama denounces slavery in the French West-Indies. Written five years before the founding of the "Friends of the Blacks Society" in France, it was certainly not calculated to please spectators, many of whom were powerful slaveholders. The Comédie accepted it in 1785 but shelved it, staging plays accepted later. It was only performed in late 1789, after the Revolution had begun and the Comédie itself was under attack, after de Gouges had tirelessly campaigned for her rights and threatened a lawsuit. All of her plays develop controversial themes. These were primarily social before 1789: the scandal of imprisonment for debt (*L'Homme généreux*), the double standard of sexual morality (*Philosophe*), the defense of a mother's sexuality (*Ninon*). After 1789 they became more explicitly political. They anticipate debate and legislation on social issues, such as monastic vows (*Couvent*) or divorce, celebrate revolutionary figures (*Mirabeau*) or events (*Démocrates, Dumourier*), or denounce conspiracies to destroy the Revolution (*France sauvée*).

Of course the social causes de Gouges championed were also defended by her Freemason friends, male and female, and by the Girondins (Kates 1985, 99-127), the political group to which she was closest. Feminist issues had already been raised in the *Journal des Dames* (Gelbart 293), and social themes were prominent in bourgeois drama, especially in plays by her friend Sébastien Mercier. But she was the first to dare represent slavery, divorce, and several other burning issues that were tabou on stage. Far from abandoning theater for politics, she engaged in playwriting as a political activity on a more conscious level after 1789. All six of her extant post-1789 plays bear revolutionary titles, contrary to the average six-to-one ratio of nonrevolutionary titles in contemporary production (Kennedy 1984, 58). In its generic distribution, her theater is also somewhat atypical. According to literary history, the late eighteenth-century French stage was dominated by bourgeois drama, but in fact many more comedies and vaudevilles than dramas were staged during the revolutionary decade (59).

De Gouges's production, however, has a proportionally greater number of dramas, and even her comedies treat serious subjects such as divorce more seriously than light-hearted vaudevilles on these themes. In other ways, the formal features—or absence of traditional forms in some of her plays such as *Démocrates, Mirabeau,* and *Dumourier* which belong to the theatrical revue and *fait historique* [historical event] category—reflect the impact of revolutionary events on the theater and her attempt to invent new forms to represent new content.

Literary historians, however, have neglected her large dramatic production to focus on the failure of her plays and the impertinence of her authorial pretensions. These defied all decorum in an age when women, more than ever, were admonished to remain in their proper sphere. They were particularly shocking in association with the theater since actresses—public women—were regarded to be little more than glorified whores. The cautionary recommendation against public display of authorship, respected by illustrious female writers of the Old Regime, had become in the wake of Rousseau a moral imperative internalized by the most intelligent women. Mme Roland writes: "I am often annoyed to see women arguing over privileges that do not suit them; even the title 'author' seems ridiculous for a woman to me. However gifted they may be in these fields, they ought not to display their talents to the public" (cited by Abray 60). Yet Olympe de Gouges, herself a disciple of Rousseau, went so far as to call for the creation of a second national theater devoted to the performance of women's plays; this in a philosophical work entitled *Le Bonheur primitif de l'homme ou les rêveries patriotiques* (1788, 2), inspired by Rousseau's discourses. Moreover, in 1790 she made an appeal on behalf of women writers to the committee formed by Beaumarchais to plead the cause of authors' rights (Hesse 475). Although the conception of "text as property" was finally recognized in the legislation of 19 July 1793, it was not extended to married women, whose texts remained their husband's property, as before the Revolution (482).

Olympe de Gouges further violated decorum and departed from the authorial strategies women had developed under the Old Regime by signing her publications, rather than publish them anonymously or under a male pseudonym.[7] Her daring might be explained by the public persona she had created for herself. As a widow, she had some rights in the eye of the law, but "de Gouges" was not her husband's name and never does her civil status as "veuve Aubry" figure on any of her works—although it does on official documents related to her trial and execution. "De Gouges" might be read as the ennoblement of the name of her legal father, Pierre Gouze, were it not for the "Olympe" she takes from her mother's middle name "Anne Olympe," so glorious next to her own common "Marie." The maternal filiation underlines Olympe de Gouges's claim that she was the issue of her mother's liaison with Le Franc de Pompignan, a nobleman who forgot his mistress and daughter after he married and became a prominent playwright and poet. Thus her name belongs neither to her husband nor to one of her fathers, but it is not exactly a pseudonym since it was the name she also used in everyday life. In signing her works first "Madame de Gouges" and later "Olympe de Gouges," her strategy was not to conceal her identity or reveal it indirectly, but to announce the public person she had become and by which she could be identified.[8] Her courageous—or foolhardy—stance would prove fatal, both to her life and to her reputation. During the Terror she was the only woman tried and guillotined for seditious writings. Although as a woman she was denied representation and the status of an active citizen, the Revolutionary Tribunal condemned her for "crimes of the pen" (Hesse 476), basing its accusations on her political pamphlet calling for a national referendum on the form of government France should have (*Les Trois Urnes ou le Salut de la Patrie*) and three political plays (*Mirabeau, La France sauvée,* and *Dumourier*) in which she showed sympathy for revolutionary leaders, heroes of their day, who by 1793 had fallen into disgrace (Blanc 1989, 199-200; Levy 1980, 254-59).

During her lifetime, her early published plays received generally favorable, if condescending reviews. But hostility increased as she asserted her authorial ambitions and managed to bring some plays to the stage, and especially as she intervened in revolutionary politics. The performances of the most controversial, *L'Esclavage* and *Dumourier* (which glorified women warriors and a victorious general under suspicion when the play was finally staged) were tumultuous and were recounted with sarcasm in newspapers of the period.[9] The few pages devoted to her in the earliest history of revolutionary theater by Etienne et Martainville merely repeat these anecdotes, with the comment that by her "pretensions," which make the "charms" but not the "weaknesses" of her sex disappear, this woman had forfeited all right to "French galantry" (58).

Olivier Blanc's groundbreaking biography revealed the extent to which political cabals, the opposition of the slaveholders, and the hostility of the Comédie Française, were responsible for the failure of these plays. But her literary productions continue to be dismissed without being read. A rather recent history of revolutionary theater that repeats Etienne and Martainville's errors has gone unchallenged.[10] In a recent anthology on revolutionary culture, failure is the theme that dominates Chantal Thomas's article, "Féminisme et Révolution: les causes perdues d'Olympe de Gouges." Although the critic names only three titles, *Mirabeau, La France sauvée, Le Couvent,* "etc.," among the plays "hardly performed," she concludes that de Gouges's contemporaries were correct in their lack of enthusiasm. "She confuses the worst stereotypes and the blandest moralizing with inspiration from nature" (1988, 309). The plays Thomas names are the only three excerpted in Benoîte Groult's 1986 anthology of de Gouges's works. While serving to draw attention to her, this anthology has performed a disservice by its unscholarly nature. It identifies texts erroneously, mixes passages from different texts under a single title, presents the plays without indicating ellipses.[11] Out of context, the scenes excerpted can lend credence to characterizations of the author as a romanticizing narcissist whose principal concern was to attract attention. Since 1986, it is on this collection that many historians have based their summary judgments of de Gouges's theater, judgments that reproduce the prejudices of the past.

Any assessment of "failure"—or success—must be contextualized. Context includes considering the disadvantaged position of women dramatists with relation to cultural institutions. That Olympe de Gouges's plays were performed at all was a triumph. Of the 2,627 plays staged by the Comédie Française since its founding 300 years ago, only 77 were written by women, and most of these were minor one-act comedies (Chevalley 41). Men, too, if they challenged established values or genres had to struggle to have their plays accepted by the powerful Comédie, but they could much more easily have them produced in other theaters.[12] Women playwrights of the Old Regime faced much greater obstacles. To succeed in bringing their works to the stage, they needed the influence and financial backing of a powerful man because any association with actors automatically compromised their honor. The obstacles and stigma for women increased after 1750 (Showalter 1988, 96). Of a total of 320 plays written by women between 1700 and 1789, thirteen plays, nine of which were in five acts, were staged at the Comédie before 1750; of the nine plays staged after 1750, only two were in five acts (Bonnifet 18-27). The first of these, *La Comtesse de Chazelles* by de Gouges's protectress, the Marquise de Montesson, failed miserably after one performance in 1785. But Montesson was able to have at least twelve other plays performed in her private theater. In 1787 *La Fausse inconstance* by Countess Fanny de Beauharnais was interrupted by jeers after the third act, due to deliberately shoddy acting.[13]

The only successful female playwright was Julie Candeille (mistress of de Gouges's friend Vergniaud), whose *Belle fermière* was played more than fifty times by the Théâtre de la République in 1792-93. Candeille was an actress in the company and performed the title role which exhibited her charms and musical talent. De Gouges's very topical *Dumourier,* written in a few days after the general's victory over the Austrians in Belgium on 14 November 1792, was announced by the Théâtre de la République on November 24, but its production was delayed in order to stage Candeille's play. In her letter to the general, de Gouges explains that she did not fight to have her play staged first because she knew that the author of *La Belle fermière* was a woman (TP 1991, 142). Candeille herself played the leading female role in *Dumourier.* De Gouges, however, claimed her play was massacred by the company when it was finally performed on January 23, two days after the execution of Louis XVI. The hostile reviews compare *Dumourier* with *La Belle fermière.* Candeille's play does not need to be judged with the "indulgence" that should be shown toward a "woman's work," since "it would honor the most distinguished man of letters." But "infinite patience" was needed to stay to the end of the "bizarre" *Dumourier,* with its "gunfire" and "senseless comings and goings." "It is beneath serious examination" (*Petites affiches de Ducray-Duminil,* 25 January 1793, 346). Obviously, Candeille's clever but traditional comedy about female rivalry and a lovelorn lady disguised as a farm woman conformed to expectations of what a woman's play should be about. These, on the contrary, were seriously violated by de Gouges's military maneuvers and women warriors.

Context also includes considering the male-defined conventions and ideological presuppositions of late eighteenth-century theatrical genres in order to understand why a woman and a feminist might reproduce conventional "morality" and the extent to which she could challenge it. De Gouges's plays must be read in conjunction with the contemporary production of male and female dramatists. Are hers more stereotypical than, for example, Mercier's and Candeille's? Is her convent play more insipid than others on this burning topic? Are her plays representing revolutionary events, such as *Dumourier,* more "bizarre" than the hundreds of rapidly written plays on occasional themes? It is true that she composed very quickly, fired by inspiration, and dictated to secretaries—but this was a common practice at the time. She claimed—and attempted to disarm criticism—that her inspiration came from nature and owed nothing to study. If de Gouges lacked a formal education, she was not illiterate, as is commonly alleged.[14] Moreover, she was an avid theater goer and had a keen dramatic sense. Despite formal and stylistic flaws, her plays are lively and provocative. Rather than dwell on their weaknesses, many of which are common to drama of the period (sentimentality, pathos, improbable recognitions, and catastrophes [Gaiffe 287-332]), and some perhaps inherent to theater of commitment, my approach will focus on their strengths and originality. I contend that rather than examples of causes "lost," her plays can be considered representative and also prophetic: Representative of the conflict of values that might account for the short-term failure of feminism and other causes, but prophetic of causes that would eventually be won—abolition of slavery, rights of illegitimate children, divorce, women's suffrage. Or causes that will be won by women and other oppressed groups in the not-too-distant future—sexual equality and political power.[15]

✤ ✤ ✤

Several recent studies suggest ways to reconsider the long neglected dramatic genres and the significance of marginalized groups. In his analysis of theoretical works on bourgeois drama, Scott Bryson highlights the coercive and normative function of the new genre as it emerged to provide a replacement for the collapsing hierarchical order of absolutism. This interesting Foucauldian thesis invites a further reassessment of a very large corpus, with a focus on the way these norms were embodied in situations, characters, and plots in plays written by both men and women.[16] According to Bryson, bourgeois drama transforms "the theater into a moral universe in which virtue is shown to reign triumphant" (4); Diderot shows the way by staging (in *Le Fils naturel*) the passage of one form of authoritarian control—paternal and external—to another, based on self-censureship, inner coherency, and identity" (17); Mercier constantly refers to the playwright as "legislator" (49). If, as was commonly held, women's nature and virtue are so different from men's, what "legislative" authority could a female playwright claim to institute? What roles does the interiorized paternal model reserve for female characters in this glorification of private virtue and domestic life? How are these reproduced in plays by women?

Revisionist reassessments of the roles assigned to women and played by women in the revolutionary drama can shed light on the presuppositions and paradoxes in dramatic representation. Though divergent in their approach, Joan Landes, Dorinda Outram, and Geneviève Fraisse have shown that revolutionary ideology, proclaiming the moral superiority of the Republic, linked Old Regime corruption with the excessive influence of women. It was constituted on the exclusion of women from the public sphere, which accelerated at the end of 1792. Outram argues that the equation of female virtue with chastity and confinement was the prerequisite for the definition of political virtue, expressed in male terms and embodied in representations of Roman republican heroes (1987, 125). Political women could not arrogate for themselves and their cause the validating power of virtue, as long as they left unchallenged the equation of sexuality with political corruption. Outram cites Olympe de Gouges's condemnation of prostitution and women's "nocturnal administration" (in the *Déclaration*) as an example of this confusion (132-33).

De Gouges did warn that the success of the Revolution depended on the regeneration of civic virtue, but did not equate this with narrow moralism. She proclaimed, moreover, that this regeneration could only be achieved by the active *participation* of women in the political sphere, not their exclusion. Centuries of repression had forced women to resort to wiles and charms to gain some power; participation would allow them to "elevate" their souls by becoming useful. Joan Scott points out that de Gouges lays the blame for women's corrupting influence not on natural difference, but on faulty institutions; female sexuality given a proper outlet might secure, not destabilize the social order (1989, 12). Scott analyzes the *Déclaration* as supplement, which adds to and supplements the 1789 *Declaration of the Rights of Man*."The 'undecidable' aspect of the 'logic of the supplement' gives de Gouges's work both its ambiguity and its critical force" (8). The ambiguities center around the use of the concept of "Nature" and women's nature: "In order to claim the general status of 'human' for women, she insisted on their particular qualifications; in the process of insisting on equality, she constantly pointed out and acknowledged difference" (9). Her formulations could be read as an endorsement of disfunctional complementarity based on sex, but also as an attempt to dissolve or transcend the categories of sexual difference (12). De Gouges refused the differentiation of bodies into fixed binary categories. In her view, the confusion of roles in nature is anarchic, not binary. This allowed her to posit that "rights were embodied and universal at the same time and this conception required not denying the existence of physical differences, but recognizing them as at once essential and irrelevant to the meaning of equality" (14). Scott concludes that the ambiguities and paradoxes in de Gouges's use of the concept of "Nature" prefigure the paradoxes of subsequent feminisms, and are the "effect of the exclusions and contradictions of the political theory within and against which it was articulated" (18).

Similar ideological tensions traverse Olympe de Gouges's plays. These created contradictions, formal and thematic, that exasperated her contemporaries perhaps because they challenged the coercive force of bourgeois drama and revolutionary propaganda on stage. In this limited space I will concentrate on the "plotted" plays, which can be read in the light of literary conventions that persisted well beyond 1789, leaving aside the revolutionary revues and the purely political circumstances that occasioned them. My remarks center around the questions of authority, nature, and virtue and examine their dramatic embodiment in male/female, oppressor/ oppressed relationships.

Female characters are assigned to a rather limited repertory of roles in typical eighteenth-century comedies and dramas[17]: young girls, sprightly or touching; older women, either ineffectual mother figures or ridiculous obstacles[18]; servants, clever and critical of their mistresses in comedy, virtuous and moralizing in drama, where they often turn out to be of noble birth and thus worthy of their young master's love. Plots often revolve around the fate of a young female, but she does not often occupy center stage because her fate depends on the actions of male characters. In tragedy and drama—if she is not saved at the last moment—she succumbs to the prejudices of a tyrannical father (Voltaire's *Zaire* [1732], La Harpe's *Mélanie* [1770]) or sacrifices herself to save her father (Mme de Graffigny's *La Fille d'Aristide,* 1750) or lover (Monvel's *Victimes cloîtrées,* 1791). In comedy, she waits for the domestic tyrant's defeat, or if she is clever (like

Rosine in Beaumarchais's *Barbier de Seville,* 1775) she cooperates with her scheming lover and his valet. Older women are more often rivals than confidantes, fighting over some attractive chevalier. In women's plays female characters tend to play the starring roles but rivalry remains an important theme, as in Beauharnais's *Fausse inconstance* and Candeille's *Belle fermière.*When women emphasize female solidarity, which is frequent, generally an older mother figure aids a young girl in accepting her seemingly unavoidable fate. In one of the most successful dramas written by a woman, Graffigny's *Cénie* (1750), the heroine is admonished by her devoted governess (who turns out to be her victimized mother) to retire to a convent rather than risk scandal by fighting for her happiness.

In revolutionary theater women often figure in groups but are not shown playing an active role in revolutionary events. Politically active women appear deviant; women's heroism derives from their role in "nature"—they bear sons for the nation and teach them patriotism. The only real heroic female figure in republican theater is the mother (Craczyk 251-54). Women playwrights seem to have internalized the message, though not without struggle. For example, the principal characters in Citoyenne Villiers's *Barra ou la mère républicaine* (1793) are two widows and their children, yet in this thoroughly feminine sphere the heroine, whose twelve-year-old son has just been killed in battle, is ready to offer her other children as canon-fodder for the fatherland.

Several features distinguish Olympe de Gouges's comedies and dramas. The young woman plays a more active role and attempts to fashion her own destiny. Female rivalry is virtually nonexistent. Mature women, quite numerous, serve as protectresses and role models for the younger ones, and encourage their emancipation. Moreover, the young woman's fate and the obstacle she faces—abusive domestic authority or institutions—are linked to another social injustice denounced by the play. Rather than the sacrifice of a solitary victim, the play stages the solidarity of oppressed groups against the masters and the oppressive institutions. Indeed, de Gouges's casts include crowds of common people, slaves, peasants, nuns, simple soldiers, and guards won over by their destitute prisoners. Several of these play roles of such importance that they rival the socially superior characters and even surpass them in heroism. Glorifying the virtue of the common man would become a frequent theme in revolutionary theater, but de Gouges anticipates it by several years. In one of her first plays, *L'Homme généreux,* the generous act of La Fleur, a simple recruiting sergeant, is compared so favorably with the generosity of the Count who pays the debts of an indigent old man, that we wonder which of them is designated by the title. In her last play, the French spy Tape-à-l'Oeil, who escapes the gallows twice and has the treacherous Austrian chaplain hung in his place, performs exploits that seem as remarquable as the victories of that "second Mars," General Dumouriez. Common women are also capable of great physical courage. In *La Bienfaisance récompensée,* a servant girl risks her life to save three men from drowning and her deed is compared with a heroic action of the Duc d'Orléans himself. What evolves in de Gouges's theater are the progressively more active, more public roles women play in the sweep of history. Yet tears and swooning, the expression of women's "natural" frailty and excessive sensibility so prominent in bourgeois drama, do not disappear.

The basic patterns are already in place in de Gouges's first play, set in the French West Indies. Two dramatic threads interweave the fate of black slaves and the fate of women. Zamor, the Governer's favorite slave, must flee with his mistress Mirza for killing (in self-defense) the intendant who was "tyranizing" her after she rejected his advances. De Gouges was attacked violently for making the murderer of a white man into a hero and for having him pardoned at the end of the play. For the threat of a slave revolt that runs through the action, the play was condemned as incendiary. (Indeed, the actors refused to wear black make-up and transposed the scene to India.) Zamor expresses the controversial message in the opening scene, in answer to Mirza's question: "Why do the Europeans have such an advantage over us, poor slaves. . . . We are humans as they are: why is there such a difference between their race and ours? (1989, 44). Zamor reduces all natural difference to color alone. Art and education gave Whites superiority and power to treat Blacks like animals. He denounces the violent Europeans who "ravish" Blacks, suggesting a parallel with Mirza's ravisher. Zamor makes analogies between racial and sexual tyranny, which de Gouges develops in her manifestoes[19]: Education gives the masters power, brutalization makes the victims mindless and passive.

The flight of the slaves is paralleled by the long sea voyage undertaken by the illegitimate Sophie, who, unlike her more passive counterparts in bourgeois drama, courageously sets out for the New World, accompanied by her husband, in search of the father who abandoned her long ago.

Zamor saves Sophie from drowning in a shipwreck, but this delay causes him and Mirza to be recaptured. True to dramatic conventions, Sophie's father will turn out to be the Governor, Saint-Fremont, who must execute Zamor whom he has raised like a son. But Zamor's generous action reveals his humanity, which is as noble as the vengeance of the judge is base, and wins him the support of the white women and the slaves. All of them implore the Governor to pardon the slayer of a white man. When Sophie, another victim of unjust laws and a father's neglect, falls at the Governor's feet he recognizes his daughter. He yields to the "call of blood," to her tears and her plea: "Grant nature the first grace she asks of you" (1989, 120). Her words recall Zamor's prayer in the first act: "God, soften our tyrants' hearts' and give back to man the rights he lost in the very bosom of nature" (46). Torn between his inclination and his duty to maintain the privileges of the colonists, the Governor pardons Zamor, but invokes *grâce* rather than natural rights, although those rights are discussed by the other characters. In 1784 it was difficult to justify the denouement by an appeal to rights that had not yet been officially recognized—the Convention legislated equal rights for illegitimate children on 2 November 1793, the eve of de Gouges's execution, and abolished slavery on 4 February 1794.[20]

Sophie's appeal to sentiment, however typical of bourgeois drama, signals a number of contradictions that become more obvious in de Gouges's plays because she accentuates the oppositional term. The disadvantaged, the women or the socially inferior, are the ones who enlighten the authority figure, sometimes with the help of a man who has freed himself from prejudice. Although this pattern is not unusual, it is inflected in two ways in her plays. On the one hand—and this is in keeping with de Gouges's humanism—the authority figure's vulnerability is underlined in an effort to understand his mistake; the Governor's own victimization by the laws of primogeniture (he is the youngest of seven children) explains his abandonment of Sophie and her mother, but this brings him closer to Zamor and his involuntary crime.[21] And yet, the father is not rejected but rather reformed, perhaps in the image of the ideal father and the ideal monarch whom de Gouges so desired. On the other hand, this bastard daughter stresses the solidarity and courage of the oppressed, especially the women so often separated by rivalry in dramatic tradition; Mme de Saint-Fremont has a relationship of mutual trust with her female slaves and protects Sophie although the young woman's arrival could constitute a threat. In the first version, de Gouges accentuates the women's alliance by introducing "Bébé," Sophie's three-year-old daughter, who is also miraculously saved from drowning and is immediately adopted by Mme de Saint-Fremont. She eliminates this novelistic complication in 1792 but shows Mme de Saint-Frémont's fear that her husband might leave her to return to Sophie's mother and then her rejection of revenge. The two women shield the slaves from the executioners' bullets with their own bodies. Yet their courage and their lesson are useless without the Governor's sanction. In the end, rather than outright emancipation, the play advocates enlightened paternalism: The Governor would like to free Zamor and Mirza in anticipation of the law, but they themselves define happiness as living with so virtuous a master. Accused of fomenting the 1791 slave revolt in Haïti with her play, de Gouges could only reaffirm this moderate solution in 1792.

These distinguishing features can be seen in *L'Homme généreux*, which treats a subject similar to Mercier's *L'Indigent* (1772), imprisonment for debt. Again, it is a real injustice that inspired de Gouges, the ruin of the poor Clamet family in Rouen caused by the father's imprisonment. She vowed to donate her royalties to repay his debts, and invited her readers to contribute to this worthy cause (1788, 1: 1-7).[22] In both plays a destitute brother and sister toil to release their father (Mercier) or prevent his arrest (de Gouges); playing on their sentiments, a rich libertine and his vile agent attempt to corrupt the brother and debauch the sister, who vigorously defends her honor. However daring in their representation of the indigent, the plots are fraught with improbabilities. Mercier's turns on a staple of drama, mistaken identity. The freed father and an upright notary reveal that Charlotte is not Joseph's sister, but the libertine's. The libertine must share his fortune with her and amend his ways, while the two estwhile siblings can unite in virtuous marriage.

De Gouges's improbabilities are less novelistic and her changes underline her revision of the theme. There are no mistaken identities but mistakes in judgment—primarily made by the hero whom the women set straight. The libertine, Flaucourt, does not appear on stage. It is occupied instead by his friend, a virtuous Count secretly in love with the poor Marianne. The count is deceived by the vile La Fontaine into believing that the girl and his own secretary—Marianne's brother—are illicit lovers. The father is saved from La Fontaine's clutches, thanks to La Fleur's and the Count's generosity but the real denouement is reached when the Count is disabused. Rather than a man of the law, de Gouges introduces a woman to perform the task: herself a victim, the illegitimate sister of Flaucourt, Mme de Valmont,[23] protects Marianne, proves her virtue to the Count, and helps him overcome the "prejudice" preventing him from marrying the daughter of a ruined bourgeois. In contrast with the frail Charlotte's utter isolation in a world of men, de Gouges creates a community of women. Marianne also cares for her sick mother offstage and protects a young apprentice, who in turn helps save her mistress from rape by La Fontaine.

The theme of female solidarity in the face of male mispersuasion becomes central in de Gouges's next play, *Le Philosophe corrigé, ou le cocu supposé*. Its title recalls *Le Philosophe sans le savoir* and its protagonists, the Marquis and the Marquise of Clainville, have the same name as Sedaine's main characters in *La Gageure imprévue* (1768). Indeed, in her excellent five-act comedy, she seems to rewrite the messages of Sedaine's very influential plays[24] as well as refute the age-old theme of women's inability to unite. Unlike Sedaine's clever Marquise who is caught in the trap she set for her husband, de Gouges's timid Mme de Clainville ends up "correcting" the false ideas of her impassive "philosophe" of a husband thanks to the assistance of her enterprising friends. Unlike the female utopia destroyed by class quarrels in Marivaux's *Colonie,* her characters—the widowed Countess, the bourgeoise Mme Pinçon, and the peasant girl Babet—maintain their league and their objective. This is a more consciously feminist project than the women's association in *Le Mariage de Figaro*. They unite to restore the rights and reputation of the Marquise, falsely accused of adultery, and teach a lesson to the men. These include the Marquis, his uncle the Commander incarnating male prerogative, a fatuous Baron, M. Pinçon, who dares to denigrate women in front of his redoubtable wife, and even the gardener Blaise who is convinced that the troubles are due to the fact that the Marquise's baby is a girl when all expected a boy. The women imagine an unlikely but dangerous stratagem: The Marquise wins back her husband's heart by disguising as a mysterious masked lady with whom he falls madly in love. The consequences, however, are quite unequal since power and the law are on the side of the husband. In becoming pregnant the Marquise risks being put away forever in a convent, even though the Marquis is the one who committed adultery, at least in intention. Before the mounting rage of the "philosopher" who even threatens the baby—until, hearing the "call of blood," he melts into tears—the Marquise is tempted to fall at his feet and confess the ruse. But her colleagues want to see the experiment to the end. Mme Pinçon pronounces the women's philosophy with such vigor that M. Pinçon retreats before these ladies' "authorship." Not only are women capable of joining forces and keeping secrets, but with education, which men so unjustly deny them, they could become intellectual and even military heroes (OCT 1993c, 119). Mme Pinçon's courage brings about the dénouement. Disguised as the Marquise's lover, she provokes the Marquis to attack her so unphilosophically that he discovers the errors of his system and the injustice of his behavior. But she does not fail to remind him that his conjugal and paternal bliss are due to the actions of several resourceful women. (141).

However provocative, Olympe de Gouges's revisionary *Philosophe* does not yet fully challenge the double standard. While the superficial importance attached to women's honor is ridiculed, the Marquise triumphs because she does remain a faithful spouse. The Marquis's infidelity with the "masked lady" is not forcefully condemned nor is his wife's right to seek happiness with another asserted. The representation of an adulteress was, of course, still taboo on stage. These factors highlight the originality of de Gouges's next play, *Molière chez Ninon, ou le siècle des grands hommes,* written a few months after Mercier's *Maison de Molière*.[25] De Gouges's Molière, however, is not the hero but only the confidant of the famous courtesan. Ninon de Lenclos is at the center of this rather untidy, twenty-nine-character "episodic" play that represents the best-known events of her colorful life. Although Enlightenment *philosophes* had already glorified this extraordinary woman who had freed herself from "prejudice" and made herself into an *honnête homme,* they were uneasy about her legendary promiscuity well into old age. When Voltaire first brought her to the stage in his society comedy *Le Dépositaire* (1769), he dramatized the famous example demonstrating her probity and friendship but stripped her of all dangerous sexuality. At forty, his Ninon is nearing the "winter of her life" and only desires to educate young men philosophically. On the contrary, de Gouges's Ninon is forty-five but still seductive, and she changes lovers in the course of the action. The cast also includes her illustrious male and female friends and past, present and future lovers. Ninon's love scenes alternate with her philosophical conversations and acts of generosity; but, we also see the scandal of her life when an exempt announces the Queen

Mother's order (later reversed) to have the courtesan locked up with the *Filles repenties* (Repentant Whores).

De Gouges overturns the legend that tarnished masculine versions of the mythic Ninon (Verdier 110, 136), the story of the adolescent who falls madly in love with the middle-aged courtesan and kills himself when he finds out she is his mother. For the *femme fatale,* de Gouges substitutes the good mother. Her Ninon protects a young girl—named Olympe!—against a tyrannical father, the Marquis of Châteauroux, who opposes her love for a young man of unknown origin. This young man will of course turn out to be Ninon's son by Marshal Coligny, who took the child away from her because of her reputation. Instead of seducing her son, Ninon ensures the happiness of two children; when she reveals that she is the boy's mother, Châteauroux agrees to marry his daughter to the son of the "respectable Mademoiselle de Lenclos." Ninon's avowal remains private,[26] yet in order to save her son from the prejudice of illegitimacy, she courageously retires into a convent. The "good mother" who sacrifices herself for her children had become, in the wake of Rousseau, an ideal which de Gouges accepted in part at least. But before the curtain falls, Molière predicts her speedy return to their enlightened society. Ninon's retreat thus represents a momentary concession to prejudice, and not lifetime expiation of guilt. The double standard denounced by the play is social, moral, and psychological; while Ninon agonizes over the fate of her children, two of her former lovers casually settle a paternity dispute with a throw of the dice. De Gouges challenges moral conventions by imagining a controversial woman who manages to combine nurturing motherhood, sexual satisfaction, and intellectual and charitable activity in the world. As a dramatic role, her heroine defies all traditional classifications. De Gouges was quite aware of the audacity of her creation. In the paratexts recounting how badly the Comédie received the play, she proclaims, in the face of all detractors, that she is "proud to be the mother" of "her lovable Ninon." By the multiple facets of her character, her Ninon will "have a good effect on all women since they share her weaknesses and can aspire to her virtues" (1788, 3: 206).[27]

Despite increased emphasis on chastity as synonymous with female virtue after the outbreak of the Revolution, de Gouges dared to bring Ninon back on stage in a patriotic production glorifying the constitutional monarchy (in 1791 still the favored form of government). Mirabeau's sudden death (2 April 1791) inspired her to write a four-act play, which was reduced to a one-act political revue when it was performed by the Italians under the title *Mirabeau aux Champs Elysées*. Mirabeau is welcomed by great figures of history, including kings (Henri IV & Louis XIV), *philosophes* (Montesquieu, Voltaire, Rousseau), statesmen (Solon, Cardinal d'Amboise, and Benjamin Franklin), and a popular young hero of the Revolution (Desilles). Several plays represented apotheoses set in Elysium, including another celebration of Mirabeau, the anonymous *L'Ombre de Mirabeau* (performed 7 May 1791). De Gouges's version is original for the political discussion she stages (which is not devoid of humor), the direction the play seeks to give to the Revolution, and the inclusion of women. In the last scene, Destiny announces that the spirits of a wise legislator and an honest minister, Solon and Cardinal d'Amboise, will be reincarnated in political figures (de Gouges probably believed in the transmigration of souls, as did many Freemasons), who will continue Mirabeau's moderate leadership of the Revolution.[28] More importantly, she introduces three great ladies of the Old Regime among the blessed shades—two illustrious women of letters of unblemished reputation, Mme de Sévigné and Mme Deshoulières, and their contemporary, Ninon de Lenclos. In the Elysian Fields, "the only place women have equal rights" (TP 1991, 125), these women celebrate Mirabeau's plan for national education, which includes the education of women. In terms that anticipate the *Déclaration,* the courtesan leads her sisters in proclaiming that the success of the Revolution depends on "elevating" women by letting them exercise political responsibility. It is not the "nocturnal administration" of Old Regime mistresses nor the chastity glorified in Republican rhetoric, but, Ninon asserts, women's active "contribution" to the Revolution that constitutes their "true glory" (126).

The indispensable "elevation" of women and other oppressed groups, who as de Gouges maintained, were not "naturally" inferior, depended on the reform of unnatural institutions. After 1789 such reforms became possible and are the central themes of her political plays. But, as Ninon warned and de Gouges lamented in her prefaces, centuries of oppression instilled in women a slave mentality which made them hate and envy each other. Women are "their own worst enemies"; whenever one dares to break out of "her sphere" to defend women's rights, she incurs the wrath of her own sex (TP 1991, 125). Culturally induced self-hatred, not sexual excess, is women's greatest weakness. Female abjection is caused by, but also invites, male tyranny. While representing ideal solidarity among Lenclos, Sévigné, and Deshoulières (who were not always the best of friends[29]) and the support they received from enlightened men like Molière and Mirabeau, de Gouges was not blind to the moral and psychological difficulties women had to overcome and men had to recognize.[30] In the political plays, the possibility of emancipation intensifies women's interior struggle.

Le Couvent ou les vœux forcés and *La Nécessité du divorce,* both written in 1790, attack the two institutions that seal women's fate but also entrap their masters in vice: forced religious vocations and indissoluble marriage vows. Again, de Gouges was among the first to represent these controversial issues directly and show characters wearing religious habits.[31] The Constituent Assembly abolished religious orders on 13 February 1790. Later the same year it debated allowing divorce, but a first divorce law was only passed by the Legislative Assembly in September 1792, and a more liberal one by the Convention in December 1793.[32] In the preface de Gouges states that she wrote *Le Couvent* while the Assembly was debating the religious question, and had proposed it to "Théâtre de Monsieur" in February 1790. But because they could not stage it soon, she offered it to the Palais Royal theater, which kept the play for two months without giving her an answer. Meanwhile, she gave another manuscript to the actor-playwright Monvel, who liked it very much—and who might have drawn inspiration from it for his immensely successful *Victimes cloîtrés,* performed in March 1791, after the January 1791 decree granting greater freedom in the theater. But, while de Gouges waited for an answer from the Palais Royal, a popular two-act comic opera, Fiévée and Breton's *Les Rigueurs du cloître,* was performed in August 1790. Her play was only staged in October after her son gave her manuscript without her consent to Labreu, director of the newly founded Théâtre Français, Comique et Lyrique, who interpolated comic scenes and attributed co-authorship to himself. By then her play, though successful, appeared to be an imitation rather than a daring creation (TP 1991, 35-36).

The authentic version, which de Gouges published in 1792, distinguishes *Le Couvent* (whose earlier titles, *La Révolution des couvents* and *L'Ecole du fanatisme* [Blanc 1989, 227]) are even more provocative) from other monastic plays. Similarities in the basic situations highlight de Gouges's departure from the pattern. Like her precursor, La Harpe, and her probable imitators, Fiévée and Monvel, she imagines a novice (Julie) who loves a young man (the Chevalier de Leuville); she is being forced to take religious vows by a parental figure (her uncle, the Marquis de Leuville) who wants her out of the way and she almost consents in order to save her lover. An enlightened priest and, after 1789, representatives of the law, intervene to prevent the sacrifice. Unlike La Harpe's Mélanie, who commits suicide, de Gouges's Julie is saved, as are the heroines of Fiévée's vaudeville and Monvel's dark melodrama. The latter two also feature the triumphant lover and representatives of the law. In the men's plays, however, the lover and the national guard are the determining forces that rescue the passive young heroine from the persecution of abbesses and monks whose villany is accentuated.[33]

De Gouges's play does not feature such stark manichean contrasts between vice and virtue. Her hypocritical grand-vicar and her abbess are not monsters of perversity, but opportunists who cling to the prerogatives that give them power. More important, however, de Gouges creates a character who does not appear in the other plays but who accentuates social injustice, the plight of the female victim of patriarchal authority. True to the patterns already observed in her theater, Julie is protected by an older nun, Sœur Angélique, forced into the convent by her own brother, who disapproved of her marriage and killed her husband. The Marquis de Leuville increases Angelique's suffering by forbidding her to reveal to Julie that she is her mother. While waiting for her play to be staged, de Gouges added a third act that intensifies the anguish of both mother and daughter. With Angélique sequestered, the abbess, the vicar, and the Marquis very nearly succeed in convincing Julie that only her self-sacrifice can save the Chevalier from the wrath of his father. Although the *curé,* the lover, and even a commissioner of the National Guard arrive on time to interrupt the ceremony, so pressured is Julie that she continues to utter her vows "voluntarily," until Angélique bursts on the scene to reveal the abuse both she and her daughter have suffered. Again, one woman's courage saves another and enlightens the oppressors,[34] but at a price. For even though the lovers are united and Marquis and the abbess reformed, Angélique, who has made her solemn vows, remains in the convent.

Olympe de Gouges's 1790 play advocating divorce two years before the first divorce law was passed, was certainly the first in a series on the question which included at least five other plays written between 1792 and 1801.[35] Enough external and internal evidence suggests that the recently discovered manuscript was indeed written by her.[36] Like *Le Couvent, Le Divorce* features debates between enlightened characters and ones who defend oppressive Old Regime institutions for their own advantage. The confirmed bachelor Rosambert opposes the indissolubility of marriage on three grounds: moral, social, and historical. He argues that its "chains," by nature repugnant to human liberty, are a rather recent church invention that only fosters marital misery, loose morals, and the disintegration of families. On the other hand, the hypocritical abbé Basilic, who profits from conjugal discord by playing wife against husband, defends the sanctity of the sacrament (OCT 1993c, 231). At stake is the fate of two couples, the unhappily married d'Azinvals and Rosambert's nephew, Germeuil, in love with d'Azinval's sister, Constance. The action illustrates the pernicious effects of marital enslavement. Though they loved each other at first, d'Azinval is inconstant because he remains unhappily married to his wife, while she exacerbates the situation and her own suffering by her resentment. Their unhappiness causes Constance to distrust Germeuil. Again, de Gouges adds an unexpected character who accentuates the suffering unnatural institutions cause the weaker party. D'Azinval's mistress, Herminie, turns out to be a respectable young woman who sincerely believed he was unattached. Mme d'Azinval overcomes her jealousy and invites Herminie to her home, while d'Azinval is lured by Rosambert into witnessing their confrontation. Rising above petty rivalry, the two deceived women express esteem and friendship for each other. Yet Herminie retires with nothing but a broken heart and Mme d'Azinval remains with a husband who hates her (III, 5). The married couple's change of heart comes about when Rosambert announces that the Assembly has legalized divorce. Now that they are free to separate, the d'Azinvals realize that they still love each other. Although Rosambert's announcement in 1790 is still just a ruse, the prospect of a law allowing couples to separate or to choose to remain together sways the old bachelor to consent to his nephew's marriage with Constance. He has proven that rather than encourage dissipation, freedom strengthens families and the social fabric. De Gouges illustrates other negative effects of the indissolubility of marriage in the characters who could so easily have been mere comic foils. It encourages male deception and the victimization of other Herminies, but also takes its toll on the bachelor, who reveals in a poignant speech describing the joy of a friend surrounded by a loving wife and children, that he paid a high price for his freedom, utter solitude (233-34).[37]

For today's audience the message of the play may seem conservative and sentimental. But all the divorce plays of the period, when they did not oppose the law, argued that it would serve to strengthen marriages. De Gouges's play stands out by its serious treatment of this complex issue. By contrast, in a vaudeville such as Desfontaines's *Le Divorce* (1793), a young wife sings and dances about divorcing (with such unforgettable couplets as, "En mariage l'ennui nait de l'esclavage" ["In marriage slavery breeds boredom"]), flirts with a shady abbé, but is returned to her senses by her fifty-year-old husband ("La Raison vient nous éclairer" ["Reason returns to enlighten us"]) and the sight of their seventeen-month old daughter, who is brought in from the country by the wet-nurse and literally tossed back and forth on stage. In Pigault-Lebrun's *Les Mœurs ou le divorce* (1794), divorce is never really discussed, it is just used as a ploy, along with a fake rival, to bring a wayward husband back to his wife.

De Gouges's last play, the "bizarre" *L'Entrée de Dumourier à Bruxelles ou les Vivandiers* whose performance caused such an uproar, presents even greater contrasts with occasional plays on similar themes. France's declaration of war against the European monarchies opposing the Revolution and the advance of the Austro-Prussia troops toward the French borders in Spring and Summer 1792 spurred a rash of patriotic plays extolling the victories of the revolutionary army over the foreign aggressor.[38] Joigny's popular *Siège de Lille ou Cécile et Julien,* a three-act musical comedy played by the Opéra-Comique on 21 November 1792 (three days before the original date set for the performance of *Dumourier*) seems fairly representative of the *fait historique* genre. Featuring patriotic songs, spectacular stage effects, masses of patriots, and ridiculous characters who have remained faithful to "aristocratic" values, it is still a domestic comedy, but in a war setting. As the Austrians lay siege to Lille, Julien, inspired by love of country and love of Cécile, performs heroic deeds that save the city and win him the girl. When Austrian bombs set fire to the city, Julien rescues the swooning Cécile from her burning house (Act II). While her old suitor with aristocratic pretentions defects to the enemy, Julien, taken prisoner, gives lessons in liberty, equality, and fraternity to the Austrian general. He then escapes and saves his compatriots, with the help of an *émigré* converted to the revolutionary cause (Act III). Although Cécile too expresses patriotic sentiments, her role consists in filial piety and charming conversation.

As the foreign menace increased, women joined the army as soldiers rather than mere camp followers. When a 30 April 1793 law prohibited female military service except as laundresses and *vivandières,* some continued to volunteer in male disguise. A number of plays were written about women soldiers, showing what curiosity this phenomenon aroused (Harten 48-50). Understandably, it seemed particularly appealing to women playwrights. In Citoyenne Desmoulins's *Héroine républicaine* (one-act musical comedy, 1794), Zelime, a commoner who joined the army and was rewarded for bravery, combines courage and beauty, and thus inspires respect as well as love in Valcour, whose parents want him to marry a rich girl. The plot hinges on getting Valcour's parents to accept Zelime, which they do after the General persuades them that in fighting together for the honor of the nation, the young warriors will both win glory. The play ends with a marriage ceremony. But, Zelime does not leave the battlefront, and sings, to the tune of "La Marseillaise": "Vive, vive le son / De l'aimable canon. / L'Amour ne peut jamais / Egaler ses attraits" ("Long live the pleasing sound of the canon. Love can never match its charms"). Desfontaines's one-act "fait historique et vaudeville," *La Fille soldat* (1794), is more typical of a general pattern, however. Julie, alias Victor, fought bravely for the Republic—before the curtain rises—but her disguise is penetrated by her sergeant, Julien, although not by village girls who are also in love with him/her. The action consists in persuading "Victor" to heed the call of "nature": s/he acknowledges her feelings for Julien, resumes her feminine garb and goes home to take care of her sick father. The play ends with the theme song: "Fille soldat / Doit à l'état / Des Marmots / Gentille milice" ("Soldier girl owes the state a nice militia of little kids").

Like Citoyenne Desmoulins, Olympe de Gouges expresses a "naive" utopian enthusiasm for women warriors (Harten 62), although in late 1792, before the 1793 law banning women from the army, her optimism was perhaps more understandable. Despite her pacifism, she was an ardent patriot, won over to the Republican cause after 10 August 1792 (even if she offered to defend Louis XVI, arguing prophetically that martyred kings live forever and that regicide would lead to a general bloodbath). And she realized that women's "usefulness" to the nation might best be demonstrated in war, perhaps the only language men really understand. *Dumourier* differs from the plays discussed above by its ambitious, almost epic scope. Set in Brussels (Acts I & V), in the Austrian and French camps (Act II) and in outlying battlefields (Acts III & IV), it includes a huge cast of characters (twenty-six speaking roles and two armies) and a more complex interaction of dramatic situations that represent conflicting loyalties: Austrian princes and generals; Dumouriez and his aides; treacherous Belgian monks collabo--rating with Gribourdin, the Austrian chaplain; Brussels municipal councilors and common citizens struggling over their allegiance; Clerfayt, son of the Austrian general, who defects to the French; Charlot, a French sutler working for the Austrians but in sympathy with his revolutionary compatriots; and six energetic women: Charlot's German wife, their daughter Charlotte, Mme Lafeuillette, wife of a drunken Belgian wine merchant, the peasant girl Suzette, and the famous Fernig sisters who fought in Dumouriez's army. Clearly de Gouges wanted to represent the major forces—religious, political, military, social, and sexual—that decided the fate of Belgium and would determine the international spread of the Revolution. A reviewer described the play as "à la Shakespeare"[39]; by its epic sweep and mixture of genres it also anticipates Romantic drama, though it differs radically in the representation of the women, who are far from doomed Romantic heroines. I would call it "proto-Brechtian."

True to revolutionary ideology, de Gouges's common people, the *vivandiers* and others, equal Dumouriez in courage, as the title indicates. Like other playwrights, she represents honest but initially misguided characters who join the Revolution. But the exuberant and often comic succession of political debates, combats, meals (Charlot manages to feed both the Austrian and the French armies), sexual encounters (Gribourdin attempts to rape Mme Charlot), and love scenes (between Clerfayt and Charlotte) might indeed have seemed confusing, if badly performed, as it was in 1793. Despite some vagueness in the fourth act, de Gouges's elaborate stage directions indicate that she visualized a complicated but coherent spectacle. What might have irritated her audience most, however, is the role she gives her female characters, which contests the place assigned to them in revolutionary ideology and constitutes a sort of "distanciation." They are not presented as curiosities, but as models for women.

With the exception of the Fernig sisters,[40] the women imagined by de Gouges evolve from (more or less) submissive wives and daughters into intrepid warriors and political leaders. Moreover, they triumph in combat and in political debate on stage. Charlotte follows Clerfayt into the French camp, but after dressing like a man and meeting the Fernigs, she can declare: "I followed my lover only to fight alongside the two Freling [*sic*] warriors, and to imitate them" (TP 1991, 204). Charlot hides his sympathies from his wife because "a woman's tongue makes as much noise as a canon" (173), but she shares them and secretly assists him in causing the mass desertion of Austrian troups. When the Charlots are imprisoned for treason, Mme Charlot's tears win her release; no sooner released, she abandons supplication and addresses the Belgians assembled on the main square of Brussels, exhorting them to open the city gates to the revolutionaries. As the Austrian archduke orders her arrest, she challenges him with superb arrogance:

> Tiger, your efforts are powerless, I defy you, you can do nothing, your reign is over. It is time for the reign of the people, your sovereign, to begin. Yes, my husband spread insurrection in your army, I declare it to you and take glory in it; and I fostered in the minds of my fellow citizens the germ of liberty that long fermented in their hearts. (OCT 1993c, 323; inadvertently omitted in TP 1991)

The women convince the city officials to join the people in overthrowing the tyrant. The Fernig sisters, who have no romantic attachments, accompany Dumouriez at the head of his army, kill five Austrians, and win battles on stage. Their role is a moral one as well, emulated by the other women: At the General's side when the French army enters Brussels, the Fernigs, joined by Carlotte, address their Belgian sisters.

> Imitate us; let us do more today than the men; let us fight to defend their rights, and at the same time avenge our sex of a tyrannical prejudice. Let us force the pride, the arrogance of these haughty men to render hommage to our valor, and let them learn at last that women are able to die by their side for the common cause of the country and the destruction of tyrants. (TP 1991, 240)

Dumouriez seconds their words, consecrates the women in their new role and, in the name of all men, sets a truly universal course for the Revolution.

> Women, you have just heard it. The sages of Athens and Rome would have seen in these two young women, two valiant warriors; the men of

the French Republic will be no less equitable toward your sex in a natural revolution that must extend to everyone, without distinction (241).

Though the play ends with sentimental and patriotic ceremonies (Charlotte and Clerfayt are wed and all plant the tree of liberty, singing "La Marseillaise"), these speeches constitute the thematic climax.

It is true that this feminist utopian revolution is sanctioned by an idealized masculine authority figure. But, even today, it might be difficult to imagine female triumphs totally independent of male recognition, and women's solidarity remains a goal. For Olympe de Gouges, circumstances were particularly harsh. A few weeks after the play was performed and published (she did that immediately and addressed copies to the Convention and to newspapers), Dumouriez was defeated at Neerwinden and defected to the enemy. The Convention regarded women's participation in revolutionary events with increasing suspicion, and finally outlawed all women's political clubs and gatherings on 30 October 1793, four days before her execution.

Two hundred years after Olympe de Gouges's death, her literary legacy can at last be appreciated for her extraordinary courage and clairvoyance. While her plays adhere inevitably to some moral and dramatic conventions, when they are read in the context of other drama of the period, they reveal their profound originality. She stands out from other playwrights, both male and female, by her consistent choice of controversial subjects, before and after 1789, at a time when much of the stage was filled with entertaining froth. Her plays denounce social abuses, like Mercier's, but her preoccupation with issues that raise explicitly the problem of women's place within family, society, and state give them a dimension that is at the same time gendered and more universal. Anticipating later feminisms, she saw the similarities among various forms of oppression based on race, class, and sex. She was not content to advocate more galant treatment and better education as did many of her sisters, but claimed a public economic and political role for women.

De Gouges's ideological stance has important dramatic consequences. Her characters rarely fit into well-defined categories and binary oppositions, black and white, passive and powerful, contrary to the general trend toward melodrama in the late eighteenth century. If her women are more active and vocal in claiming their rights, her men are often also more nuanced because they are more sympathetic and vulnerable. The comparison of her plays with men's plays on similar themes reveals her strategy of revision. Although the male authority figure is not overthrown, he is displaced from center; he is corrected and must share moral authority with the strong independent women who invariably erupt on stage in her plays. Mme de Valmont, a double for the author, enlightens the "generous man" and the league of women "corrects" the "philosophe." In "le siècle des grands hommes" [the century of great men] Ninon outdoes Molière himself in moral courage. Three women enter Elysium and prophesy that the Revolution can only succeed if women are included. The Fernig sisters and even the fearful Charlotte take their place at the head of the revolutionary army with Dumouriez. These characters constitute the disturbing supplement, the excess that deranges the neat patterns and ideological presuppositions of the genres to which her plays belong. They can result in figures that defy all categories such as Ninon, or violate classical norms and rules of female conduct to such an extent that they create a new theater, as in *Dumourier*. Her female characters also manifest typically "feminine" traits; despite signs of physical frailty, however, the younger ones learn strength from mature maternal figures. Women's relationships in de Gouges's theater are characterized not by rivalry over men, so frequent in plays by men, but by moral emulation.

Traditionally, women playwrights emphasized female roles. But de Gouges seems to distinguish herself from her predecessors by refusing to accept victimization; inspired, perhaps, by the promise of change brought by the Revolution, she stresses the solidarity and the public triumph of women, and men's recognition of their success. This is the most important message that Olympe de Gouges, as dramatic "legislator" wanted to convey and to have her male and female audience internalize. Since even today this ideal has not yet been achieved, it could only strike Old Regime patriarchy and the "virtuous" all-male Republic as dangerous and demented.

Notes

1. She published them in February 1786 to refute allegations that she employed male ghost writers. (It was frequently charged that women's plays were written by their lovers; this was rumored about her contemporaries Fanny de Beauharnais and Julie Candeille.) The preface exposes the role played by Beaumarchais, to whom she had presented her

continuation of *Le Mariage de Figaro,* in sabotaging her efforts to bring her play to the stage. She recounts her struggles to have her plays performed in various prefaces and postfaces, as well as in a clever fifty-page pamphlet, *Les Comédiens démasqués, ou Madame de Gouges ruinée par la Comédie Française pour se faire jouer* (1789). De Gouges included *Chérubin* and five other plays in her three-volume *Œuvres* (1788).

Four editions of Olympe de Gouges's political texts and plays appeared in 1993, after this article was completed. For the reader's convenience, however, I refer whenever possible to the most recent editions, abbreviated as follows: political texts, *Ecrits politiques 1788-1791* (EP 1993) and *Ecrits politiques II 1792-1793* (EP II 1993), ed. Blanc; the post-1789 plays and prefaces and the 1786 *L'Homme généreux, Théâtre politique* (TP 1991) and *Théâtre politique II* (TP 1993), ed. Thiele-Knobloch; the pre-1789 plays and the plays in manuscript, *Œuvres complètes: Tome I Théâtre* (OCT 1993), ed. Castan. For the pre-1789 prefaces and other paratexts (not included in OCT but forthcoming in a volume IV), I refer to her *Œuvres* in three volumes (1788). All translations mine.

2. Mili calls for a reappraisal of revolutionary theater based on its strengths, its didactic, and utilitarian function (50).

3. My observations are based on a corpus of some fifty late eighteenth-century plays out of the 500 listed in Gaiffe's index (558-77), and the thousands written during the Revolution (Kennedy 1984, 49). Due to space considerations I do not include my corpus in Works Cited.

4. Eleven published plays, if we consider the quite different versions of her play on slavery: *Zamor et Mirza, ou l'heureux naufrage* (1788, III) and *L'Esclavage des noirs,* published in 1792. The prompter's manuscript (1789), entitled *L'Esclavage des nègres,* constitutes an intermediate version (Archives de la Comédie française). The attribution of another play is uncertain. *Le Prélat d'autrefois, ou Sophie de Saint-Elme,* by "Pompigny and Degouges," was performed and published in 1794 & 1795, after her death. Her son, Aubry de Gouges, might have passed his mother's manuscript to Pompigny. I shall not discuss *Le Prélat.*

5. The unfinished manuscript of *La France sauvée* is included in the Olympe de Gouges dossier at the Archives nationales. Another manuscript, *La Nécessité du divorce* (1790), was discovered at the Bibliothèque nationale by Gisela Thiele-Knobloch and myself, working independently. Although many of de Gouges's papers were destroyed, it is likely that she gave copies of plays to Mme de Montesson, herself a playwright. Mme de Montesson was the morganatic second wife of the Duc d'Orléans, father of Philippe d'Orléans, the future Philippe-Egalité, to whom de Gouges dedicated the first two volumes of her *Œuvres* and with whom she had a long and stormy association. Mme de Montesson's papers passed into the Soleinne collection, which was sold and dispersed in the 1840s.

6. See Olivier Blanc's bibliography (1989, 226-27). It is based on the document signed by Judge Thilly of the Revolutionary Tribunal and references de Gouges made to her plays

in her political texts. Five titles in the inventory may refer to her plays published under different titles and a few, perhaps, to works written by her friends.

7. Her name—either "Madame de Gouges" or "Olympe de Gouges"—appears on the title page of all her published plays, with the exception of *Les Démocrates*.

8. For discussions of revolutionary feminists' "noms de guerre," see Duhet 1972, 78 and Delon 1988, 283. For other discussions of de Gouges's name, Scott 1989, 8 and Blanc 1989, 25 and 1993.

9. Some favorable, or at least galant reviews of published plays appeared in: *Almanach des muses* 1787, 89, 92; *Journal littéraire de Nancy* 1785, 86; *Mercure de France* 3/4/86; *Journal général de France* 3/30/86; *Journal encyclopédique* 8/88; of the *Œuvres* in *Journal général de France* 3/13/88. Significantly, the very negative reviews begin with *L'Esclavage* and the performed plays, for example, in: *Le Moniteur* 12/28/89; *Mercure de France*, 12/89; *Les Actes des Apôtres*, end 89; *Petites affiches Ducray-Duminil*, 1/93.

10. Marvin Carlson belabors Etienne et Martainville's description of her as "old and ugly" (65), although there is no mention of her looks in the hostile contemporary reviews of *Dumourier* (January 1793), and her name is listed in fifth place (out of 149) in an *Hommage aux plus jolies et vertueuses femmes de Paris*, published in 1792 (Blanc 1989, 35, 211). Carlson describes her as an "eccentric old lady who possessed an uncanny ability for writing unsuccessful plays on apparently foolproof subjects" and attributes to her a play staged in 1790—when the "old lady" was forty-two—that she never wrote (55). Other entries repeat how old, ugly, irascible and unsuccessful she was (148-9). His last mention of "the half-mad old Olympe de Gouges," recounts the arrest, trial, and execution of "the octogenarian" (154). His note for this entry refers to an unreliable history by E. Jauffret, *Le Théâtre révolutionnaire*, published in 1869.

11. For example, "Préface pour les dames," is identified as a preface to *Mirabeau*, 1791 (Groult 1986, 115-19) when de Gouges published it preceding *Mémoires de Madame de Valmont* (1788, II). "Encore une préface" (150-2) mixes fragments from two different prefaces to *Mirabeau*. "Réflexions sur les hommes nègres" (83-7) omits several pages with no indication of ellipses. *La France sauvée* is described as a "five act prose drama, written in 1792, in which Olympe de Gouges stages herself, giving lessons in patriotism to valets, in manners to the Princesse de Lamballe, and in political clairvoyance to Marie-Antoinette herself" (160). The excerpts reproduced are the first nine scenes of the first act, which show Barnave in amorous pursuit of the king's sister and Olympe herself issuing audacious warnings to the queen's ladies in waiting while Marie-Antoinette, hidden in an armoire, vows to corrupt her patriotism. In fact, since the royal family's abortive flight to Varennes in 1791, deputy Barnave had been suspected not just of collaboration with the monarchy, but of a romantic involvement with the queen herself. Olympe de Gouges did present herself at the Tuileries to admonish Marie-Antoinette to join other women of the nation in contributing to the Festival of the Law, to which she said the Queen herself is subject (Blanc 1989, 129). Accused of collaboration, de Gouges published an account of the incident and her correspondence with Lamballe and others to justify her actions

(*Correspondance de la cour, Compte moral rendu par Olympe de Gouges* [EP II 1993b]). The anthology fails to mention that the play was never completed, and was used against her in her trial. The summary fails to mention that the remaining six scenes of the first act, and the four extant scenes of the second, develop what is probably the principal subject of the play: The conspiracy and factions that led to the fall of the monarchy on 10 August 1792 (but as they were played in the Tuileries palace itself). They reveal Barnave's ambition and resentment, Clermont-Tonnerre's opportunism, the King's pusillanimity and the Queen's ruthlessness as she attempts to corrupt Pétion, the Mayor of Paris, into betraying the Constitution. They represent the clash warring troups, the treacherous "Chevaliers du poignard" guarding the royal family and the patriotic national guard.

12. After twenty years as playwright, Mercier succeeded in having a play performed by the Comédie in 1787, and only because *La Maison de Molière* was a kind of hommage to Comèdie's view of itself as "Molière's house." On the other hand, he managed to have his dramas (such as *La Brouette du Vinaigrier*, 1775) staged by minor companies and become great hits. Association with such theaters and actors would totally dishonor a woman.

13. Beauharnais, and other female playwrights, also protested the Comédie's treatment of their plays (Chevalley 44-45, and Beauharnais's preface to *La Fausse inconstance*, Paris 1787). But since de Gouges was more vocal and insistent in defending her rights, she was labelled obsessed and ridiculous.

14. Born in Montauban in southwest France, de Gouges spoke Occitan before learning French well when she came to Paris at eighteen. Her handwriting and signature are strained, but many people who wrote with difficulty (and her secretaries, too, made spelling and grammar mistakes), could read well. Her works show that she had read widely, if not classically. She mentions revising at least five of her plays. It is hard to imagine that a woman who frequented prominent political and literary circles (the household of the Duc d'Orléans, the Condorcets, Brissot, Pétion, and playwrights such as Mercier, Cubières, Dorat) was actually illiterate. (On her background and friends see Blanc 1989, chapters 1-2 and 1993.)

15. Readers will be able to judge for themselves. In addition to the recent editions cited in Note 1, several volumes are forthcoming: Œuvres complètes II & III: Romans et Pensées; IV: Pamphlets (1789-93), ed. Castan. At least two plays (*L'Esclavage, Mirabeau*) were performed during the Bicentennial. Olympe de Gouges is the heroine of *The Butcher's Daughter*, an award-winning play by Wendy Kesselman, staged by the Cleveland Repertory Company in March-April, 1993.

16. The last general study of bourgeois drama dates back to Gaiffe's (1910).

17. Lanson's and Gaiffe's studies do not include a systematic analysis of female roles in sentimental comedy and bourgeois drama. My observations are provisional and based on a limited corpus. Of course there are exceptions, in particular, the complex female characters in Marivaux and Beaumarchais.

18. In the most influential dramas the mother is absent (Diderot's *Fils naturel* and *Père de famille*, 1757, 1758, Mercier's *Broutte du vinaigrier*, Sade's *Oxtiern*, 1791) or trivial (Sedaine's *Philosophe sans le savoir*, 1765). But ill-tempered or ridiculous older women abound in sentimental comedy and drama (e.g. the tyranical *Baronne de l'Orme* in Voltaire's *Nanine*, 1749, the snobbish sister in Sedaine's play, the ambitious aunt in Beaumarchais's *Eugénie*, 1767).

19. In the *Déclaration* she makes the parallel explicit: "The woman whom a man buys, like the slave on the African coasts." (Levy 1980, 93).

20. But slavery was restored in 1802 and only definitively abolished in 1848; natural offspring would lose their rights under the 1804 Civil Code and only recover them in January 1972! For a discussion of the "cultural revolution of 1793-94"—which de Gouges anticipated in her writings—see Bianchi.

21. The father in bourgeois drama tends to be an irreprochable authority figure (as in Diderot's *Père de famille* and Sedaine's *Philosophe*) even if virtually absent (Diderot's *Fils naturel*), or a hard-hearted tyrant who sees the light at the end (La Harpe's *Mélanie*, Mercier's *Zoé*).

22. Olivier Blanc informs me that under the Restoration, Clamet's daughter, with the Duchesse de Berry's support, asked the Comédie for a reading of the play.

23. This character is obviously a double for the author. She suffers the same injustice from her family as the heroine in de Gouges's autobiographical letter-novel, *Mémoire de Madame de Valmont contre l'ingratitude et la cruauté de la famille des Flaucourt avec la sienne* (1788, III).

24. Revision was her strategy in *Le Mariage inattendu de Chérubin;* her page, reformed, upstages the philandering Count by treating women with respect.

25. Mercier shows the great playwright struggling to perform *Tartuffe* while enduring, philosophically, the rivalry of the Béjart women (his former mistress and his future wife).

26. Ninon's dignified admission contrasts with the humiliation endured by Countess Almaviva when she confesses her adultery in Beaumarchais's *La Mère coupable* (1792).

27. Enthusiasm for Ninon was by no means shared by all women. In her history of women's influence on literature, Mme de Genlis expresses relief that she does not have to discuss the courtesan because she wrote so little. She condemns her severely in a note: "Ninon, by her wit, her depravity and her love affairs, had the most baneful influence on morals" (1811, 183-84).

28. De Gouges's play is not a simple-minded panegyric of this complex figure. She admired Mirabeau's eloquence and his revolutionary ideas, his ability to contain the excesses of the Royalists and the radicals, but she denounced his debauchery and corruption. As she points out in the prefaces, she had attacked him in her writings and exhorted him to reform his "heart" to match the elevation of his mind (TP 1991, 102). Yet of all the members of the National Assembly to whom she had sent her political writings, Mirabeau was the only one to acknowledge them and praise the author for her patriotism

(94). In the play she introduces the shade of a young boy, Fortuné, who recounts how Mirabeau secretly assisted him and his destitute mother. She claims that this episode, based on a real event, proves his capacity for disinterested generosity. The extent to which Mirabeau had been "bought" by the monarchy to defend its interests would only be revealed months after his death. True to her humanism and pacifism, de Gouges praises him for defending the Constitution and avoiding bloodshed, and for what she perceived as his willingness to admit women into the revolutionary process.

29. Lenclos had affairs with both Sévigné's husband and son. But in old age, Sévigné expressed admiration for her rival's moral and intellectual qualities.

30. The fragment of *La France sauvée* suggests that France might be saved if the Queen could be "educated" to rise above intrigue, manipulation, and Old Regime strategies that made her into a tyrant and a slave at the same time.

31. Until 1790 royal censors forbade the representation of Church costumes and ceremonies on stage. Earlier plays on forced vocations either set the action in antiquity or avoided showing nuns. The first play to feature nuns in habits was Laujon's *Le Couvent ou les fruits du caractère*, performed in January 1790. But this inoffensive play is not about forced vocations, merely about the often negative effects of a convent education on snobbish girls. (Estève 177-190).

32. The liberal divorce law was repealed in 1804 and only restored in 1975.

33. Monvel's Eugènie only appears in the last act, chained in a deep convent dungeon. Her lover, Dorval, the center of the action from the beginning of the play, breaks through the wall as she is about to expire.

34. In contrast, the mother in *Mélanie* defends her daughter at first, but succumbs to her tyranical husband; in Monvel's play the mother is the one who forced her daughter into the convent. Mother-daughter suffering and solidarity in *Le Couvent* recall the women's bond in *Cénie* (Mme de Graffigny), except that de Gouges's mother challenges patriarchal oppression directly.

35. The police signature on the manuscript of *La Nécessité du divorce* is dated 26 October 1790. Welschinger (262-63) lists four plays inspired by the divorce law: *Le Double divorce ou le bienfait de la loi*, anonymous, 1792; *Le Divorce*, a vaudeville by Desfontaines, May 1793; *Les Mœurs ou le divorce*, by Pigault-Lebrun, September 1794; *Le Mur mitoyen* (against divorce), by Barré and Bourgueil, February 1796. In addition, there is a play with a title similar to de Gouges's, *L'Utilité du divorce*, written by Prévost, director of the Théâtre Sans-Prétention, and performed in 1801. In the Soleinne catalogue, *La Nécessité du divorce* is also attributed to Prévost, although the plays are completely different.

36. De Gouges advocated divorce as early as 1789, in her pamphlet *L'Ordre national*. She mentions a play on divorce among others she has written in a 1791 pamphlet, *Sera-t-il Roi* (EP 1993a, 192), and a play entitled *La Nécessité du divorce* was inventoried among her papers (Blanc 1989, 195-96). The discussions in the play resemble passages in the

Déclaration, where de Gouges states that indissoluble "marriage is the tomb of trust and love" and proposes a "Social Contract Between Man and Woman" based on reason and nature. A central character in the play, the bachelor opposed to the indissolubility of marriage, is named Rosambert, which evokes the name of the bachelor with whom de Gouges had a long liaison but by mutual agreement never married, Jacques Biétrix de Rozières. I am grateful to Olivier Blanc for calling the homophony to my attention.

37. Several plays were written on crusty old comic bachelors (the most famous is Collin d'Harleville's *Vieux célibataire* [1792], who regret they missed out on the joys of family life. Typically, they are also made to realize that by not procreating, they failed to fulfill their obligation to society and state. Rosambert is original in his insistence on liberty and his critique of indissoluble marriage as contrary to nature.

38. At least fifty were written about the seige of Toulon by the English fleet in 1793. (See Guenot)

39. *Journal de Paris,* 17 Feb. 1793, 216. This article, however, comments on the published text rather than the performance. Blanc surmises that the anonymous reviewer might have been Mercier (1989, 218, n. 5).

40. Félicité and Théophile Fernig, 22 and 17 years old, daughters of an ardent patriot, had donned male garb and started leading military skirmishes against the Austrians in May 1792. They were brought with their father to Dumouriez's headquarters in September and served as aides-de-camp. They fought at Valmy, Jemappes, and Anderlecht (the battle staged in the play) and were cited in the general's report to the Convention Assembly (*Dictionnaire de Biographie Française* 13: 1051-52).

ง # III

To Interpret History:
Mme de Staël and George Sand

11

Liberating Exchanges: Mme de Staël and the Uses of Comparison

Susan Tenenbaum

While Germaine de Staël has not been a neglected figure in intellectual history, her fame has largely attached to her work as a literary critic and novelist, as well as reflected in an abiding fascination with her legendary persona. Recently, however, scholars have turned to rediscover Staël as a political thinker (Kadish 113-21; Sourain 42-51). I emphasize the term "rediscover," since the impact of Staël's political writing on her own day was considerable, and her legacy so vital that her biographer Albert Sorel dubbed her the "muse of Restoration liberalism" (197). Yet Staël has long been dismissed as a polemicist whose political writings offer little of enduring value and criticized for arguments that are, in the words of Jean Touchard, "essentially confused" (2: 522). In this paper, however, I shall be guided by the counsel of the poet and historian Lamartine, who assessed most generously that quality of eclecticism, which later critics were less eager to applaud:

> Her voice was like an antique chorus, in which all the great voices of the drama unite in one tumultuous concord. (1: 198-99)

Following Lamartine, I suggest that Staël's practical political involvements and divided intellectual allegiances establish a claim on our attention. The intellectual tensions in her work reflect her predicament as a thinker at the crossroads of eighteenth- and nineteenth-century cultures, and reveal an insatiably inquisitive mind eager to assimilate wide-ranging currents of ideas and apply them to the problems of her revolutionary era. If these problems were tied to the particular circumstances of her day, Staël simultaneously perceived them as enduring political questions: What are the determinants of political stability? the prerequisites of a free society? the causes of revolution? These larger questions were, in turn, intimately bound to problems of practical politics: the building of consensus in an age of partisan extremism; the designing of constitutions; the arresting of revolutionary change.

The breadth of Staël's vision, combined with her practical involvement in the politics of her day, make Staël an exemplar of the engaged intellectual whose writings may be studied as a locus of interaction between politics and theory. The present essay focuses on one dimension of this encounter: Staël's use of the comparative method as an instrument of partisan politics. It will be argued that her use of comparison in defense of the principles of 1789 (the embodiment, for Staël, of the "true" revolution) represented a subtle shift in revolutionary discourse away from the early rhetoric of abstract right toward more empirical modes of legitimation. This political argument was, in turn, embedded in a broader attempt by Staël to defend her role as political thinker in the context of prevailing normative assumptions concerning the sexual division of public and private spheres. Accordingly, a discussion of Staël's gender-based defense of her political involvements will serve to frame analysis of her partisan use of the comparative method.

To engage the question of Staël's political activism is to confront a central irony: Staël's insistent defense of her public role was coupled with her striking failure to endorse political rights for women. Staël's refusal to protest the exclusion of women from citizenship issued from a complex set of attitudes regarding woman's appropriate role. On one level, it reflected what Landes and Outram have described as the internalization of Rousseauian-inspired norms relating to sexual difference, norms which compromised the political demands of even outspoken advocates of women's rights like Wollstonecraft and de Gouges. On the level of practical politics, however, Staël used Rousseauian norms only to subtlely subvert them in the service of her political aspirations. For example, she turned to her advantage Rousseau's theme of "the corruption of virtue by public women," arguing that her legal proscription from public office attested to her lack of personal ambition (her uncorruptibility) and, accordingly, to her suitability as political mediator (Staël 1904, 137). Further, Staël's linkage of the feminine with the possession of heightened sensibility drew upon the Rousseauian ideal of feminine virtue (Okin, 108-39), while according it a public role in defiance of Rousseau's proscription. On Staël's approach, woman's sensibility, nurtured outside the realm of political power, becomes a touchstone of political morality.

> ... sensibility is not suited to statesmen; that is to say, those who govern must not allow emotion to cloud their reflexions. But true sensibility always accords with reason. ... it provides a swifter judgment that reason later confirms. The Germans, who consulted their women as oracles, never allowed them to participate in practical affairs. They looked to women's impressions as their moral compass, yet always retained for themselves stewardship of the state (Staël 1904, 254)[1]

Staël's conception of her public role was more immediately informed by the tradition of the French salon, which offered the example of female empowerment within a framework of legal subordination (DeJean 1989; Goldsmith; Lougée). The daughter of the celebrated *salonnière* Suzanne Necker, Germaine de Staël sought to recast the role of the salon, adapting it to the changed circumstances of her revolutionary age. For Staël, the salon remained a pivotal site for shaping the discourse of political society; but whereas under the Old Regime the salon had cultivated an aristocratic culture based on elaborate artifice and aestheticism, the institution now had to be grounded in an ethic of sincerity and utilitarian purpose (Staël 1967, 1: 301-05). On this understanding, the salon would continue to straddle a public/private status, yet would assume a more overtly political role in the competition to fix public meanings in the wake of the revolution. The shift to practical political involvements, with its appeal to a wider audience of "public opinion" (Baker 167-99), necessitated new intellectual strategies on the part of the *salonnière*. It is within this context that Staël sought to transform the use of the comparative method.

While the invocation of remote historical periods and foreign cultures was commonplace among seventeenth-century *salonnières,* such early uses of comparison served as a form of exoticism and as a stimulus to literary invention. Fidelity to historical and social fact was consistently subordinated to French conventions of good taste (Ratner, 58-60). The passage from comparison as a playful exercise in narrative and style to the "realistic" perspectives of Staël was continuous and complex, yet critically mediated by the work of Montesquieu. Staël, who had annotated *De l'Esprit des Lois* at an early age, assimilated Montesquieu's sociological method to recast the *salonnière* as presider over an international society of dialogue that privileged substance over style, and carried practical implications for the politics of her day.[2] Corinne, the title heroine of Staël's celebrated novel, may be seen as a representative figure of this new social type. Corinne's dual English-Italian heritage symbolized Staël's embrace of the "other" as a participant in French political discourse, and exemplified the comparatist's capacity for sympathetic engagement with diverse cultures. In the novel, a coterie of admirers representing France, England, and Italy comprise an informal salon over which Corinne presides.[3] These social encounters are marked by neither verbal preciosity nor by the revelation of private sentiment, but by the exchange of descriptive accounts of national character and culture. Participants eagerly contribute appreciative as well as critical assessments of each other's history, culture, and political society, offering a model of sociability rooted in intellectual exchange and a spirit of practical reform. This ideal of conversation as pedagogy was, as I shall explore in the body of this paper, wedded to Staël's use of comparative analysis as a weapon in domestic politics, and pointed to a revived role for the *salonnière* as a shaper of public discussion in the post-revolutinary era.

Throughout her public career Staël turned repeatedly to the comparative method to defend the Revolution of 1789. It was this initial phase of the Revolution that provided a base for political moderates like Staël, who situated themselves between the opposing extremes of radicalism and reaction. For Staël, the events of 1789 represented the "true" revolution, issuing from general historical causes and animated by a core set of liberal values: constitutionalism, representative institutions, the protection of civil liberties, and limited political equality. Staël deployed the comparative method to legitimate this reading of 1789, as well as to condemn what she held to be the Revolution's aberrant phases—the Terror and the Napoleonic era. Staël's use of comparison for these purposes provides a striking illustration of the "general abandonment of the language of politics originally adopted to justify the Revolution" (Welch 5). This language, invoking abstract argument from natural right, laid the foundation of an absolutist discourse that, according to Staël, accommodated no middle ground. To defend the Revolution against its enemies on the Left and Right, Staël sought to modify its justificatory framework by introducing contextual arguments which tempered, though did not displace, earlier appeals to abstract principle. Thus she offered historical evidence in support of the principles of 1789 and inventoried the heterogeneity of social orders to discredit the encompassing classicism of the radical revolution. In both these enterprises, the comparative method figured prominently.

Before turning to these explicitly partisan dimensions of Staël's analysis, however, I should first like to bring to the surface several key intellectual tensions that characterize Staël's work as a comparatist. These tensions owe as much to the divergent traditions of argument she sought to synthesize, as to her shifting political alignments and polemical strategies. At least three distinct perspectives on the role of comparative analysis may be distilled from her writings:

Comparison to Illuminate Socio-Cultural Differences

Staël's celebration of the unique character of each national society bore the imprint of her Montesquieuian inheritance and was later nourished by her contact with German nationalist thought. Montesquieu had ascribed to each society a distinctive "general spirit," arising from its unique combination of physical and moral causes (292-315). In *De la littérature* Staël extended Montesquieu's method to explore the sociology of culture. This analytical framework was applied in *De l'Allemagne,* where Staël stressed the importance of each nation's cultural self-expression, arguing that only authentic national cultures were worthy of admiration.

Comparison to Modify Socio-Cultural Differences

Staël's valuation of the multiplicity of national cultures was tempered by her cosmopolitanism. Thus, she was critical of exaggerated national differences and turned to comparison as a means of modifying these differences by a mutual "balancing" or "checking" of national characteristics. *De l'Allemagne,* for example, juxtaposes the "excessively worldly" French and the "excessively religious" Germans with a view to moderating the pronounced tendencies of each nation, reconciling both on a cosmopolitan middle ground.

Comparison to Illuminate a Theory of Historical Progress

The theme that history is governed by general laws directed toward the realization of a universally valid social order and a universal human nature threads through Staël's major writings. In her work prior to the *Considérations,* Staël compared two broad historical types: ancient and modern societies. In the *Considérations* she adopted a three-stage theory of history. Both frameworks identified modernity with the development of a liberal constitutional state and a private sphere rooted in the "natural" needs of society. Unlike the first category of comparison, the present category appeals not to the richest expression of national differences, but to the historical emergence of a common humanity.

Staël is thus seen to straddle positions as a cultural relativist and as an exponent of universal standards deriving from a secular natural law. Though, as I shall argue below, this tension was powerfully reinforced by the strategic requirements of her politics, it was nourished on a deeper level by the intellectual traditions of her day. Montesquieu, for example, drew no mutually exclusive distinctions between appeals to comparative and natural law (Richter 20-30). And to the extent that Staël sought to synthesize currents of ideas as disparate as natural law, utilitarianism and romanticism, her thought was simultaneously enriched and confused. My present concern is not, however, with her intellectual sources but with how Staël's posture as a political moderate informed her use of comparative analysis.

Although during the course of the Revolution Staël shifted her allegiance between monarchical and republican forms of government, she consistently identified herself as a centrist and a supporter of constitutionalist principles. Before examining how these political convictions gave shape to Staël's studies of England, Italy, Germany, and Russia, I shall briefly consider how they figured in her theory of progress.

The idea of historical progress was shaped by Staël into a strategy of intertemporal comparison designed to discredit her political enemies on the left and the right. It furnished a double-edged weapon with which to repudiate Jacobin reverence for classical antiquity, as well as to disavow the veneration of tradition by reactionary Royalists. In collaboration with

Benjamin Constant, Staël framed the ancient/modern dichotomy directed against Jacobin ideals of classical democracy. Using this dualist model of intertemporal comparison, Staël indicted her opponents on the grounds of ahistoricism: Jacobins refused to recognize that changes in social conditions had rendered their ideals of civic virtue, community, and social democracy anachronistic and oppressive in the context of the modern state. Staël's dualist model underscored the polarities between ancient and modern social orders. As opposed to modern society, the ancient polity was characterized by smallness of scale, the absence of domestic life (given women's inferior status, the gratifications of domesticity remained secondary to active involvement with one's equals in the affairs of state), and a rudimentary economy. Modern society, by contrast, was marked by a highly developed commercial sector and a richly rewarding domestic life. The rise of the private sector as the locus of worthwhile endeavor, Staël argued, transformed the classical Jacobin ideal of civic self-sacrifice into an instrument of political oppression (Staël 1904, 89-95).

Staël's adoption of a three-stage model of progress in the *Considérations* reflected a shift in the balance of political forces under the early Restoration; the reactionary aristocracy had replaced the Jacobins as the principal threat to Staël's vision of liberal order. Their demands for a return to the authoritarian arrangements of the Old Regime countered her own efforts to legitimate the "gains" of the Revolution. Omitting all reference to classical antiquity, Staël's model now comprised three stages: feudalism, despotism, and representative government. These stages were distinguished by the degree of liberty secured by each: feudalism—limited liberty; despotism—no liberty; representative government—liberty extended to all citizens. By depicting feudalism as a system of limited monarchy in which the power of the crown was curbed by the privileges of the nobility, Staël fashioned a political strategy that was at once conciliatory and critical. Conceding that the feudal constitution contained anticipations of her cherished liberal form of government—"it is liberty that is ancient, and despotism which is modern" (Staël 1983, 70)—Staël acknowledged the historical claims of the nobility. Yet she also implicitly criticized the reactionaries' characterization of the Revolution as criminal or aberrant.[4] Her model served to affirm the Revolution's continuity with the historical struggle for liberty and to celebrate its universalization of liberal principles in 1789.

Turning from Staël's comparative historical typologies to her treatment of contemporaneous societies, the model of England found in the *Considérations* represents the most complete portrait of Staël's ideal of the modern free society. The models of Italy, Germany, and Russia set out, respectively, in *Corinne, De l'Allemagne,* and *Dix années d'exil* occupy a more ambivalent status in her work. They neither embody Staël's preferred forms of government nor do they receive her blanket censure. Instead, they encapsulate various traits which, during the course of the Revolution, Staël deemed essential to the triumph of her cherished values. Thus she lauded the "enthusiasm" of the Germans and the "military spirit" of the Russians during a period when the overthrow of Napoleon was uppermost in her thoughts. These models also served Staël's political purposes on another level: by focusing on the manifold variety of European cultures, she implicitly repudiated Napoleonic designs for French hegemony. Ultimately, however, such concessions to relativist standards are superseded by her belief in the universal validity of a liberal social order. On this view, Staël's comparative investigations of Germany, Italy, and Russia function in a manner analogous to her concept of despotism, namely, they counterpoint her model of a free society.

Staël's homage to England in the *Considérations* had historical roots reaching back to the Huguenots, who celebrated English liberty in order to condemn French despotism following the Revocation of the Edict of Nantes. Enlightenment philosophes like Montesquieu, Voltaire, and Rousseau regarded themselves as either Anglophiles or Anglophobes (Acomb). And, most immediately, the English model had played a strategic role in debates throughout the revolutionary era. Members of the *noblesse* promoted an aristocratic image of England as a means of defending their position first against the Crown, and later against the Third Estate. Against this aristocratic vision, Anglophile reformers like Necker depicted England as a model of an enlightened, liberal, and commercial order (Bonno). It was this image of England that Necker transmitted to his daughter, and which she enshrined in the *Considérations* as a model to be imitated by France:

> We cannot believe that Providence has placed this fine monument of social order so near to France, only to give us the pain of never being able to equal it. (Staël 1983, 530)

To claim England as a model, Staël had to overcome not only her grim personal experience of English intolerance of "superior women," but also a relativism which disallowed the wholesale importation of alien social forms. Staël's advocacy of English institutions, while nourished by her desire to compose the *Considérations* as a testament to Necker and a vindication of his policies, was nonetheless rooted in practical political judgments. Political conditions in France appeared to auger well for the reception of the British model: England had established her credentials as the foremost opponent of Napoleon and liberator of France; the King and nobility had been restored to French political life; and, as George Kelly has observed, all other constitutional solutions had already been exhausted (514).

Staël's model of England replicated the sweep of Montesquieuian analysis. She ascribed to England an animating passion—love of liberty—and explored how this motive informed English legal, political, social, and cultural institutions. She lauded England's balanced constitution, founded on a tripartite sharing of power by King, Lords, and Commons, and praised its protection of individual rights. She explored how the English love of domesticity functioned as a barrier against state interference and pioneered a concern for the sociology of leisure by describing the English penchant for solitary walks as suited to the dynamics of a free and privatized society (Staël 1983, 523-64).

Staël's liberal criterion of good government had earlier served as a potent weapon against Napoleon, but Napoleon's hegemonic designs on Europe nurtured her wariness of any universalistic claims. Thus she rallied resistance to the Emperor by championing the pluralistic expression of national cultures. French domination of Italy was a focus of her novel *Corinne,* which depicted Italy as corrupt and enervated under foreign rule, but as possessing the resources of a rich culture and an inspirational past. The novel is a sociological tour de force. Plotlines dissolve into political argument and cultural expositions; protagonists are caricatures of their national traits rather than distinctive personalities. In the novel, Staël appealed to historical example to renew and rejuvenate the Italian people. Ancient ruins, often described in guidebook detail, serve as metaphors of lost dignity and inspirations to national rebirth. If Staël had elsewhere alluded to the dangers of classical principles in modern society, she here conceded their relevance to Italian politics. To the ancients, freedom meant the absence of alien rule; it also referred to the capacity to participate in public life, an ideal with which to awaken Italy's dormant civic consciousness. Corinne, who embodied the spontaneity and imagination Staël deemed characteristic of Italian culture, pointed the way to Italy's political redemption.

Like *Corinne, De l'Allemagne* was focused on an historically fragmented society which, under Napoleon, was being forged into a centralized state. Among the purposes of the treatise was to awaken a consciousness of national identity in order to incite rebellion against French hegemony. By joining these goals, Staël opposed the views of German intellectuals like Hegel and Fichte, who defended French rule precisely on the grounds that it was instrumental to the formation of a modern German state. Like Italy, Germany was depicted by Staël as characterized by a divorce between politics and intelligence, albeit diverse national causes channeled Italian energies into the fine arts and German energies into philosophy. Staël distinguished "enthusiasm," an elevation of the soul linked to apprehension of the sublime, as the animating passion of the German nation (5: 186-99). Enthusiasm lent an abstract contemplative quality to German philosophy, which led to the deprecation of worldly interests. While this disposition militated against political activism, it nonetheless nourished a romantic aesthetic that, for Staël, could be used to indict the prevailing French classicism. Whereas the romantic was organic, progressive, and complex, the classical was mechanical, closed, and simple (2: 127-40). Because Staël equated the tenets of classicism with the principles of despotic rule, her espousal of romantic aesthetics challenged the ideological foundations of the Napoleonic system, and thus brought into question its entire apparatus of control.

Staël's profile of Russia is found in her memoir, *Dix années d'exil*, which records her travels through that nation in 1812. Although the work was not intended as a political tract, the sections pertaining to Russia were drafted in the wake of the French invasion and directly reflect her Manichean view of the 1812 War. Her largely sympathetic portrait of Russian life owed much to her perception of Russia as the instrument of Napoleon's defeat. She applauded Russia's primitive martial vigor, yet recognized it to be incompatible with the spirit of a free society; she admired Czar Alexander, yet acknowledged his power to be "despotic."

Staël's designation of martial vigor as the animating passion of the Russians was informed by earlier Western views of Russian primitivism, as well as by her own political sympathies. The image of Russia, massed as a nation and directing its unbridled barbaric energies against the Napoleonic menace, had captured her imagination. Staël's politics once again merged with her sociological concerns, as she offered a sustained investigation of the physical and moral causes that combined to form the distinctively Russian character type. She called attention to the harshness of the Russian terrain and the severity of its climate; to the absence of a middle class that would support liberal institutions; to education interrupted at an early age by military service; and to an economy marked by extremes of luxury and privation (1966, 176-237).

In the case of Russia, as with England, Italy, and Germany, Staël's practical political involvements served as a spur to her scholarship. The defense of the ideals of 1789 nourished Staël's many styles of comparison, and her use of this method carried important historical and intellectual consequences. Historically, Staël's turn to comparison represented a shift away from the rights-based language of legitimacy that marked the early stages of the Revolution. Whether she drew on intertemporal comparison to repudiate the anachronistic vision of her opponents, or on the analysis of English institutions to support her cherished political ideals, Staël introduced empirical considerations which complicated and enriched the abstract perspectives of her forebearers. Similarly, Staël's celebration of social diversity, while ambivalently coupled with her espousal of liberal institutions, nurtured a sensitivity to social context as it served the political purpose of marshalling opposition to Napoleon. These empiricist tendencies introduced by Staël marked the beginning of a second stage of French liberalism that would culminate in the work of thinkers like Guizot and Tocqueville. Incorporating and enlarging a tradition of comparison reaching back to Montesquieu, Staël reinvigorated the role of the *salonnière* as shaper of discourse in a revolutionary age.

Notes

1. All translations of Staël are mine. An earlier version of this paper was presented at Hofstra University in 1989 and is forthcoming in the conference proceedings published by Greenwood Press.

2. Staël extended Montesquieu's categories to include comparative investigations of national literature and conversational style, topics traditionally the province of the *salonnière*.

3. Staël cast Corinne as an "improvisatrice," a reciter of spontaneous verse. In conversation with her admirers, however, Corinne assumed a more pedagogical tone.

4. These charges were leveled by critics like Burke and deMaistre.

12

Speech Acts: Germaine de Staël's Historiography of the Revolution

Karyna Szmurlo

> Once the power of speech gains admission to political interests, it becomes of the greatest importance . . .
> —Germaine de Staël, *De la littérature*

> The power of the National Assembly to transform the world comes first through words: the power to suppress, change, and name.
> —Christie McDonald, "Words of Change: August 12, 1789" in *The French Revolution 1789-1989. Two Hundred Years of Rethinking* (Petrey 1989a)

As a critic of the Revolution, Germaine de Staël is interested in the link between semiotics and politics. Whether rejoicing in the sonorous intensity of deliberative assemblies or elaborating on the theory of eloquence, she tries to detect the transgressive/regressive action of speech within a social context. "It is the spoken word which has called legions from the earth" and has driven armies to be victorious. "Words make things happen . . ." (CA 272, 336).[1] Because of the emphasis placed on the pairing of the verbs to do/to speak, Staël's approach takes on a particular energy in light of the recent studies originating in English analytic philosophy. J. L. Austin, in his book *How to Do Things with Words,* discusses the priority of the "performative" function in relation to the simply "constative" role of transmitting the truth. As an illustration of an act by enunciation, he takes the classic example of the marriage ceremony, in the course of which the question "Do you take this woman to be your lawful wedded wife?" and the response "I do," are neither descriptive nor constative, but performative. A political speech inspired by passion is a substitute for power that is immediately borne out. As Sandy Petrey has recently demonstrated, "The Revolution—a momentous process of language acquisition as well as the seizure of state power, consistently sought the means to speak itself while exercising the power to make itself" (1988, 21).[2]

Necker's daughter, whose conversational brilliance was admired in all the most prestigious continental salons, found in the Revolution a wide range of possibilities. Though she was denied direct intervention in political arenas, Staël never stopped writing about politics and was never willing to repress the desire for action. Her numerous texts provide evidence of passionate involvement (*Réflexions sur le procès de la reine,* 1793; *Réflexions sur la paix adressées à M. Pitt et aux Français,* 1794; *Réflexions sur la paix intérieure,* 1795; *De l'influence des passions,* 1796; and the only recently published *Des circonstances actuelles,* 1979). It is, however, *Considérations sur la Révolution française,* begun in 1812, years after the secular clash, that contains the fullest demonstration of the reciprocal relationship between politics and the voice's rise to power. This demonstration is inscribed in the work's main project: the reconsideration of the logic of the Revolution, emphasizing clarity and logical sequence as opposed to chaos. As Michel Delon has noticed, Staël "claims to go beyond individuals to understand the play, even should it be a tragedy"; and here "the play" means "the construction or constitution of a meaning" (1989, 168). From this conceptualization (or taking control) of events, springs forth an uncontainable linguistic commentary.

Presented in terms that are doubly "performative," the Revolution unrolls as a prodigious spectacle with masses of actors involved in the enactment of history. Staël is an eyewitness, capable of confirming the truth of speeches and reporting them in her narrative of events. But within this decorum of spectacle, speech is endowed with a power for change and plays the major role, constituting, so to speak, the essential basis of the cognitive process in *Considérations.* Unlike La Harpe, who in *Du fanatisme dans la langue révolutionnaire* (1797) contented himself with violent attacks on linguistic aberrations (since, according to him, "words, like things, have been monstrosities"), Staël attempts to grasp the historic dynamism at work in the "performance" of speeches (14). The brilliance of eloquence (the calling of the States General and its debate) is superseded by a progressive disintegration of speech (from the end of the Assembly and the Terror, to Napoleon's taking of power). In Austinian terms, Staël's commentary moves from discursive "felicities" to "infelicities" typical of "unhappy functioning of the performative" (C 14). More important, her investigation evolves within the problematics of social context and referential speech, the two axioms of performative theory. What the language "does" depends on social specificity in time and space.

> Apart from the institution, the words do not do things but simply make noise. Conversely, efficacious utterance of words confirms the institution's solidity. Performative speech is by definition—in its essence— socially specific. Its power is inseparable from a precise collective vision of what counts as authority in which sets of circumstances.
> (Petrey 1988, 21)

Before Staël begins to write about the Third Estate's coming to voice, that is, its denomination as the National Assembly, she retraces the social pressures as well as the maturation process permitting such a victory. From the beginning, progressive accumulation of power is associated with communication. A brief survey shows the "sociability" of the absolute monarchy politically based in terseness and silence in opposition to the new "sociability" structured around general opinion (clubs, women's salons, press, philosophers, and men of letters).[3] During this memorable period of widespread support for liberty and interaction among social classes (1788 until the end of 1791), "history turned into gossip" and "as long as the scaffolds had not yet been erected, speech was still a mediator" (C 229). This circuit of horizontal communication, experienced as an actual "physical force" that "acts upon men even when they are unaware of it," weakens the hierarchical, vertical, and well-armed network of monarchy (C 81). "Louis XIV set up this exaggerated etiquette which deprived kings . . . of all straightforward and natural communication with men; consequently he did not know when circumstances became threatening" (C 76-77). Louis XVI, still rooted in the past and surrounded by people who spoke only flattery, was doomed, as were they. While France impatiently compared the modernity of the English parliamentary eloquence, the king maintained the politics of camouflage, intrigue, and fear.

The courtisan language, "a misleading echo changing the things it repeats," is invariably opposed to the democratized unveiling speeches (C 153). This insistence on the mediation principle not only coincides with the necessity of explicitness and referentiality in performative theory, but considerably enriches it when investigated in the context of the late eighteenth century. The declining Enlightenment exalted the power of the man able to realize himself as both an organic and spiritual being, able to construct his own historicity on the basis of his own dynamism. The philosophical/political vocabulary placed less emphasis on language as a system of communication than on biologism—individual *energeia*.[4] Staël, as a precursor of modern linguistics, approached Humboldt as she moved away from the static philosophy of the sensualists (Condillac, Tracy) to generic concepts disseminated by the German transcendentalists. The latter saw language as an energy in perpetual evolution and analyzed it in relation to the development of mankind's cognitive processes. In her study on the ideologue, J. M. Degérando, *Des signes et de l'art de penser considérés dans leurs rapports mutuels,* Staël insists on the interaction between mind and language, before concluding that it is "only through language that man begins to think and act creatively" (Mueller-Vollmer 208). This unity of the mental and the discursive has a direct influence on the effectiveness of political speech. Like Kant or Hegel, who linked law, religion, or esthetics to the linguistic phenomenon and made use of the interdependent nature of those realms, Staël establishes a "speech ethics" in which the act of eloquence depends on the equivalency between speech and moral energy. Words "spacialize" a person. The phenomenon of transparency repeatedly seen in numerous forms throughout Staël's texts reveals itself in a political speech as the "sound of truth," that "sublime ensemble" capable of moving the masses (L 407, 390). This totalizing tone is explicit: "Speech would be an *action,* if the soul's energy were completely reflected there, if sentiments were raised to the level of ideas, and if tyranny thus saw itself attacked by all that condemned it" (L 35).[5]

It is from this perspective that Staël evaluates the enigmatic power of revolutionary eloquence still reverberating centuries later in the sculpture of

Rude or the choruses of Berlioz. She experiences it as "military music" that makes ideas flow in the blood and that "transforms logical conviction into electric impulses." Oratorical splendors, enhanced by Greek or Roman rituals, assure proximity of crowds, along with the pleasure of their disorderly rhythms and "the intoxication men feel through one another when they join together" (L 118).[6] This communal euphoria, not without resemblance to Durkheim's concept of festival, is a measure of the democratization of language. François Furet's study *Penser la Révolution française* in which the Revolution is explained as a fundamentally linguistic event, shows methodological similarities to Staël's analysis despite its different purpose and different field of investigation. Curiously, critical tools are provided by the same pivotal concepts in both reexaminations of the events: the unity between speech and political power, the phenomenon of transparent speech, and, as it will be argued, an imaginary construct proper to the Revolution. Furet emphasizes that "language was substituted for power, for it was the sole guarantee that power would belong to the people, that is, to nobody" (1978, 48). The voice of the people's tribunes invested with the power to speak in the nation's name becomes synonymous with law, results in decrees, in social pacts, and determines events. Even after many years, Staël remembers Mirabeau's voice as he made the Assembly adopt his famous proposal to recall the troops summoned secretly by Louis XVI (C 159). Under different circumstances, she describes Mirabeau arguing in defense of a finance decree introduced by Necker, his gestures and scathing words painting "the horrors of bankruptcy. There was nothing more impressive than his voice . . . There was a strength of life which one could feel in his words and which was prodigiously effective" (C 199).

The contrast between the rhetorical clarity leading to social pacts and the vagueness precipitating the fall of the monarchy takes on the form of the authentic discursive confrontation during the debates of the General Assembly. The nobles, unable to articulate the restoration of absolute power, gradually lose ground. This impasse of words results, first of all, from the "circular" and unproductive modulation of the debate: "Whenever the Third Estate raised the tone, the nobility, accustomed to giving in to power, yielded, but as soon as the crisis died down, it went right back to its old arrogance" (C 144). This recurrence of two incompatible codes produces the effect of a dialogue of deaf or, perhaps, a crisis of metalanguage, such as Jakobson describes in relation to aphasic disturbances.[7]

> While the privileged class representatives discussed their powers, their interests, their etiquettes, in short everything that was of concern only to them, the Third Estate issued an invitation to join with them in their concern about scarcity and finances. What an advantage these people's deputies enjoyed when they called for a gathering of all the deputies on the same grounds! (C 147)

The truth of circumstances is contrasted with the illusory. The stubborn clinging to the permanent nature of signs is clearly seen by Staël as a power manoeuver attempting to prevent an evaluation based on social values: "A privileged body, whatever it may be, can only receive its license from history; its force in the present derives only from the fact that it existed in the past (C 107). While the deputies insist upon vital and urgent questions and participate in the renewed power of the nation they represent, the nobles, along with Louis XVI and Marie-Antoinette, return to a transhistoric, "nonexistent" past and refuse to leave "these three words: *c'était ainsi jadis* (it was like this before)" (C 144).

Throughout her analysis, Staël explores the imperative of actuality which corresponds to the "axiom of existence" in the performative utterance. In the chapter "Reference as a Speech Act," Searle emphasizes the referent's reality: "Whatever is referred to must exist" (77). In *Considérations,* the opening of the States General, full of signs visibly manifesting an authentic disposition of powers, demonstrates the crisis of the aborted referent. The representatives of the bourgeoisie, "men of letters, merchants, a great many lawyers" appear in suits and black coats, as a grey, indivisible mass. "No individual's name . . . was yet famous among the six hundred deputies from the Third Estate, but there were many honorable men, and many men to be feared" (C 140). Their imposing numbers and self-assured gazes are in sharp contrast with the artifice of the nobles' costumes, their swords and plumes, and the *mise en scène* of "a throne for the king" (C 140). Moreover, the staging and the speeches about "the way it used to be" are repeatedly called "frivolities" to stress even further the "breakdown of reference" (Austin, 137). Staël's use of this word corresponds to Condillac's definition, recently commented upon by Derrida: "Frivolity consists in being satisfied with tokens. It originates with the sign, or rather with the signifier which, no longer signifying, is no longer a signifier. The empty, void, friable, useless signifier" (118). On the contrary, a valid utterance (anchored in the context) can move history. It was during a violent session of parliament that "the word was spoken upon which France's fate was to depend" (C 114). The Abbé Sabatier replied to the magistrates, who were loudly demanding a financial accounting, with a phrase that assured his immediate imprisonment while at the same time triggering an historical action: "You sirs, are demanding the state of receipts and expenses, and it is the States General that you need. . . . This thought, though expressed in a play on words threw light upon everyone's confused desires. . . . From this moment on the revolution was a fact" (C 114). The people's deputies, conscious of their real supremacy, decide to "have recourse to more energetic means," literally illocutionary force, and to reverse secular values through the official act of naming. "Siéyès proposed that they constitute themselves *purely* and *simply* as the National Assembly of France and that they invite the members of the two orders to join in this assembly; this decree passed, and this decree was the Revolution itself" (C 147).

The binary concept of real/efficient and illusory/ineffective reappears in the relationship between Louis XVI and his Minister of Finances. Necker's prestige as he attempts to save the country from the insurrection derives from his ability to mediate between the king and the popular party. When he prepares his famous *Compte rendu,* it is to make "known to all the real state of the finances" and to give proof of his conviction that publicity is the "guarantee of faithfulness in engagements" (C 90). Fully aware of the authority of the people ("You are stronger now, wisdom is yours!"), Necker studies public opinion as the "compass" that the king must follow (C 134). Again, in Austin's terms: Necker excels in persuasive, "perlocutionary" speech, whose most important characteristic is a "happy" influence (121).[8] His gift for negotiation and convincing people will become the king's last resource; without military power after July 14, Louis XVI will make use of Necker's speeches to influence the deputies directly.

By contrast, each of the king's addresses prepared in advance by numerous advisers, marks his further slide toward the scaffold and compromises every effort made by the minister. Louis XVI conducts himself as one taking part in "the performance of certain spectacles in which actors gesture while someone else says the words" (C 149). The inauthenticity of these sessions is further emphasized by the arrogance and improbability of commands that seem to abrogate the general will. Far from pacifying, his words incite anger and increasingly aggressive reaction of the bourgeoisie.

Staël's notations pertaining to time have an almost breathless tone that accentuates the exhaustion of a Racinian-like tragedy. At the beginning: "Means still existed, perhaps, to save the State from a revolution" (C 112); "the popular party became more powerful in the time lost by the court in uncertainty" (C 155), and "in two weeks the resources (for communication) were lost" (C 157). The king's speeches are the epitome of Austinian "misfires" subverting the teller's intentions (121).[9] What is more, with the declaration on June 23, Louis XVI unleashes violence. After having held up the royal session by his trip to Marly, "where public opinion made itself even less heard than at Versailles," the incorrigible king returns to set the Assembly straight (C 153). Rather than following Necker's suggestion and captivating, "from his very first words," the impassioned deputies with a discussion of taxes, Louis XVI begins by revoking "the decrees which the Third Estate had enacted as a National Assembly and had sanctioned with the Tennis Court Oath" (C 153). This revocation of an already acquired authority drives the crowd to rebellion. "The first words outraged the Third Estate, and from that moment on it listened no more" (C 153). After the king's departure, the Assembly sits "permanently" to declare itself in session regardless of what has just taken place. Staël, fully conscious of the dialectical crossing of forces, insists on the defensive/offensive mechanism of speech repeatedly validating itself. "Given the trend, the royal session, far from attaining the goal formerly proposed, increased the momentum of the Third Estate by providing the occasion for a new victory" (C 156). The king's speech provoked immediate reaction from the popular party and led to the redefinition of its authority. A few days later the urgent nature of this rectification was confirmed by the storming of the Bastille. "Performative language became not a source of stability but the stakes of a struggle" (Petrey 1988, 28).

The analysis of the street cries and slogans (all italicized in the narrative) demonstrates the same confrontation. In the chronicled montage of anguish, each word gives proof of extraordinary generative abilities and becomes "a little arena for the clash and criss-crossing of differently oriented accents, ... the living interaction of social forces" (Voloshinov 41).[10] This time, however, Staël attempts to show internal contradictions that will explode the revolutionary act. The Revolution reveals itself as a "signifying" process continually threatened by underground forces. From the beginning, the jargon of clubs and numerous expressions, all belonging to the vocal realm, seem to "prostitute the truth" as they safeguard the democratic principles under the aristocratic forms (CA 293). Instead of solidifying general opinion, they divide, stir masses, and lead to carnage. The danger of semantic malaise—always triggered by referential laxity—is initially perceived during the period in which the Assembly flirted with the king. After the constitution of 1791, the disparity between the name and the thing was an indication of history's illusory aspect. During the comedy of "gossip" (or, to borrow Northrop Frye's terminology, the spectacle of reconciliation between the Father and the Son), the new generation sought the blessing of the old order, which had been based on arbitrary laws. But the king was a captive and the nobility absent, having gone abroad en masse. Nevertheless, convinced that suffering was ended and freedom established, "the people sang, and the newspaper peddlers filled the air with their loud proclamations of *Vive le roi!* announcing the king's great acceptance and the monarchical constitution" (C 249, 250). They thought they reached "the reality of things," when all they had obtained was "an empty sound" ("On crut atteint la réalité des choses, dont on n'avait obtenu que le nom" C 249).

Certain terms put into circulation by the Assembly disclose even further the unreal aspect of things. Despite their lameness and invalidity, these words—described by Staël as nominal errors—unleash carnage. For example, the title chosen for one of the committees in the Assembly, the *Comité des recherches,* revives the ghost of *lettres de cachet.* Even when the Assembly, was no longer "in many respects the mistress of its own deliberations, . . . had no power, no agents at its command and, . . . (even), moreover, there was complete freedom of speech," the popular imagination conjured up "the inquisitorial institutions adopted by religious and political tyrants" (C 191). The right of absolute veto (*veto absolu*) offered the king released obsessive fantasies. Although the veto was no more than "a ceremony of the Crown" and devoid of power, "people talked about the veto as if it were some sort of monster that would devour little children" (RP 51; C 202). These burning words announce the impasse: The return to a haunting past. Whether through a mirage of reconciliation or through hatred of the absolute system, the phantasmagoria of days gone by poisons the Revolution as it passes through an untruth that is "mythological," in the Barthesian sense of the word. For this reason, certain prerogatives taken by the Assembly seem troubling despite giving every appearance of reconciliation. The system of royal democracy (*la démocratie royale*) and the king's title as first public official (*le premier fonctionnaire public*) literally caused the Minister of Finances "great pain," because he saw it as "the greatest danger for the throne and for liberty." In his desperate final attempts to save the king, Necker had good reason to "protest against this means of reconciliation at the same time that he offered it" (C 204). Two chairs set on the podium, one for the king and the other for the president, induce the same reaction from Michelet: "It was abolishing the throne!" (1979 1:616). The destruction of semantic balance, typical of "a paradigmatic collapse," has the effect of a guillotine. When "two terms separated by the strongest distinctions . . . are suddenly brought together in the same person . . . meaning . . . is abolished, . . . and this subversion is fatal" (Barthes 191).

As proper names are swept clean of attributes, the ghost of the Aristocrat/Royalist inflames a parallel ferocity: no more titles, no more functions. Stripped of tradition, of familial memory, of history, names emerge in all their nakedness. Every distinction reverberates as a violation of democratic power. The day after the decree removing reference to landholdings from names borne by many families for centuries, Montmorenci becomes "Bouchard," La Fayette becomes "Mottié," and Count Mirabeau changes to "Riquetti l'aîné," etc. . . . (C 222). Any sign of luxury stirs fear. When Staël describes an attack in the dark of night on boulevard Saint Germain by a crowd shouting for her death, she explains, "They were not reviling me, because I was scarcely known at the time; but, in the eyes of the mob, a large carriage and clothes trimmed in braid stood for people they had to murder" (C 281).

This "mythic" hatred infiltrates the world through slander. Obscene pamphlets, which have as their target the royal family, particularly Marie-Antoinette, by now reduced to a symbol of evil, are all the more dangerous for being fabricated and reported by a public opinion invested with speech as power—the power of uttering truth. Public speech proliferates, functions hyperbolically, and echos throughout the queen's trial and in the mutterings of the crowd that accompanies her to the guillotine. The word "Libertine" replaces "Aristocrat" and a myth of unquenchable lust usurps the privileges of former power (Thomas 1989 b, 54). In response to the pornographic image of the queen as sinner, a foreign enemy of the French people, Staël draws a picture of the suffering mother, the protector of children. She brings to bear all the resources of femininity as described by Rousseau, as if maternity could redeem the unbridled sexuality depicted in caricature.[11] Her urgent defense, *Réflexions sur le procès de la reine* (August 1793), creates the impression of an actual fight, not only because Staël identifies with the queen when speaking of slander aimed at "women who are all sacrificed in such a loving mother" (RP 32), but also because she feels the murderous authenticity of public speech. "Hatred directed at an effigy is effective hatred. Symbolic violence intends to be realized in acts, . . . to encounter its target and to burn with it in the same rage for destruction" (Thomas 1989 b, 54).

The major portion of *Considérations* retraces the corruption of the founding energy into a manipulative force that excites, deceives, and dominates. Messianic platforms mutate into scaffolds and transparent unifying language fragments, turning to chaos. In the Assembly's final moments, the collectivity loses its rights as the representative of opinion, and the ideology of unanimity threatened by individual expansionism undergoes a progressive deconstruction. As Furet maintains: "Conspiracy is a delirious reaction to (vacant) power" offered to those who were kept from it in the past (1981, 54). Staël's theatrical metaphors express the same sort of uncontainability as a deterioration of "the ritual of the spectacle as it breaks apart, undermined by basic drives." The stage overflows, invading the audience (Delon 1989, 172).[12] On the level of words, this flood shows up in rhetorical confusion, lack of communication, and finally opacity. Revolutionary discourse splinters into infinite pieces, turns into a competitive arena where political power is proven through linguistic competence, and descends like "Dante from circle to circle, ever deeper into hell" (C 303). Furet's argument that "the Revolution replaced the conflict of interests for power with a competition of discourses for the appropriation of legitimacy" is illustrated throughout *Considérations* (1981, 49). On numerous occasions, Staël returns to the name of the *Comité du salut public,* where a cynical tour de force disguises its factional strategy: "A lethal expression, reducing moral sacrifice to what is referred to, by agreement, as the interests of the state—that is, the passions of the people who govern" (C 316). In the climate of mounting multilingualism Danton and Robespierre change into alchemists of speech. Mirabeau—"a marvel of good and bad," wrapped up in his passions as if they were "Laocoon's serpents"—climbs up the podium to manipulate with his "demogogic words" the nobility, the king, and the Third Estate (C 216). Robespierre leaves "traces of a secret plan in confused speeches" (C 314). Among his closest colleagues (Collot-d'Herbois and Billaud-Varennes), there stir, as at the core of every faction, the same ambitions that corrupt communication. The people's tribunes, Furet says, participated successively in a single great revolutionary act, "the discourse of equality," that was impossible to embody. This investing of politics with vague, symbolic meanings is central to Staël's explanation for the advent of the Terror, namely, that there was an excess of "abstract equality" (C 223). Orators-actors, in their double identity, haggled over the truth, brilliantly defined nearly a century later by Nietzsche, as the "pathos of belief or alibi of domination, . . . a discursive illusion behind which is hidden some partial game of power, interest or desire" (Felman 3). Marat's invectives against the royal family magnify this insatiable thirst: "Never had such distorted human speech been heard; the roars of wild animals could be translated into that language" (C 275). At the height of the persecutions, eloquence struck and severed necks like an ax. It was necessary to fight against the encircling snares of "these speeches that were sharp as daggers, containing death in every sentence" (C 305). The only way to end the nightmare was to stifle the voice. Robespierre, in fact, at the moment of his death "could not even speak to defend himself, he who had spoken so much to proscribe." His jaw "shattered by a pistol blow" symbolizes the scandal of the eloquent body and the scandal of speech as a machine, perverted and set in motion by the Revolution (C 315).

Under Napoleon, the most depraved multilingualism is displayed as burlesque hyperbole. Bonaparte determines to "lie actively" (C 365). A politics of wordy opacity effectively serves his intention to make people believe "things that were completely opposite, to disconcert minds through this whirlwind of speeches" (C 362). This "coryphaeus"—denigrated to a "subtle and vigorous athlete"—orchestrates his will through the various channels: newspapers, the voices of writers, of the senate, or the shouts ordered in the tribunes (C 364). He filters it down into the speeches of his deputy consuls who translate "the same text into two different languages": Cambacérès serving as an interpreter for the revolutionaries and Lebrun speaking before the Royalists (C 366). But Bonaparte, himself an able manipulator who could twist language in any direction, looms suddenly as a lying Don Juan—preserving Jacobins from the monarchy's return, flattering royalist hopes with the restoration of the Bourbons, promising Siéyès a constitution, and seducing the people with images of eternal peace. To top off these burlesque flipflops, he can speak as an oriental, as "the most learned of mullahs," praising Allah and Muhammed in front of the pyramid of Cheops on his expedition to Egypt (C 354). Throughout this masquerade, an effort to lay out a theory of terrorist speech becomes apparent. Along with surprise tactical threats, such as "Do you want me to turn you over to the Jacobins?" Bonaparte skillfully exploits the nation's imaginary constructs to disorient and divide it (C 386). Finally, to justify himself, he reaches out for tactics of argumentation that distort the truth of history. "Abstract questions were only discussed to establish tyranny; just as in Cromwell's time, the Bible was read to provide passages to authorize absolute power" (C 361).

This eruption of playfulness indicates another dimension of *Considérations*. Up to this point, the free-flowing relationship between words and the status of truth has been carefully recorded, but here it bursts forth as unpardonable scandal. Staël "materializes," in the classically Bakhtinian, degrading meaning of the word, the corruption of speeches. Bonaparte, like a "chess-master" playing against humanity, replaced freedom with his monstrous ego, reversing the Revolution and cutting up "the red cap to make a big Legion of Honor sash" (C 397). And yet, when entering the political arena, he openly accepted the Revolution, pledging himself to it publicly; but his rhetoric involved a sequence of promises that could not be kept, false promises of the sort that Austin openly lists as "abuses" (121). Bonaparte's speeches stole the republican enthusiasm of the nation and literally outsmarted truth.

Once again the revolutionary crisis is inscribed as a drama of non-communication and disguised truth. Over and over the lapses in community ideology resemble the distortions in a house of mirrors. "Frequently, certain common ideas in circulation stray farthest from a public good sense, because most men take them to be *truths* . . . But in partisan times the same interests inspire the same speeches, without their being any *truer* the hundredth time they are given" (C 512). Shoshana Felman clarifies this weakening of truth through linguistic dissipation with a definition that, while making use of Austin's theory, distinguishes between "truth in speech" (illusive, Nietzschean, with seduction in mind) and "truth in act" (resulting in commitment and doing). The latter is always accompanied by a clash and total reversal: "Far from being the result of a process of seduction by a power or a code, quite the opposite, by definition it is what subverts every power and destroys every code" (3).[13] The adventure of a revolutionary speech retraced in *Considérations* seems to be bound up in the perversion of "truth in act" into "truth by naming." The circulation of promises that cannot be kept corrupts generosity and the epitome of an antinarcissistic promise—the revolutionary oath/pact—mutates into a scandal of truth: "Strictly speaking, truth is none other than a commitment that binds me, that promises me to someone else; . . . and commitment is neither ontological nor epistemological but performative" (Felman 7).

However, when one analyzes pronominal and verbal modalities, the text of *Considérations* can be read as an active validation of the desire to belong and to act. The work, whose original intention was to provide an apologetic transcription of Jacques Necker's work, turns into a display of his daughter's political competence. Paternal discourse vanishes into the remarks of Germaine, who, as has recently been noted, reinvents history. Lucia Omacini's study of Staëlian persuasion in theoretical writings is most revealing. *Considérations* clearly differs from earlier texts. In *Des circonstances actuelles,* for example, the recurrence of "I declare," "I attest," and the inserted dialogue "one could say to me" confirm the "specular," dialogic structure of the work indicating a transfer of power repressed in real life (Omacini 1979, 378). On the contrary, in *Considérations,* the I disappears, giving way to a collective subject we, which moves in the "dilated time . . . of eternal presence." The frequent use of the impersonal mode emphasizes the "messianic" aspect of the message and gives the impression "of an all-embracing discourse" (386). The use of tenses, strikingly incompatible with the rules of the historical genre, is even more significant. According to Omacini, Staël describes the mistakes of history—with violence and injustice—in the preterite, and places the truth in the present and the future (379). In the proliferation of the conditional, the mode of desire, and in the continual intertwining of the factual and the possible, Michel Delon perceives an exploration of temporality, which "forever provisional" can always be remodelled (1991, 33). The conditional proves also an attempt at concrete action begun in the past but projected into the future: "Staël seems to move into still another conditional tense—what would have happened if she had had the opportunities afforded her father" (Hogsett 1991, 40). Furthermore, the pairing of the verbs to wish/to have to in *Circonstances actuelles* evolves, argues Omacini, into to be able/ to know in *Considérations*. While in the work of her youth, Staël can only wish to influence others and to transfer her desire for action, in *Considérations*—confirmed by the authority of experience—the liberated subject is able and knows how to act.[14]

Comprehension of the dynamics of history implies success and consequently is placed on the side of language. Seen from a critical distance, epistemological space constitutes the most disclosive attribute of the revolutionary past; power reversals can be deduced from modalities of enunciation. Thus, the Revolution emerges as the product of Man, his commitment and his speech acts. Such is the optimistic message contained in *Considérations,* an exemplary act of generosity addressed to Man— battling still for freedom.

Notes

1. Abbreviations indicate the following works: (C) *Considérations sur la Révolution française;* (L) *De la littérature;* (CA) *Des circonstances actuelles* (1979), (RP) *Réflexions sur le procès de la reine, Œuvres complètes* (1967). All translations are mine.

2. This reading has been inspired by Petrey's interpretations of performative theory within the historical context. "The French Revolution is replete with examples of what Austin called performative speech, language that does not say what is but transforms it. From the self-conversion of the Third Estate into the National Assembly in 1789 to the restoration and re-restoration of the Bourbon regime in 1814-15, the years of the Revolution were a continuous illustration of the power of words to enact what their users willed" (1989, 2, 3).

3. I borrow the term "sociability" from Furet. "Une sociabilité politique: j'entends par là un monde organisé de relations entre les citoyens (ou les sujets) et le pouvoir, aussi bien qu'entre les citoyens (ou les sujets) eux-mêmes à propos du pouvoir. La monarchie absolue suppose et comporte un type de sociabilité politique par lequel toute la société est rangée concentriquement et hiérachiquement autour d'elle, qui est le centre organisateur de la vie sociale" (1978, 58).

4. I refer to the essential research done in this area by Mueller-Vollmer, especially to his study "From Poetics to Linguistics: Wilhelm von Humboldt and the Romantic Idea of Language" in *Le Groupe de Coppet.* See also, in the same volume, Becq 83-98, and Delon "L'idée d'énergie au tournant des Lumières."

5. For a development on the concept of moral veracity in eloquence, see Principato.

6. For a more elaborate analysis of the hyperbolic aspect of oratory art, one always present in Staël's study, see Bonnet "La 'sainte masure,' sanctuaire de la parole fondatrice" (1988). For the monumental dimensions of eloquence in iconography and sculpture, see Roger "Le débat sur la langue révolutionnaire" (1988) and Gutwirth 1992.

7. I refer in particular to the essay "Two Aspects of Language and Two Types of Aphasic Disturbances" in *Language and Literature*.

8. "we distinguished . . . the illocutionary act which has a certain force in saying something (and) the perlocutionary act which is the achieving of certain effects by saying something" (121).

9. In the category of "infelicities" Austin distinguishes between "misfires"—without effect, or having the opposite effect—and "abuses"—promises made in bad faith (121).

10. In his analysis of the Bakhtinian vision of language, Petrey indicates that during revolutionary times "even so small a linguistic unit as the single word spoken by a single speaker carries within itself the ideological thrust of vast collective conflict" (1988, 44). Bakhtin's collaborators insist on the difference between societies in revolt and the linguistic dynamics of peaceful societies that mask contradictions. "The ruling class strives to impart a supraclass, eternal character to the ideological sign, to extinguish or drive inward the struggle between social value judgments which occurs in it" (Voloshinov 23).

11. The coupling of the terms "maternity" and "sexuality" is further discussed by Gutwirth (1989 b, 121-40). Staël rebels against the slander directed at women: "What peace, what happiness can any court return to a woman attacked in the papers? Her family may be permanently disturbed; her husband may have lost his respect for her; a man who loved her may have left her because she has lost that affecting charm endowed by a quiet life devoted entirely to the object who took her gift. Finally, do these slanderers know the depths to which they have put life in turmoil? They accuse a gentle soul with their cruel opinion. They only hurt the souls they should be treating kindly. . . " (CA 119).

12. According to Hunt, the relation between the myth of an all-embracing whole and the political conspiracies recalls the tension analyzed by Derrida in *De la grammatologie* between the "metaphysics of presence" and the threat of violation produced in the act of writing. "In this sense, revolutionary rhetoric was constantly 'deconstructing' itself, that is, at once positing the possibility of a community without politics and inventing politics everywhere" (1984, 49).

13. For an extensive debate on the perversion of truth, see Felman's study *Le Scandale du corps parlant* (Paris: Seuil, 1980) or Catherine Porter, trans. *The Literary Speech Act* (Ithaca: Cornell UP, 1983).

14. Staël's reconsideration of history through the performance of speeches coincides with her coming to voice as a writer. Recent critical commentaries have convincingly demonstrated the extent to which the antinomy mutism/voice is inseparable from the work of Staël-novelist. See Gutwirth 1978; Hogsett 1987; Vallois; also Bowman and DeJean both in Gutwirth et al. 1991, respectively 55-68 and 122-37.

13

Unmasking *Indiana:* George Sand and the French Revolution(s)[1]

Lauren Pinzka

In George Sand's first novel, Indiana, written in 1832, the reader witnesses Sand's attempt to make sense of four decades of her nation's history, an effort that she consciously makes yet one whose course she cannot entirely control. *Indiana* illustrates Gabrielle Spiegel's description of the dialectical relation between text and context:

> All texts occupy determinate social spaces, both as products of the social world of authors and as textual agents at work in that world, with which they entertain often complex and contestatory relations. In that sense, texts both mirror and generate social realities, are constituted by and constitute the social and discursive formations which they may sustain, resist, contest, or seek to transform.... (77)

Any discussion of Sand's literary treatment of history must be predicated by an acknowledgement of the illusory status of the "reality" of historical events, the accounts of which are a linguistic construction, as is Sand's novel. There is no historical "truth" to which we can refer; history is constructed from texts which also include historical fiction.

Sand wrote her novel well after the turbulent events of 1789, the Reign of Terror (or "Terrors" as Furet explains [1990, 796-97]) and the First Empire, but had experienced them vicariously through the eyes of her aristocratic grandmother with whom she spent her childhood. It is significant to the political ramifications of *Indiana* that it was written just after the political upheaval of 1830. The surprisingly understated treatment of this second French Revolution confirms Henry Peyre's observation in *Qu'est-ce que le romantisme?* that the dust must first settle before history can integrate itself into a fictional form (89). Peyre observes that the traumatic memory of emigration, the Terror, compulsory military service under Napoleon, and territorial invasion in 1814 and 1815 emotionally hindered much of the French intelligentsia from any immediate examination of events. It was in particular the children of the victims of the Revolution who studied, with hindsight, the costs and benefits of those years both in fictional and nonfictional expression. It was not until the ascension of Charles X to the throne and the subsequent popular dissatisfaction with his retrograde policies that the Revolution came to be a popular fictional subject.[2]

Nonetheless, Sand underplays the actual Revolution. Its memory, though dulled by the passage of time, was still largely what historian Emmet Kennedy calls "a nightmare" (1989, 378) for her generation. As he remarks in his recent work on that period, "Most politicians and historians incorporated revolution in their work to exorcise it, neutralize it, make it tolerable. But however much they excoriated it, it would not go away" (1989, 378). Such is the role of history in Sand's *Indiana*. The Revolution and the Terror are far from the central topics or even the setting of her novel, yet their presence hovers over the entire work like a bad dream. For Sand, the French Revolution is more than a few magical dates (Chastagnaret 446). In *The Body and the French Revolution,* Dorinda Outram affirms that this crucial period in French history was not a question of dates and of beginnings and endings, but of the values that it produced (1989, 37). *Indiana,* a rich portrait of those values, is a commentary on the French Revolution through its critique of the Restoration and Revolution of 1830.

I will examine Sand's remarks about both revolutions, but more important to my reading of the text is what she chooses not to say, or rather what she says, but in an obscured fashion. By emphasizing the role of the unconscious in the composition of the literary text, I do not underestimate the importance of Sand's conscious literary choices, her astute knowledge of her audience, and her desire to consciously rework traditional forms. To the contrary, my paper will reveal Sand to be a far more complex thinker than is commonly believed. In particular, Sand's public image of a socialist and a pacifist is belied by a careful reading of her work. Some of her stated political views are also helpful in resolving what appear to be contradictory political positions and will reveal Sand in divergence from her public persona as "la bonne dame de Nohant." I will also consider the role of gender in some of those contradictions.

The methodology will seem unorthodox at first; I will read Sand's novel both from a historical and a psychoanalytic point of view. Although psychoanalytic readings focus on the transposition of unconscious fantasies to the scene of literary creation, thereby highlighting issues like the author's "acting out" of family scenarios, I focus on the repression of historical forces in the novel. I will show that Sand's denial system is related to a key issue in psychoanalysis, eroticized violence, or sado-masochism. The unconscious has a relation to history in that those memorializing it, men and women alike, are forever split subjects. As Lacan elaborates in "La Signification du Phallus," "the subject designates its being only by barring what it signifies" (112).[3] Elsewhere he evokes Freud's recognition of "the self's radical ex-centricity to itself" ("Instance" 284). Furthermore, Sand's marginalized position as a woman inevitably has a bearing on her literary production. Psychoanalysis provides some insight into this thorny question.

This paper is divided into two parts: an examination of what is called in psychoanalytic theory the "manifest content" of Sand's revised fantasy-text, that is the text as it appears at first reading, followed by a glimpse at the "latent content" of Sand's text as revealed through denial and obsessive word choice. I will attempt to uncover the traces of fantasy unconsciously reproduced in literary production and censored by the process of secondary elaboration, the smoothing over of narrative inconsistencies to "make sense" of fantasy as well as to make it acceptable to the self-censor. The obsessive references to "the hidden," "the buried," the impossible desire of penetrating one another's thoughts, and most of all, the veiled portrait of Ralph, invite the reader to search for the repressed desire masked by the text. *Indiana*'s "mask" is more than concealment, however. It provides for a fruitful discussion of history, politics, and narrative point of view.

History and Politics in *Indiana*

Restoration politics are at the core of *Indiana,* informing the conception of the characters, influencing the plot, and generating pages of political analysis. Like most writers, Sand's primary means of conveying the complexities of her time is through the creation and reproduction of symbols. Some correspond to well-known historical stereotypes, but it is through the development of characters as symbols that Sand achieves a more elaborated political analysis. A typical example of her tendency towards cliché appears early in the novel when she introduces Raymon's mother as one of those women "who have eluded the scaffolds of 93, the vices of the Directory, the vanities of the Empire, the rancor of the Restoration" (78). Sand more reveals a desire to perpetuate symbols of political events than to analyze them. The process of enumeration equalizes the significance of the historical events in question, each with its assigned defect. Her text thus functions as mirror and generator of social reality (Spiegel 77).

Confirming the use of "scaffolds" as a haunting symbol of the Revolution, Sand's narrator explains that Raymon, the aristocrat, fears the reinstitution of "the scaffolds" and the flow of "innocent blood" (167). The Revolution of 1830, which takes place in the narrative space of this work, is dramatically presented in the context of its symbol when Indiana arrives in France only to be confronted with the revolt: "But how surprised and fearful was she, on debarking, to see the tricolor floating above the walls of Bordeaux!" (290). Instantly the political struggle is linked to the symbolic tricolor, then followed by a more familiar representation of Revolution: bloodshed. The following sentence terms the political events "a violent agitation" which point toward an imminent "bloody struggle." "Blood" semantically unites both revolutions and will show itself to be a dominant theme of the work as well. Napoleon and the Old Regime are also reduced to a symbolic representation: Delmare and Raymon are depicted as "one under the sword of Napoleon, the other under the scepter of Saint Louis; M. Delmare, planted at the foot of the Pyramids; Raymon, seated beneath the monarchial shade of the oak of Vincennes" (169).

The above example also demonstrates the manner in which Sand creates characters who embody specific political positions and who repeatedly reenact history through their fictional existences. She accomplishes her task primarily through Delmare, the Bonapartist; Raymon, the hereditary monarchist; Ralph, the Republican; and Indiana, the pacifist who rejects all man-made law. Her narrator is often critical of her characters while favoring Ralph and Indiana's more liberal views. Nonetheless, Sand's own class prejudices obviously influence her presentation of characters. A discussion of each of these characters permits an elaboration of the coexistence between text and context, between historical processes and fictional representation in her novel.

Delmare, as worshipper of the fallen Napoleon, is obsessively labeled a despot and tyrant. He is portrayed as "a man of iron" (86), brutal, imperious, and combative, corresponding to the popular image of Napoleon as an impulsive and brutish warrior. The character of Delmare exemplifies much that was true of the Bonaparte regime: ambition, military prowess, the self-made man (Kennedy 1989, 377), and the subordination of women (Delmare claims that women are to obey, not to advise [204]). Carol Richards brands Delmare as the embodiment of the infamous Napoleonic code that stripped women of all civil rights (16). However, it is significant that this code was written by the very men who made the revolution, that is, the legists and anti-monarchists. Furthermore, the "Family-State Compact," forged in sixteenth- and seventeenth-century France, demonstrates to what extent women had been legally constrained well before the Revolution (Hanley 24). Despite its original promise of equality for women's liberation, the Revolution was but a "process of exclusion . . . a purging of the female from the body politic" (Outram 1989, 126). It would be historically blind to brand Napoleon as particularly harsh towards women when in fact he was maintaining a long French tradition. Indeed, Delmare is matched by Raymon in his subjugatory tendencies although he relies more on brute force than does his aristocratic counterpart whose method is largely rhetorical. However, Indiana's servitude to her brutal master, which legally ends only when he dies, is a dramatization of the plight of French women both before and after the French revolution.

Delmare's social class is another link to his Bonapartist stance. He is a former colonel turned industrialist and landowner, thereby exemplifying the social classes who came to power under the Empire.[4] Sand links him semantically to his class by emphasizing his "good business sense" and his "capital" (85). His status as landowner marks him as a successful man of the Napoleonic years, *"propriétaires"* the foundation of the Napoleonic state (Bergeron 151).[5] Sand's use of the term both reflects a social reality and reinforces the acquisitive nature of capitalism; although hardly unique to bourgeois capitalists, Delmare's treatment of his wife implies a proprietary nature as well: "In marrying Delmare, she [Indiana] only changed masters" (88). Sand therefore perpetuates the stereotype of the Bonapartist bourgeois capitalist but opens her novel with Raymon, the aristocrat, pretending to steal industrial secrets from Delmare, thereby demonstrating her knowledge of aristocratic participation in industry. Revisionist historians have uncovered ample evidence that aristocrats were full participants in the rise of capitalism as early as in pre-Revolutionary France (Chaussinand-Nogaret 1985 a, 87ff). Although Delmare belongs to the class that will benefit in many ways from the Revolution of 1789, Sand chooses to have her Bonapartist colonel fall into financial ruin while her aristocrats prosper, a historically viable choice since much of the old nobility maintained its prominence after the Revolution and many bourgeois entrepreneurs failed (Bergeron 126, 143ff). Sand's choice of the failed bourgeois and successful aristocrat contradicts the Marxist interpretation of the Revolution as the prerequisite for bourgeois capitalism. Capitalism was well under way before the Revolution which severely disrupted it. Furthermore, after the Revolution, much of the wealth remained in the hands of the old nobility who also not only owned huge amounts of land but participated in "bourgeois" professions both before and after the Revolution (Bergeron 172, 126, 133; Chaussinand-Nogaret 1985 a, 167).

As Lynn Hunt notes, Napoleon remained faithful to the revolutionary project of modernization without striving to achieve democracy. The capitalism that did flourish (it was not uniformly successful) during his "ephemeral dynasty" (*Indiana* 85) was a product of his links to the Old Regime and to the building of an empire, and by no means a consequence of the Revolution (Hunt 1984, 95). As *Indiana* progresses, Delmare's growing allegiance is to Raymon, the aristocrat, with whom he shares considerably more than with Ralph, the Republican. This link is deeply rooted in French history as the aristocracy had coopted bourgeois values of merit and individualism well before the Revolution (Chaussinand-Nogaret 1985 a, 22-48); by 1789 the Third Estate and the nobility were virtually the same class since they earned their money in the same professions, received the same education, and enjoyed the same cultural pursuits (Chaussinand-Nogaret 1985 a, 167; Schalk 210-11). Even during the "Great Terror" when nobles were routinely being guillotined in Paris, there was frequent cooperation between aristocrats and bourgeois officeholders on local levels (Chaussinand-Nogaret 1985 a, 170).

Sand's personal feelings about Napoleon may have influenced her portrait of Delmare. In her autobiography and correspondence, she draws a more sympathetic portrait of Napoleon than one might expect of a woman who both despised the legal code that bound her and abhorred much of what he stood for. In fact, she admired his brilliance while deploring his retrograde policies (*Histoire* 1: 373).[6] In particular, she objected to his sympathy for the Old Regime and his hypocritical stance on religion, namely the imposition of the Concordat when in fact he was a non-believer (*Histoire* 1: 406). Delmare will also be a social hypocrite far more interested in *la forme* than in truth (*Indiana* 134). Notwithstanding, Sand viewed Napoleon as an honorable man consistently betrayed by his entourage (*Histoire* 1: 690). Is it coincidental that Delmare is also a betrayed and abandoned figure, dying alone on a remote island? Although the narrator consistently attacks Delmare's political positions, Sand softens her portrait of Delmare towards the end of the novel and shows that he is all bluster (207-10).

While Delmare is associated with the fallen Napoleon, Raymon is associated with the fallen aristocracy. His political views are stereotypical of his social class which in fact was far more liberal than commonly believed (Chaussinand-Nogaret 1985 a, 157-67). Raymon personifies the degraded aristocrat. The narrator continually undercuts his political positions to demonstrate their fallacy. Raymon defends the current system only because it has served him well (166-67); the Charter is justified by national needs, which the narrator points out to be those of the crown (168) and in turn those of his class as well (260). Injustice and abuses are tolerable if they prevent scaffolds (167). In the months preceding *les trois glorieuses,* the three days that led to the overthrow of Charles X, Raymon's analysis shows an overriding concern for his own class interest. He is infuriated when the King, by his own stupidity (permitting the absolutist Polignac ministry), threatens to bring Raymon and his class down with him. Never does he express concern for the plight of any group other than his own (260-61). By having Raymon oppose the king's absolutism and wish at one point that he could join the revolutionaries (262), Sand illustrates the complexity of the position of many aristocrats who often had liberal leanings but unsurprisingly, their own class interests at heart.[7] Ultimately, Raymon, like Indiana, is oblivious to the political events surrounding him. Towards the end of the novel, she finds him comfortably ensconced in her former home which he has now purchased after Delmare's bankruptcy: "The political storms had not removed a hair from his head . . ." (295). In *The French Generation of 1820,* Alan Spitzer writes that the generation to which

Raymon belonged was one of great promise and of great disappointment, that instead of regenerating French society, they merely merged with it (274, 282). At any rate, Sand chooses to provide little class analysis to explain the outbreak of violence in 1830 beyond a description of the repressive practices under Polignac (260-62), leaving us with only the aristocratic point of view and reflecting perhaps class prejudices of her own but also confirming Peyre's observation that it was too soon for any real commentary on such recent political events.

Nonetheless, Raymon's social class provides for a scathing attack on the Restoration. Raymon, we learn, "appreciated the advantages of birth for what they were worth" (72). In Sand's phrase, aristocratic terms like birth ("*naissance*") and advantages ("*avantages*") are associated with bourgeois notions of worth. The juxtaposition reflects the commingling of the two classes' value systems, a process begun centuries earlier and completed as early as the mid-eighteenth century (Chaussinand-Nogaret 1985 a, 34). Aristocrats increasingly downplayed "birth" in favor of "merit" as their *raison d'être* but were far from abandoning inheritance as the cornerstone of their caste (Schalk 218-19). Allying himself with the bourgeoisie by befriending Delmare, Raymon even considers marrying a "plebeian" (but does not in the end) since "to all appearances, this class would rise from the debris of the other, and to keep himself on the surface of the movement, he must become the son-in-law of an industrialist or of a speculator" (264). Sand perpetuates Raymon's mistaken belief that aristocrats never dirtied their hands with commerce. Similarly to Stendhal's Julien Sorel, Raymon considers it a question of "his honor" (178) to obtain results from his relations with Indiana. He complains that "he had yet to obtain anything from this love" (178). The amusing juxtaposition of the aristocratic concept of honor with the bourgeois emphasis on product again shows to what extent the aristocracy had adopted bourgeois values. However, aristocrats liked to believe that bourgeois honor was individualistic whereas the nobility's honor as a *class* was always at stake (Chaussinand-Nogaret 1985 a, 47).

Although Raymon is Sand's chief symbol of the French aristocracy under the Restoration, Indiana's aunt, Mme de Carvajal, provides an example from an older generation. Once the monarchy has been restored, she discards Bonapartism, speculates advantageously in stock and becomes a respected court figure. In her salon, "only the Restoration was praised" (85-86). Her social position reflects many a social reality: The participation of the nobility in the Bonapartist regime and in the development of capitalism (Bergeron 126, 133), as well as the superficiality (*"les apparences"*) of the Restoration period (*Indiana* 215). Sand has chosen to depict aristocratic salons, of which there were but few remaining under the Restoration. She privileges them in relation to the burgeoning utilitarian bourgeois *cercles* which served young businessmen as the salons had the aristocracy (Kennedy 1989, 26).

Raymon's social class is underscored with constant allusions to blood, haunting traces of the Revolution. He is marked as the victim of violence, elliptically the violence of the Revolution. The book significantly opens with Delmare shooting Raymon, implying the self-made man's victory over inherited privilege. (The victory is short lived.) This violent act occasions Ralph's chilling remark, "human blood has been spilled about" (62). Raymon is subsequently described several times as "all bloody" and will continue to be associated with blood throughout the novel as in "a bilious man, whose blood circulated quickly" (193). The word *terror* is frequently invoked in connection with this character, although not exclusively. Raymon is also linked to the "crime" (193) perpetrated against Noun, which symbolizes his class's abuse of the populace.

The case of the novel's most positive characters, Ralph and Indiana, deserves special attention. Ralph is linked to the Republic, to positive ideals of equality and pacifism. He is symbolic of many trends of Sand's own thought. Yet he is termed and considers himself an egotist (despite his self-sacrificing posture throughout the novel), and decries a government which permits abuses and prejudices, while forbidding the discussion of "our interests" (166-67). His ideology corresponds to the nineteenth-century belief in a new social order, based on self-interest, and termed the science of society ("the greatest good for the greatest number") and focus was turned to the interests of society rather than that of "man in the singular or of the knowledge of God" (Kennedy 1989, 381). Ralph's philosophy reflects this changed perspective, a direct outcome of revolutionary thought (Kennedy 1989, 381). Sand's narrator summarizes his republican dream as follows: "He wanted to exclude all abuses, all prejudices, all injustices, a project entirely founded on the hope of a new race of men" (167). He rejects Louis XVIII's charter, aspiring to a greater expanse of freedom for the French (168). Sand minimizes, however, both Raymon and Ralph's political stances as signs of their egotism: like children, her narrator writes, one supports a system that has served him well while the other despises a life that has treated him unfairly. Both were judging from their own limited perspective and incompetence (166-67). Sand also chooses to make her liberal noble an Englishman, underscoring his marginal status in French society. Given Ralph's progressive views (while egotistical, far from Delmare and Raymon's) and his clear signs of androgyny, it is possible that Sand projected some of herself onto Ralph and chose for him the condition of foreigner as a statement on her own outsider-status as a woman in French society.

Indiana, with whom Sand claimed not to identify,[8] embodies opposition to masculine political values which are systematically denigrated by the narrator; her actions are continually characterized as "resistance," a term whose political overtones suggests a legitimate political position in its own right: refusal to participate in the system. Despite Sand's stereotypical portrait of her main character as an ignorant Créole, Indiana proves herself to be a resourceful woman compared to many nineteenth-century French heroines, and her political acumen develops along with the trajectory of the novel. She expresses herself most articulately in a letter to Raymon where she attacks not only the concept of divine monarchy and the influence of the Catholic Church, but predicts that God will sweep both away (249), suggesting that her guise of political indifference veils the passions of a true revolutionary.

Revolution in *Indiana*[9]

We have located three preponderant political positions in *Indiana:* the Royalist, Bonapartist, and Republican. Conspicuously absent is that of the revolutionary. Its very lack implies its presence as well as Sand's desire to efface it along with its essential violence from her liberal world view. Just as important as her political stance were the cultural constraints that deemed it unseemly that a woman should openly condone violence, although Sand would hardly be alone in breaking with the stereotype of female pacifism (Charlotte Corday is a notable example). However, her avoidance of the revolutionary stance only forces it to appear in subtextual forms: Hence, the abundance of references throughout the novel to heads (of which "to lose one's head" is particularly preponderant), blood ("bloody," "*en sang*";

"cold-blooded," "*sang froid*"; "frozen blood," "*sang glacé*"; "veins," "*veines*"), cutting ("*trancher*"), crime and terror. The terse fashion in which Sand dismisses the outbreak of the Revolution of 1830 in a few sentences and recounts it from the point of view of her most apolitical character, Indiana, supports the theory that she is suppressing a dominant force of her era. Her attempt to repress it out of well-known distaste for political violence is unsuccessful once the subtext of Indiana is rendered manifest. Sand hints at such when referring repeatedly to the Restoration as a masquerade. Aristocrats metamorphose into "that crowd of masks" (77) while political moderation "mask[s] . . . antipathies" (129). "Political sentiment" serves as a "mask" for expressing one's hatred and desire for revenge (171). Sand projects onto the entire period the desire to mask the violence that it no longer wishes to see.

The metaphor itself recalls one of the key concepts of revolutionary thought: transparency. Lynn Hunt argues that "political discourse was structured by notions of transparency, publicity, vigilance, and terror" (1984, 44). During the Revolution, the traditional French obsession with conspiracy was so exacerbated that revolutionaries spoke incessantly of unmasking plots (1984, 38-39). Perhaps the mask of the Restoration is obliquely a reference to its distance from revolutionary clarity. The Revolution and its violence may be masked, but in the words of Emmet Kennedy, it will not go away, hence the prevalence of *sang* and *terreur*. One can see evidence of the violence of the Revolution of 1830, but in disguised form. A key example is a reference to Indiana's ironic disillusionment after thinking that Raymon's perfidious character has been revealed (whereas only the tip of the iceberg has manifested itself) as "the illusions of three days" (126). The epithet is later transformed into "the whims ("*caprices*") of three days" but Indiana significantly evokes the term "with terror." The repeated insistence on the fact that she was happy for only three days, coupled with the evocative "illusions" suggests that Indiana's brief and blind passion for Raymon is an erotic representation of *les trois glorieuses,* occurring just shortly before *Indiana* was written. Noun's subsequent suicide suggests the defeat of the dreams of the people who were perhaps again committing political suicide. Supporting this view is Indiana and Ralph's attempted suicide following the description, minimized as it is, of the Revolution of 1830.

The violence of revolution is also hidden under Indiana's passive resistance as slave to Delmare's master. In perhaps the most intriguing scene of the novel, Indiana dresses as the now dead Noun and tries to seduce Raymon. Her intent is to shock him into admitting that he had pursued an affair with her chambermaid. So convincing is she as Noun that Raymon faints. On awakening, he bitterly accuses her of having done him incomparable harm. "You have just shown me how full it [your heart] is of revenge and cruelty. . . . and once you discover with what delirious passion I love you, you dig your female nails into my heart to find a bit of blood that may still flow for you . . ." (193). His harsh words produce the desired effect. She immediately reverts to her more customary role of submissiveness: "She gave in like a weak child; she abandoned her lips to him without resistance. She was nearly dead" (194). After changing her mind and freeing herself from him, "Raymon tore her with authority from her hiding place" and but for her "moral resistance" would have raped her (195). This scene demonstrates Indiana's courage in the face of adversity but also a more troubling facet of her character as she continues to long for Raymon well after his cruel nature is revealed. For now that he has been humiliated by Indiana, he vows not only to "possess" Indiana but to "reduce" her as well (200). In a clear sadistic fantasy, he envisages himself as becoming her master for the sheer pleasure of abandoning her and seeing her at his feet. His wish comes true later in the novel when she returns to France to throw herself at his feet: "Dispose of me, of my blood, of my life; I am yours, body and soul. I have traveled three thousand leagues to belong to you, to tell you this; take me, I am your possession, you are my master" (297). Raymon clearly enjoys the moment:

> I [the narrator] do not know what infernal idea suddenly crossed Raymon's mind. He withdrew his face from his clenched hands, and looked at Indiana with a diabolical *sang-froid;* then a terrible smile wandered across his lips and made his eyes sparkle, for Indiana was still beautiful. (297)

In fact, throughout *Indiana,* men express strong desires to physically harm her, beginning with her violent father (88). At one point Delmare fantasizes about strangling her, dragging her by her hair, and trampling on her until she begs for mercy and implores his grace, but she was so pretty that he could not hurt her, like a child who takes pity on the bird he wants to kill (210). Again Sand depicts a man (assimilated to a child) engaging in a strong sadistic fantasy with Indiana as victim. Indiana herself imagines at one point the rough hand of her husband grabbing her, knocking her down, and dragging her in the gutter (226), a fantasy probably influenced by real experience. Delmare is true to his reputation after he reads her love-letters to Raymon: He grabs her by the hair, knocks her over, and kicks her in the forehead with his boot (269).

Although Indiana is ostensibly attracted to Raymon despite, and perhaps because of his cruelty, she tolerates Delmare's brutality without seeming to enjoy it. Much of Sand's portrait points to sexual masochism. A case could be made for Louise Kaplan's argument, informed by the work of Krafft-Ebing, that women practice a distinctive form of masochism, termed "sexual bondage," whereby it is the woman's emotional torment in the relationship that provides the essential ingredient of her sexual pleasure and not the physical pain she often encounters (210-15).

However, Sand's richness as a novelist allows her female protagonist a more complex personality than that of a masochist. In fact, Sand recognizes the dual nature of masochism, that is that sadism and masochism are alternating phases of the same psychic phenomenon, the infliction of pain, punishment, or humiliation for purposes of sexual gratification (Freud, *SE* 14: 127-28). The difference between the two is determined by the object of the action, that is, whether the subject receives or inflicts pain (*SE* 14: 127-28). Freud contends that sadists vicariously enjoy the pleasure they imagine their victims to be feeling and are thus masochists at heart (*SE* 14: 129). However, most sadists are men because women are usually socialized to inhibit aggressive responses (*SE* 22: 116). Through sadism, Sand thus allows her female protagonist to demonstrate the often excluded parts of the traditional representation of women. Indiana shows a surprising predilection for the hunt, "this abridged version of war with its strains, its ruses, its calculations, its combats, and its chances" (162). "This excitement" (162) enhances her mundane life. Indiana, who has been described as Delmare's "prey" (94), occasionally displays an equal passion for the role of the predator.

The narrator tells us that her courage was "more than masculine" (162), suggesting an androgynous portrait and an acceptance of the traditional and unfortunate division of gender attributes that equates courage with masculinity. (On the other hand, "more than" could suggest that Indiana's feminine courage was superior to a masculine variety.) There are other indications of Indiana's dual nature. The narrator concludes that Indiana's ability to manipulate her brutal husband through passive resistance demonstrates that "she was cruel out of virtue, as he was good out of weakness" (210). Laplanche and Pontalis succinctly explain that sado-masochism is "the chosen expression of the most fundamental principal of psychical functioning . . . and . . . in so far as it is 'the essence of the instinctual,' it binds every wish, whether aggressive or sexual, to the wish to death" (103). Indiana's repeated attempts to commit suicide after Raymon's rejection link her further to sado-masochistic impulses. It is noteworthy that "the hunt was the only passion that Ralph and Indiana had in common" (162). This detail reveals that beneath their pacifist exteriors lies a hidden attraction for what has overtly been compared to warfare.

Indiana has already linked herself to revolution in her letter to Raymon, written while she is on the Ile Bourbon. She tells him that while he believes that God has authorized him to "usurp the empire of the earth," she is convinced that in time, "like grains of sand, His breath will blow you away" (249). Without overt reference to revolution, its image obliquely introduces a series of metaphors comparing revolution to violent events of nature: "the storm" (295) and "the whirlwind" (235). The latter trope reappears in a natural setting in the scene where a younger Ralph shows his devotion to his childhood friend, Indiana, by stealing eggs from birds' nests. Sand suggests political allegory through reference to the bird named "queen of the seas" (*"la reine des mers"*), who flies in air metaphorically termed the birds' "homeland" (*"patrie"*). The birds, angered by Ralph's theft, "rose in black whirlwinds (*"tourbillons"*) only to fall to the ground" as "Indiana laughed at their movements" (*"évolutions"*) (257). Both the *"tourbillons,"* already associated with revolutions, and the phonetically similar *"évolutions,"* suggest an oblique reference to or an unconscious allusion to the Revolution with Ralph as revolutionary activist.

In this scene from Indiana's childhood, it is Ralph who transgresses, assuming Raymon's habitual role earlier in the novel. Just as Ralph's portrait is veiled when Indiana is not at Lagny, his character is hidden under "a stone mask" (315). His face is also described as "the immobile mask of Sir Ralph, his petrified countenance" (182). The word *mask* has clear connotations of revolutionary conspiracy. It is Ralph's task to bleed Raymon once he has been wounded. It is thus suggested that bloodshed is necessary to achieve political utopia. Underneath Ralph's passive exterior is the subaltern force of violent revolution, already exhibited when he steals from "the queen" in a revolutionary act.

Ralph appears most strikingly as violent revolutionary when he divulges to Indiana the true motive of Noun's suicide. The narrator's description of his act is telling: "Ralph had just thrust the knife in and pierced a dreadful wound" (184). Although he immediately regrets hurting Indiana, "the outward calm with which he carried out this cruel operation gave him the air of an executioner in Indiana's eyes." She labels his act "your revenge," whereas the narrator terms it "the clumsy execution," and insists on its "violence." To complete the tableau of the Terror with its executioners, the action turns to Raymon who then enters the grounds of the château: "But on entering, he felt his head become cold" (184). Both Raymon and Indiana are the victims of Ralph's brutality, assimilated to "the excesses of '93" as Raymon has already termed them (168). Furthermore, Ralph's status as outsider (he is British) conforms to the stereotype but also to the political reality of the revolutionary of 1789 (Hunt 1984, 184). Ralph is, however, a baronet, allowing Sand to show that liberal aristocrats like herself did exist.

Another link between Ralph (and Indiana for that matter) and revolution is his stoicism which leads him to unsuccessfully attempt suicide. The neo-classical fixation with death, revived by the Romantics, arose from a reworking of classical stoicism between the sixteenth and eighteenth centuries. The impact of the new stoicism on revolutionary behavior was significant, particularly on the number of suicides attempted and achieved. Self-control, self-discipline, sacrifice of personal emotions, tolerance, moderation, all were attributes of those who adhered to this philosophy (Outram 1989, 68-79), and are all traits that characterize the silent, faithful Ralph who waits until both he and Indiana are about to commit suicide to express his love for her. New stoics, however, maintained an active role in politics and primarily committed suicide to control their own death, thus avoiding public humiliation (Outram 1989, 97). Stoic suicide disappeared with Napoleon, but we know that Ralph appeals to "tastes from another century, known as *philosophic*" (*Indiana* 51). Ralph's neo-stoicism links him to revolutionaries even if his suicide is enacted for different reasons, and is in fact more in the romantic mode.

Beneath his stoic façade, Sand suggests Ralph's hidden violence through the repetition of conditionals and negations which have the effect of affirming his violent desires. In the scene of Ralph swearing to Raymon's mother that he will not harm her son, he provides supposed evidence of his innocuousness, couched in the following hypnotic series of denials:

> I surprised their first kiss, and I did not throw M. de Ramière down from his horse. I often intercepted their messages of love in the woods, and I did not destroy them with a whip. I encountered M. de Ramière on the bridge that he was crossing to go find her; it was nighttime, we were alone ... however, I did not throw that man into the river (237).

Many other instances of this phenomenon can be observed throughout *Indiana* where the possibility of violence is affirmed by its repeated denial. As Lyotard explains in *Discours, figure,* negation does not mark an object, but a relationship. Existence is affirmed by its negation, the latter becoming a substitute for a repressed desire, "a certificate of origin" (123). Lyotard provides the following definition: "Negation is the mutation of the drive into desire through its passage into language" (127). Included in each of Ralph's negated statements is their affirmation, the expression of a repressed wish.

The above example points to another side of Ralph's complex character, that is, its "feminine" side. I borrow Rita Felski's aptly put explanation of the term *feminine:* "a set of ideological configurations, that is, a cluster of nineteenth-century symbolic connotations between the female gender and a specific, though often contradictory, range of psychological and cultural attributes" (1104 n.1). The culturally bound and binary gender codes of "femininity" and "masculinity" underlay most Western representations of men and women; I have already given as an example the Sandian narrator's categorization of Indiana's courage as "masculine." Granted that there is no pre-discursive reality, and that meaning is created by a linguistic system of differences, the binary pairs of male and female and their normalized gender attributes "feminine" and "masculine" inform our conception of reality. Lacan goes so far as to assert that the very notion of femininity is constituted as lack and that femininity is a mask, a masquerade ("Phallus" 113-15). In other words, the very division has historically functioned as a linguistic system of difference that defines "femininity" as the absence of masculinity; therefore, the feminine is never the mark of the subject. For Lacan, our fate is "the constitutive ignorance of the *self*" ("Mirror" 96) because the masculine "subject" is a fictive construction, requiring the suppression of the sexual positions excluded in the process of identity formation and the suppression of the pre-individuated pleasures associated with the repressed maternal body. Julia Kristéva identifies that repressed state as the "semiotic," and claims that the essentialized feminine unconscious serves as a perpetual source of subversion within the Symbolic. A point often misunderstood in Freud's work and a cornerstone of psychoanalytic theory is the positing of primary bisexuality and the cohabitation of culturally defined "masculine" and "feminine" dispositions within the individual; the predominance of one or the other will affect identification with the mother or the father (*SE* 19: 28-31). The subject represses object-choices unacceptable to the Symbolic order and internalizes the tabooed object of desire (*SE* 19: 28-29). We must choose between two sexual dispositions and two object choices, the mother and the father. Freud would agree with Michel Foucault that our choices are culturally overdetermined. In *The History of Sexuality,* the latter emphasizes the normative nature of both sex and sexuality (1:83), fictitious unities that gain meaning through discourse (1: 151, 156). *In Gender Trouble,* Judith Butler concludes that sexual dispositions refer not to "primary sexual facts of the psyche, but produced effects of a law imposed by culture and by the complicitous and transvaluating acts of the ego ideal" (64). Her central thesis is that gender is performance, the result of a process whereby behavior is "naturalized" (70).

Sand undermines those very gender codes in her portrait of Ralph. She disrupts "[t]he construction of coherence [that] conceals gender discontinuities" (Butler 135). Béatrice Didier in particular observes the odd manner in which Ralph's desires manifest themselves. He speaks of destroying love notes with a whip, surely an impractical means of doing so. Didier notes as well that it never occurs to Ralph to challenge Raymon to a duel, which would be the normal means of settling a dispute; instead he expresses a desire to pull him from his horse and to throw him into the river. Didier links this denied/expressed desire to his method of choice for suicide—drowning, which in its passivity and liquidity, is linked to the feminine in its cultural associations (1969, 90). Margaret Higonnet points out that Freud interpreted suicide by drowning as a means by which the individual fulfilled his or her wish to bear a child (Freud *SE* 18: 162n, qtd. in Higonnet 69). Although suicide is by no means an exclusively female act, the nineteenth-century feminized it through association with passive self-surrender, love, and illness (Higonnet 71). As a method, drowning suggests passive surrender, and liquidity, the intrauterine environment; it is thus a doubly "feminized" act.[10]

Didier's observations are supported by other indications of culturally defined "femininity" in Ralph, not the least his role as nurturer towards Indiana. The first description we encounter of the character is studded with nouns some of which denote virility but nearly all in the feminine gender: "The rather casual vigor (*"la vigueur"*) of his form, the clarity (*"la netteté"*) of his brown eyebrows, the polished whiteness (*"la blancheur"*) of his forehead, the calm (*"le calme"*) of his limpid eyes, the beauty (*"la beauté"*) of his hands, even the rigorous elegance (*"la rigoureuse élégance"*) of his hunting costume . . ." (51). The only masculine noun, *"le calme,"* is a characteristic most frequently associated with women, as are beautiful hands. The veiled portrait of Ralph is another obvious allusion to femininity as is his inarticulateness, the pre-verbal linked to the pre-Symbolic, a state of symbiosis with the mother that precedes entry into language (*infans* literally means "without language"). Pierrette Daly notes that his inability to articulate his sentiments links him to Indiana and Noun, whose words are often paraphrased by the narrator.[11] Ralph explains in ironic eloquence that nature had denied him "what it grants the most vulgar of creatures, the power to express my feelings through glances and words" (315).

I have shown that Ralph's character contains both revolutionary violence and culturally coded femininity. There is, however, an evolution in this association. I have already maintained that the character is introduced in a suggestively feminine manner but also in a hidden one, as the veiled portrait so eloquently symbolizes. Throughout the novel, Ralph is outwardly phlegmatic and peaceful, although he is continually associated with the perpetration of violence, revolutionary and otherwise. The end of the novel, however, suggests a passage away from both masculine violence and masculine political systems (his professed Republican sympathies) towards a feminine lifestyle, commencing with the feminine drowning. Another indication of this passage towards the "feminine" (which counters the author's personal passage towards the "masculine" through the adoption of a male pseudonym and narrator[12]) is the repeated use of the feminine plural pronoun to refer to Indiana and Ralph on their return to the Ile Bourbon:

> These two people [*"personnes," n.f.*] had allocated this time to rest . . .
> But they [*"elles," f.pl.*]) undoubtedly did not imagine it thus; for,

> having taken the *faham* together . . . , they [*"elles"*] dressed with a particular care, as if they [*"elles"*] intended to spend the evening in the city, and, taking the mountain path, they [*"elles"*] arrived after a one-hour walk at the gully of Bernica (310).

Similarly to Ralph's series of denials, the repetition of *"elles"* has a nearly hypnotic effect, and again, places Ralph clearly in the feminine camp.

It could be justifiably asserted that this "passage to the feminine" represents the triumph of traditionally essentialized feminine values of nature, harmony, and family over the masculine values of violence, ambition, success, and society. Sand's choice to associate Republicanism with femininity has historical foundations as well. During the Revolution, feminine allegorizations of classical derivation were adopted to the exclusion of all paternalistic figures reminiscent of the monarchy. The symbol of the Revolution was of course Marianne, the Roman goddess of Liberty (Hunt 1984, 32).[13] By associating Ralph with femininity, Sand is showing her allegiance to revolutionary and republican ideals. Nancy Rogers observes that she also breaks with the Napoleonic and old regimes by having her heroine consciously reject her husband's name and by discarding the use of rank and titles. At the end of the novel, Mme Delmare and Sir Ralph have become Indiana and Ralph. Furthermore, Indiana has no child to further her father's or husband's lineage (Rogers 63, 72).

However, Sand's work cannot be reduced to simply a feminist message. Kathryn Crecelius asserts in *Family Romances* that Sand is attempting to reconcile herself to the new bourgeois social order emerging from the Revolution of 1789 (79). She is promoting, in her union of Indiana and Ralph, a collapse of class barriers through intermarriage, yet Ralph promotes a clearly bourgeois lifestyle:

> It requires too much energy to break with the world, too much pain to acquire that energy . . . Go, young man, pursue the course of your destiny: have friends, a position, a reputation, a country . . . Do not break the chains that tie you to society (343).

Indeed, *Indiana* sketches a portrait of a society in upheaval after two revolutions, a society struggling with the questions of legitimacy and proprietorship. Two solutions for the individual are proposed: a Romantic flight from

(Indiana and Ralph's choice) and a pragmatic embrace of bourgeois society (Ralph's advice to others).

The surface level of the text reveals conflicting ideologies; the subtext hints at yet another. The strong undercurrent of violence that I have unearthed in this study suggests that Sand is sublimating her own attraction to violence in the creation of this fantasy-text, art being one of the means of such sublimation. I have already suggested that as a woman, she was more inclined to repress such a troubling tendency, given societal gender-bound codes prohibiting female expression of such "negative" affect.

The novel's conclusion leaves a troubling chink in the armor of a clear feminist message. Why is the feminine ideal marked with the stigma of incest and crime? The narrator feels strangely "repentant" as he questions Ralph who, twice on one page alone, refers to "our crimes" and "our crime" (342). The narrator also compares himself to "a thief caught in the act," adding, "[i]t seemed to me that I had wronged him" (336). He denies the existence of Ralph's crimes ("that man had no crime in his memory"), despite the latter's repetitive reference to it. Perhaps Sand's text, like the "hieroglyphic impressions," the "mysterious characters" (333) that Ralph and Indiana find on the island, cannot be fully understood. However, I suggest a possible explanation for that guilt, externally manifested as a taboo relationship. Perhaps a source of the guilt associated with their union is the sublimation of the violence to which both are drawn, Ralph as we have already seen, and Indiana in the obvious pleasure she obtains as Raymon's victim. We are reminded of Ralph and Indiana's mutual passion for the hunt, a metaphor for war, and another socially sanctioned form of violence. Freud maintained the necessity of the repression of our instinctual desires in order to live in civilization. Michael Roth, in *Psycho-Analysis in History,* summarizes Freud's argument from *Civilization and Its Discontents:*

> Civilization is seen as a process humanity undergoes—a process that modifies the demands of instinct. Three results of changes in the erotic instincts are . . . character traits . . . sublimations (art, science, ideology), and renunciation (168).

Ralph and Indiana ironically sublimate their desires for both sexual release and violence (the sado-masochistic impulse, the fusion of Eros and

Thanatos) outside of civilization, or at least outside warlike, revolutionary Europe. Their political action becomes the freeing of slaves, in fact the single positive emancipatory act portrayed in the novel, and a probable reference to the suppression of Toussaint's slave revolt in Santo-Domingo.

Sand's novel represents her own sublimation. However, Lucienne Frappier-Mazur explains that Sand "may identify in fantasy with feelings and drives that may or may not have found any actualization in the events of her own life, but, conversely, she is the originator of those fantasies which, for this reason, ultimately refer back to herself" (332-33). I look to other information about Sand to support my contention. We learn in Sand's autobiography of her admiration for Robespierre, "one of the greatest men in history" (*Histoire* 1: 113). Sand states that she would have been a Jacobin had she lived during the tumultuous events of the 1790s, although she later admits that in hindsight, she feels differently (*Histoire* 1: 168). As late as 1841, she justified the Terror as a necessary means of self-defense, and in 1852 repeated that the Terror was excusable since there was no universal suffrage. Robespierre, she claimed, was obliged to institute capital punishment despite his opposition to it (*Correspondance* 5: 506; 11: 14; qtd. Vermeylan 164-65).

Although Sand appears to have been correct that Robespierre was a principled man, and, unlike many others, not motivated by personal gain, a quotation from one of his tracts leaves little room for doubt of his role in the Terror:

> Terror is nothing other than justice, prompt, severe, and inflexible; it is therefore an emanation of virtue. . . . Break the enemies of liberty with terror and you will be justified as founders of the Republic. The government of the revolution is the despotism of liberty against tyranny.[14]

It was Sand's conviction that Robespierre had been scapegoated by historians when, in fact, most great leaders had committed acts that "make nature shudder and revolt the conscience" (*Histoire* 1: 113). Sand was thus conscious of Robespierre's deeds and beliefs, yet felt that they were justified. Many modern historians have chosen to explore the scope of the Revolution's brutality in an attempt to understand it and perhaps as a response to Marxist idealism, to demystify the revolutionary process. For Dorinda

Outram, both the middle and lower classes, whose bodies had always been scorned by the aristocracy, were chiefly responsible for the killings of the Revolution. She is particularly struck by the obsession with cannibalism and dismemberment (1989, 63), in part seen in the extraordinary use of the guillotine and the cases of citizens' justice in the prison massacres.

The link between revolution and violence would appear obvious, less so the link between democracy and violence. Sand's support of the first appears to have included the latter. Lynn Hunt explains how one leads to the other:

> Democracy, terror, socialism, and authoritarianism were all made possible by the expansion of the political space and the organized participation for the popular classes. The terror was unthinkable without the previous experience of democracy; it was the disciplinarian side of the democratic community, invoked in time of emergency and justified by the needs of virtue and the nation's defense (1984, 224-25).

Historians previously believed that a chief influence on Robespierre, Marat, Saint-Just, and other revolutionary figures was Rousseau's *Du contrat social*. Bernard Manin claims that Rousseau's political writings were opportunistically appropriated by the new government but generally misread, and that his anti-violent and democratic principles were systematically ignored (831, 835). Furthermore, his *Du Contrat social* had not been reprinted in the seventeen years preceding the Revolution (830-31). He did, however, influence the broader public, particularly through his dramatizations of egalitarianism in *Emile* and *La Nouvelle Héloïse* (837-39). Manin writes that "[t]he revolutionaries may not have followed the detailed prescriptions of the *Social Contract,* but they did draw images and general propositions about the nature of man, society, and history from it" (840). Rousseau was also read and admired by Napoleon and George Sand. Despite Manin's insistence on Rousseau's anti-violent stance, one can find a striking passage from *Du Contrat social:* "Every evildoer who attacks social rights becomes by his crimes a rebel and traitor to his country. . . . he makes war on it. . . . when a guilty man is executed, it is less as a citizen than as an enemy . . . the right of war is to slay the vanquished" (90-91). Rousseau adds, however, that excessive recourse to capital punishment is a sign of weakness or indolence in the government, and that generally one should try to reform criminals who pose no danger to society (91). Rousseau's myth of primitive man living in a state of nature, which he equates with a state of terror, justifies the creation of society to vanquish the animal fear in men. Force is sanctioned as a measure of self-defense (Ungvari 14). Lynn Hunt explains that organized opposition was not permitted during the revolutionary period; instead of the development of liberal politics, that is, a mechanism for the representation of interests, opponents were systematically purged (1984, 229). In other words, all opposition was judged treacherous, thereby presenting a threat to the state. Without simplifying the causes for the excesses of the Terror, we note that despite Rousseau's reputation as a pacifist, some of his writings called for the very behavior so abhorrent to us now.

Several historians have seen a link between the rise of Romanticism and the excesses of the Revolution. Rousseau of course was pivotal in the development of that movement in France, although his puritanical stance on the arts can in no way be seen as having influenced the more unseemly traits of Romanticism. Emmet Kennedy cites Edmund Burke's influential *Philosophical Enquiry into the Origin of Our Ideas of the Sublime and Beautiful* (1757). Terror elevates the individual towards the sublime, far surpassing mere pleasure. Terror evokes "nobility of feeling, grandeur, and depth" (1989, 106). By late century, a proclivity had developed for horror, murder, corpses, incest, and perverse pornography; the gothic novel was at its peak; the marquis de Sade was composing his salacious writings. Kennedy attributes these tastes to a fascination with sensory immediacy. If the passions exist, it is for them to be satisfied. Without original sin, an assent to good became natural (Kennedy 1989, 105). Locke's pleasure-pain principle of moral theory where good was identified with the pleasurable, however gross and cruel it may be, may have contributed to the hedonistic sensibility of the era and ultimately to the Terror. In his epic poem, *Organt,* Saint-Just deplores the absence of virtue in the Old Regime, in particular in the Church. He illuminates the role of terror in speaking to all the emotions, conditioning the individual and the nation to the requirements of the new regime. Terror is ultimately an instrument of regeneration (Kennedy 1989, 106).

Indiana, written during the second wave of French Romanticism in the 1830s, reflects both its literary antecedents and the tastes of its period. The emphasis in *Indiana* on terror, floating cadavers (Noun's suicide that haunts Indiana), and mistaken identities (Indiana and Noun) are but a few of the features that mark it as a romantic novel. That the Revolution is linked to violence is not surprising; that violence is linked to republicanism is perhaps more so. Lynn Hunt explains that the association is historically based. For the French, transition to a republican government was always abrupt and difficult because it had connotations as a political option: "It signalled profound upheaval and triggered memories of deep conflict and class antipathy. The Revolution, in this sense, made the achievement of republican and representative government more difficult" (Hunt 1984, 235).

The example of *Indiana* confirms that at least on an unconscious level, Sand did associate republicanism with violent revolution. My finding can also be understood in the context of unconscious fantasy systems of the group in contrast to those of the individual. Didier Anzieu explains that unconscious processes, though universal, can vary on the level of the individual according to his or her experiences; they can also vary according to societal groups. Composed of common constituents, individual and collective fantasies can overlap, but it is in fact rare. He continues:

> The same man acts in his private life according to his private fantasy structure and, in a group, he acts according to the fantasy structure of that group. . . . A given civilization lives for a thousand years on the same fantasy structure. The latter underlies what one calls traditions.[15]

We can understand that Sand, while overtly expressing the "feminine" and socialist stance against violence, may have internalized a group fantasy structure that attracted her to the more "masculine" perpetration of violence. The erotic appeal of violence is clearly part of our Western tradition, that is, our Western fantasy structure. Although her admiration of Robespierre was ostensibly based on his idealism and moral rectitude, it is possible that his brutality had more appeal than she was willing to admit.

Another issue that I have skirted until this point is the frequently noted ambiguity of Sand's sexual identity.[16] Although her famed transvestism and adoption of a male pseudonym were by no means unique to the nineteenth century, her, as well as many of her contemporaries', interest in androgyny may have been a response to the late eighteenth-century predilection for classificatory systems that stressed anatomical differences between the sexes. Converging with the radical politics of the Revolution, new bourgeois political theory required the elaboration of more "natural" relations in society to counteract the political implications of egalitarianism. Rousseau's insistence on both social equality and the importance of feminine domesticity is a case in point.[17] It is not surprising that her male protagonist displays androgynous features, as he often espouses her political views in the novel, functioning perhaps as a sort of alter-ego, a feminized man. Naomi Schor notes that the doubling of Indiana and Noun with the scenes of female transvestism incurring an exchange of female identities functions as "a blurring of difference *within* difference" (1986 a, 369). Sand is refusing "to anchor woman—but also man—on either side of the axis of castration" (1986 a, 369). Sand's attraction to the perpetration of violence may have been a reflection of her own gender ambivalence that shows itself in what Schor terms her "bisextuality" (1986 a, 368), and her own refusal to conform to the "masquerade" of femininity. "The masquerade," writes Irigaray, "is what women do . . . in order to participate in man's desire, but at the cost of giving up their own."[18]

But if in fact I can cast Sand as a lover of revolution, which most of her writings contradict at least on the surface, we are left with still another contradiction. Unlike most proponents of revolution, Sand never chooses to sanitize either the Revolution of 1789 or 1830. The notion of revolution had undergone an entirely new set of associations during the Enlightenment and had come to be portrayed as an act of nature that could not be inhibited. In post-Revolutionary thought, it continued to be divested of its violent associations (Ungvari 2-3), yet Sand prefers to insist on underscoring precisely those associations. During the Revolution, there was a continuous process of renaming, intrinsic to the shaping of a new ideology. Ronald Paulson speaks of this "process of substitution,"[19] invoking Edmund Burke who had succinctly explained: "Things are never called by their common names." For example, the word *massacre* would be changed to "agitation," "effervescence," or "excess."[20] In the above references from *Indiana,* Sand does use the whitewashed term *agitation,* yet juxtaposes it with "bloody struggle" and in a revealing change of heart, she writes, "the prefect had nearly been massacred the night before" (290). In earlier additions, Sand had written "assassinated" in the place of "massacred."[21] Neither word reflects a desire to mask the violence of the Revolution, although Sand's more graphic choice reflects a temporal distancing from the immediacy of the events of 1830, perhaps thus exhibiting less sympathy for the artisans of the Revolution.

We have already seen that Sand's narrator likens revolution to "political storms (*"orages"*) and "the whirlwind" of revolutions." Here the benevolent comet of Enlightenment *philosophes* has given way to revolution as act of nature "that cannot be halted by human force" (Ungvari 2, 10). Her word choice is remarkably close to that of proponents of revolution like Robespierre who spoke of the "revolutionary storm (*"tempête"*)," and Desmoulins who qualified the events surrounding him as the "revolutionary torrent" (Ungvari 10).

Sand's position on revolution is thus more complicated than at first it would appear. She evokes the Enlightenment image of revolution as an irresistible force of nature, yet refuses to sanitize it. She appears to favor pacifist republicanism, yet shows a perhaps unconscious link between the advent of that system and bloodshed. An enthusiast of Robespierre, she may be acknowledging that bloodshed is a justifiable, even necessary, part of constructing a better world. To understand these contradictions, I return to Freud's belief that civilization is based on the process of instinctual repression. Masked beneath the civility of Sand's heroes lies an attraction to violence, a pull towards victimization and domination. The excesses of the late eighteenth and early nineteenth centuries show a lifting of that veneer of civilization and the emergence of sado-masochistic tendencies, which had subsisted in the group fantasy structure. Furet claims that the political climate of the Revolution was the chief cause of the Terror; he cites Mme de Staël's observation in *Considérations sur la révolution française* that some of its viciousness was in response to the harsh social relations of the Old Regime that inclined individuals not only to dominate but humiliate one another (1983, 303; cited in Furet 1989, 149-50), or as Furet calls it, "an egalitarian fanaticism born of an inegalitarian pathology in the Old Regime" (1989, 149-50). Some of the violence of that fanaticism spills over into the clichés of romantic love, many rehabilitated from the courtly tradition. Ralph and Indiana choose renunciation, as does their creator, modifying "the demands of instinct" (Roth 168). But in true Romantic form, they are drawn to "nobility of feeling, grandeur, and depth," terror's elevation of the individual towards the sublime (Kennedy 1989, 106). The mask of the Restoration hides the nightmare and the allure of the Terror. The George

Sand of bucolic *romans champêtres* and messianic religions of humanity is not an inaccurate characterization; rather, it is incomplete.

Notes

1. I wish to thank Rosemarie Scullion and several anonymous referees for their helpful comments on this paper.

2. Sandy Petrey writes: "From one perspective, the historic upheavals that began in 1789 and continued through Napoleon's fall in 1815 are less important for literary scholars than for social and political historians. The Revolutionary decades produced few works that have entered the canon of masterpieces. . . . From another perspective, however, the Revolution is integral to all literary developments in modern France" (1989 b, 567). The "canon of masterpieces" is certainly suspect as an absolute standard of literary worthiness. However, few would dispute the claim that the 1830s constituted an intellectual high point in French literary history and that it included a serious attempt to look backwards at the tormented years of the Revolutionary period. Obviously, much was written during and just after the Revolution, a fact to which this volume richly attests. The works written a generation later demonstrate a perspective informed by the passage of time and a good deal of hindsight.

3. All translations mine unless otherwise indicated.

4. Bergeron emphasizes that Napoleon's rule favored both the old aristocracy and the bourgeoisie, but in particular the military (62, 120). Landed property was officially recognized as the foundation of society (70). The maintenance of feudal rents created a new class of landowners (124), many of whom bought confiscated property of the old aristocracy (126). Many bourgeois landowners were also industrialists (130-31) as the post-revolutionary years did provide an opportunity for many entrepreneurs (143), although many failed (172 ff).

5. "*Propriétaires*" included those living off the income of their property, retirees (Delmare is on a half-pension from the imperial army, his other link to Napoleon), or nobles, farmers, or others who preferred to claim as their occupation that of "*propriétaire*" (Bergeron 151).

6. Cited in Vermeylan 170. All subsequent references to Sand's autobiography (hereafter called *Histoire*) have also been previously cited in Vermeylan 166-75 unless otherwise indicated.

7. Chaussinand-Nogaret describes the *volte-face* of the nobility just after 1789 as such a phenomenon. It was largely supportive of liberal reforms until it realized that its ranks were not going to be leaders of the new regime (1985 a, 169).

8. ". . . I never portrayed myself with feminine traits" (*Histoire* 2: 160, qtd. in Didier 12-13).

9. Some of the ideas contained in this section appeared in an earlier version of this article published in *George Sand Studies* under the title "George Sand: Rewriting Revolutions."

10. Françoise Massardier-Kenney demonstrates that an outright equation between femininity and liquidity is inaccurate in *Indiana* (68). Her comment points to another often observed breakdown of gender in Sand's work.

11. See *Indiana* 103, for an excellent example of this. See also Naginski 63 ff. for further discussion of this point.

12. See Vareille for a discussion of Sand's passage to the masculine and for another reading of Sand's text as fantasy. Naginski devotes an entire chapter to the question of Sand's androgyny and its influence on her writing.

13. See Hunt for an analysis of the decline of Marianne as revolutionary symbol (1984, 229), reflecting women's increasing exclusion from the centers of power as the Revolution progressed; Hercules, an anti-feminist symbol who preceded Marianne as symbol, is discussed on pp. 94-116.

14. "Rapport sur les principes de morale publique qui doivent guider la Convention nationale dans l'administration intérieure de la République." Feb. 5, 1794, qtd. in Hunt 1984, 46. Translation hers.

15. Anzieu, Didier. "Freud et la Mythologie." *Nouvelle Revue de Psychanalyse* 1 (1970): 142, qtd. in Bellemin-Noël 65.

16. In Sand's own words: "I could see that my education, because of fortuitous circumstances, had been somewhat different from that of other women, and *had modified my being* . . . . I was also aware that the stupid frivolity of fineries, and the impure desire to please all men, had no hold on my spirit . . . *I was therefore not entirely a woman* . . . my soul possessed an enthusiasm for the beautiful, a thirst for truth, *and yet I was a woman* like all the others, weak, irritable, dominated by imagination, easily prone to the soft-hearted feelings and anxieties of motherhood" (*Histoire* 2: 126-27; qtd. in Naginski 21; translation hers). Sand's conflicts about her own gender identity stem from her essentialist stance, leading her to denigrate all that is culturally feminine.

17. Robert Nye (48-49) summarizes Thomas Laqueur's argument from "Orgasm, Generation and the Politics of Reproductive Biology" (2-4) and Londa Schiebinger's "Skeletons in the Closet: The First Illustration of the Skeleton in 18th Century Anatomy" (42-82), *The Making of the Modern Body: Sexuality and Society in the 19th Century.* Ed. Thomas Laqueur and Catherine Gallagher (Berkeley: U. Calif. Press, 1987).

18. *Ce sexe qui n'en est pas un* (Paris: Editions de Minuit, 1977) 131, qtd. in Butler 47.

19. *Representations of Revolution* (1789-1820) 15, qtd. in Ungvari 11.

20. Edmund Burke, "Preface to the Address of M. Brissot," qtd. in Ungvari 12.

21. Didier brings this point to the reader's attention in her endnotes following the text of *Indiana*, 393 n.290.

14

Mad Sisters, Red Mothers, Wise Grandmothers: Women's Non-Realist Representations of 1789

Margaret Cohen

Unexplained Absences

It is a strange, if recognized, fact that July Monarchy realism produced no panoramic representations of the French Revolution. Yes, there is Balzac's *Les Chouans*. Critics agree, however, that this novel, the first that he claimed as his own, is hardly one where his realist project has assumed its mature form. And most of Balzac's canonical realist novels, like Stendhal's *Le Rouge et le noir,* are set in post-Napoleonic France. So, too, while Hugo declares, "the Revolution . . . that is the source of nineteenth-century literature," Hugo's own direct novelistic representation of the Revolution is considerably later: he writes *Quatre-Vingt Treize* in the years following the Paris Commune (Hugo 306-07).[1] Why should the Revolution not have been a favored subject for a genre concerned with representing social change and class conflict, and notably the conflict between aristocracy and bourgeoisie enacted so spectacularly in the years around 1789?

It is also a strange, if recognized, fact that women did not write realism in July Monarchy France (1830-48). The explanation for this absence certainly does not derive from the fact that no French women were writing at the time that realism became the dominant novelistic genre in France. During the first wave of French realism, French women were writing novels concerned with collective contemporary social reality as perhaps never before; indeed, as one contemporary politician and *homme de lettres,* N.-A. de Salvandy, put it in a preface to a woman's novel from this time: "The wish of the Saint-Simonians is accomplished in the republic of letters" (ii).[2] These novels, however, did not conform to the generic conventions of realism. Rather, they constituted an independent novelistic subgenre which I have elsewhere characterized as the feminine social novel (Cohen forthcoming).

If women did not write realist novels, it also was not because there were no significant feminine literary talents around: George Sand produced arguably her best works in the period 1831-48 and was considered by her European contemporaries to be at least as important as Balzac. Since then, however, and until recently, she fell into relative neglect, treated either as a scarlet woman, "a woman who had Chopin, Liszt, Delacroix, Louis Blanc, Taine, Merimée, Renan, Flaubert, Balzac, and Musset for correspondents, friends or lovers," as her Gallimard Folio editor put it in 1973, or the pastoral writer of bedtime stories for good bourgeois children like Marcel Proust (Fermigier 17).[3] Finally, women's absence from the consolidation of French realism cannot derive from a basic incompatibility between women writers and realist strategies of narration. The example of England shows us Jane Austen, Charlotte Brontë, George Eliot, and Mrs. Gaskell, whose works were central to the development of this paradigm in its English form.

Is there some link between the absence of French women writers and French Revolutionary subject matter from July Monarchy realism? Might this double absence derive from a single characteristic of the genre? The following pages argue that both absences can be linked to an ideological project of French realism: The attempt to stabilize a turbulent society in the throes of economic and political change. Not only did women's material social position make women novelists both uninterested and unable to accomplish the task that realism took as its own; it led them to represent the Revolution with an ideological aim radically different from that of their male realist counterparts.

The Ideological Project of French Realism

Following the Marxist understanding of French realism, and notably Sandy Petrey's recent *Realism and Revolution,* let me suggest that the designation, realism, when applied to works from the period 1830-48, can as much be used to characterize texts with a shared ideological project as with a shared writerly technique.[4] The first wave of French realism is a genre concerned with rendering legible the social (dis)order that 1789 and its consequences substituted for a stable social hierarchy organized around the monarchy and the transcendental signifier of the King. This (dis)order is a situation of extreme hermeneutic uncertainty where incompatible models for political and economic organization, but more, for social value itself, compete with each other, overlay each other, masquerade as each other. As a text like Balzac's *Le Père Goriot* demonstrates, the education of Rastignac is an education in how to read a situation where the name of the father both no longer operates and is retained as a commodity among other commodities, where the aristocratic value of blood and the bourgeois value of gold conflict and compete with each other, where the bourgeois view of society as a social contract struggles with a traditional vision of society organized in familial terms.[5] Balzac's novel provides a panorama of Parisian society embodied in Rastignac's last contemplation of the city from the cemetery where dead fathers are interred; a panoramic vision of social totality available, however, not from a distance, but rather through a labyrinthian tour of the interstices of the city and the various forms of social commerce harbored there.

A definition of the realist novel according to its ideological project helps to explain the curious absence, in the first wave of French realism, of direct representations of the French Revolution. If the first wave of realism is engaged in stabilizing a social situation produced by the struggles of the French Revolution, the violent history of the Revolution hardly provides events which remedy the social (dis)order that it brings in its wake. Illegible, contradictory, and transgressive of multiple social orders, the Revolution's history is too unsettling to serve this ideological project that the realist novel takes as its task. The realist novel thus treats the Revolution that is both its precondition and its demon with great circumspection, often representing it with non-realist strategies, as a glance once more at that exemplary realist text, *Le Père Goriot,* makes clear. The Revolution is represented allusively, allegorically, and within the confines of private life, personified as "old 93," as the Duchesse de Langeais terms Goriot, or reenacted through the language of decapitation surrounding Vautrin's discovery by the police inspector Gondureau. Hugo's declaration that "the Revolution . . . that is the source of nineteenth-century literature" only encompasses July Monarchy realism, then, if we acknowledge that realism does not represent historical reality with the mimetic strategies that realism's own account of its method leads us to expect. It is precisely because of the intimate link between realism's project and the Revolution that the Revolution appears in realist literature in such a curiously oblique way.

A characterization of the realist novel in terms of its ideological project suggests, in addition, an explanation for why women did not write realism. For given women and men's asymmetrical material positions within French bourgeois-liberal society of the time, how could we expect women and men to participate in realism's project of ideological stabilization in the same way? One of the prime ways French realism of this period seeks to render legible social relations is through its use of gender representation. Translating public social struggle into the realm of sentimental relations, the novels of Balzac and Stendhal represent men's public fortunes as a function of their private lives. Thus, Balzac's *Le Père Goriot* depicts the ambitious young Rastignac's rise to public power as his initiation into the manipulation of women ranging from an impoverished bourgeoise to the reigning queen of the Faubourg Saint-Germain. Through this procedure, July Monarchy realism gives its reader mastery over public conflict in two important ways. Bestowing psychological and intellectual form on confusing public struggle, it allows a fractured society to be dominated from the standpoint of individual contemplation. This is the standpoint incarnated in the celebrated ending to *Le Père Goriot,* where Rastignac encompasses all of Paris in one panoramic glance. Simultaneously, however, it allows the individual to take refuge from public social struggle in the intimacy of private life. So, *Le Père Goriot* suggests that Rastignac most effectively masters the conflicts between aristocracy and bourgeoisie by attending to his own sentimental education.

But by the terms of this project, women themselves are hardly "real." Relegated by bourgeois-liberal ideology to the domain of the private, women are barred from political participation and treated as minors when it comes to disposing of property. They are thus part of the personal realm which realism uses to resolve political struggle, and they experience it in a very different way from their male contemporaries. Rather than the place where public conflicts are to be resolved, the private sphere is the site of women's own social subordination. For women writing at the time, it was hence not a question of using private life to resolve public struggles, but rather of exposing private struggles too often veiled from public view. "Poor woman, so unhappy that it might be called a novel," Caroline Marbouty's narrator exclaims in the opening to her 1844 feminine social novel, *Une Fausse Position* (Marbouty 1:47). With this statement Marbouty indicates the difficulties of recognizing the reality of women's private sufferings given their dominant novelistic portrayal; the fact that their private sufferings are associated with a novelistic economy of aesthetic and ideological pleasures.

Red Mothers, Wise Grandmothers, Mad Sisters

July Monarchy women writers had no hesitations about making clear the deliberate nature of their antipathy to realism. So, for example, Sand reiterates a celebrated comparison between herself and Balzac, reproduced here as it appears in her 1851 discussion of her *Compagnon du Tour de France*. "Since when is the novel forcibly the painting of what is, of the hard and cold reality of contemporary men and things?" she asks, and then goes on to report a dialogue that she had on this subject with Balzac (n.d., 131). "In short," she tells Balzac, picking up an old contrast familiar from Aristotle on Sophocles and Euripides, as well as from the seventeenth-century French literary establishment on Corneille and Racine, "you want and know how to paint man as he is, under your eyes, so be it. In contrast, I feel myself drawn to painting him as he wishes to be, as he should be" (n.d., 131).[6]

The remainder of the paper considers what it means to represent man as he "should be" by considering Sand's relation to the Revolutionary primal scene. Despite her oblique treatment of the event, she uses it, I argue, in substantially different fashion from her masculine counterparts. While the male realists remedy in the aesthetic realm the social (dis)order that the Revolution has wrought, Sand is interested in exploiting the Revolution's destabilizing power. In particular, she appeals to it to question the class and gender hierarchies of July Monarchy society. In addition, she invokes the Revolution to question bourgeois-liberal society's use of gender and class discourse as a tool of ideological work.[7]

Let me pass from a general discussion to specific textual analysis, examining a text from this period by Sand set during the first French Revolution, *La Petite Fadette*. *La Petite Fadette,* a novel about the French Revolution? Written following Sand's disillusioning political experience in the Revolution of 1848, this text has generally been treated as Sand's flight from politics into the realm of the pastoral, if not into pollyannaish moralizing. Even such an excellent critic of Sand as Reinhold Grimm, who recognizes the importance of the cross-class social representation found in Sand's country novels from the early 1840s, differentiates these later pastoral novels from Sand's earlier, more politicized work (Grimm 65).

But in treating *La Petite Fadette* as pastoral, Grimm, it seems to me, gets the text's genre slightly wrong. While Sand's narrative is set in the country, its landscape is not a pastoral one, for, located in a specific place, rural Berry, *La Petite Fadette* is also grounded in a specific historical moment, the first French Revolution. If Grimm misses Sand's historical references to the Revolution in this text, it is, however, not surprising, for Sand situates her text in concrete history in an extraordinarily discreet way. Why she does this, is a question to which I will return.

That *La Petite Fadette* is set during the Revolution emerges in the text's last pages when its narrator, the *chanvreur,* the hemp-hackler, discusses the fate of its most troubling character, the twin who can find no place in the happy family circle formed at the story's end. Instead, the nineteen-year-old Sylvain Barbeau leaves to be a soldier, for "it was the time of the great, magnificent wars of the emperor Napoleon," as "in ten years of weather, of fatigue, of courage and of brave conduct, he became captain, and got the cross on top of it" (1967, 242). The *chanvreur*'s historical precision situates the temporal framework of his narrative within several years. Napoleon accedes to power in the late 1790s and Sylvain must enter the Grande Armée by 1804 in order to spend ten years there. Performing the arithmetic, we discover that the twin's date of birth most likely falls between 1779 and 1781, and that the narrative runs from this time until Napoleon's rise to power.

The most obvious revolutionary problem presented in *La Petite Fadette* is the failure of fraternity among radical revolutionaries. Landry and

Sylvain's childhood and adolescence bear a noticeable resemblance to the most radical moments of the Revolutions of 1789 and 1848, for, like the *sans culottes* of 1793 and the socialists of 1848, Sylvain and Landry attempt and fail to form a society founded on the principles of radical equality. For our purposes, however, I want to insist on a second revolt against the authority of the père Barbeau that Sand recounts, the revolt of the character who lends her name to the text. "I don't esteem you," Fadette tells Landry, "neither you nor your twin, nor your father and mother, who are proud because they are rich and who believe that one only does one's duty in doing a favor for them" (1967, 114). When Landry questions Fadette on the reasons for her critical attitude towards his father's order, Fadette cites its intolerance of women's socially active behavior, mentioning its condemnation of her mother who left to follow the army as a *vivandière,* sutler, when Fadette was ten:

> They [the other children] reproached me with the fault of my mother and wanted to make me blush about her. Perhaps in my place a *reasonable* girl, as you say, would have taken it lying down, thinking that it was prudent to abandon the *cause of her mother* and let her be insulted to keep herself from being insulted too. But me, you see, I couldn't. It was stronger than me. . . . And since I cannot and do not know how to defend her, I avenge her, in saying to others the truths that they merit hearing, and in showing them that they're not worth those at whom they throw stones. (1967, 138-39)

That Fadette identifies her mother's memory with a political word, "cause," is peculiar, for the content of her mother's cause seems exclusively personal. Or does it? A year younger than the twins, Fadette was abandoned around 1792, as her mother's military engagement occurs when the French people rallied to defend the Revolution against foreign intervention. Leaving her daughter with a "red apron," when she goes off to war, Fadette's mother also bequeaths to her a legacy of radical feminine revolutionary activity (1967, 158).

Multiple details associated with Fadette's mother and Fadette before her transformation by Landry recall the militant revolutionary woman, a figure familiar from representations of the French Revolution as well as its reality. Associated with images of popular womanhood, the militant woman, like Fadette, is not known for her careful appearance. Like Fadette's mother, the sutler, she is linked to food, and like Fadette's mother, she is often associated with sexual licentiousness. Like Fadette, her social engagement occurs in response to economic scarcity rather than to political conflict, as her major arena of action throughout the eighteenth and nineteenth centuries is the bread riot. To protest economic hardship, she uses precisely the arms taken up by Fadette in her mother's cause. According to Michelle Perrot, militant revolutionary women's primary aggressions were linguistic, as they employed the rhetorical tools of irony and insult (79). Failing that, they resorted to throwing stones, and when Fadette explains her behavior to Landry in the speech quoted above, she performs a figurative equation of the two tactics: "And since I cannot and do not know how to defend her, I avenge her, in saying to others the truths that they merit hearing, and in showing them that they're not worth those at whom they throw stones," we saw her state (1967, 139).

That Fadette's revolt against social inequality is the revolt of the militant revolutionary woman emerges also in Landry's arguments against her, for Landry echoes the responses of many male bourgeois revolutionaries to the threat posed by revolutionary women. While the bourgeois revolutionaries owed the success of their revolution in part to women's active intervention (the October 1789 march on Versailles is perhaps the most celebrated example), they found that revolutionary women rebelled not only against economic injustice, but also against a domestic understanding of a women's place. But far too invested in bourgeois gender ideology to transform woman's social presence into political rights, the bourgeois revolutionaries gradually excluded them from all political participation in the new republic. A concise summary of the bourgeois revolutionaries' objections to revolutionary women is provided by convention delegate André Amar in his report from 29 October 1793 recommending the dissolution of women's political clubs. He opened this report by attacking women's militant public behavior and dress, which he represented as masculine: "Several women, so called Jacobins, from a so-called revolutionary society, were walking around the market place with pants and a red cap" (299). Amar went on to oppose such behavior to women's appropriate social conduct:

> What character is appropriate to women? Custom and even nature have assigned her function: to begin the education of men, to prepare

children's minds and hearts for public virtues, to direct them early on towards the good, to elevate their souls and to instruct them in the political cult of liberty: these are their functions, after household cares; woman is naturally destined to make virtue loved. . . . Women have more than another way of doing service to their country; they can enlighten their husbands, communicating to them precious reflections, fruit of the calm of a sedentary life; and fortify in them love of country [*patrie*] by everything that private love gives them in the way of empire. (299-300)

Proclaiming women to be the privileged guardians of private values, Amar relegated them exclusively to the private realm. And if, like the bourgeois revolutionaries, Landry has been aided several times by a woman's active power, he condemns it for similar reasons. " 'You have nothing of a girl and all of a boy,' " Landry tells Fadette, and he continues, " 'It's good to be strong and quick; it's good, too, not to be afraid of anything, and it's a natural advantage for a man. But for a woman, too much is too much, and you seem to want to make yourself noticed' " (1967, 136). Objecting to the fact that Fadette displays herself in public at all, Landry objects also to the content of this display. He genders Fadette's aggressive strength and intelligence as masculine, and suggests that Fadette should instead adopt a demure and self-effacing demeanor, becoming " 'sweet and obedient,' " " 'clean and well-cared for' " (1967, 136).

Elsewhere I have discussed how Landry and Fadette's central conflict echoes in multiple ways the debate between the militant women and the bourgeois revolutionaries (1989, 32 ff.). Important for me now is the fact that Sand represents the Revolution not to stabilize but rather to question the current social order, and, more specifically, to reawaken the feminine experience which this order has chosen to exclude. Like Balzac, that is, Sand recognizes the contemporary destabilizing power of the ghosts of Revolution. But, as a subject excluded from the *res publica,* where bourgeois-liberal society situates its most important socially transformative transactions, Sand has stakes in this destabilization that are considerably different. While Balzac seeks to lay the ghosts of the Revolution to rest, Sand resuscitates them for their disruptive power, using them to challenge one of the most stable existing social categories in ideological circulation at the time;

namely, gender difference, which much contemporary ideology used to naturalize political and economic conflict as fact.[8]

My argument for Sand's use of the Revolution to attack bourgeois gender ideology may seem surprising to those readers who remember the end of *La Petite Fadette*. For it would seem that, despite Fadette's canny attack on Landry's position, Sand then retreats from her challenge to a woman's non-domestic social place. Transforming her heroine from a militant popular woman into a model bourgeois young lady, Sand lets Fadette find happiness by abandoning her socially critical behavior. Fadette enters the family of that embodiment of hierarchical order, the père Barbeau, and there fulfills the prime feminine directive enunciated by Amar, becoming a mother and educating new Barbeau children. But although Fadette retreats from political activity, she does not fill the submissive role allotted to women by bourgeois revolutionaries such as Amar. It is, indeed, in her simultaneous retreat and refusal of submission that Fadette's challenge to liberal ideology is most pronounced. "They have more than one way of serving their country," we saw Amar propose; "they can enlighten their husbands, communicate to them precious reflections, fruit of the calm of a sedentary life; and fortify in them love of country [*patrie*] by everything that private love gives them in the way of empire." Fadette does indeed enlighten her husband, but she does not enlighten him in a manner which bolsters the order of the *patrie*. Rather, she continues to question the père Barbeau's valorization of property, and her questions have greater effect from within this hierarchy than from outside it. She not only educates Landry and Sylvain into morality and sentiment but also reminds them of the radical social equality that they had abandoned with their childhood, then spreading her message of equality from the twins to the community at large.

Summing up Fadette's challenge to liberal ideology, we might put it thus: When women engage in the violent and/or political tactics of bourgeois revolutionaries, they mistake a liberal and implicitly masculine account of social power for the totality of forms of social power available in contemporary society. Rather than accepting liberal accounts of social power as the whole story, Sand suggests, women should profit from the insight that their exclusion from these relations provides, and she uses Fadette to question not only the subordinate view that liberal society takes of the domestic realm to which it relegates women, but also its distinction between public and private realms itself. In "A Woman's Place," I have looked in detail at how

Fadette's story questions the public/private distinction dear to liberal ideology. While Fadette gets her social message from her mother, I have argued, she gets her techniques of social influence primarily from her wise grandmother, the folkhealer, and popular wise-woman, la mère Fadet, who is a figure from a pre-liberal society where the distinction between public and private is not in place in the same way.

Sand's use of the Revolution as a way to destabilize the dominant gender ideology of July Monarchy society is found throughout her novels from the July Monarchy. I give, for the sake of economy, only one other example: the utopian ending of her 1846 *Le Meunier d'Angibault,* which is brought about through unleashing the disruptive power of a walking revolutionary ghost. That we are in the realm of the relation between gender ideology and revolutionary issues is already indicated by the peculiar space in which Sand's preface sets her tale. "The novel is," Sand tells us, "the result of a promenade, of a meeting, of a day of leisure, of an hour of *far niente,*" a promenade which she made with her children in 1844 (1976, 1). It is, however, not only the result of a domestic woman's praise of the pleasures of private life, but also the encounter, in the course of this praise, with a reminder of the revolutionary past. Sand sets her tale at a "pretty mill" in our valley, which used to be owned by "an old man, who, since his liaison in Paris with *M. de Robespierre* (so he always called him) had let grow around the locks of his stream everything which could grow" (1976, 1). Finally, she tells us, she derives it from her encounter with a mad woman, driven crazy by love.

The body of Sand's novel expands the encounter between domestic femininity, revolutionary abandon, and libidinal excess toward which her preface gestures. I leave, for the purposes of economy, the twists of the plot aside. Let me simply observe that they turn around a series of love affairs, thwarted because of the gender and class ideology dominant in July Monarchy France. And that Sand creates a ghost of the revolutionary past to destroy these values and bring about a happy ending.

This ghost is la Bricoline, the sister of one of the thwarted lovers and once a young bourgeois woman in love with a man below her in social station. Driven mad by her father's refusal to agree to a marriage based on love rather than property, she turns to a phantasmagorical apparition, and one whom her sister qualifies as "dérangée." We notice the play on "rank," in this description of her madness, and it is a program of unranking that her seemingly senseless ravings proclaim to the attentive ear. Wandering around the crumbling ruins of an aristocratic château now ruled over by her *parvenu* father, she speaks a Pauline discourse of love across social difference (her lost lover's name was Paul), and underlines that she derives this discourse from the revolutionary past. "What I have been seeking for fifty-four years ... was *tenderness*," she tells her sister in her madness; this is a novel, we remember, set in the mid-1840s (1976, 292).

To find this tenderness, she sets fire to the aristocratic château and her father's neighboring farm. And if Sand establishes the architectural structures of her rural landscape as a fit emblem for the existing July Monarchy hierarchy, a new egalitarian social order is born from the ashes of their decimation. Also instrumental in this happy ending, it might be added, is once more a wise grandmother evincing the virtues of popular womanhood that we have discussed in the context of *La Petite Fadette*. Suppressed under the parvenu father's rule, the popular grandmother recovers her voice and her money, as well as deriving the power to bestow it as a maternal inheritance at the novel's end. In this new order, la Bricoline's bourgeois sister frees herself of specifically bourgeois gender stereotypes, rediscovers her popular roots and marries the working-class man of her choice. In addition, an aristocratic woman marries the utopian socialist proletarian with whom she has long been in love, a man who had refused her because of his own belief in the fixed divisions of bourgeois class hierarchy.

✣ ✣ ✣

In closing, I want to underline not only the different stakes that men and women writing at the time had in the representation of the French Revolution, but also the challenge that Sand's use of the Revolution poses to our existing critical definitions of realism. In Sand's attack on liberal society's valorization of public, political, and implicitly masculine social power, we find an explanation for the oblique methods that she uses to represent the Revolution very different from the explanation for the oblique representation of this event by the realist men. Sand represents the Revolution in oblique fashion, I would suggest, not because she is uncomfortable with its unlaid ghosts, but rather because she attempts to devise narrative strategies consonant with the specifically feminine social power that her text takes as its theme. The allegorical, moral, and sentimental discourses in which she couches what we consider to be her oblique representation of the Revolution are, after all, among the discourses that women used to make sense of their daily life in July Monarchy France. Fusing these discourses with historical fact, Sand regrounds them in the social context that produced them. She thus both negates bourgeois-liberal ideology's claim that women's experience is severed from public, political history and suggests that the seemingly ahistorical discourse in which women frame their experience has itself a specific social validity. Linking this discourse to the events of public history, she simultaneously refuses to collapse it back into these events altogether.

If I opened by suggesting women's problematic relation to the first wave of French realism, I close by suggesting this proposition's obverse: that women writers from the time may be engaged in a realism which we can only understand once we question the difference that gender makes in defining a subject's discursive access to the real. How does our current vision of the mimetic novel depend on implicitly masculine models of creativity and reality? And how might a history of realism look if it were written taking as its referential dimension the "reality" of women's experience within bourgeois-liberal society instead?

Notes

1. This translation and all following are mine, unless otherwise indicated. Portions of this essay appeared as "A Woman's Place: *La Petite Fadette* v. *La Voix des Femmes*" in *L'Esprit Créateur,* Summer 1989, Vol. XXIX, No. 2. I thank the editors of *L'Esprit Créateur* for permission to reprint.

2. The Saint-Simonians, we remember, prophecied the advent of a WOMAN MESSIAH whose new moral order of love and sentiment would save the world.

3. In the United States, Naomi Schor and Nancy Miller have initiated Sand's rehabilitation. See Miller 1988, as well as Schor 1986 b, Schor 1987, and Schor 1988.

4. Important earlier names in this lineage include Lukács, Macherey, and Jameson.

5. See Petrey 1988, 83 ff.

6. On Sand and realism, see Schor 1988. The question of Sand's relation to the July Monarchy feminine social novel is too complex to elaborate here. In addition to Schor's article cited here, see her book *George Sand and Idealism* (New York: Columbia University Press, 1993), which was published after this chapter was written.

7. I employ the term following Poovey, to designate how representations mediate and mask contradictions among material practices, as well as between material practices and ideological representation.

8. On this subject more generally, see Scott 1988, notably parts II and III.

Contributors

JENENE J. ALLISON is Assistant Professor of French at the University of Texas at Austin. Recent publications include articles on Marivaux and the epistolary novel. She has just completed *Revealing Differences: The Fiction of Isabelle de Charrière* (Univ. of Delaware Press, forthcoming).

MARGARET COHEN is Assistant Professor of Comparative Literature at New York University. She is the author of *Profane Illumination: Walter Benjamin and the Paris of Surrealist Revolution* (Berkeley Univ. Press, 1993) and has published articles on subjects ranging from Benjamin and Breton to problems of gender and genre.

NINA CORAZZO is Assistant Professor in Art History at Valparaiso University. She is currently working on a paper entitled "The Red Bonnets and the Society of Revolutionary Republican Women, 1793."

SUZANNE DESAN is Associate Professor of History at the University of Wisconsin at Madison. She has recently published *Reclaiming the Sacred: Lay Religion and Popular Politics in Revolutionary France* (Cornell Univ. Press, 1990), as well as an article on Jacobin women's clubs in the French Revolution. She is currently working on the impact of the French Revolution on divorce, marriage, and the family.

MARY FAVRET is Assistant Professor of English and Women's Studies at Indiana University. She is the author of *Romantic Correspondence: Women, Politics, and the Fiction of Letters* (Cambridge Univ. Press, 1992) and co-editor of *At the Limits of Romanticism: Essays in Historicist and Material Criticism* (Indiana Univ. Press, 1994).

CATHERINE R. MONTFORT, editor, is Associate Professor of French and Women's Studies at Santa Clara University. Her books and papers range from a study of the mythical imagery in the epic poetry of Agrippa d'Aubigné to an analysis of gender issues in the writing of Annie Ernaux and include articles on Mme de Sévigné, Voltaire, Mme de Staël, Maupassant, and Simone de Beauvoir. Her current research is focused in two areas: the reception of Sévigné's letters in early nineteenth century France, which carries on the work begun in her *Les Fortunes de Mme de Sévigné au XVIIème et au XVIIIème siècles* (Jean-Michel Place, 1982); and research directed at reevaluating the message and intended audience of Charlotte Corday's letters from prison. Her most recent paper on Corday is forthcoming in *Studies on Voltaire and the Eighteenth Century.*

LAUREN PINZKA is an Instructor at Yale University. She has published several psychoanalytical studies of *Mme Bovary* and an article on Sand and the French Revolution. She is currently at work on a comparison of the use of cross-dressing, gender, and sado-masochism in the works of Flaubert and Sand.

KARYNA SZMURLO is Associate Professor of French at Clemson University. She is the co-editor of *Germaine de Staël: Crossing the Borders* (Rutgers Univ. Press, 1991), and is currently working on a manuscript exploring the link between politics and semiotics, *Performative Discourses: Germaine de Staël.*

SUSAN TENENBAUM is Assistant Professor of Political Science at Baruch College, CUNY. She is the author of numerous articles in the areas of political philosophy and public policy. She is presently at work on *The Political Thought of Germaine de Staël.*

MARY TROUILLE is Assistant Professor of French at Illinois State University. She recently completed a book titled *Sexual Politics and the Cult of Sensibility: Eighteenth-Century Women Writers Respond to Rousseau* (Cornell Univ. Press). Her current research is centered on the reception history of works by eighteenth-century women writers as a means of studying canon formation and its relation to shifting social and literary models.

JANIE VANPÉE is Associate Professor of French at Smith College. She has published essays on Rousseau, Greuze, and Laclos, and is currently writing a monograph on de Gouges: *Olympe de Gouges's Legacy: Writing for Woman's Rights.*

GABRIELLE VERDIER, Associate Professor of French at New York University, is the author of *Charles Sorel* (G. H. Hall, 1984) and numerous articles on seventeenth-century prose fiction and women writers. She is preparing a monograph on Olympe de Gouges and eighteenth-century women playwrights.

MARILYN YALOM is the Senior Scholar at the Institute for Research on Women and Gender at Stanford. Her publications include books and articles in the fields of French literature and history, comparative literature, and women's studies. Among these are her books titled *Le Temps des Orages: Aristocrates, Bourgeoises et Paysannes racontent* (Maren Sell, 1989), and *Blood Sisters: The French Revolution in Women's Memory* (Basic Books, 1993). She is also the editor, with Susan Bell, of *Revealing Lives: Autobiography, Biography and Gender* (State University of New York, 1990).

Works Cited

Abray, Jane. 1975. "Feminism in the French Revolution." *American Historical Review* 80.1: 43-62.
Acomb, F. 1950. *Anglophobia in France*. North Carolina: Duke Univ. Press.
Adickes, Sandra. 1991. *The Social Quest: The Expanded Vision of Four Women Travelers in the Era of the French Revolution*. New York: Peter Lang.
Adresse au beau sexe, rélativement à la révolution présente. Paris. 1790.
Agulhon, Maurice. 1981. *Marianne into Battle: Republican Imagery and Symbolism in France, 1789-1880*. New York: Cambridge Univ. Press. Trans., Janet Lloyd. Trans. of *Marianne au combat: L'imagerie et la symbolique républicaines de 1789 à 1880*. Paris: 1979.
Albistur, Maïté, and Daniel Armogathe. 1977. *Histoire du féminisme français*. 2 vols. Paris: Des femmes.
Alméras, Henri d'. 1910. *Charlotte Corday d'après des documents contemporains*. Paris: Libraire des Annales Politiques et Littéraires.
Amar, André. An II. Speech during the National Convention Session of 9 Brumaire. *Réimpression de L'Ancien Moniteur* 18: 299-300.
Andries, Lies. 1988. "Récits de survie: Les mémoires d'autodéfense pendant l'an II et l'an III." Bonnet 261-75.
Applewhite, Harriet B. and Darline Gay Levy. 1984. "Women, Democracy and Revolution in Paris, 1789-1794." Spencer 64-79.
———, eds. 1990. *Women and Politics in the Age of the Democratic Revolution*. Ann Arbor: Univ. of Michigan Press. Archives Nationales, côte W no. 277, dossier 82.
Armstrong, Nancy. 1987. *Desire in Domestic Fiction: A Political History of the Novel*. New York: Oxford Univ. Press.
Auger. 1807. *Revue philosophique, littéraire et politique* 53 (avril-juin): 466-80.
Austin, J. L. 1975. *How to Do Things with Words*. Cambridge: Harvard Univ. Press.
Badinter, Elisabeth. 1983. *Emilie, Emilie: L'ambition féminine au XVIIIème siècle*. Paris: Flammarion.
———. 1989. *Paroles d'hommes (1790-1793)*. Paris: P.O.L.
Badinter, Elisabeth, and Robert Badinter. 1988. *Condorcet, un intellectuel en politique*. Paris: Fayard.
Baillot, P. 1793. *Chant de la Côte-d'Or pendant la guerre de la liberté*, 3 juin 1793. Bibliothèque municipale de Dijon, Fonds Juigné, no. 58, receuil CXII.

Baker, Keith M. 1990. *Inventing the French Revolution.* Cambridge: Cambridge Univ. Press.

Balayé, Simone. 1979. *Madame de Staël: Lumières et liberté.* Paris: Klincksieck.

———. 1986. "*Delphine* de Madame de Staël et la presse sous le Consulat." *Romantisme* 51:39-47.

Ballanche. An IX-1801. *Du Sentiment considéré dans ses rapports avec la littérature et les arts.* Lyon: Ballanche et Barret; Paris: C. Volland.

Barthes, Roland. 1970. *S/Z.* Paris: Seuil.

Beauvoir, Simone de. 1949, 1976. *Le deuxième sexe.* 2 vols. Paris: Gallimard.

Becq, Annie. 1977. "Politique, esthéthique et philosophie de la nature dans le Groupe de Coppet: le concept d'organisme." *Le Groupe de Coppet: Actes et documents du deuxième colloque de Coppet 10-13 juillet 1974.* Geneva: Slatkine. 83-98.

Bell, Susan Groag. 1976. "Christine de Pisan (1364-1430): Humanism and the Problem of a Studious Woman." *Feminist Studies* 3 (Spring-Summer): 173-84.

Bellanger, Claude. 1969. *Histoire générale de la presse française.* Vol. 1. Paris: PUF. 5 vols.

Bellemin-Noël, Jean. 1978. *Psychanalyse et littérature.* Paris: PUF.

Bérard, Suzanne Jean. 1979. "Une curiosité du théâtre à l'époque de la Révolution, les 'faits historiques et patriotiques.'" *Romantische Zeitchrift für Literaturgechicte* 3: 250-77.

Bergeron, Louis. 1981. *France under Napoleon.* Trans., R.R. Palmer. Princeton: Princeton Univ. Press.

Béringuier, Nadine. 1991. "From *Clarens* to *Hollow Park,* Isabelle de Charrière's Quiet Revolution." *Studies in Eighteenth-Century Culture* 21: 219-43.

Beugnot, Jacques-Claude. 1959. *Mémoires.* Ed., Robert Lacour-Gayet. Paris: Hachette.

Bianchi, Serge. 1982. *La Révolution culturelle de l'an II.* Paris: Aubier.

Blanc, Olivier. 1981, 1989. *Olympe de Gouges.* Paris: Syros.

———. Forthcoming 1993. "Une femme quitte la ville: Olympe de Gouges." *Autrement* (issue on Montauban).

Blandin-Desmoulins, citoyenne de Dijon. 1793. "Réponse au citoyen Prudhomme," 10 February 1793. *Révolutions de Paris* 16-23 February.

Bloch, Maurice and Jean H. Bloch. 1980. "Women and the Dialectics of Nature in Eighteenth-Century French Thought." *Nature, Culture and Gender.* Ed. Carol P. MacCormack and Marilyn Strathern. Cambridge: Cambridge Univ. Press. 25-41.

Blum, Carol. 1986, 1989. *Rousseau and the Republic of Virtue: The Language of Politics in the French Revolution.* Ithaca: Cornell Univ. Press.

Bodek, Evelyn Gordon. 1976. "Salonières and Bluestockings: Educated Obsolescence and Germinating Feminism." *Feminist Studies* 3 (Spring-Summer): 185-99.

Boissel, Thierry. 1988. *Sophie de Condorcet: Femme des Lumières (1764-1822).* Paris: Presses de la Renaissance.

Bonnet, Jean-Claude, ed. 1986. *La mort de Marat.* Paris: Flammarion.

———. 1988. *La carmagnole des muses. L'homme de lettres et l'artiste dans la Révolution.* Paris: Colin.

Bonnifet, Nadeige. 1987-88. "Répertoire des femmes auteurs dramatiques de langue française du XVIe, XVIIe, et XVIIIe siècles et de leurs œuvres." Institut d'Etudes théâtrales. Université de Paris, III. Mémoire DEA.

Bonno, G. 1932. *La constitution britannique devant l'opinion française de Montesquieu à Bonaparte*. Paris: Champion.

Bouilly, Jean-Nicholas. 1822. "Madame de Sévigné." Comédie en trois actes représentée pour la première fois au Théâtre Français, le 6 juin 1805. *Suite du répertoire du Théâtre Français*. Tome 8. Paris: Mme Veuve Dabo. 241-364.

Bowman, Frank. 1991. "Communication and Power in Germaine de Staël: Transparency and Obstacle." Gutwirth et al. 55-68.

Bray, Bernard. 1969. "Quelques aspects du système épistolaire de Mme de Sévigné." *Revue d'Histoire Littéraire de la France* 69: 491-505.

Brive, Marie-France, ed. 1989-1991. *Les femmes et la Révolution française*. Actes du Col. Int. 12-13-14 avril 1989. 3 vols. Toulouse: Université Du Mirail.

Broglie, Gabriel de. 1985. *Madame de Genlis*. Paris: Perrin.

Bryant, Lawrence. 1986. *The King and the City in the Parisian Royal Entry Ceremony: Politics, Ritual, and Art in the Renaissance*. Geneva: Droz.

Bryson, Scott. 1991. *The Chastised Stage. Bourgeois Drama and the Exercise of Power*. Saratoga, CA: Stanford French and Italian Studies, ANMA Libri.

Burke, Edmund. 1967. *The Correspondence of Edmund Burke*. Eds., Alfred Cobban and Robert A. Smith. 24 vols. Chicago: Univ. of Chicago Press.

Butler, Judith. 1990. *Gender Trouble: Feminism and the Subversion of Identity*. New York: Routledge.

Carlson, Marvin. 1966. *The Theater of the French Revolution*. Ithaca: Cornell Univ. Press.

Cerati, Marie. 1966. *Le club des citoyennes républicaines révolutionnaires*. Paris: Editions Sociales.

Charrière, Isabelle de. 1979-1981. *Œuvres complètes*. Ed., Jean-Daniel Dandaux et al. 10 vols. Amsterdam: G.A. van Oorschot.

———. 1991. *Une Liaison dangereuse: correspondance avec Constant d'Hermenches, 1760-1776*. Ed., Isabelle Vissière and Jean-Louis Vissière. Paris: Editions de la Différence.

Chastagnaret, Yves. 1988. "George Sand et la Révolution française." *Dix-Huitième Siècle* 20: 431-48.

Chaussinand-Nogaret, Guy. 1985a. *The French Nobility in the Eighteenth Century*. Trans., William Doyle. Cambridge, UK: Cambridge Univ. Press.

———. 1985b. *Madame Roland: Une femme en Révolution*. Paris: Seuil.

Chénier, André-Marie. 1826. "Ode IX." *Œuvres posthumes*. Paris: Guillaume. 275-78.

Chevalley, Sylvie. 1964. "Les femmes auteurs dramatiques et la Comédie-française." *Europe* 427-28 (nov.-déc.): 41-47.

Cohen, Margaret. 1989. "A Woman's Place: *La Petite Fadette* v. *La Voix des Femmes*." *L'Esprit créateur* 29. 2: 26-38.

———. Forthcoming: "The Feminine Origins of the French Social Novel."

Colwill, Elizabeth. 1989. "Just Another Citoyenne? Marie-Antoinette on Trial, 1790-1793." *History Workshop Journal* 28: 63-87.

———. 1990. "The 'Bonds of Womanhood' in the March to Versailles." Unpublished paper. Western Society for French History. Santa Barbara, CA.

Couet de Gironville. An IV. *Charlotte Corday décapitée à Paris le 16 (sic) juillet 1793, ou mémoire pour servir à l'histoire de la vie de cette femme célèbre*. Paris: Gilbert.

Cordelier, Jean, 1967. *Madame de Sévigné par elle-même*. Paris: Seuil.

Cornevin, Marianne. 1989. *La véritable Madame Roland*. Paris: Pygmalion.

Courtney, C.P. 1980. "A Preliminary Bibliography of Isabelle de Charrière (Belle de Zuylen)." *Studies on Voltaire and the Eighteenth Century* 186: 7-157.

Craczyk, Annette. 1989. "L'image de la femme dans le théâtre révolutionnaire." Brive 251-54.

Crecelius, Kathryn. 1987. *Family Romances*. Bloomington: Indiana Univ. Press.

Crow, Thomas E. 1985. *Painters and Public Life in Eighteenth-Century Paris*. New Haven: Yale Univ. Press.

Culler, Jonathan. 1982. *On Deconstruction: Theory and Criticism after Structuralism*. Ithaca: Cornell Univ. Press.

Daly, Pierrette. 1981. "The Problem of Language in George Sand's *Indiana*." Singer 22-27.

Darnton, Robert. 1982. *The Literary Underground of the Old Regime*. Cambridge, Mass: Harvard Univ. Press.

———. 1989. "What was Revolutionary about the French Revolution?" *New York Review of Books* 19 Jan.: 4.

Darrow, Margaret. 1989. *Revolution in the House: Family, Class, and Inheritance in Southern France, 1775-1825*. Princeton Univ. Press.

Dash, Comtesse. 1855. (Pseudonym for the Vicomtesse de Poiloüe de Saint-Mars.) *Mademoiselle Robespierre*. 2 vols. Paris: Coulon-Pineau.

Datlof, Natalie, et al., eds. 1982. *George Sand Papers*. Conference Proceedings, 1978. Hofstra University Center for Cultural and Intercultural Studies 2. New York: AMS Press.

Dauban, Charles-Aimé. 1864. *Etude sur Mme Roland et son temps, suivie des lettres de Mme Roland à Buzot et d'autres documents inédits*. Paris: Plon.

Dauxois, Jacqueline. 1988. *Charlotte Corday*. Paris: Albin Michel.

Decours, Catherine. 1985. *La lettre à Alexandrine écrite dans les derniers jours de Marie-Anne-Charlotte de Corday d'Armont*. Paris: Orban.

Defrance, Eugène. 1909. *Charlotte Corday et la Mort de Marat: Documents inédits sur l'histoire de la Terreur tirés des Archives Nationales de la Bibliothèque de la ville de Paris, et notamment des Bibliothèques Municipales de Caen et d'Alençon*. 2nd ed. Paris: Mercure de France.

Deguise, Alix. 1989. *Trois femmes: le monde de Madame de Charrière*. Geneva: Slatkine.

DeJean, Joan. 1989. "Salons, Preciosity, and Woman's Influence." Hollier 297-303.

———. 1991. "Portrait of the Artist as Sappho." Gutwirth et al. 122-37.

DeJean, Joan and Nancy Miller, eds. 1988. "The Politics of Tradition: Placing Women in French Literature." *Yale French Studies* 75:1-258.

Delon, Michel. 1977. "L'idée d'énergie au tournant des Lumières." *Le Groupe de Coppet: Actes et documents du deuxième colloque de Coppet 10-13 juillet 1974*. Geneva: Slatkine.

———. 1988. "Le nom, la signature." Bonnet 277-95.

———. 1989. "La métaphore théâtrale dans les *Considérations sur la Révolution française*." *Le Groupe de Coppet et la Révolution française*. Lausanne: Institut Benjamin Constant. 163-73.

———. 1991. "Germaine de Staël and Other Possible Scenarios of the Revolution." Gutwirth et al. 22-23.

Derrida, Jacques. 1987. *The Archeology of the Frivolous. Reading Condillac*. Trans. John P. Leavy. Lincoln: Univ. of Nebraska Press.

Desan, Suzanne. 1990. *Reclaiming the Sacred: Lay Religion and Popular Politics in Revolutionary France*. Ithaca: Cornell Univ. Press.

———. 1992. "'Constitutional Amazons': Jacobin Women's Clubs in the French Revolution." *Re-creating Authority in Revolutionary France*. Ed., Bryant T. Ragan and Elizabeth Williams. New Brunswick, NJ: Rutgers Univ. Press. 11-35.

———. 1993. "Marriage, Religion, and Moral Order: Debates about Divorce during the Directory." *The Meaning of Citizenship in the French Revolution*. Ed., Renée Waldinger. Westport, Conn.: Greenwood Press.

Dictionnaire de biographie française. Vol 13.

Didier, Béatrice. 1969. "Ophélie dans les chaînes: Etude de quelques thèmes d'*Indiana*." *Hommage à George Sand*. Ed., L. Cellier. Paris: PUF. 89-92.

———. 1989. *Ecrire la Révolution 1789-1799*. Paris: PUF.

Diesbach, Ghislain de. 1983. *Madame de Staël*. Paris: Perrin.

Dorbe, Mlle. 1792. "Discours à la Société des amies de la Constitution pour l'anniversaire du grand homme Mirabeau," 10 April 1792. Archives municipales de Bordeaux, 178.

Dubois, Jean-Baptiste. An XII-1803. *Delphinette ou le Mépris de l'opinion*. 3 vols. Paris: Bertrandet.

Duchêne, Jacqueline. 1985. *Françoise de Grignan ou le mal d'amour*. Paris: Fayard.

Duchêne, Roger. 1970. *Madame de Sévigné et la lettre d'amour*. Paris: Bordas.

———. 1972-78. *Madame de Sévigné: Correspondance*. 3 vols. Paris: Gallimard (Bibliothèque de la Pléïade).

———. 1982. *Madame de Sévigné ou la chance d'être femme*. Paris: Fayard.

Duhet, Paule-Marie. 1971. *Les femmes et la Révolution, 1789-1794*. Paris: Gallimard-Julliard.

———, ed. 1981, 1989. *Cahiers de doléances des femmes en 1789 et autres textes*. Paris: Des femmes.

Dupaty, Emmanuel. 1829. "Ninon chez Mme de Sévigné." Comédie en un acte et en vers, mêlée de chants. Représentée pour la première fois sur le théâtre de l'Opéra-

Comique, le 26 septembre 1808. *Collection des Théâtres Français: Fin du Répertoire.* Tome 31. Senlis: Tremblay. 1-60.
Dussault, Jean Joseph François. 1806. "Lettres de Madame de Sévigné à sa fille et à ses amis." *Journal des Débats,* 1806. Rpt. *Annales littéraires.* 2:65-70.
———. 1807. "Quelques réflexions générales à l'occasion d'une notice de M. Grouvelle, où madame de Sévigné est transformée en philosophe." *Le Spectateur français au XIXème siècle ou Variétés morales, politiques et littéraires, recueillies des meilleurs écrits périodiques.* Paris: Gignet et Michaud. 4: 46-52.
Estève, Edmond. 1917. "Le théâtre monacal sous la Révolution: ses précédents et ses suites." *Revue d'Histoire Littéraire de la France* (avr.-juin): 177-222.
Etienne, C.-G., and A. Martainville. 1802. *Histoire du théâtre français depuis le commencement de la Révolution jusqu'à la réunion générale.* Vol. 1. Paris: Barba. 4 vols.
Farrell, Michèle. 1991. *Performing Motherhood: The Sévigné Correspondence.* Hanover: Univ. Press of Hanover.
Féletz. 1802. *Journal des Débats,* 5 nivôse-26 décembre.
———. 1807. *Journal de l'Empire,* 7 et 12 mai.
Felman, Shoshana. 1982. "Le scandale de la vérité." *Discours et pouvoir.* Ed., Ross Chambers. Ann Arbor: Michigan Romance Studies 3. 1-28.
Felski, Rita. 1991. "The Counterdiscourse of the Feminine in Three Texts by Wilde, Huysmans, and Sacher-Masoch." *PMLA* 106: 1094-1105.
Les femmes dans la Révolution française. 2 vols. Paris: EDHIS, 1982.
Fermigier, André. 1973. Preface. *François le Champi.* By George Sand. Paris: Gallimard.
Fiévée. 1797. *Gazette de France,* 24 juillet et 19 août.
———. 1803. Mercure de France, 11 nivôse an XI-ler janvier.
Fink, Beatrice, ed. 1989. *Isabelle de Charrière, Belle van Zuylen. Eighteenth Century Life* 13:1-94.
Fleishmann, Hector. 1910. *Charlotte Robespierre et ses Mémoires.* Paris: A. Michel.
Fleury. n.d. *Mémoires de Fleury.* [Paris]: n.p.
Foucault, Michel. 1978. *The History of Sexuality.* Trans., Robert Hurley. 3 vols. New York: Pantheon.
Fraisse, Geneviève. 1989. *Muse de la Raison: La démocratie exclusive et la différence des sexes.* Aix-en-Provence: Alinéa.
Frappier-Mazur, Lucienne. 1984. "Desire, Writing, and Identity in the Romantic Mystical Novel: Notes for a Definition of the Feminine." *Style* 18.3: 328-64.
Freud, Sigmund. 1981. "The Ego and the Id." *The Standard Edition of the Complete Psychological Works of Sigmund Freud.* Trans., James Strachey. 24 vols. London: The Hogarth Press and Institute of Psychoanalysis. 19: 3-66.
———. "Femininity." SE 22: 112-35.
———. "Instincts and Their Vicissitudes." SE 14: 117-40.
Fulchiron, Hugues. 1989. "La femme, mère et épouse dans le droit révolutionnaire." Brive 1: 377-86.
Furet, François. 1978. *Penser la Révolution française.* Paris: Gallimard.

———. 1981. *Interpreting the French Revolution*. Trans., Elborg Forster. Cambridge: Cambridge Univ. Press.

———. 1990. "A Commentary." *French Historical Studies* 16.4: 792-802.

———. 1989. "The Terror." Furet and Ozouf 137-50.

Furet, François, and Mona Ozouf. 1989. *A Critical Dictionary of the French Revolution*. Trans., Arthur Goldhammer. Cambridge, MA: Belknap Press of Harvard Univ. Press. Trans. of *Dictionnaire critique de la Révolution française*. Paris: Flammarion, 1988.

Gaiffe, Félix. 1910. *Le drame en France au XVIIIe siècle*. Paris: Colin.

Gallo, Max. 1971. *Robespierre the Incorruptible: A Psychobiography*. New York: Herder. Trans. of *Maximilien Robespierre: Histoire d'une solitude*. Paris: Perrin, 1968.

Garaud, Marcel, and Romuald Szramkiewicz. 1978. *La Révolution française et la famille*. Paris: PUF.

Gardiner, Judith, 1982. "On Female Identity and Writing by Women." *Writing and Sexual Difference*. Ed., Elizabeth Abel. Chicago: Univ. of Chicago Press. 179-88.

Gauchet, Marcel. 1988. "Droits de l'homme." Furet and Ozouf 685-95

Gautier, P. 1921. *Madame de Staël et Napoléon*. Plon: Paris.

Gay, Peter. 1984. *The Bourgeois Experience: Victoria to Freud*. Vol. 1. of *Education of the Senses*. New York: Oxford Univ. Press.

Gazette de France Nationale, 16 juillet, 20 juillet 1793.

Gelbart, Nina Rattner. 1987. *Feminine and Opposition Journalism in Old Regime France: 'Le Journal des Dames'*. Berkley: Univ. of California Press.

Genlis, Stéphanie-Félicité Ducrest de Saint-Aubin, comtesse d. An XI-1803. *La femme philosophe. Nouvelle Bibliothèque des Romans*. Paris: Maradan. 5: 151-244.

———. 1811. *De l'influence des femmes sur la littérature française, comme protectrice des lettres et comme auteurs; ou Précis de l'histoire des femmes françaises les plus célèbres*. Paris: Maradan.

Geoffroy. 1806. "Du style épistolaire et des 'Lettres de madame de Sévigné'," (édition de M. l'Abbé de Vauxelles). *Le Spectateur français au XIXème siècle*. 3: 306-20.

Giroud, Françoise. 1988. *Les femmes de la Révolution de Michelet*. Paris: Carrère.

Godechot, Jacques, ed. 1983. *Considérations sur la Révolution française*. Paris: Tallandier.

Godet, Philipe. 1973. *Madame de Charrière et ses amis, d'après de nombreaux documents inédits*. 2 vols. 1906. Geneva: Slatkine.

Godineau, Dominique. 1988. *Citoyennes tricoteuses: Les femmes du peuple à Paris pendant la Révolution française*. Aix-en-Provence: Alinéa.

———. 1990. "Masculine and Feminine Political Practice during the French Revolution, 1793-Year III." Applewhite and Levy 61-80.

Godwin, William. 1968. *Memoirs of Mary Wollstonecraft*. London, 1798. Ed. W. Clark Durant. London: Constable & Co.

Goldsmith, Elizabeth. 1988. *Exclusive Conversations*. Philadelphia: Univ. of Pennsylvania Press.

Goodman, Dena. 1989a. "Enlightenment Salons: The Convergence of Female and Philosophic Ambitions." *Eighteenth-Century Studies* 22.3: 329-50.

———. 1989b. "Filial Rebellion in the Salon: Madame Geoffrin and Her Daughter." *French Historical Studies* 16: 28-47.

———. 1992. "Public Sphere and Private Life: Toward a Synthesis of Current Historiographical Approaches to the Old Regime." *History and Theory* 31: 58-77.

Gordon, Daniel. 1992. "Philosophy, Sociology and Gender in the Enlightenment Conception of Public Opinion." *French Historical Studies* 17: 882-911.

Gouges, Olympe de. 1788. *Œuvres de Madame de Gouges*. 3 vols. Paris: l'auteur et Cailleau.

———. 1986a. "Lettre de Mme de Gouges à la Comédie Française." Groult 140-41.

———. 1986b. "Projet d'un second théâtre et d'une maternité." Groult 78-82.

———. 1989. *L'esclavage des noirs, 1792*. Pref. Eléni Varikas. Paris: Côté-femmes.

———. 1991. *Théâtre politique: le couvent ou les vœux forcés, 1790-92; Mirabeau aux Champs-Elysées, 1791; L'entrée de Dumouriez à Bruxelles ou les Vivandiers, 1793*. Pref. Gisela Thiele Knobloch. Paris: Côté-femmes.

———. 1993a. *Ecrits politiques 1788-1791*. Ed. Olivier Blanc. Paris: Côté-femmes.

———. 1993b. *Ecrits politiques II 1792-1793*. Ed. Olivier Blanc. Paris: Côté-femmes.

———. 1993c. *Œuvres complètes. Tome I. Théâtre*. Ed. Félix-Marcel Castan. Montauban: Cocagne.

———. 1993d. *Théâtre politique II: L'Homme généreux (1786); Les Démocrates et les Aristocrates ou les curieux du Champ de Mars (1790); La Nécessité du Divorce (1790); La France sauvée ou le tyran détrôné (1792); Le Prélat d'autrefois ou Sophie de Saint-Elme (1795)*. Ed. Gisela Thiele-Knobloch. Paris: Côté-femmes.

Grimm, Reinhold. 1977. "Les romans champêtres de George Sand." *Romantisme* 64-70.

Groult, Benoîte. 1977. *Le féminisme au masculin*. Paris: Denoël/Gonthier.

———, ed. 1986. *Olympe de Gouges, Œuvres*. Paris: Mercure de France.

Grouvelle, Ph.-A. 1823. "Notice sur la vie et la personne de Mme de Sévigné." *Lettres de Madame de Sévigné, de sa famille et de ses amis*. Ed. Gault-de-Saint-Germain. Paris: Dalibon. 291-328.

Guenot, Hervé. 1987. "Le théâtre et l'événement: la représentation dramatique du siège de Toulon (août 1793)." *Littérature et Révolution française*. Annales littéraires de l'Université de Besançon, no. 354. Paris: Belles Lettres. 261-302.

Guillois, Dr. Alfred. 1904. *Etude médico-psychologique sur Olympe de Gouges*.

Guinguené. 1803. *La Décade philosophique*, 30 nivôse an XI-20 janvier; 30 pluviôse an XI-19 février.

Gutwirth, Madelyn. 1978. *Madame de Staël, Novelist: The Emergency of the Artist as Woman*. Urbana: Univ. of Illinois Press.

———. 1989a. "*1788: The Marquis de Condorcet Publishes 'Lettres d'un Bourgeois de New-Haven.' Civil Rights and the Wrongs of Women*." Hollier 558-66.

———. 1989b. "Nature, cruauté et femmes immolées: Les réflexions sur le procès de la reine." *Le Groupe de Coppet et la Révolution française*. Lausanne: Institut Benjamin Constant. 121-40.

---. 1992. *The Twilight of the Goddesses: Women and Representation in the French Revolutionary Era.* New Brunswick: Rutgers Univ. Press.

Gutwirth, Madelyn, Avriel Goldberger, and Karyna Szmurlo, eds. 1991. *Germaine de Staël: Crossing the Borders.* New Brunswick: Rutgers Univ. Press.

Hanley, Sarah. 1989. "Engendering the State: Family Formation and State Building in Early Modern France." *French Historical Studies* 16.1: 1-27.

Harten, Elke, and Hans-Christian Harten. 1989. *Femmes, culture et révolution.* Paris: Des femmes. Trans. Bella Chabot, Jeanne Etoré, and Olivier Mannoni. Trans. of *Frauen, Kultur und Revolution.* 1988.

Harth, Erica. 1992. *Cartesian Women: Versions and Subversions of Rational Discourse in the Old Regime.* Ithaca: Cornell Univ. Press.

Hébert, Jacques-René. 1792. *Le Père Duchesne* 202 (20 December); 204 (25 December).

---. 1793. *Le Père Duchesne* 243 (20 June).

Hesse, Carla. 1989. "Reading Signatures: Female Authorship and Revolutionary Law in France, 1750-1850." *Eighteenth-Century Studies* 22.3: 469-87.

Higonnet, Margaret. 1986. "Speaking Silences: Women's Suicide." Suleiman 68-83.

Histoire générale de la presse française des origines à 1814. 3 vols. Paris: PUF, 1969.

Hogsett, Charlotte. 1987. *The Literary Existence of Germaine de Staël.* Carbondale: Southern Illinois Univ. Press.

---. 1991. "Generative Factors in Consideration on the French Revolution." Gutwirth et al. 34-41.

Hollier, Denis, ed. 1989. *A New History of French Literature.* Cambridge, MA: Harvard Univ. Press.

Honegger, Claudia and Bettina Heintz, eds. 1981. *Listen der Ohnmacht.* Frankfurt: Europäischer Verlaganstalt.

Huet, Marie Hélène. 1982. *Rehearsing the Revolution: The Staging of Marat's Death, 1793-97.* Trans., Robert Hurley. Berkeley: Univ. of California Press.

Hufton, Olwen. 1971. "Women in Revolution, 1789-1796." *Past and Present* 53: 90-108.

---. 1992. *Women and the Limits of Citizenship in the French Revolution.* Toronto: Univ. of Toronto Press.

Hugo, Victor. 1967-70. *Œuvres complètes.* Ed., Jean Massin. Vol. XII. 18 vols. Paris: Club Français du Livre.

Hunt, Lynn. 1980. "Engraving the Republic: Prints and Propaganda in the French Revolution." *History Today* 30: 11-17.

---. 1984. *Politics, Culture, and Class in the French Revolution.* Berkeley: Univ. of California Press.

---. 1985. "Révolution française et vie privée." Vol. 4 of *Histoire de la vie privée de la Révolution à la Grande Guerre.* Ed., Michelle Perrot. Paris: Seuil. 5 vols. 1985-1987. 21-51.

---, ed. 1989. "The French Revolution in Culture." *Eighteenth-Century Studies* 22.3: 293-487.

———. 1990. "The Unstable Boundaries of the French Revolution." Vol. 4 of *A History of the Private Life*. Ed., Michelle Perrot. Trans. Arthur Goldhammer. Cambridge, MA: Belknap.

———, ed. 1991. *Eroticism and the Body Politic*. Baltimore: Johns Hopkins Univ. Press.

———. 1992. *The Family Romance of the French Revolution*. Berkeley: Univ. of California Press.

Intrigues de Madame de Staël à l'occasion du départ de Mesdames de France. Paris: De l'Imprimerie d'un Royaliste, 1791.

Jackson, Susan K. 1985. "The Novels of Isabelle de Charrière, or, a Woman's Work is Never Done." *Studies in Eighteenth-Century Culture* 14: 299-306.

Jacob, Louis. 1938. *Robespierre vu par ses contemporains*. Paris: Colin.

Jakobson, Roman. 1987. "Two aspects of Language and Two Types of Aphasic Disturbances." *Language and Literature*. Cambridge: Belknap.

Jameson, Fredric. 1981. *The Political Unconscious*. Ithaca: Cornell Univ. Press.

Jauffret, Eugène. 1970. *Le théâtre révolutionnaire*. 1869. Geneva: Slatkine.

Jehlen, Myra. 1990. "Gender." *Critical Terms for Literary Study*. Ed., Frank Lentricchia and Thomas McLaughlin. Chicago: Univ. of Chicago Press.

Jodin, Mademoiselle. 1790. *Vues législatives sur les femmes*. Paris.

Johnson, Mary Durham. 1980. "Old Wine in New Bottles: The Institutional Changes for Women of the People during the French Revolution." *Women, War and Revolution*. Ed., Carol R. Berkin and Clara M. Lovett. New York: Holmes. 107-43.

Jordonova, Ludmila J. 1980. "Natural Facts: A Historical Perspective on Science and Sexuality." *Nature, Culture and Gender*. Ed. Carol P. MacCormack and Marilyn Strathern. Cambridge: Cambridge Univ. Press. 42-69.

Joubert, Joseph. 1850. *Pensées, Essais, Maximes et Correspondance*. 2 vols. Paris: Le Normant.

Journal de Paris, 17 février 1793.

Journal des Débats, mars 1800; 22 mai 1803.

Julia, Dominique. 1981. *La Révolution: Les trois couleurs du tableau noir*. Paris: Belin.

Jullien, Rosalie. 1881. *Journal d'une bourgeoise pendant la Révolution, 1791-1793, publié par son petit-fils, Edouard Lockroy*. Paris: Levy.

Kadish, Doris. 1991. "Narrating the French Revolution: The Example of *Corinne*." Gutwirth et al. 113-21.

Kaplan, Louise. 1991. *Female Perversions: The Temptations of Emma Bovary*. New York: Doubleday.

Kates, Gary. 1985. *The 'Cercle Social,' the Girondins and the French Revolution*. Princeton: Princeton Univ. Press.

———. 1990. "'The Powers of Husband and Wife Must be Equal and Separate': The Cercle Social and the Rights of Women, 1790-91." Applewhite and Levy 163-80.

Kelly, George A. 1965. "Liberalism and Aristocracy in the French Restoration." *Journal of the History of Ideas* 26: 509-30.

Kelly-Gabol, Joan. 1977. "Did Women have a Renaissance?" *Becoming Visible: Women in European History.* Ed., Renate Bridenthal and Claudia Koonz. Boston: Houghton. 137-64.

Kennedy, Emmet. 1984. "Traitement informatique des répertoires théâtraux pendant la Révolution française." *Traitements informatiques de textes du 18ème siècle.* Ed. Anne-Marie and Jacques Chouillet. Textes et documents, série VII. INaLf-CNRS-ENS de Saint Cloud. 43-60.

———. 1989. *A Cultural History of the French Revolution.* New Haven: Yale Univ. Press.

Kennedy, Michael. 1982. *The Jacobin Clubs in the French Revolution: The First Years.* Princeton NJ: Princeton Univ. Press.

Kitchin, Joanna. 1965. *Un journal 'philosophique': "La Décade" (1794-1807).* Paris: Minard.

Knibiehler, Yvonne. 1984. "Chronologie et histoire des femmes." *Une histoire des femmes est-elle possible?* Ed., Michelle Perrot. Marseille: Rivages. 50-57.

Knibiehler, Yvonne, and Catherine Fouquet. 1977. *Histoire des mères du Moyen Age à nos jours.* Paris: Montalba.

Knibiehler, Yvonne, et al. 1983. *De la pucelle à la minette: Les jeunes filles de l'âge classique à nos jours.* Paris: Messidor/Temps Actuels.

Krief, Huguette. 1989. "La condition de la femme dans la littérature romanesque féminine pendant la Révolution française." Brive 1: 263-72.

Lacan, Jacques. 1971. "L'instance de la lettre dans l'inconscient ou la raison depuis Freud." *Ecrits.* 2 vols. Paris: Seuil. 1: 249-89.

———. "La signifcation du phallus." *Ecrits* 2: 103-15.

———. "Le stade du miroir comme formateur de la fonction du *Je.*" *Ecrits* 1: 89-97.

L. C. [La Chabeaussière]. An XI. "Delphine, en un acte." *Décade philosophique* 3ème trimestre: 439-40.

Lacour, Léopold. 1900. *Trois femmes de la Révolution.* Paris: Plan-Nourrit.

Lacy, Margriet Bruyn. 1982. "Madame de Charrière and the Constant Family." *Romance Notes* 23: 154-58.

———. 1990. "Belle Van Zuylen/Isabelle de Charrière (1740-1805): Tradition and Defiance." *Canadian Journal of Netherlandic Studies* 11.2: 33-36.

La Fontaine. 1965. *Œuvres complètes.* Ed., Jean Marnier. Paris: Seuil.

La Harpe, Jean-François. 1797. *Du fanatisme dans la langue révolutionnaire ou de la persécution suscitée par les barbares du dix-huitième siècle, contre la religion chrétienne et ses ministres.* 3rd ed. Paris.

Lajer-Burcharth, Ewa. 1991. "David's 'Sabine Women': Body, Gender, and Republican Culture under the Directory." *Art History* 14: 397-430.

Lamartine, Alphonse de. 1849. *History of the Girondists.* 2 vols. New York: Harper Bros.

Landes, Joan B. 1988. *Women and the Public Sphere in the Age of the French Revolution.* Ithaca: Cornell Univ. Press.

Lanson, Gustave. 1885. *Nivelle de la Chaussée la comédie larmoyante.* Paris: Hachette.

Laplanche, J., and J.-B. Pontalis. 1973. *The Language of Psychoanalysis.* Trans., Donald Nicholson Smith. New York: Norton.

La Tour du Pin, Henriette-Lucy, marquise de. 1979. *Mémoires de la Marquise de La Tour du Pin: Journal d'une femme de cinquante ans (1778-1815), suivis d'extraits inédits de sa correspondance (1815-1846).* Paris: Mercure de France.

Le Bas, Elisabeth. 1901. *Autour de Robespierre. Le conventionnel Le Bas.* Ed. Stéfane-Pol. (Pseudonym for Paul Coutant.) Paris: Flammarion. 102-50.

Levizac, M. de. 1803. *Lettres choisies de Mesdames de Sévigné et de Maintenon.* 2nd ed. Paris: Gabriel Dufour.

Levy, Darline Gay, Harriet Branson Applewhite, and Mary Durham Johnson, eds. and trans. 1979. *Women in Revolutionary Paris, 1789-1795.* Urbana: Univ. of Illinois Press. [Chicago Univ. Press, 1980].

Levy, Darline Gay, and Harriet B. Applewhite. 1990. "Women, Radicalization, and the Fall of the French Monarchy." Applewhite and Levy 81-107.

———. 1992. "Women and Militant Citizenship in Revolutionary Paris." Melzer and Rabine 79-101.

Lézardière, Pauline de. 1792. *Théorie des lois politiques de la Monarchie française.* Paris.

Lougée, Carolyn. 1976. *Le paradis des femmes.* Princeton: Princeton Univ. Press.

Louvet de Couvrai, Jean-Baptiste. 1939. *Mémoires de Louvet de Couvrai.* Ed. A. Aulard. Paris.

Lukács, Georg. 1964. *Studies in European Realism.* New York: Grosset.

Luria, Gina. 1974. Introduction. *Julia.* By Helen Maria Williams. 2 vols. 1790. New York: Garland Publishing.

Lux, Adam. n.d. *Charlotte Corday.* N.p.: n.p.

Lyotard, Jean-François. 1985. *Discours, figure.* Paris: Klincksieck.

MacArthur, Elizabeth R. 1987. "Devious Narratives: Refusal of Closure in Two Eighteenth-Century Epistolary Novels." *Eighteenth-Century Studies* 21: 1-20.

Macherey, Pierre. 1978. *A Theory of Literary Production.* London: Routledge.

Madelin, Louis. 1910. *La Révolution française.* Paris: Hachette.

Manin, Bernard. 1989. "Rousseau." Furet and Ozouf 829-40.

Marand-Fouquet, Catherine. 1989. *La femme au temps de la Révolution.* Paris: Stock.

Marat, Jean-Paul. 1869. *L'Ami du Peuple* 684 (19 September 1792). *Œuvres de J.-P. Marat.* Ed., A. Vermorel. Paris: Décembre-Alonnier. 230.

Marbouty, Caroline. 1844. *Une Fausse Position.* 2 vols. Paris: Librairie d'Amyot.

Maromme, Mme Loyer de. 1862. "La jeunesse de Charlotte Corday." Ed., Casimir Périer. *La Revue des deux mondes* 1er avril: 597-617.

Marrinan, Michael. 1980. "Images and Ideas of Charlotte Corday: Texts and Contexts of an Assassination." *Arts Magazine* April: 158-76.

Massardier-Kenney, François. 1990. "*Indiana*: Lieux et personnages féminins." *Nineteenth-Century French Studies* 19.1: 65-71.

Mathiez, Albert. 1958. *La Révolution française.* Paris.

May, Gita. 1964. *De Jean-Jacques Rousseau à Madame Roland.* Geneva: Droz.

———. 1970. *Madame Roland and the Age of Revolution.* New York: Columbia Univ. Press.

———. 1984. "Rousseau's Antifeminism Reconsidered." Spencer 309-17.

Mayo, Robert D. 1962. *The English Novel in the Magazines 1740-1815.* Evanston, Illinois: Northwestern Univ. Press.

Maza, Sarah. 1989a. "The Rose-Girl of Salency: Representations of Virtue in Prerevolutionary France." *Eighteenth-Century Studies* 22: 395-412.

———. 1989b. "Women's Voices in Literature and Art." Hollier 623-27.

———. 1991. "The Diamond Necklace Affair Revisited (1785-86): The Case of the Missing Queen." Hunt 63-89.

———. 1992. "Women, the bourgeoisie, and the Public Sphere: Response to Daniel Gordon and Daniel Bell." *French Historical Studies* 17: 935-50.

Melchior-Bonnet, Bernadine. 1969, 1989. *Charlotte Corday.* Paris: Tallandier.

Melzer, Sara E. and Leslie W. Rabine. 1992. *Rebel Daughters: Women and the French Revolution.* New York: Oxford Univ. Press.

Mercure de France, Messidor an VIII 1800, Fructidor an IX 1801.

Michelet, Jules. n.d. *Les femmes de la Révolution: Héroines, victimes, amoureuses.* Ed. P. Labracherie and J. Dumont. Paris: Hachette.

———. 1854. *Les femmes de la Révolution.* Paris: Delahays.

———. 1952. *Histoire de la Révolution française.* Ed. Gérard Walter. Paris: Gallimard.

———. 1979. *Histoire de la Révolution française.* Paris: Laffont-Bouquins.

Mili, Muriel. 1989. "Le théâtre de la Révolution 1789-1799. Présentation, problématique, perspectives." *Actes du Colloque Théâtre et Révolution.* Ed., Lucile Garbagnati and Marita Gilli. Annales littéraires de l'U. de Besançon. Paris: Belles Lettres. 45-51.

Miller, Nancy. 1987. *The Poetics of Gender.* New York: Columbia Univ. Press.

———. 1988. *Subject to Change.* New York: Columbia Univ. Press.

Minier-Birk, Sigyn. 1983. "Les *Lettres écrites de Lausanne* de Madame de Charrière: rapports familiaux et exigences sociales au XVIIIe siècle." *Selecta: Journal of the Pacific Northwest Council on Foreign Languages* 4: 23-27.

———. 1987. *Madame de Charrière: Les premiers romans.* Paris: Champion-Slatkine.

Moi, Toril. 1989. "Feminist Female Feminine." *The Feminine Reader: Essays in Gender and the Politics of Literary Criticisms.* Ed., Catherine Belsey and Jane Moore. New York: Blackwell. 117-32.

Le Moniteur universel. 29 brumaire an II [19 Nov. 1793].

Monselet, Charles. 1857. *Les oubliés et dédaignés.* Paris.

Montesquieu, baron de. 1966. *The Spirit of the Laws.* Trans. Thomas Nugent. New York: Hafner.

Montfort [-Howard], Catherine. 1982. *Les Fortunes de Madame de Sévigné au XVIIème et au XVIIIème siècles.* Etudes littéraires françaises 18. Paris: Jean-Michel Place.

———. 1992a. "Grouvelle et Madame de Sévigné: Une admiration intempestive." *Correspondances.* Ed. Wolfgang Leiner and Pierre Ronzeaud. Etudes littéraires françaises 52. Tübingen: Gunter Narr. 447-53.

———. 1992b. "Ordre et contestation chez Madame de Sévigné." *Ordre et contestation au temps des classiques.* Ed., Roger Duchêne and Pierre Ronzeaud. 2 vols. Tübingen: Biblio 17. 2:17-31.

———. Forthcoming. "For the Defense: Charlotte Corday's Letters from Prison." *Studies on Voltaire and the Eighteenth Century.*

Mueller-Vollmer, Kurt. 1977. "From Poetics to Linguistics: Wilhelm von Humboldt and the Romantic Idea of Language." *Le Groupe de Coppet: Actes et documents du deuxième colloque de Coppet 10-13 juillet 1974.* Geneva: Slatkine. 196-215.

Naginski, Isabelle. 1991. *George Sand: Writing for her Life.* New Brunswick: Rutgers Univ. Press.

Napoléon. 1823. *Mémorial de Sainte-Hélène, ou Journal où se trouve consigné, jour par jour, ce qu'a dit et fait Napoléon durant dix-huit mois, par le comte de Las Cases.* 8 vols. Paris: L'auteur.

Nathans, Benjamin. 1990. "Habermas' 'Public Sphere' in the Era of the French Revolution." *French Historical Studies* 16: 620-44.

Nye, Robert A. 1989. "Honor, Impotency, and Male Sexuality in 19th Century French Medicine." *French Historical Studies* 16.1: 48-77.

Offen, Karen. 1990. "The New Sexual Politics of French Revolutionary Historiography." *French Historical Studies* 16.4: 909-22.

Okin, Susan. 1979. *Women in Western Political Thought.* Princeton: Princeton Univ. Press.

Omacini, Lucia, ed. 1979. *Des circonstances actuelles.* Paris/Geneva: Droz.

———. 1982. "Pour une typologie du discours staëlien: les procédés de la persuasion." *Benjamin Constant, Madame de Staël et le Groupe de Coppet. Actes du quatrième colloque de Coppet 20-23 juillet 1988.* Oxford: Voltaire Foundation. 371-91.

Opinion de femmes: De la veille au lendemain de la Révolution. Paris: Côté-femmes, 1989.

Orcey, G. d'. 1893. "La sœur de Robespierre, épisode de la Terreur." *Revue Britannique.* Vol. 6.

Orr, Linda. 1992. "Outspoken Women and the Rightful Daughter of the Revolution: Madame de Staël's *Considérations sur la Révolution française.*" Melzer and Rabine 121-36.

Outram, Dorinda. 1987. "Le langage mâle de la vertu: Women and the Discourse of the French Revolution." *The Social History of Language.* Ed., Peter Burke and Roy Porter. Cambridge: Cambridge Univ. Press. 120-35.

———. 1989. *The Body and the French Revolution: Sex, Class, and Political Culture.* New Haven: Yale Univ. Press.

Ozouf, Mona. 1976. *La fête révolutionnaire, 1789-1799.* Paris: Gallimard.

Palissot de Montenoy, Charles. An XI-1803. "Genlis." *Mémoires pour servir à l'histoire de notre littérature depuis François Ier jusqu'à nos jours.* 2 vols. Paris: Gérard. 1: 357-61.

Palmer, Robert. 1985. *The Improvement of Humanity: Education and the French Revolution.* Princeton: Princeton Univ. Press.

WORKS CITED

Parker, Alice. 1985. "Madame de Tencin and the 'Mascarade' of Female Im/personation." *Eighteenth-Century Life* 9: 65-78.
Paulson, Ronald. 1983. *Representations of Revolution (1789-1820)*. New Haven: Yale Univ. Press.
Pelous, Jean-Michel. 1980. *Amour précieux, amour galant (1654-1675)*. Paris: Klincksiek.
Perrot, Michelle. 1981. "Rebellische Weiber. Die Frau in der französischen Stadt des 19. Jahrhunderts." *Listen der Ohnmacht*. Ed., Claudia Honegger and Bettina Heintz. Frankfurt Europäische Verlaganstalt. 71-98.
Petrey, Sandy. 1988. *Realism and Revolution*. Ithaca: Cornell Univ. Press.
———. ed. 1989a. *The French Revolution 1789-1989: Two Hundred Years of Rethinking*. Lubbock: Texas Tech Univ. Press.
———. 1989b. "Seventeen Eighty-Nine." Hollier 566-72.
Peyre, Henri. 1971. *Qu'est-ce que le romantisme?* Paris: PUF.
Pinzka, Lauren. 1990-91. "George Sand: Rewriting Revolutions." *George Sand Studies* 10.1-2: 42-49.
Piozzi, Hester Thrale. 1914. *The Intimate Letters of Hester Piozzi and Penelope Pennington, 1788-1821*. Ed., Oswald Knapp. London: George Allen.
Planté, Christine. 1989. "Constance Pipelet: La Muse de la Raison et les despotes du Parnasse." Brive 1: 285-94.
Poovey, Mary. 1988. *Uneven Developments: The Ideological Work of Gender in Mid-Victorian England*. Chicago: Univ. of Chicago Press.
Pope, Barbara Corrado. 1977. "Angels in the Devil's Workshop: Leisured and Charitable Women in Nineteenth-Century England and France." *Becoming Visible: Women in European History*. Ed., Renate Bridenthal and Claudia Koonz. Boston: Houghton. 296-324.
Popkin, Jeremy. 1990. *Revolutionary News: The Press in France, 1789-1799*. Durham, NC: Duke Univ. Press.
Principato, Aurelio. 1989. "La tradition rhétorique et la crise révolutionnaire: l'attitude de Madame de Staël." *Le Groupe de Coppet et la Révolution française*. Lausanne: Institut Benjamin Constant.
Proctor, Candide E. 1990. *Women, Equality, and the French Revolution*. New York: Greenwood Press.
Radet, J.B. An XI. *Colombine Philosophe Soi-Disant*. Comédie en un acte et en prose, mêlée de vaudevilles représentée pour la première fois sur le théâtre du vaudeville, le 17 Prairial.
Ratner, Moses. 1971. *Theory and Criticism of the Novel in France from L'Astrée to 1750*. New York: Cambridge Univ. Press.
Rebérioux, Madeleine. 1989. Préface. *1789: Cahiers de doléances des femmes et autres textes*. Ed., Marie-Paule Duhet. Paris: Des femmes. i-xii.
Reid, Martine. 1989. "Language under Revolutionary Pressure." Hollier 572-79.
Reval, Gabrielle. 1931. *Madame Campan, Assistante de Napoléon*. Paris: Albin Michel.

"Révolution et littérature." *Revue d'Histoire Littéraire de la France* 4-5 (juillet-octobre 1990): 571-830.

La Révolution et l'ordre juridique privé: Rationalité ou scandale? Actes du colloque d'Orléans, 1986. 2 vols. Paris: PUF, 1988.

Revue de l'enseignement des femmes, I.1 (1845): 1-2, 9-10.

Richards, Carol V. 1982. "Structural Motifs and the Limits of Feminism in *Indiana*." Datlof 12-20.

Richmond, Ian, and Constant Venesoen, eds. 1987. *Présences féminines: Littérature et Société au XVIIe siècle français*. Tübingen: Biblio 17.

Richter, Melvin. 1977. *The Political Theory of Montesquieu*. New York: Cambridge Univ. Press.

Robespierre, Charlotte. 1835. *Mémoires sur ses deux frères*. Paris: dépot central, faubourg Saint-Denis. No. 16.

Roger, Philippe. 1988. "Le débat sur la langue révolutionnaire." Bonnet.

Rogers, Adrienne. 1984. "Women and the Law." Spencer 33-48.

Rogers, Nancy. 1981. "George Sand and Germaine de Staël: The Novel as Subversion." Singer 61-74.

Roland, Marie-Jeanne Philpon, Madame. 1900-15. *Lettres de Madame Roland*. Ed., Claude Perroud. 4 vols. Paris: Imprimerie Nationale.

———. 1905. *Mémoires de Madame Roland*. Ed., Claude Perroud. 2 vols. Paris: Plon.

———. 1966. *Mémoires de Madame Roland*. Ed., Paul de Roux. Paris: Mercure de France.

———. 1967. *Mémoires*. 1795. Paris: Crémille.

Ronsin, Francis. 1990. *Le contrat sentimental: Débats sur le mariage, l'amour, le divorce, de l'Ancien Régime à la Restauration*. Paris.

Rosa, Annette. 1988. *Citoyennes: Les femmes et la révolution française*. Postface d' Elisabeth Guibert-Sledziewski. Paris: Messidor.

Rosenblum, Robert. 1974. *Transformations in Late Eighteenth-Century Art*. Princeton: Princeton Univ. Press.

Rossard, Janine. 1972. "Le Désir de mort romantique dans 'Caliste'." *PMLA* 87: 492-98.

Roth, Michael. 1987. *Psycho-analysis as History*. Ithaca: Cornell Univ. Press.

Roudinesco, Elisabeth. 1989. *Théroigne de Méricourt: Une femme mélancolique sous la Révolution*. Paris: Seuil.

Rousseau, Jean-Jacques. 1955. *Du contrat social*. Les Classiques du peuple. Paris: Editions Sociales.

———. 1961. *Julie, ou la Nouvelle Héloïse*. Vol. 2 of *Œuvres complètes*. Ed. Bernard Gagnebin and Marcel Raymond. 4 vols. Paris: Gallimard.

Rousselot, Paul. 1883. *Histoire de l'éducation des femmes en France*. 2 vols. Paris: Didier.

Sade, Marquis de. 1793. *Sélection des Piques, Discours Prononcé à la Fête décernée par la Section des piques aux mânes de Marat et de LePelletier*, le 29 septembre.

Salm, Constance de [Constance Pipelet]. 1842. *Œuvres complètes*. 4 vols. Paris.

Salvandy, N.-A. de. 1833. Preface. *Natalie*. By Madame de Montpezat. Paris.

Sand, George. n.d. "Quelques mots sur mes romans." *Souvenirs et impressions littéraires*. Paris: Hetzel.
———. 1964-. *Correspondance*. Ed., Georges Lubin. 23 vols. Paris: Garnier.
———. 1967. *La Petite Fadette*. Paris: Garnier Flammarion.
———. 1970-71. *Histoire de ma vie. Œuvres autobiographiques*. Ed., Georges Lubin. 2 vols. Paris: Pléiade. 1: 113-690; 2: 126-60.
———. 1976. *Le Meunier d'Angibault*. Plan de la Tour: Aujourd'hui.
———. 1984. *Indiana*. Ed., Béatrice Didier. Paris: Gallimard (Collection Folio).
Schalk, Ellery. 1986. *From Valor to Pedigree: Ideas of Nobility in France in the Sixteenth and Seventeenth Century*. Princeton: Princeton Univ. Press.
Schama, Simon. 1989. *Citizens: A Chronicle of the French Revolution*. New York: Knopf.
Schor, Naomi. 1986a. "Female Fetishism: The Case of George Sand." Suleiman 363-72.
———. 1986b. "Reading Double: Sand's Difference." *The Poetics of Gender*. Ed., Nancy Miller. New York: Columbia Univ. Press. 248-69.
———. 1987. "Portrait of a Gentleman." *Representations* 113-33.
———. 1988. "Idealism in the Novel: Recanonizing Sand." *Yale French Studies* 75: 56-73.
Scott, Joan Wallach. 1988. *Gender and the Politics of History*. New York: Columbia Univ. Press.
———. 1989. "French Feminists and the Rights of 'Man': Olympe de Gouges's Declarations." *History Workshop Journal* 28 (Autumn): 1-21.
Searle, John. 1969. *Speech Acts*. Cambridge: Cambridge Univ. Press.
Seward, Anna. 1811. *The Letters of Anna Seward Written Between the Years 1784-1807*. 6 vols. Edinburgh: Constable.
Showalter, English, Jr. 1977. "Madame de Graffigny and Her Salon." *Studies in Eighteenth-Century Culture* 6: 377-91.
———. 1988. "Writing Off the Stage: Women Authors and Eighteenth-Century Theater." *Yale French Studies* 75: 95-111.
Singer, Armand E., ed. 1981. *West Virginia George Sand Conference Papers*. Morgantown: Department of Foreign Languages, W. Va. Univ.
Slama, Béatrice. 1989. "Ecrits de femmes pendant la Révolution." Brive 1: 291-306.
Sledziewski, Elisabeth G. 1989. "Naissance de la femme civile: La Révolution, la femme, le droit." *Révolutions du sujet*. Paris: Klincksieck. 99-126.
Smith, Bonnie. 1989. *Changing Lives: Women in European History since 1700*. Lexington, MA: DC Heath.
Snyders, Georges. 1965. *La pédagogie en France aux XVIIe et XVIIIe siècles*. Paris: PUF.
Solé, Jacques. 1989. "Did the French Revolution Undermine the Traditional Family." *Questions of the French Revolution: A Historical Overview*. Pantheon: New York. Trans., Shelley Temchin. Trans. of *La Révolution en questions*, 1988. 209-15.
Sonnet, Martine. 1987. *L'éducation des filles au temps des Lumières*. Préf. Daniel Roche. Paris: Cerf.

Soprani, Anne. 1988. *La Révolution et les femmes de 1789 à 1796.* Paris: MA éditions.
Sorel, Albert. 1907. *Mme de Staël.* Paris: Hachette.
Sourian, Eve. 1991. "Delphine and the Principles of 1789." Gutwirth et al. 42-51.
Spencer, Samia, ed. 1984. *French Women and the Age of Enlightenment.* Bloomington: Indiana Univ. Press.
Spiegel, Gabrielle M. 1990. "History, Historicism, and the Social Logic of the Text in the Middle Ages." *Speculum* 65.1: 59-86.
Spitzer, Alan B. 1987. *The French Generation of 1820.* Princeton: Princeton Univ. Press.
Staël-Holstein, Anne-Louise Germaine Necker, baronne de. 1904. *Des circonstances actuelles qui peuvent terminer la Révolution française.* Ed., John Vienot. Paris: Fischbacker.
———. 1954. *De la littérature.* Ed. Paul Van Tieghem. Geneva: Droz.
———. 1958. *De l'Allemagne.* 5 vols. Paris: Hachette.
———. 1966. *Dix années d'exil.* Intro. Simone Balayé. Paris: Bibliothèque 10/18.
———. 1967. *Œuvres complètes.* 17 vols. Paris: Treuttel & Wurtz, 1820-21. Paris, 1861. Geneva: Slatkine.
———. 1979. *Des circonstances actuelles.* Ed. Lucia Omacini. Geneva: Droz.
———. 1983. *Considérations sur la Révolution française.* Ed. J. Godechot. Paris: Tallandier.
———. 1987. *Corinne, or Italy.* Trans. and ed. A. Goldberger. New Brunswick: Rutgers Univ. Press.
Stanton, Domna C. 1981. "The Fiction of Préciosité and the Fear of Women," *Yale French Studies* 62: 107-34.
Starobinski, Jean. 1982. *1789: The Emblems of Reason.* Trans. Barbara Bray. Charlottesville: Univ. of Virginia Press.
Stendhal. 1962. *Correspondance.* Ed., Henri Martineau and Del Litto. 3 vols. Paris: Gallimard (Bibliothèque de la Pléiade).
Stewart, Joan Hinde. 1989. "1787: Designing Women. Isabelle de Charrière Publishes 'Caliste'." Hollier 553-58.
Suleiman, Susan, ed. 1986. *The Female Body in Western Culture.* Cambridge: Harvard Univ. Press.
Sullerot, Evelyne. 1966. *Histoire de la presse féminine en France des origines à 1848.* Paris: Colin.
Sydenham, Martin. 1961. *The Girondins.* London: Athlone.
Thomas, Chantal. 1988. "Féminisme et Révolution: les causes perdues d'Olympe de Gouges." Bonnet 308-12.
———. 1989a. "Heroism in the Feminine: The Examples of Charlotte Corday and Madame Roland." Petrey 67-82.
———. 1989b. *La reine scélérate: Marie-Antoinette dans les pamphlets.* Paris: Seuil.
Todd, Janet M. 1975. Introduction. *Letters From France.* By Helen Maria Williams. 1795-6. Delmar, New York: Scholars' Facsimiles and Reprints.
Touchard, Jean. 1959. *Histoire des idées politiques.* 2 vols. Paris: PUF.

Trouille, Mary. 1989. "Revolution in the Boudoir: Mme Roland's Subversion of Rousseau's Feminine Ideals." *Eighteenth-Century Life* 13 (May): 65-85.

Trousson, Raymond. 1985. "Isabelle de Charrière et Jean-Jacques Rousseau." *Bulletin de l'Académie Royale de Langue et de Littérature Françaises* 63.1: 5-57.

Tuetery, Alexandre. 1890-1894. *Répertoire général des sources manuscrites de l'histoire de Paris pendant la Révolution française*. Vol. 10, nos. 812-46. Paris.

Ungvari, Tamas. 1990. "Revolution, A Textual Analysis." *Nineteenth Century French Studies* 19.1: 1-21.

Vallois, Marie-Claire. 1987. *Fictions féminines: Mme de Staël et les voix de la Sibylle*. Stanford French and Italian Studies 49. Stanford: Anma Libri.

Van Tieghem, Paul, ed. 1959. *De la littérature*. Geneva: Droz.

Vareille, Jean-Claude. 1983. "Fantasmes de la fiction, fantasmes de l'écriture." *George Sand: Colloque de Cerisy*. Ed., Simone Vierne. Paris: SEDES. 125-36.

Vatel, Charles. 1864-72. *Charlotte de Corday et les Girondins*. 3 vols. Paris: Plon.

Vercruysse, Jeroom. 1989. "The Publication of the *Œuvres complètes*: Navigating the Risky Waters of the Unforeseeable." *Eighteenth-Century Life* 13: 69-78.

Verdier, Gabrielle. 1992. "Libertine, Philanthropist, Revolutionary: Ninon's Metamorphoses in the Age of Enlightenment." *Continuum* 4 (2). New York: AMS Press. 102-147.

Vermeylan, Pierre. 1984. *Les idées politiques et sociales de George Sand*. Brussels: Université de Bruxelles.

Villeterque. 1802. *Journal de Paris*, 2 nivôse an XI-23 décembre.

Villiers, Chéron de. 1865. *Marie-Anne-Charlotte de Corday d'Armont: Sa vie, son temps, ses écrits, son procès, sa mort*. Paris.

Villiers, Marc. 1910. *Histoire des clubs de femmes et légions d'amazones*. Paris: Plon-Nourrit.

Vissière, Isabelle. 1988. *Isabelle de Charrière: Une aristocrate révolutionnaire. Ecrits 1788-1794*. Paris: Des femmes.

———. 1989. "Duo épistolaire ou duel idéologique? La correspondance de Madame de Charrière et de Benjamin Constant pendant la Révolution." *Benjamin Constant et la Révolution française 1789-1799*. Geneva: Droz. 23-37.

Voloshinov, V.N. 1973. *Marxism and the Philosophy of language*. Trans., L. Matejka and I.R. Titunik. New York: Seminar Press.

Vray, Nicole. 1989. *Les femmes dans la tourmente*. Rennes: Editions Ouest-France.

Walpole, Horace. 1980. *Horace Walpole's Miscellaneous Correspondence*. Ed., W.S. Lewis and John Riely. 3 vols. New Haven: Yale Univ. Press.

Walter, Gérard. 1968. *Actes du Tribunal révolutionnaire*. Paris: Mercure de France.

Welch, Cheryl. 1984. *Liberty and Utility*. New York: Columbia Univ. Press.

Welschinger, Henri. 1880. *Le théâtre de la Révolution, 1789-1799*. Paris: Charavay.

White, Hayden. 1989. "Romantic Historiography." Hollier 632-38.

Williams, Helen Maria. 1828. *Souvenirs*. Paris: n.p.

———. 1975. *Letters From France*. Introd. Janet M. Todd. From the 5th ed. of *Letters Written in France* and 1st ed. of *Letters Containing a Sketch of the Politics of*

France. 2 vols. 1795 and 1796. Photorpt. Delmar, New York: Scholars' Facsimiles and Reprints.

Winegarten, Renée. 1985. *Mme de Staël*. Dover, UK: Berg.

Wollstonecraft, Mary [?]. 1795. "Madame Roland's Appeal to Impartial Posterity." Review of *An Appeal to Impartial Posterity* [English version of Mme Roland's memoirs]. *The Analytical Review* 22 (July-December): 145-52.

———. 1982. *Vindication of the Rights of Women*. London: Harmondsworth.

Wood, Dennis. 1982. "Isabelle de Charrière et Benjamin Constant: à propos d'une découverte récente." *Studies on Voltaire and the Eighteenth Century* 215: 273-79.

Woodward, Lionel-D. 1930. *Une anglaise amie de la Révolution française*. Paris: Honoré Champion.

Yalom, Marilyn. 1989. *Le temps des orages: Aristocrates, bourgeoises, et paysannes racontent*. Paris: Maren Sell.

———. 1990. *Revealing lives: Autobiography, Biography, and Gender*. Ed. Susan Groag Bell and Marilyn Yalom. Albany, N.Y.: SUNY.

———. 1993. *Blood Sisters: The French Revolution in Women's Memory*. Basic Books.